# OBJECT DESIGN

# Object Design

*Roles, Responsibilities, and Collaborations*

REBECCA WIRFS-BROCK

ALAN MCKEAN

✦✦Addison-Wesley

Boston • San Francisco • New York • Toronto • Montreal
London • Munich • Paris • Madrid
Capetown • Sydney • Tokyo • Singapore • Mexico City

The publisher offers discounts on this book when ordered in quantity for bulk purchases and special sales. For more information, please contact:

U.S. Corporate and Government Sales
(800) 382-3419
corpsales@pearsontechgroup.com

For sales outside of the U.S., please contact:

International Sales
(317) 581-3793
international@pearsontechgroup.com

Visit Addison-Wesley on the Web: www.awprofessional.com

Library of Congress Control Number: 2002112293

ISBN: 0-201-37943-0
Text printed on recycled paper
12345678910—CRW—0605040302
First printing, November 2002

# Contents

*Foreword by Ivar Jacobson   xv*
*Foreword by John Vlissides   xvii*
*Preface   xix*

CHAPTER 1   Design Concepts   1

Object Machinery   2

Roles   3

Object Role Stereotypes   4

Roles, Responsibilities, and Collaborations   5

Object Contracts   7

   *Conditions-of-Use and Aftereffect*
   *Guarantees   8*

Domain Objects   8

Application-Specific Objects   10

Interfaces   12

Classes   13

   *Two Roles   13*

Composition   16

# Contents

Inheritance   16

Object Organizations   17

Components   18

Patterns   18

*Applying Double Dispatch to a Specific Problem*   20

*The Real Benefits of Using Patterns*   25

Frameworks, Inc.   25

Architecture   27

Architectural Styles   28

*Centralized Control Style*   30

*Dispersed Control: No Centers*   30

*Delegated Control*   31

*Examining Interactions: A Layered Architecture Example*   32

*Locating Objects in Layers*   34

Design Description   36

Summary   36

Further Reading   37

CHAPTER 2   Responsibility-Driven Design   39

A Process for Seeing, Describing, and Designing   40

*Launching the Production: Project Definition and Planning*   44

*Setting the Stage: Early Description*   44

*Staging the Production: Design*   47

*"Seeing" from Multiple Perspectives*   49

Writing the Script: Analysis Descriptions   49

*Usage Descriptions*   50

*Other Specifications*   58

*Glossaries*   58

*Conceptual Objects*   58

Casting the Characters: Exploratory Design   60

    *CRC Cards*   61

    *Inventions: Using Patterns*   62

    *Pursuing a Solution*   67

    *Bouncing Between Ideas and Details*   68

Tuning the Production: Design Refinement   70

    *Designing for Flexibility and Extension*   71

    *Designing for Reliability*   73

    *Making Our Design Predictable, Consistent,*
    *and Comprehensible*   73

Summary   74

Further Reading   74

CHAPTER 3    Finding Objects   77

A Discovery Strategy   78

Looking for Objects and Roles, and Then
Classes   79

Why Tell a Design Story?   80

Search Strategies   84

What's in a Name?   88

Describing Candidates   93

Characterizing Candidates   98

Connecting Candidates   99

Looking for Common Ground   101

Defend Candidates and Look for Others   104

Summary   106

Further Reading   107

CHAPTER 4    Responsibilities   109

What Are Responsibilities?   110

Where Do Responsibilities Come From?   111

# Contents

Strategies for Assigning Responsibilities   125

    *Recording Responsibilities*   126

    *Making Initial Assignments*   128

    *Getting Unstuck*   138

Implementing Objects and
Responsibilities   140

Testing Your Candidates' Quality   145

Summary   146

Further Reading   146

CHAPTER 5   Collaborations   149

What Is Object Collaboration?   150

    *Preparing for Collaboration*   150

    *Recording Candidate Collaborations*   151

The Design Story for the Speak for Me
Software   152

Collaboration Options   153

    *Who's In Control?*   155

    *How Much Should Objects Trust One
Another?*   155

Strategies for Identifying Collaborations   158

    *Looking at an Individual Object's Role:
Stereotypes Imply Collaborations*   159

    *Looking at Individual Responsibilities: They
Imply Collaborations*   166

    *Designing the Details of a Complex
Responsibility*   168

    *Designing Collaborations for a Specific
Task*   169

    *Identifying Applicable Patterns*   170

    *Identifying How Architecture Influences
Collaborations*   172

    *Solving Problems in Collaborations*   173

Simulating Collaborations   176

    *Planning a Simulation*   177

    *Running a Simulation*   180

Designing Good Collaborations   183

    *The Law of Demeter: A Case Study*   184

Making Collaborations Possible   187

    *Guidelines for Making Connections*   188

    *Designing Reliable Collaborations*   190

When Are We Finished?   191

Summary   193

Further Reading   193

CHAPTER 6   Control Style   195

What Is Control Style?   196

Control Style Options   197

Making Trade-offs   198

    *Centralizing Control*   198

    *Delegating Control*   200

    *The Limits of Control Decisions*   201

Developing Control Centers   205

A Case Study: Control Style for External User
Events   206

    *Centralizing Control in the
MessageBuilder*   208

    *Refactoring Decision Making into State
Methods within the MessageBuilder*   220

    *Abstracting Away Decisions*   221

    *Delegating More Responsibility*   224

    *Designing the Control Style for the Guessing
Neighborhood*   225

    *Designing a Similar Control Center: Can We
Be Consistent?*   230

Summary   237

## Contents

CHAPTER 7    Describing Collaborations   239

Telling Collaboration Stories   240

A Strategy for Developing a Collaboration
Story   241

Establishing Scope, Depth, and Tone   242

Listing What You Will Cover   243

Deciding on the Level of Detail   243

*Showing a Bird's-Eye View*   244

*Showing Collaborators Only*   245

*Showing a Sequence of Interactions Among
Collaborators*   250

*Showing an In-Depth View*   251

*Showing a Focused Interaction*   253

*Showing an Implementation View*   254

*Showing How to Adapt a Collaboration*   254

*Where UML Diagrams Fall Short*   258

Choosing the Appropriate Form   263

Tell It, Draw It, Describe It: Guidelines   264

Organizing Your Work   270

*Adding Emphasis*   271

*Unfolding Your Story*   271

*Understanding What's Fundamental*   272

*Putting It All Together*   273

Preserving Stories   274

Summary   275

Further Reading   275

CHAPTER 8    Reliable Collaborations   277

Understanding the Consequences of
Failure   278

Increasing Your System's Reliability   280

Determining Where Collaborations Can Be
Trusted   280

*Trusted Versus Untrusted Collaborations* 281

*Implications of Trust* 284

Identifying Collaborations to Be Made Reliable 285

*What Use Cases Tell Us* 286

*Distinguish Between Exceptions and Errors* 287

*Object Exceptions Versus Use Case Exceptions* 288

*Object Exception Basics* 288

*Exception- and Error-Handling Strategies* 294

*Determining Who Should Take Action* 296

Designing a Solution 299

*Brainstorm Exception Conditions* 299

*Limit Your Scope* 300

*Record Exception-Handling Policies* 302

Documenting Your Exception-Handling Designs 303

*Specifying Formal Contracts* 307

Reviewing Your Design 311

Summary 312

Further Reading 313

CHAPTER 9   Flexibility 315

What Does It Mean to Be Flexible? 316

Degrees of Flexibility 317

The Consequences of a Flexible Solution 319

Nailing Down Flexibility Requirements 320

Recording Variations 324

Variations and Realizations   327

   *Identifying the Impact of a Variation*   328

   *Exploring Strategies for Realizing Flexibility*   329

   *Using Templates and Hooks to Support Variations*   330

The Role of Patterns in Flexible Designs   338

   *Varying an Object's Behavior with the Strategy Pattern*   338

   *Hiding Interacting Objects with Mediator*   339

   *Making a Predefined Object or System Fit Using Adapter*   340

   *How Do Patterns Increase Flexibility?*   340

How to Document a Flexible Design   342

   *Consider Your Audience*   344

   *Describing How to Make a Variation*   345

Changing a Working System's Design   350

Summary   352

Further Reading   353

CHAPTER 10 On Design   355

The Nature of Software Design   356

Tackling Core Design Problems   357

Frame the Problem   358

Dealing with Revealing Design Problems   361

   *A Story About Managing Shared Information*   362

   *A Story About Connection Problem Complexity*   363

   *A Story About a Design Problem That Never Got Easier*   364

   *Can Revealing Problems Be Wicked, Too?*   365

Strategies for Solving Revealing Problems   366
    *Redefining the Problem*   368
    *Synthesizing a Solution*   369
Working on the Rest   370
Designing Responsibly   371
Further Reading   374

Bibliography   375

Index   381

# Foreword

## by Ivar Jacobson

Software development is very different than it was over 10 years ago when Rebecca first introduced us to Responsibility-Driven Design. Use cases are now widely used to gather system requirements. The Unified Modeling Language is now the common tool for describing software designs and architectures. Object-oriented languages are everywhere. Business pressures demand that we develop systems quickly and react to changing market demands.

Good software design, however, remains essential. *Object Design* advances the state of the art as well as the practice of software design using objects. It offers a powerful way of thinking about software in terms of roles, responsibilities, and collaborations. Use cases specify the role of your system when interacting with its users. Designers transform use cases into responsibilities of objects. This higher-level view of a design, which focuses on responsibilities that are tied to your system's usage, helps you step away from implementation details and focus on what the appropriate software machinery should be. Once you understand that, then you can decide how to implement your design using classes, interfaces, and inheritance hierarchies.

*Object Design* presents a "theatre of design ideas." It is full of stories, design examples, and commonsense advice. It offers a vocabulary for characterizing object roles, application control styles, and design problems. It presents practical strategies for finding candidate objects and offers sound advice for naming them.

This book is more than an introduction to design. It also offers in-depth treatments of design topics that will be of interest to the most experienced software designers. It explores how to effectively use design patterns, make trade-offs, and reason about design alternatives. It demonstrates the consequences that seemingly simple design decisions have on the distribution of responsibilities among collaborators. In the chapter on control style, the authors present one solution to a problem and then work through several alternatives, discussing each of their relative merits. Another chapter is devoted to designing reliable collaborations and establishing "trusted" collaboration regions. This book takes design seriously!

There isn't just one way to think about and describe a design. Informal techniques and tools can complement more formal ones. In this new, agile world, we need to use a variety of tools and techniques to communicate design ideas. Whether you are new to object technology or an experienced developer, this book is a rich source of practical advice.

*Ivar Jacobson*
*Rational Software Corporation*
*August 2002*

# Foreword

## by John Vlissides

**W**hat makes for effective pedagogy? Well, first you avoid words like "pedagogy." Next, you learn all about your subject because a robust mental model is a prerequisite to enlightening others. Then you need a stockpile of examples that illustrate the model—varied examples that hit it from different angles. Finally, you must present the material smoothly and progressively like the graceful blooming of a rose under time-lapse photography.

If that's the gist of good teaching, then this book is its embodiment. Rebecca and Alan are master expositors, and they have done a masterful job conveying Responsibility-Driven Design, their model of object-oriented expertise. Conceived in the late 1980s, Responsibility-Driven Design has developed into a principled yet pragmatic approach with a big following. It was perhaps the first methodology to capitalize on the fundamental advance of objects—moving away from a mathematical, algorithmic view of programming to one of autonomous objects, each with its own responsibilities, collaborating in time and space much as people do. Object languages had captured the mechanisms that made an advance possible; Responsibility-Driven Design captures the thinking and practices that make objects live up to their promise.

This book explains the concept and practice of Responsibility-Driven Design in the context of modern software technology, rich with examples in contemporary object language, informed by the growing body of software patterns, and couched in notational (read "UML") standards. Unlike many works with comparable goals, there's nothing daunting about this book. The authors ease you into the material and keep you engaged with a steady revelation of wisdom. From beginning to end, this book teaches effectively.

But this isn't just a book for beginners. It's filled with practical techniques and advice for all practitioners, experts included. The more expertise you have, the harder it is to know what you don't know, and the more susceptible you become to over design and the dreaded second-system syndrome. The authors' treatments of flexibility and the nature of software design is especially insightful, revealing the relationship of variability to problem focus, strategies for solving "wicked" problems, and the synergies between agile and Responsibility-Driven Design. No matter what your technical persuasion, regardless of the school of design you practice, the wisdom here will enlighten you.

You're holding the definitive work on Responsibility-Driven Design of object software. More importantly you're embarking on what may be the most efficient path to designing better software.

*John Vlissides*
*IBM T.J. Watson Research*

# *Preface*

This book is about designing object software. Like many human endeavors, design is part art, part engineering, and part guesswork and experimentation. Discipline, hard work, inspiration, and sound technique all play their parts. Although software design is a highly creative activity, the fundamentals can be easily learned. Strategies and techniques exist for developing a design solution, and this book is packed with practical design techniques that help you get the job done. We hope you will become adept at thinking in objects and excited about devising solutions that exploit object technology.

You can consider design choices only in light of what you know to be relevant and important. To achieve good results, you need to learn how to discriminate important choices from mundane ones and how to acquire a good set of techniques that you intelligently practice. The informal tools and techniques in this book that don't require much more than a white board, a stack of index cards, a big sheet of paper, and chairs around a table. Oh yeah, be sure to bring your brain, too!

But more important than a grab bag of techniques are the fundamental ways you view a design. Although the techniques we present in this book are independent of any particular implementation technology or modeling language or design method, our approach to object design requires a specific perspective:

> Objects are not just simple bundles of logic and data. They are responsible members of an object community.

This approach, called Responsibility-Driven Design, gives you the basis for reasoning about objects.

Most novice designers are searching for the right set of techniques to rigidly follow in order to produce *the* correct design. In practice, things are never that straightforward. For any given problem there are many reasonable solutions, and a few very good solutions. People don't produce identical designs even if they follow similar practices or apply identical design heuristics. For each problem you approach, you make a different set of tactical decisions. The effects of each small decision accumulate. Your current design as well as your current lines of reasoning shape and limit subsequent possibilities. Given the potential impact of seemingly inconsequential decisions, designers need to thoughtfully exercise good judgment.

Your primary tool as a designer is your power of abstraction—forming objects that represent the essence of a working application. In a design, objects play specific roles and occupy well-known positions in an application's architecture. Each object is accountable for a specific portion of the work. Each has specific responsibilities. Objects collaborate in clearly defined ways, contracting with each other to fulfill the larger goals of the application.

Design is both a collaborative and a solo effort. To work effectively you need not only a rich vocabulary for describing your design but also strategies for finding objects, recipes for developing a collaborative model, and a framework for discussing design trade-offs. You will find these tools in this book. We also explore how design patterns can be used to solve a particular design problem and demonstrate their effects on a design. We present you with strategies for increasing your software's reliability and flexibility. We discuss different types of design problems and effective ways to approach them. This book presents many tools and techniques for reasoning about a design's qualities and effectively communicating design ideas. Whether you're a student or a seasoned programmer, a senior developer or a newcomer to objects, you can take away many practical things from this book.

## HOW TO READ THIS BOOK

This book is organized into two major parts. The first six chapters— Chapter 1, Design Concepts, Chapter 2, Responsibility-Driven Design, Chapter 3, Finding Objects, Chapter 4, Responsibilities, Chapter 5, Collaborations, and Chapter 6, Control Style—form the core of Responsibility-Driven Design principles and techniques. You should get a good grounding by reading these chapters.

Chapter 1, Design Concepts, introduces fundamental views of object technology and explains how each element contributes to a coherent way of designing an application. Even if you are a veteran designer, a quick read will set the stage for thinking about object design in terms of objects' roles and responsibilities. Chapter 2, Responsibility-Driven Design, provides a brief tour of Responsibility-Driven Design in practice. Chapter 3, Finding Objects, presents strategies for selecting and, equally important, rejecting candidate objects in an emerging design model. Chapter 4, Responsibilities presents many techniques for defining responsibilities and intelligently allocating them to objects. Chapter 5, Collaborations, gives many practical tips and examples of how to develop a collaboration model. Chapter 6, Control Style, describes strategies for developing your application's control centers and options for allocating decision-making and control responsibilities.

Chapters 7–10 explore challenges you may encounter as you develop your design. Each chapter covers a specific topic that builds on the design concepts and techniques presented in the first part of the book. Chapter 7, Describing Collaborations, explores options for documenting and describing your design. Chapter 8, Reliable Collaborations, presents strategies for handling exceptions, recovering from errors, and collaborating within and across a "trusted region." Chapter 9, Flexibility, discusses how to characterize software variations and design to support them. Chapter 10, On Design, discusses how to sort design problems into one of three buckets—the core, the revealing, and the rest—and treat each accordingly.

## ACKNOWLEDGMENTS

A lot of people have helped us in this endeavor, and we wish to acknowledge and thank them.

First, we would like to thank our design clients and students, who over the years have kept us on our toes, have offered much support and enthusiasm for our ideas, and have kept our focus on the practical.

We'd also like to thank our colleagues and friends with whom, over the years, we've had many thoughtful design discussions. While at Instantiations, and later at Digitalk, we found good design practices and techniques a frequent and energizing part of daily discussions. Our fellow consultants and trainers kept us honest: If a design technique or concept didn't work for a real client with a real problem, it was ditched. As a consequence, what's in this book has been proven in the trenches. And thanks to the engineers at Instantiations, who while they built amazing object-oriented applications and tools to support Smalltalk development, offered pearls of wisdom whenever we were able to divert their attention from their keyboards long enough to discuss their current design challenge.

We'd also like to acknowledge our editor, Paul Becker, the publication staff at Addison-Wesley, and our reviewers. Paul, you offered constant, unwavering support. Thanks.

## Rebecca's Acknowledgments

I would like to acknowledge several people who have been a spark of inspiration or a source of strength. First, I'd like to acknowledge my coauthor, Alan McKean. You truly are a student of design. You like to think and talk and reflect. You are excited about exploring ideas and turning them into things of value you can teach your students. Thanks for being my constant collaborator, coauthor, and friend. I'd also like to acknowledge Dave Squire, who (long ago as my manager at Tektronix) gave me this challenge: "Either write a book on design, lead the color Smalltalk project, or manage the engineering team. You've got to pick one and just do it." Ignoring Dave's advice, I managed to do all three. And I've been juggling the roles of designer, author, and manager ever since. Thanks, Dave, for believing I had something to write about that others would want to read. Sharon Holstein encouraged me more than she knows when she commented on my first solo efforts at writing in the *Smalltalk Report*. She told me that she liked reading what I wrote because it was just like having a conversation with me. John Schwartz is another colleague who sharpened our ideas. John read and ripped on each and every chapter of this book. I learned to not only accept but also relish his advice, and our book is better because of it. Finally, I'd like to acknowledge the constant support and occasional words of wisdom from my best friend and the best designer I know on this planet: my husband, Allen Wirfs-Brock. Allen, you know how to chip in ideas at just the right time and give me that gentle prod or word of encouragement.

## Alan's Acknowledgments

My ideas about design are very broad. *The Universal Traveler*, by Don Koberg and Jim Bagnell, a design book from the 1970s, puts it well:

> "Design is the process of making your dreams come true."

I would like to acknowledge many of the people who moved me along that path of fulfillment.

R. Buckminster Fuller, architect, industrial designer, philosopher, mathematician, poet, and humanitarian, for demonstrating how to live a life in which genius involved both heart and mind. He helped me know that I could make the world a better place.

Murshida Vera Corda, Sufi teacher, for showing me that laughter is the ultimate language. She opened my doors of perception.

Richard Britz, architect, teacher, builder, and friend, for inspiring me with his devotion to good work. Surely a member of my karass.

Sarah Douglas and Art Farley, professors at the University of Oregon, for starting me along the Smalltalk path.

Rebecca Wirfs-Brock, business partner and friend, for hiring me at Instantiations. Our work together has been more collaborative and stimulating than I had even hoped.

Walter and Marjorie McKean, my parents, who gave me their all. Their devotion to each other is an inspiration to everyone who knows them.

My wife, Brenda Herold, and my son, Jesse Vasilinda, my life's companions. Most of all, for showing me that love is a verb.

# Chapter 1

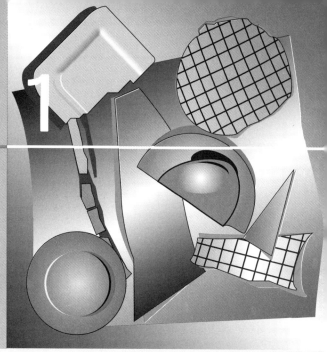

## Design Concepts

**A**lan Kay's favorite metaphor for software objects is a biological system. Like cells, software objects don't know what goes on inside one another, but they communicate and work together to perform complex tasks. In contrast, monolithic software is like a mechanical clock containing innumerable gears. Each gear functions unintelligently and only in relation to other adjacent gears. That design is hopelessly flawed. "When you're building gear clocks, eventually you reach a certain level of complexity and it falls in on itself," says Kay.

A software object may be machinelike, but, crafted by a thoughtful designer, it can be very smart. It makes decisions; it does things and knows things. It collaborates with potentially many other objects. Living in an enclosing machine, it is a whole on one level and a part on another. As with a machine, or a cell, the behaviors of an object are strictly limited to those that are designed into it. Cells and objects follow programmed instructions. But the dynamic behavior of a software system emerges from the interactions of many objects—each contributing, each playing a responsible role.

## OBJECT MACHINERY

Like all good questions, "What is an object?" raises a number of others. How do objects help us think about a problem? How are object applications different? Once we have found an object solution, can we use it again for other purposes?

All but the simplest of devices, both hardware and software, are designed from parts. These parts interact according to someone's plan. In a physical machine, these parts touch one another or communicate through a shared medium. Their interactions may give way to force, transfer motion, or conduct heat.

Software machinery is similar to physical machinery. A software application is constructed from parts. These parts—software objects—interact by sending messages to request information or action from others. Throughout its lifetime, each object remains responsible for responding to a fixed set of requests. To fulfill these requests, objects encapsulate scripted responses and the information that they base them on (see Figure 1-1). If an object is designed to remember certain facts, it can use them to respond differently to future requests.

So how do we invent these software machines?

At the heart of object-oriented software development there is a violation of real-world physics. We have a license to reinvent the world, because modeling the real world in our machinery is not our goal.

Building an object-oriented application means inventing appropriate machinery. We represent real-world information, processes, interactions, relationships, even errors, by inventing objects that don't exist in the real world. We give life and intelligence to inanimate things. We take difficult-to-comprehend real-world objects and split them into

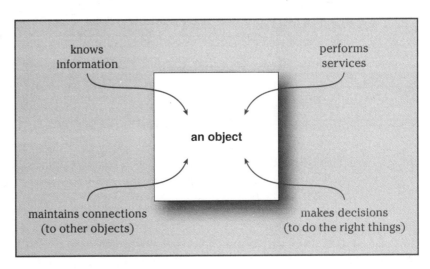

Figure 1-1
*An object encapsulates scripts and information.*

simpler, more manageable software ones. We invent new objects. Each has a specific role to play in the application. Our measure of success lies in how clearly we invent a software reality that satisfies our application's requirements—and not in how closely it resembles the real world.

For example, filling out and filing a form seems simple. But to perform that task in software, behind the simple forms, the application is validating the data against business rules, reading and refreshing the persistent data, guaranteeing the consistency of the information, and managing simultaneous access by dozens of users. Software objects display information, coordinate activities, compute, or connect to services. The bulk of this machine is our invention! We follow a real-world metaphor—forms and files—but our object model includes a much richer set of concepts that are realized as objects.

Because they have machinelike behaviors and because they can be plugged together to work in concert, objects can be used to build very complex machines. To manage this complexity, we divvy the system's behaviors into objects that play well-defined *roles*. If we keep our focus on the behavior, we can design the application using several complementary perspectives:

| | |
|---|---|
| An application | = a set of interacting objects |
| An object | = an implementation of one or more roles |
| A role | = a set of related responsibilities |
| A responsibility | = an obligation to perform a task or know information |
| A collaboration | = an interaction of objects or roles (or both) |
| A contract | = an agreement outlining the terms of a collaboration |

## ROLES

No object exists in isolation. It is always part of a bigger machine. To fit in, an object has a specific purpose—a role it plays within a given context. Objects that play the same role can be interchanged. For example, there are several providers that can deliver letters and packages: DHL, FedEx, UPS, Post, Airborne. They all have the same purpose, if not the same way of carrying out their business. You choose from among them according to the requirements that you have for delivery. Is it one-day, book rate, valuable, heavy, flammable? You pick among the mail carriers that meet your requirements.

"We take a handful of sand from the endless landscape of awareness around us and call that handful of sand the world. Once we have the handful of sand, the world of which we are conscious, a process of discrimination goes to work on it. This is the knife. We divide the sand into parts. This and that. Here and there. Black and white. Now and then. The discrimination is the division of the conscious universe into parts."

—Robert Pirsig

> A role is a set of responsibilities that can be used interchangeably.

It is useful to think about an object, asking, "What role does it play?" This helps us concentrate on what it should be and what it should do. We have been speaking of objects and roles loosely. What is the real difference? When a role is always played by the same kind of object, the two are equivalent. But if more than one kind of object can fulfill the same responsibilities within the community, a role becomes a set of responsibilities that can be fulfilled in different ways. A role is a slot in the software machinery to be filled with an appropriate object as the program runs.

## OBJECT ROLE STEREOTYPES

Just as an actor tries to play a believable part in a play, an object takes on a character in an application by assuming responsibilities that define a meaningful role.

A well-defined object supports a clearly defined role. We use purposeful oversimplifications, or *role stereotypes*, to help focus an object's responsibilities. Stereotypes are characterizations of the roles needed by an application. Because our goal is to build consistent and easy-to-use objects, it is advantageous to stereotype objects, ignoring specifics of their behaviors and thinking about them at a higher level. By oversimplifying and characterizing it, we can ponder the nature of an object's role more easily. We find these stereotypes to be useful:

- Information holder—knows and provides information
- Structurer—maintains relationships between objects and information about those relationships
- Service provider—performs work and, in general, offers computing services
- Coordinator—reacts to events by delegating tasks to others
- Controller—makes decisions and closely directs others' actions
- Interfacer—transforms information and requests between distinct parts of our system

Software machinery is made of computation of information, maintenance of relationships, control of external programs and devices, formatting of information for display, responding to external events and inputs, error handling, and decision making.

Once we assign and characterize an object's role, its attendant responsibilities will follow. An object may fit into more than one stereotype.

But is it playing one or two roles? Often we find that a service provider holds information that it needs to provide its service. In doing so, it assumes two stereotypes—information holder and service provider—but only one role because the responsibilities are all wrapped up together for the same customers to use. If its information is being used solely to support its service, it assumes two stereotypes but only one role. But if it is perceived as serving two different types of clients for different purposes, it is likely playing two roles.

Some objects are hard to stereotype because they seem to fit into more than one category. They're fuzzy. How can you choose? You must decide what you want to emphasize. A transmission is a service provider if you emphasize the multiplication of power by the gears. It is an interfacer if you emphasize its connections to the engine and wheels. Can objects have more than one stereotype? If you want to emphasize more than one aspect, that's OK. There are blends of stereotypes, just as there are blends of emphasis.

## ROLES, RESPONSIBILITIES, AND COLLABORATIONS

An application implements a system of responsibilities. Responsibilities are assigned to roles. Roles collaborate to carry out their responsibilities. A good application is structured to effectively fulfill these responsibilities. We start design by inventing objects, assigning responsibilities to them for knowing information and doing the application's work. Collectively, these objects work together to fulfill the larger responsibilities of the application.

Objects and their responsibilities provide the common core for our new development process, techniques, and tools.

One object calls on, or collaborates with, another because it needs something. Both parties are involved. One needs help; the other provides a service. Objects work in concert to fulfill larger responsibilities. Designing collaborations forces us to consider objects as cooperating partners and not as isolated individuals. Design is an iterative and incremental process of envisioning objects and their responsibilities and inventing flexible collaborations within small neighborhoods.

Clearly defined objects that stick to the point when implementing their roles are easier to understand and maintain.

The services that an object holds and the information that an object provides define how it behaves when it exists alongside other objects. In early design, it is enough to know that particular responsibilities are clustered into objects. First and foremost, an object is responsible for providing and doing for others. A design model arranges responsibilities among objects. We will explore this issue in greater detail later, but, for now, consider this:

> An object embodies a set of roles with a designated set of responsibilities.

As shown in Figure 1-2, an application is a community of objects working together. They collaborate by sending requests and receiving replies. Every object is held responsible. Each contributes its knowledge and services.

Making objects smarter also makes the system more efficient. Objects can stick to their specific tasks, rather than worrying about details that are peripheral to their main purpose.

An object can be more intelligent if it does something with what it knows. The smarter it gets, the fewer details a client must know to use its services. So the client is liberated to do its work rather than take on the details of figuring out something that it could have been told. Blending stereotypes makes the responsibilities of clients using these hybrids easier, streamlined, and to the point. Such clients can focus on their problem, not on putting little details together that their helpers could have done. Making objects smarter has a net effect of raising the IQ of the whole neighborhood.

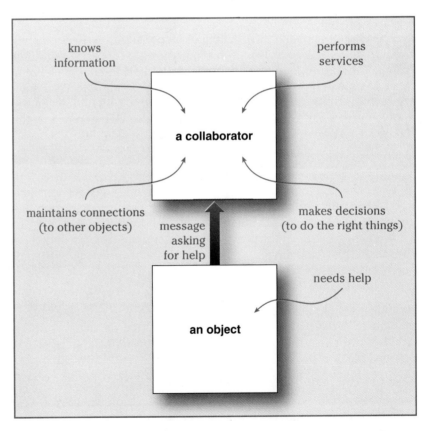

Figure 1-2
*Objects collaborate to solve larger problems than they can handle alone.*

When objects do collaborate, they are designed to follow certain protocols and observe specific conventions: Make requests only for advertised services. Provide appropriate information. Use services under certain conditions. Finally, accept the consequences of using them. Object contracts should describe all these terms.

However, some of the value of a given object is determined by its neighbors. As we conceive our design, we must constantly consider each object's value to its immediate neighborhood. Does it provide a useful service? Is it easy to talk to? Is it a pest because it is constantly asking for help? Are its effects the desired ones? The fewer demands an object makes, the easier it is to use. The more it can take on, the more useful it is. If an object can accommodate many different kinds of objects that might be provided as helpers, it makes fewer demands about the exact kinds of objects it needs around it to perform its responsibilities. Although we don't want an object's clients to have to know all these details, we designers must consider this as we balance what each object offers to its clients with the requirements and demands that it places on its neighbors.

Roles! Responsibilities! Collaborations! We use the roles-responsibilities-collaborations model in each of our activities to keep our focus on the behaviors of our software machinery. As our understanding of the problem grows, the roles and responsibilities of our objects evolve. We design and redesign the community's neighborhoods and the ways they interact. We reinvent the object roles and shift responsibilities among them until they "fit," work together, satisfy external constraints, and their responsibilities clearly support their purposes. We pin down more of the details until we reach the point where we can eventually bind the responsibilities to executable code.

## OBJECT CONTRACTS

In well-bounded situations, it is possible to know a good deal about whom an object interacts with, the circumstances under which it is used, and what long-term effects an object has on its environment. These are spelled out in object contracts. They deepen our knowledge of an object's responsibilities and build our confidence in our design. Without saying how these things are accomplished, they show the conditions under which these responsibilities are called upon (conditions-of-use guarantees), and what marks they leave when they are finished (aftereffect guarantees).

An object contract describes the conditions under which it guarantees its work and the effects it leaves behind when its work is complete.

## Conditions-of-Use and Aftereffect Guarantees

Knowing who collaborates with whom says nothing about when collaborations can succeed. "What do they expect from me? Under what conditions do I guarantee my services? My methods may only be called in this order!" For the designer to be confident that the object will perform the request, the requirements it places on its context must be described in its conditions-of-use. For each responsibility, any objects or internal values (or both) that affect its behavior should be noted, and any controls on them should be described.

Contracts are really meaningful only in the programmer's mind. Objects don't look for advertisements and read contracts; a programmer does, and writes code with those contracts in mind.

This fine print of a contract specifies the conditions-of-use for each service and specifies the aftereffects of using each of the object's services. When an object is used outside its specified conditions-of-use, it is not obligated to fulfill the request! If an Account object has responsibilities for withdrawing cash, what are the conditions-of-use? One is that the balance be greater than or equal to the amount being withdrawn! Or it may be more complex than that, depending on the bank's policies regarding individual customers. The extra effort in describing these conditions-of-use pays off in increased reliability and robustness.

Remember, an object's contracts with others describe how it interacts with them, the conditions under which it guarantees its work, and the effects it has on other members of the community. For our purposes in design, it is sufficient to know that particular services are clustered in interfaces and that these services will call on each other and succeed given the correct conditions.

## DOMAIN OBJECTS

Domain objects provide a common ground in which developers and users can meet and discuss the application. Domain objects represent concepts that are familiar to users and experts in a specific field of interest. We reason about a banking application using accounts, deposits, withdrawals, interest rates, and the like. In an airline booking application, we speak of reservations, airplanes, seats, destinations, schedules, and so on, as concepts that we will find in our software object model. Later, we develop the underlying structures and code and run scenarios for using the software. Given that users and experts are familiar with these domain concepts, they can discuss these aspects of the application easily. They feel comfortable manipulating these domain objects' information directly, and they understand the procedures for requesting their services.

For the developers, these domain objects are only the starting point for constructing a model of the domain and for developing the internal representations of these and additional concepts that will exist in the software machinery. Although the original, "common" concepts might not prove valuable in the executable system, they should be traceable through the design because they clearly express the stakeholders' understanding and issues surrounding the application.

In an object-oriented application, the domain is made of information and services that the user needs, along with structures that relate the two (see Figure 1-3). For example, an inventory control system consists of monitoring the stock on hand (information), adding and removing the stock (services), and supporting policies for maintaining related stock (relations). These three aspects (information, services, and structures) apply to virtually all data-centric applications, and we use them to guide our development of objects that fulfill these roles.

The objects in a domain model embody the application's logic in their interactions. The domain model captures, at the most abstract level, the semantics of the application and its responses to the environment. It doesn't represent all concepts of a domain but only those that are necessary to support the application's intended

Although not every software design effort starts by creating a domain model, most designs consist of certain objects that represent concepts familiar to experts in a particular domain supported by the application.

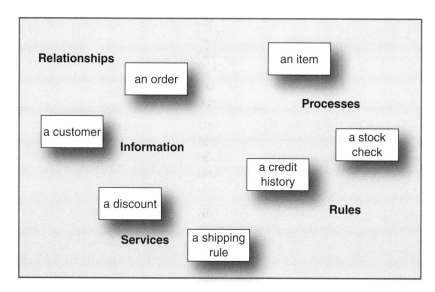

Figure 1-3
*A domain model does not represent the entire domain as it is in the real world. It includes only the concepts that are needed to support the application.*

scenarios of usage. The individual objects in the domain model hold the real, concrete responsibilities for responding to the user actions and for creating the new information that the user requires. If we are only describing a car and aren't building a model to execute on a computer, it's enough to construct a domain model that includes, among other things, a frame, an engine, a transmission, a steering wheel, a steering box, a steering column, wheels, and brakes. But when we must run it on a computer and design user interactions, we find that the domain of real-world race cars lacks many important behaviors. We need a richer set of objects and a richer domain—that of a simulated race car in a computer game. It is important to choose the right domain for your design problem and to recognize that objects designed to work in one domain won't easily slip into another, seemingly similar domain.

For example, in a race car simulation, the cockpit, racetrack, and competing cars must appear on the screen as visual images. What object from the domain of the real-world race car will do this? There isn't one! So for this specialized purpose, we must invent an object that presents the program images and captures user input: an interfacer.

## APPLICATION-SPECIFIC OBJECTS

Similarly, we need objects to translate the computer's user inputs (mouse clicks, joystick movements) to commands to appropriate objects in the racing application. These objects transform or filter user information and then call other appropriate objects to action. Or they may sequence movement from one screen to another, switching views of the race track and replaying the images and sounds of exciting crashes. These computer and application-specific objects—the interfacers, coordinators, and special service providers—supplement the domain model of the simulated race car with program-specific behaviors and glue the application together.

> Object-oriented software is a community of objects. In this community, each citizen provides information and computing services to a select group of its neighbors. The design of well-formed patterns of collaboration lies at the heart of any object design.

As we shift our view from the model of the domain to objects that are important to the actual workings of the software, we encounter many such application objects. For example, when a typical application is launched, there is at least one special startup object that creates the first population of objects. When this group is initialized and ready, the startup object passes control to them. The application is off and running. As the user navigates through the application, this initial group of objects responds to user actions, either by directly fulfilling the requirements of the application or by creating and delegating work to a new batch of objects that have been designed for specific purposes. As execution continues, new citizens of this object community are born, live, and die, according to the needs (and design) of the application.

Designers construct an executable application that is "true" (by some argument) to other stakeholders' views, even as it adds many new application-specific objects: objects that monitor inputs and user events; application-specific data formatters, converters, and filters that act out their roles behind the scenes; and other objects that reach out to the external world of databases, devices, networks, and other computer programs (see Figure 1-4). Developers naturally need a more detailed view.

The user's and the designer's views represent two different levels of thinking about applications and objects. The user view holds a representation of the highest-level concepts—the information, services, and rules of the domain under consideration. The designer invents aspects of coordination and connectivity to other systems and devices, reasoning about the application in a fundamentally different, lower level: the level of computer processes, computations, translation, conditional execution, delegation, and inputs and

The user interface, application specifics, domain concepts, and even persistent stores can be viewed logically or concretely. Users and domain experts typically are concerned only with a more abstract, or logical, view. Developers are interested in all views of the system and they must move among implementation details, design, and more abstract concepts if they want to communicate effectively.

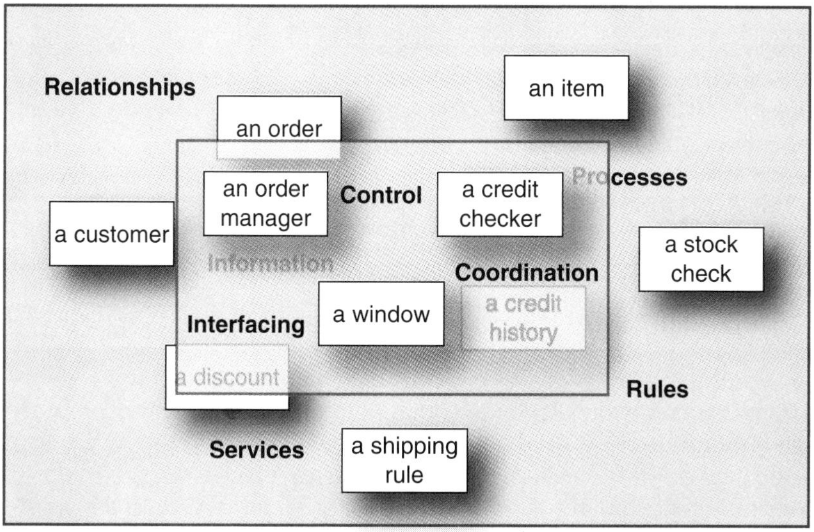

Figure 1-4
*An application model supplements the domain model with computer-specific objects for responding to the user, controlling execution, and connecting to outside resources.*

outputs. The key to developing a successful application lies in our ability as designers to wed these two views without compromising either.

## INTERFACES

Eventually, an object expresses its responsibilities for knowing and doing for others in methods containing code. An interface describes the vocabulary used in the dialog between an object and its customers: "Shine my shoes. Give me my shoes. That'll be five bucks, please. Here's your receipt." The interface advertises the services and explains how to ask for them.

It is often important to know more than just what an interface declares. To use an object's services, the conditions under which a service can be invoked may be important. Or an important side effect may need to be revealed.

Consider a gear in a machine. The number of teeth and the spacing between the teeth defines the gear's interface. This determines whether a gear will fit into a machine. But what if we replace one gear with another, built from a different alloy than the other gears? This new gear fits the interface, but as the gears turn, it may tend to overheat or break because it has different stress load characteristics. Its interface says nothing about this real-world limitation.

> We separate an object's design into three parts: its public interface, the terms and conditions of use, and the private details of how it conducts its business.

The more we publish about the behavior of an object, the more likely it is that it will be used as its designer intended. From a client's viewpoint, an object is more than its interface:

> An object implements interfaces and affects other objects.

> Only the designers of an object's inner machinery should care about how an object implements its responsibilities.

So what about information hiding? We're not talking about exposing everything about an object, but only the services and terms that are of concern to the client. We purposely hide the workings of our object's machinery. An object is a semiautonomous member of the community, stating, "It's none of your business how I do my job, as long as I do it according to our agreement! I don't want customers peeking inside to see how I conduct my business." It is the implementation of the object, not what to expect from it, that should be hidden.

## CLASSES

The term *class* is used, in mathematics and in everyday life, to describe a set of like things. It describes all of these elements in a general way but allows each *instance* of the class to vary in non-essential features. Whereas the class is abstract and conceptual, the instances are concrete, physical objects. The visual image that appears to us at the mere mention of a tree contains the essential features that enable us to recognize any of the instances of tree when we see one. We easily distinguish between a car and a truck when one vehicle adheres to one description or the other, sport utility vehicles aside.

This everyday notion of a class also applies to software objects. We build our applications from sets of like objects. But a software class has some features that are specific to the software world. An object-oriented programming language allows a programmer to describe objects using classes and to define their behaviors using methods. There are additional requirements of an object-oriented programming language, but these two are key. They provide us with all that we need to build an application from objects.

Unlike a mathematical class, a software class is not simply an abstraction. Like the instances that it describes, it is concrete. To see it, you don't have to conjure it from nothing because it is described on index cards, diagrammed with a design notation, and written in programming code. You can pick it up, turn it over, read its description. It is an object. The features that we give the class are the features that we desire in its instances. Every responsibility for "knowing," "doing," or "deciding" that we assign to its instances becomes concrete in the class definition and the instance methods that the class contains.

## Two Roles

If a software class provides two distinct sets of services, usually to two different sorts of clients, the class is said to play two roles. First, it plays a role that has no real-world analog. During program execution, a class acts as a factory for manufacturing, or instantiating, the instances required by the program (see Figure 1-5). It populates the computer memory with physical, electromagnetic objects, and it binds these memory areas to sets of instructions that they are responsible for. Our design objects—the abstract machines, roles, and clusters of responsibility that we invent to satisfy our design requirements—become classes in program code.

Classes play two roles. First, they act as factories, instantiating instances and implementing responsibilities on their behalf. Second, they act as an independent provider, serving clients in their neighborhood.

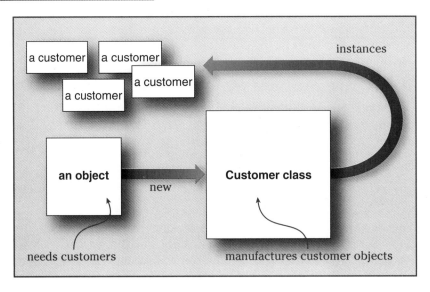

Figure 1-5
*A class, when acting as a factory, manufactures (instantiates) objects that the application needs.*

Classes hold the "shape" of the objects that they make.

A class holds the blueprints for building instances. By defining a set of instance methods, it declares the names of the behaviors that other client objects can use. When an instance responds to a request from a client, it performs the corresponding method scripted in its class. The details of how the instances perform a task are pinned down in the instance's class definition and in its collection of instance method definitions. By browsing the instance's class and its instance methods, you can see whether the instance performs its responsibilities alone or delegates portions of its task to other objects in its neighborhood.

Relations among classes describe the myriad potential relations among run-time instances.

Classes are the building blocks of our application. Just as we describe a single object through the attributes and operations defined in its class, we describe the relations among instances via corresponding relations among classes. For example, the millions of *owner* relations between people and cars can be abstracted into a single owner relation between the classes of the two.

In addition to its role as an object factory, the class can act as an object itself, with its own set of responsibilities. In this role, it provides information and services to other objects through its own interface. Often, its only clients are the instances that it has produced, but in other cases, it acts as the sole provider of data and services to a number of different kinds of objects. In fact, as shown in Figure 1-6, when a single object of its kind is sufficient, a class can be designed to shed its instance factory role and assume the role of the object that is needed.

Given the same conditions, all instances of a given class behave in the same way. They form a set of like objects. Each has a structure identical to the others, along with a set of methods that it shares with the others of its kind. Because each instance is a separate object with its own internal data areas, it can hold private data that it shares with no other. When asked to perform one of its responsibilities, it can base its response on this private data. A smart object encapsulates data that affects its decisions about how it fulfills its responsibilities.

Each instance performs its tasks in two contexts. It behaves according to rules established by the community in which it lives, and it controls its actions according to its own private rules and data. The rules are usually embedded in the methods as conditional statements in a programming language. An object's state is reflected by data held in instance variables. These variables define the internal structure of an object and are one way an object sees others in its

Despite a shared definition, instances will often behave differently because their behavior can depend on the values of their private data or different helpers in their neighborhood.

"The object has three properties, which makes it a simple, yet powerful model building block. It has state so it can model memory. It has behavior, so that it can model dynamic processes. And it is encapsulated, so that it can hide complexity."

—Trygve Reenskaug

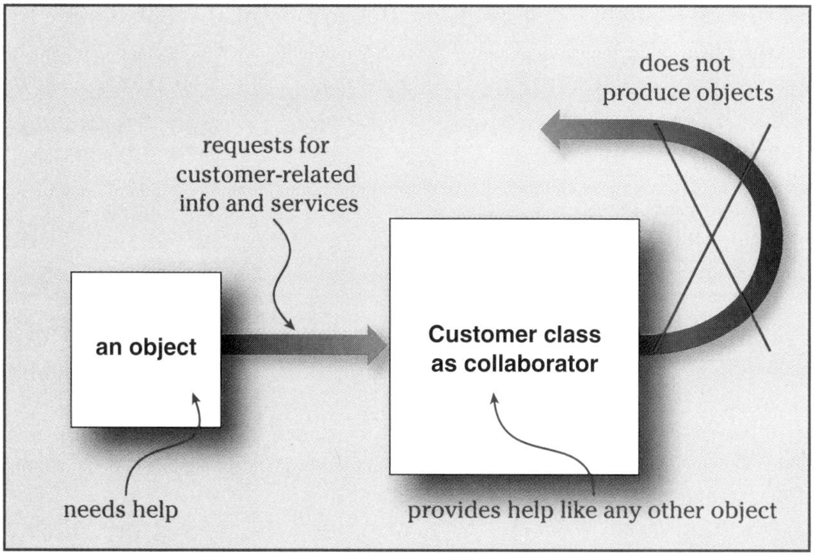

Figure 1-6
*A class can also act as an object when the application needs only one of its kind.*

neighborhood; an object can hold references to others. These references allow an object to "see," and subsequently interact, with others. These references say nothing about how they interact—only that the potential exists for collaboration.

## COMPOSITION

A family tree describes the structural relations of a group of people. Someone is added to the tree in one of two ways: by marriage or by birth.

There are only two types of relationships in an object model: composition and inheritance. Both have analogs in a family tree. A composition relation is like a marriage between objects. It is dynamic, it happens during the participating objects' lifetimes, and it can change. Objects can discard partners and get new partners to collaborate with. Inheritance relations are more like births into the family. Once it happens, it is forever. Just as both marriage and ancestry appear in the same family tree, composition and inheritance coexist in a single object model.

We can extend an object's capabilities by composing it from others. When it lacks the features that it needs to fulfill one of its responsibilities, we simply delegate the responsibility for the required information or action to one of the objects that the object holds onto. This is a very flexible scenario for extension. As the program continues execution, it plugs components together, dynamically, according to the conditions of the application.

For objects to communicate, they must know about each other for the duration of their collaborations. Composition is one way to create those paths of communication. Passing a helper object along with a request, or creating a new instance, are two other ways that an object gains visibility of potential collaborations.

## INHERITANCE

An instance *uses* another's responsibilities through collaboration. An instance *assumes* another's responsibilities through inheritance.

Inheritance is another way to extend an object's capabilities. But whereas composition is dynamic, inheritance isn't. It's static. The merging of the superclass responsibilities and the extension of its subclasses are done at compile time and not run time. Objects are not plugged together; instead, the descriptions used to compile them (the classes) are.

Every inheritance relationship between two classes involves two roles: the *superclass* role and the *subclass* role. Each acts out its role during development. With few exceptions, a subclass assumes all of the responsibilities outlined in the superclass and adds new responsibilities of its own. The subclass inherits all of the features encoded in the superclass and has the responsibility for instantiating objects having those features. The subclass extends the superclass. In this arrangement, the superclass contains features that are common to all of its subclasses, and each subclass not only creates its own instances but also adds features to them that are not described in the superclass. A subclass extends the superclass by adding attributes and operations. An instance's responsibilities are the union of all of the responsibilities in its own class and all of the responsibilities of the superclasses that it inherits from.

Classes sometimes relinquish their responsibility for producing instances to their subclasses. These *abstract classes* define many of the features of instances, but they require subclasses to fill in some details and to do the actual manufacturing.

## OBJECT ORGANIZATIONS

As you begin to decompose your application into logical pieces, you may identify objects or roles and define classes that implement specific roles. You may also find design elements that have a certain logical integrity but, on further inspection, can themselves be decomposed into smaller pieces. A common term for a logical grouping of collaborators is subsystem. Another term we use is object neighborhood. Within these organizations, objects dynamically form alliances and work together in a loosely knit community. By contracting with each other, such a confederation of objects serves a larger purpose than is possible for any individual.

Each object in a confederation promises to fulfill the responsibilities outlined in its contracts. Thus, each object can depend on the others for a reliable and predictable response to its requests. Confederations are composed of potentially many objects and often have a complex collective behavior. The synergy of the cooperative efforts among the members creates a new, higher-level conceptual entity.

Viewed from the outside, a confederation offers a unified front. Figure 1-7 shows an example. It isn't just a "bunch of objects"; it forms a good abstraction. Although individually each object has a specific role and responsibilities, it is the collective behaviors of the objects that define the confederation to the rest of the application. There is no conceptual difference between the responsibilities of an object and those of a subsystem of objects; it is simply a matter of scale and the amount of richness and detail in your design. Often, other objects interact with a confederation in limited ways. There may be a single object—a gatekeeper—that stands as the public representative of the larger group.

> It's common to say that a subclass "specializes" its superclass because the added responsibilities make the subclass's role less general than that of the superclass.

> Inheritance relations demonstrate the Peter Principle. The higher in a hierarchy a class resides, the less capable of really doing anything it becomes.

> System architects may partition an application into subsystems early in design. But subsystems can be discovered later, as the complexity of the system unfolds.

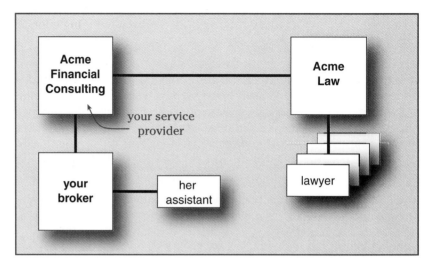

Figure 1-7
*This confederation of objects forms a company devoted to specific tasks.*

## COMPONENTS

Although a single class may not be a useful unit of reuse, a component that packages a number of services can be. Components enable medium-grained reuse.

There are other ways to package and organize pieces of a design. Components typically are design elements that are intended to be used in a number of different applications. But designers create components for other reasons, too. You can update or replace a component without reconfiguring the rest of the system. The insides of a component are hidden; its services are made available through a well-defined interface. Well-designed components, regardless of their implementation, can be plugged in and used by any object-oriented application. To be adapted for use, a component can provide interfaces that allow clients to plug in helper components or to set properties that control various aspects of its operation. You can design components to be used independently or to be plugged together to build larger components or systems.

## PATTERNS

So far we've presented fundamental object design concepts. But there is more to object design than applying these basic techniques. The early adopters of object technology generated many successful object applications and strategies for solving problems. Wouldn't it be marvelous if we had those experts at our sides during our own projects to roll their expertise into our own problem-solving efforts? Well, this community of experts has developed a means to do just that: Patterns.

There is nothing mysterious about patterns. They simply capture the experience of expert practitioners by presenting solutions to commonly recurring problems in a readable and predictable format. But what good is a solution if the problem is not well understood? What are the trade-offs? When is the solution applicable? Because problems and their solutions have an equally important context, patterns include descriptions of other aspects of the problem and its solution.

Erich Gamma and several of his colleagues wrote the *Design Patterns* book (Addison-Wesley) in 1994. Their format for a pattern covers a lot of territory. It includes:

- Pattern name and classification
- Intent
- Also known as
- Motivation
- Applicability
- Structure
- Participants
- Collaborations
- Consequences
- Implementation
- Sample code
- Known uses
- Related patterns

Most of the newer pattern books aren't so inclusive. Some patterns simply give a name to a problem and its solution. Other formats lie somewhere between these two extremes. For our purposes, let's boil a pattern down to this list:

- Name: Communicates the pattern easily
- Problem: Describes a recurring problem
- Forces: Describes what considerations need to be balanced

- Context: Describes where the solution is appropriate
- Solution: Can be tailored to a specific problem
- Consequences: Let's be real!

This is not to say that the other elements have no value. But this intermediate level of detail lets you be productive without getting bogged down in precision. However you break them down, patterns offer clear benefits to developers:

- Vocabulary: In a team of any size, communications are a vital element of a successful project. Patterns establish a concise way of describing how a group of objects solve a problem, either behaviorally, structurally, or both.
- Expertise: Patterns capture the expertise of years of development. Because they are applicable to any domain, they can model the behavior and structure of a group of interacting concepts.
- Understanding: Documenting how the system uses patterns enables new developers to quickly see the logical organization.

By condensing many structural and behavioral aspects of the design into a few simple concepts, patterns make it easier for team members to discuss the design. Let's look at a common problem and see how an appropriate pattern contributes to a good design.

## Applying Double Dispatch to a Specific Problem

To implement the game "Rock, Paper, Scissors" we need to write code that determines whether one object "beats" another. The game has nine possible outcomes based on the three kinds of objects (see Figure 1-8). The number of interactions is the cross product of the kinds of objects.

### A Solution

*Case* or *switch* statements are often governed by the type of data that is being operated on. The object-oriented language equivalent is to base its actions on the class of some other object. In Java, it looks like this:

```
// In class Rock
public boolean beats(GameObject object) {
    if (object.getClass.getName().equals("Rock") {
        result = false;
    }
    else if (object.getClass.getName().equals("Paper") {
        result = false;
    }
    else if (object.getClass.getName().equals("Scissors") {
            result = true;
    }
    return result;
}
```

This is not a very good solution. First, the receiver needs to know too much about the argument. Second, there is one of these nested conditional statements in each of the three classes. If new kinds of objects could be added to the game, each of the three classes would have to be modified.

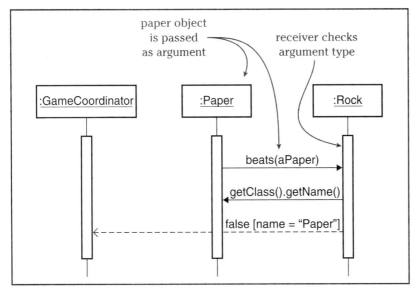

Figure 1-8
*This UML sequence diagram shows the process of deciding who wins, based on checking object type.*

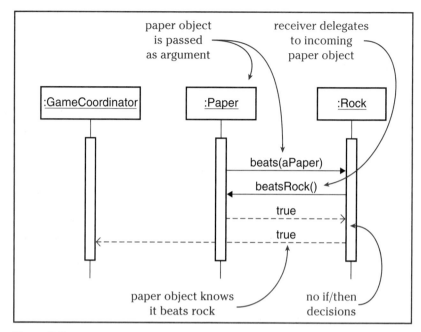

Figure 1-9
*This UML sequence diagram shows the process of deciding who wins, based on polymorphism.*

## A Better Solution

We would like to come up with a solution that would let us avoid touching any working methods. Figure 1-9 shows an example that uses the double dispatch pattern to do that.

Note that rock does not need to know what kind of object it is comparing itself against. The second message clearly identifies the situation to the second object. Another Rock or a Paper will return false, but a Scissors will return true.

Here are the GameObject, Rock, and Paper definitions in Java:

```java
public interface GameObject {
    public boolean beats(GameObject o);
    public boolean beatsRock(GameObject o);
    public boolean beatsPaper(GameObject o);
    public boolean beatsScissors(GameObject o);
}
```

```
public class Rock implements GameObject {
    public boolean beats(GameObject o);
        // the receiver is a Rock. Ask the argument about rocks.
        return o.beatsRock();
    }
    public beatsRock() {
        // could return either false or true
        return false;
    }
    public beatsPaper() {
        // a Rock doesn't beat a Paper
        return false;
    }
    public beatsScissors() {
        // a Rock beats a Scissors!
        return true;
    }
}
```

```
public class Paper implements GameObject {
    public boolean beats(GameObject o) {
        // the receiver is a Paper. Ask the argument about papers.
        return o.beatsPaper();
    }
    public beatsRock() {
        // a Paper beats a Rock
        return true;
    }
    public beatsPaper() {
        // could return either false or true
        return false;
    }
    public beatsScissors() {
        // a Paper doesn't beat a Scissors!
        return false;
    }
}
```

Extending the application to include another kind of GameObject simply requires adding a new declaration of the comparison method to the GameObject interface, defining the new method in the existing classes, and creating a new class that implements the new Game-Object interface.

## The Double Dispatch Pattern

Here's the pattern description:

**Name:** Double Dispatch

**Problem:** Select an action based on the type of two objects appearing in combination.

**Context:** Sometimes you need to write code that makes decisions about what to do based on the class of one of the parameters to a method.

**Forces:** Case or switch statements are often used in procedural languages to decide what action to take. But deciding what to do based on the class of a parameter can result in code that is hard to maintain; each time you add a new class, working code will have to be modified.

Polymorphism allows an object to send the same message to objects belonging to many different classes. Code in each of these classes can subsequently make different decisions and perform the same requested operation differently.

**Solution:** Instead of writing code that specifically checks the class of a parameter, add new methods having the same name (a secondary method) to each class of all the potential parameter objects. Write the original method to simply call this new secondary method, passing the original receiver as an argument. It is the responsibility of each object receiving this secondary message to know specifically what should be done. Typically, each secondary method turns around and invokes a specific operation on the original receiver (hence the name *Double Dispatch*).

You can tie the specific operation to the class of object by appending the class name of each class that implements a secondary method to the name of this specialized operation. If necessary, pass the original receiver as an argument to these specialized operations as well.

**Consequences:** Double Dispatch eliminates case or switch statements based on the class of a parameter. This makes the code that implements the design more maintainable. It doesn't completely solve the maintenance problem, but it supports extension by adding methods and not by modifying them. Double dispatching does have its drawbacks. Adding a new class of parameter means adding a secondary method to it, unless you are able to add a single method to a superclass and have it inherited by its subclasses. It also may mean adding a class-specific method to the original object (or deciding to invoke an existing operation). A case statement, however, is usually a worse solution.

## The Real Benefits of Using Patterns

Imagine that during a design review, one of the team members mentions that a group of objects uses Double Dispatch. The discussion then centers on an analysis of the problem to see whether the pattern fits, the motives for choosing to use it, and a consideration of the trade-offs involved. The use of the pattern shifts the focus to a higher-level design concern. Little time is spent describing the mechanics of the object collaborations because they are condensed into two little words: double dispatch.

## FRAMEWORKS, INC.

The business equivalent of a framework is a franchise. Having proven that there is a market for its services, a company incorporates and sells a generic design for its business: a franchise. A franchise provides a general design for providing its products or services and dictates that franchise owners follow the franchising company's rules. Franchise owners tailor their businesses to their specific markets, within the limits of the franchise contract. With a franchise, services become better defined and widely known and used. Because of their familiarity with the business processes, owners often buy multiple franchises, reusing the business design in different locations. A franchise pools business owners' resources to advertise, train employees, and provide just-in-time services beyond those that a single company could offer.

Similarly, a framework is a general design for solving a software problem (see Figure 1-10). Unlike a pattern, which is an idea of how to solve a familiar problem, a framework provides a library of classes that developers can tailor or extend to fit a particular situation. The success of a framework depends on how useful it is to these developers and how easily they can tailor its services to their needs.

Here are some of the problems that frameworks have been applied to:

- GUI: The Java Swing framework offers a set of features useful for building an interactive user interface.
- Simulation: The early Smalltalk-80 language included a framework for building discrete event simulations.
- Programming environments: The Eclipse IDE (integrated development environment) has a plug-in architecture that lets tool providers supply different compilers, refactoring tools, and debuggers.

- Web applications: Microsoft's .NET framework is a unified set of tools for building distributed applications. It includes frameworks for building user interfaces, performing transactions and concurrency, interoperating between platforms, and building Web services.

Frameworks offer a number of advantages to the developer:

- Efficiency: A framework means less design and coding.
- Richness: Domain expertise is captured in the framework.
- Consistency: Developers become familiar with the approach imposed by the framework.
- Predictability: A framework has undergone several iterations of development and testing.

different sound cards have different behaviors,
but each fits into the framework

board/interrupts/clock/signals
provide a framework that calls on parts

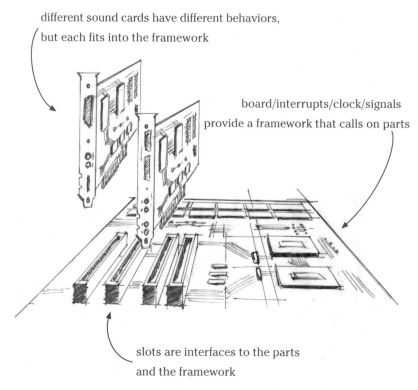

slots are interfaces to the parts
and the framework

Figure 1-10
*A framework codifies the rules of how things should be done.*

But they don't come without costs:

- Complexity: Frameworks often have a steep learning curve.

- If you only have a hammer, everything looks like a nail: Frameworks require a specific approach to solving the problem.

- Performance: A framework often trades flexibility and reusability for performance.

Frameworks are sometimes used as is. In this case, they provide default behaviors that their designers deemed to be useful across many potential applications. But most frameworks are meant to be extended to completion. They provide generic solutions but lack specific behaviors that vary by application. The behaviors that are left incomplete are hooks: implementations that are deferred to the developers for specific applications. When coding these hot spots, a programmer must accept an inversion of control. This takes some getting used to. Typically, our code calls other objects and asks them to do work on our behalf. To use some functionality in a library, for example, you typically instantiate a library object and then call on it to provide a service.

In the case of a framework, you must implement the hooks using code that fits into the framework. The hooks are those areas of the framework that the framework code will call. Instead of being in control, our objects are plugged in and must correctly implement hooks that are called by framework code. To use the features of a framework, you define classes that implement specific interfaces. To use a framework, you fill in the missing functionality, following the constraints dictated by the framework designers.

## ARCHITECTURE

There is no single, defining architecture of an application. Often we see box-and-line drawings purporting to be *the* architecture. Goofjuice! An architecture is a collection of behaviors and a set of descriptions about how they impact one another. Box-and-line drawings describe only the structure. They completely ignore the behavior. A revealing architecture demonstrates the assumptions that each subsystem or component in the application can make about its neighbors, whether it be their responsibilities, error-handling abilities, shared resource usage, or performance characteristics. Because there are many objects in an application, we need different ways of viewing its parts that hide most of their details. The internal details of how a group of objects accomplishes a task should not be the issue when you consider its architecture. At the architectural level, the interfaces must tell it all.

Any single architecture description tells only part of the software's story. For example, the organization of system functions implies little about how the modules are divided among team members for development. The process synchronization characteristics are conspicuously missing from the descriptions of how components are distributed across machines and networks. Because there are many requirements of our software, we often require many views of our "architecture" to convince us that it meets them.

Which views shed the most light on our applications' characteristics, of course, depends on the application. But several of these views are prominent: conceptual views, control flow, and, for object-oriented applications, views of components and subsystems as well as objects and interactions. It is important to identify and document patterns of collaboration. Simply documenting the interfaces of the objects or components would not show how they collaborate. Writing the client-server contracts as part of the architectural descriptions clarifies the roles of each and provides a better understanding of the complexity of the design. Each development project should determine what subset of these architectures is appropriate. In fact, choosing which architectural views to represent and study is a key element of early design.

## Architectural Styles

Just as design patterns offer ways to distribute responsibilities among collaborators to solve generic design problems, there are *styles* for organizing software objects. There are a number of aspects to consider when you think about architectural style. Two of the most common viewpoints are component interaction styles and control styles. Both need to be considered. Component interactions are concerned with issues that we commonly see addressed with block structure diagrams. These typically show components or layers of the system and generally describe how they are allowed to interact. Typical examples of these styles are layered, pipes-and-filters, and blackboard. Figure 1-11 shows a layered architecture.

Control style dictates the approaches to distributing responsibilities for decision making and coordination within or between layers or components. We can construct a solution along a continuum of control from highly centralized to overly distributed.

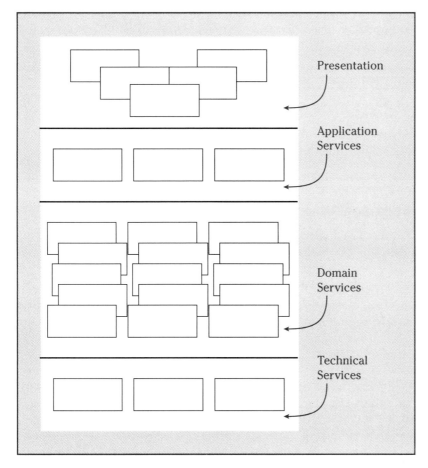

Figure 1-11
*A layered architecture separates objects according to their roles in the application.*

Each combination of architectural styles supports one or more characteristics that we may value in a project:

- Usability
- Availability
- Security
- Performance
- Maintainability
- Flexibility
- Portability

Architectural styles have well-known liabilities. For example, pipes-and-filters is computationally expensive due to the need to cast all data into a common form, usually text.

To support these and other qualities before any analysis, design, or coding takes place, we can start by choosing architectural styles that support them. Using a particular mix of styles will not guarantee that desired qualities will prevail, but we have the window of opportunity left open in which to build them.

Selecting architectural styles is largely dependent on an assessment of the desired attributes of the application. Most applications require a mix of these qualities and a combination of architectural styles. Choosing the right architectural styles can have a big impact.

So before examining a popular component interaction style—the layered style—let's examine the continuum of control styles we can employ.

## Centralized Control Style

A procedural program makes a clear distinction between data and algorithms. Algorithms, whether they are called procedures or functions, use and operate on data. We can simulate a procedural style by creating a single smart object, filled with algorithms, and surround it with numerous, data-structure-like objects that hold only information: pure information holders (see Figure 1-12). When the smart object needs to compute, it asks the information holders for the information it needs, processes it, and either puts it back or puts it in some other information holder. The procedures operate on data. The procedures tend to be redundant because other objects need to operate on the data, too. Many objects use the information holders, and many messages flow around the system.

But despite being procedural, a centralized style does have some advantages. The application logic is centered in only a few objects: the smart ones. Code may be more difficult to read because it is embedded in a lot of the other logic, but you have only a few places to look.

Now try to describe who uses which objects. Any one of the information holders has many clients. The processing of their information is outside of them and is spread across many classes. What if you wanted to shift the responsibility for knowing a piece of information from one to another? Many other objects would break because of the many dependencies.

## Dispersed Control: No Centers

In the other extreme, we spread the logic across the entire population of objects, keeping each object small and building in as few

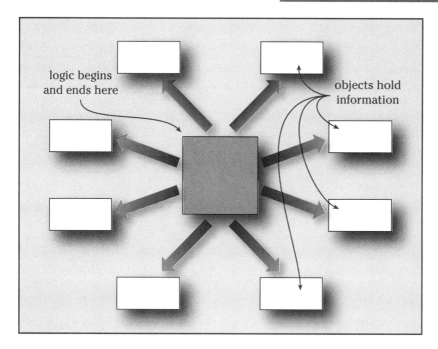

Figure 1-12
*Centralized control concentrates logic into a single object.*

dependencies among them as possible. As Figure 1-13 shows, there are no centers to the design.

When you want to find out how something works, you must trace the sequence of requests for services across many objects. And they are not very reusable because no single object contributes much.

## Delegated Control

A delegated control style strikes a compromise or balance between these two extremes. As Figure 1-14 shows, each object encapsulates most of what it needs to perform its responsibilities, but, on occasion, it needs help from other, capable objects. Every object has a substantial piece of the pie. It isn't hard to trace through the few objects involved to see how something works. On the other hand, because each object is largely capable of fulfilling its own responsibilities, it is more reusable. Reusing even the larger responsibilities means including only a few collaborators. System functions are organized into pools of responsibility that can be used in relative isolation.

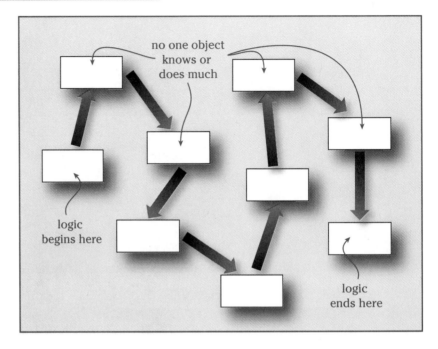

Figure 1-13
*Dispersed control spreads the logic across many kinds of objects.*

## Examining Interactions: A Layered Architecture Example

Let's take a closer look at the layered architectural style. We use it to illustrate how it guides our design of system responsibility. We maximize simplicity and reusability by using a layered style. This architectural style groups responsibilities into layers. Each layer has a well-defined number of neighboring layers, typically one or two. Objects living in each layer communicate mostly with other objects within the same layer. But there are times when the services that an object needs are not to be found within its layer, and it will reach out to an adjacent layer for the selected services. Here is a typical organization of responsibilities in the layers: One layer is devoted to interfacing with the outside world. An adjacent layer coordinates responses to outside events. A third layer provides information and services that span the entire domain, and another layer provides technical services for connecting to external devices and programs. The layered style can contribute to simplicity, maintainability, and reusability. Information systems, which often fit into this component interaction style, typically have a long life span, requiring that they be easy to maintain, scale, and port to new platforms.

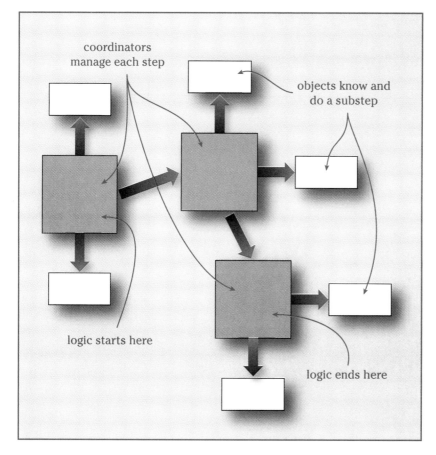

Figure 1-14
*Delegated control creates pools of application logic.*

Using this style gives us flexibility in deciding at run time which objects will collaborate. It also lets us develop objects in each layer without concern for which objects in adjacent layers we will collaborate with. Figure 1-15 shows a sample of collaborating objects, layers, and loose coupling.

This architecture of a Web-based information system application separates areas of functionality into layers of functionality (layered style), defines groups of objects within each layer, and broadcasts events across network connections.

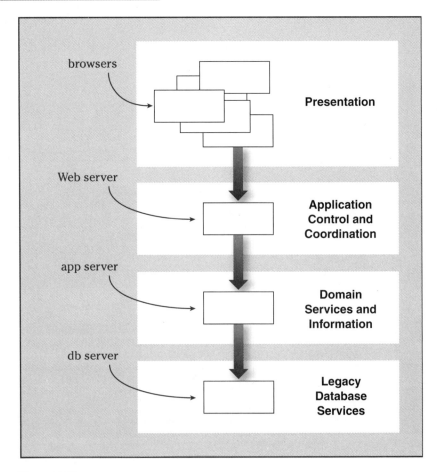

Figure 1-15
*Interactive information systems often use layered architectures.*

## Locating Objects in Layers

We can combine the features just discussed with our notion of object stereotypes to demonstrate a very general layout of objects in an object-oriented information system application. As we discussed earlier, we use these stereotypes to characterize objects' roles: information holder, structurer, service provider, coordinator, controller, and interfacer. How might we build a layered style application from them? Where would objects of each stereotype live? The architecture of a layered system of objects looks something like the diagram in Figure 1-16.

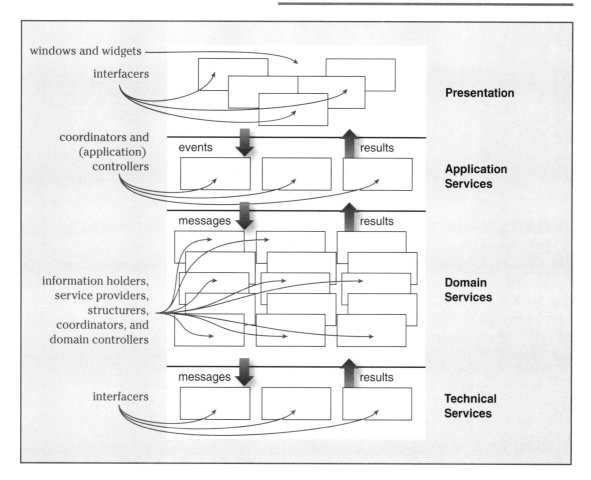

Figure 1-16
*Each layer contains characteristic object roles.*

Communication between objects tends to follow these rules:

- Objects collaborate mostly within their layer.
- When they do reside in different layers, client objects are usually above server objects. The messages (requests) flow mostly down.
- Information (results) flows mostly up.

- When messages flow up, client objects are in lower layers, and they are loosely coupled to their server objects. This usually uses an event mechanism.
- Only the topmost and bottommost layers are exposed to the "outside" world. They hold platform-specific objects: widgets in the top layer, and network, device, and external system interfacers in the bottom layer.

## DESIGN DESCRIPTION

CRC cards were invented by Ward Cunningham and Kent Beck in 1988 as a means of describing early design ideas about classes, their responsibilities, and collaborations. Instead of classes, we use them to describe candidate objects, which eventually are realized by one or more interfaces and classes.

As part of a design process, it is essential to communicate your ideas. During development there are many ways to think about your design, and many ways to informally describe it. Descriptions can range from design stories to roughly drawn sketches, to conceptual "art" that serves as a focal point for discussions, to handwritten CRC cards describing candidates. Design is an inherently messy process, and along the way many descriptions are discarded after serving their purpose.

But there is a time and a place for creating more precise descriptions. The Unified Modeling Language (UML) is a good way to describe your design using a standard graphical modeling language. It provides a vocabulary for describing classes, objects, roles, interfaces, collaborations, and other design elements. It is a large language that includes many more elements than we use in this book. But the UML is more than a graphical notation. Behind each symbol are well-defined semantics. This means that you can specify a UML model using one design tool, and another tool can interpret that model unambiguously.

Any design model or modeling language has limits to what it can express. No one view of a design tells all. That is why in this book we use a rich toolkit that includes both low-tech and more precise ways to describe our designs.

## SUMMARY

Object-oriented applications are composed of objects that come and go, assuming their roles and fulfilling their responsibilities. Typically, the initial set of objects that we find represents domain concepts that designers as well as users are comfortable talking about. Other objects are invented with specific responsibilities for controlling and coordinating the user interface, managing the connections to the outside world, and governing the flow of control in the application. The software itself has properties that emerge. These systemic behaviors are accounted for by the software patterns, frameworks, and architectures. They contribute to system-level properties. Together, they form a collection of perspectives on the system under development.

The "products" of development—the objects, responsibilities, collaborations, contracts, patterns, frameworks, and architectures—are the focus of a systematic development process, a method. With many levels and abstractions to account for, we must be opportunistic in the way we approach the tasks. We shift perspective to reveal a new problem or another facet of an old one; we look for new solutions and explore half-formed ideas. Above all, we keep the focus on what is important right now. This process is the topic of the next chapter.

## FURTHER READING

Timothy Budd's wonderful book, *An Introduction to Object-Oriented Programming* (Addison-Wesley, 2001), includes a thorough discussion of object-oriented concepts and programming principles. Although a college text, it is handy for professional developers, too. Programming languages come on the scene with great rapidity (they don't disappear so quickly, but new ones constantly appear). This book is in its third edition. One of the best things about it is the presentation of the same applications implemented in various object-oriented languages ranging from Smalltalk to Java, C#, C++, Object Pascal, and Oberon.

In addition to inventing the Model-View-Controller concept, Trygve Reenskaug wrote a definitive book on thinking about objects in terms of roles. *Working With Objects* (Manning, 1995), written with Per Wold and Odd Arid Lehne, explores how patterns of interacting objects can be abstracted into patterns of interacting roles. We have been inspired by Trygve's work over the years and believe that modeling roles is essential to creating well-factored, flexible designs.

The classic *Design Patterns: Elements of Reusable Object-Oriented Software* (Addison-Wesley, 1995), by Erich Gamma, Richard Helm, Ralph Johnson, and John Vlissides, launched the software pattern movement. This book contains twenty-some patterns organized into behavioral, creational, and structural patterns. If you want to learn more about the original design patterns that launched the pattern movement, pick up Gamma's book. If you are a Java programmer, you'll learn even more by reading *Design Patterns Java*™ *Workbook* (Addison-Wesley, 2002). In this book, Steve Metsker clearly explains each and every pattern in the *Design Patterns* book from a Java programmer's perspective.

The best source for learning about the UML is *The UML Language User Guide,* (Addison-Wesley, 1999) written by Grady Booch, James Rumbaugh, and Ivar Jacobson. Others have tried to boil down this rich language to its fundamentals, but they lose something in the process.

# Chapter 2

# Responsibility-Driven Design

**B**etty Edwards, author of *Drawing on the Artist Within*, argues that many so-called creative talents can be taught. She poses this delightful thought experiment:

> *What does it take to teach a child to read? What if we believed that only those fortunately endowed with inborn creative ability could learn to read? What if teachers believed the best way to instruct was to expose children to lots of materials, then wait to see who possessed innate reading talent? Fear of stifling the creative reading process would dampen any attempts to guide new readers. If a child asked how to read something, a teacher might respond, "Try whatever you think works. Enjoy it, explore, reading is fun!" Perhaps one or two in any class would possess that rare talent and spontaneously learn to read. But of course, this is an absurd belief! Reading can be taught. So too, can drawing.*

Her book challenges our assumptions that drawing requires rare and special "artistic" talent and that formal teaching of basic drawing skills stifles creativity. Basic drawing techniques, like reading techniques, can be taught. No wonder many of us can't draw! Learning to draw is a matter of learning basic perceptual skills—the special ways of seeing required for accurate drawing.

Object design does not require rare and special "design" talent. Although design is a highly creative activity, the fundamentals can be easily learned. You can become adept at object design with enough practice and experience seeing the nature of the design problem and learning fundamental strategies for producing an acceptable solution.

This chapter presents basic steps for developing object applications following an approach called Responsibility-Driven Design. We first describe the actions and activities for which our software should be "responsible." We describe our software's responsibilities in terms that application users as well as developers understand. Then we turn our attention to designing software objects that appropriately implement these responsibilities.

## A PROCESS FOR SEEING, DESCRIBING, AND DESIGNING

We wish to be very clear on one point: Although this book presents object-oriented development activities in a linear fashion, this is rarely how design proceeds in practice. Software design processes are highly fluid and opportunistic, even though the final results are firmly fixed in code. Our presentation of this flurry of activity is limited by the constraints of the printed page.

Responsibility-Driven Design is an informal method. It offers many techniques for honing your thinking about how to divvy an application's responsibilities into objects and coordinating their performance. Our primary tool is the power of abstraction—forming objects that represent the essence of a working application.

The name of our method emphasizes the thread that runs through every activity: our focus on software responsibilities. Responsibilities describe what our software must do to accomplish its purpose. Our work progresses from requirements gathering through roughly sketched ideas and then on to more detailed descriptions and software models. Surprisingly, at the beginning of our process, we don't focus on objects. Instead, we focus on describing our system by capturing the viewpoints of many different stakeholders. We need to

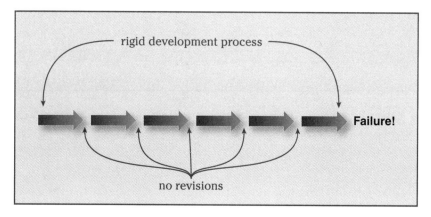

Figure 2-1
*Rigid, tightly planned development often leads to failure.*

consider multiple perspectives in our solutions. Responsibility-Driven Design is a clarification process. We move from initial requirements to initial descriptions and models; from initial descriptions to more detailed descriptions and models of objects; from candidate object models to detailed models of their responsibilities and patterns of collaboration.

We do not follow a straight design path as shown in Figure 2-1. As shown in Figure 2-2, our design journey is filled with curves, switchbacks, and side excursions. When tracking down design solutions,

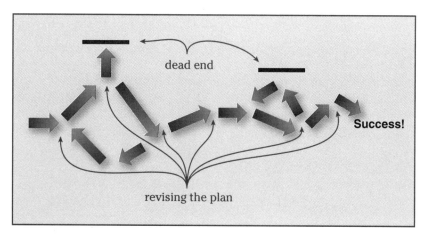

Figure 2-2
*The Responsibility-Driven Design path is a flexible one.*

we often switch among different design activities as we discover different aspects of the problem. We are opportunistic. We use a variety of tools that help us gain perspective, discover information, and craft solutions. Our work is fluid and malleable.

Our ordering of activities and our focus will, of necessity, change (see Figure 2-3). Planning, adding new features, setting goals, characterizing the application via a prototype, creating an object model, identifying the hard problems—these are only some of our tasks. These tasks vary in their purpose, rigor, scope, emphasis, context, and applicable tools.

With all but the simplest software, we can't fathom what lies ahead. With so much complexity, we won't always make optimal decisions. Progress isn't always steady. Along the way we discover new information and constraints. We must take time to breathe and smooth out these recurring wrinkles.

To address our lack of 20-20 foresight, we plan pauses to reexamine, adjust, and align our work to a changing set of conditions. This allows us to incorporate our growing understanding into what we build. As shown in Figure 2-4, our process is iterative and incremental. We are simply shifting emphasis along our development timeline from requirements gathering and specification to analysis, design, testing and coding. We can always retreat to earlier activities and rediscover more of the features of our problem.

Our linear presentation of design activities is due to constraints imposed by printed, numbered pages. As you read this book, ask yourself, Where can I bring this technique to bear on my problem? What thinking tool would be most effective to use right now? Be opportunistic!

Marvin Minsky says our intelligence comes from our ability to negotiate solutions and resolve conflicts among competing goals. If part of your mind proposes solutions that another part finds unacceptable, you can usually find another way. When one viewpoint fails to solve a problem, you can adopt other perspectives.

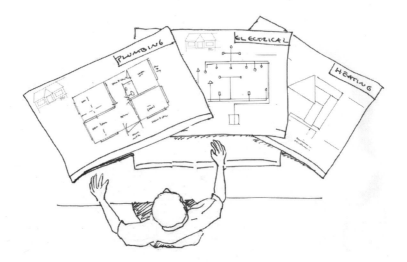

Figure 2-3
*We continually move our focus from one problem area to another, recasting relationships and finding new details.*

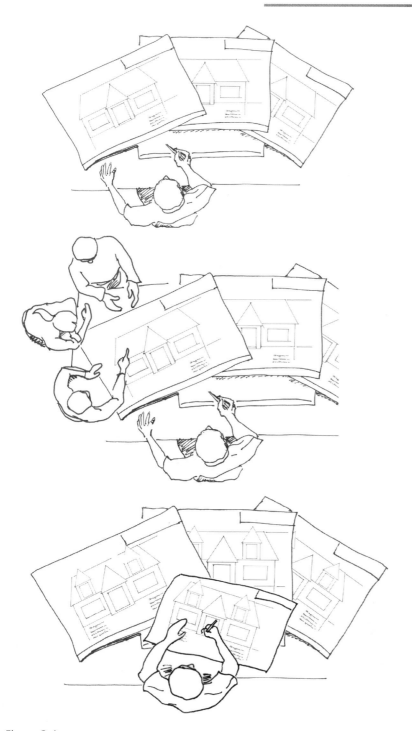

Figure 2-4
*Discovery involves stating an idea, reflecting it back to stakeholders for feed-back, and then incorporating changes and new insights in the revised model.*

As designers, we naturally think that software objects are the center of the software universe. However object-oriented *we* may be, though, many other participants and perspectives go into the conception, design, and construction of a successful application. Just like a theater production, software development involves much more than meets the eye during a performance. And although objects may take center stage for our work, it is important to recognize the impact that different perspectives and activities have on our design.

## Launching the Production: Project Definition and Planning

We adopt a conventional approach to describing our object development process. First things first. It's desirable to define project goals, construct a plan for achieving them, and receive buy-in before jumping into a big effort.

In long or complex productions, we need to survey and document the users' requirements and demonstrate how our software system will serve those who have some "skin in the game"—the stakeholders who will be impacted by our success or failure. Even in quick projects, a little planning goes a long way. This leads us to form a concise statement of the project, which includes a statement of purpose, an overview, and a definition of the scope and benefits.

Project planning sets the stage for our design ideas. It is our plan for action. Keeping in mind that our main goal is to please our users and project sponsors, a project plan describes the following:

- How the software will be developed
- The values that are important to the project and the people involved
- The people and their roles, the processes, and the expected outcomes
- The expected deliverables

Although not the focus of this book, project planning and definition are fundamental. Once we have a plan of action, we consider structures and processes. Our goal is to understand what our software should do and how it will support its users.

> "It is very much a matter of artistry. The developer, like ancient bards whose epic poems were not written down but recited from memory, must choose structures that will be readily remembered, that will help the audience not to lose the thread of the story."
>
> —Michael Jackson

## Setting the Stage: Early Description

Initially, we narrow our scope and our descriptions. We begin with rough sketches, fudging in those areas that demand detail that we can't yet provide. We iterate through cycles of discovery, reflection, and description. Bit by bit we add details, pin down the ambiguous, and resolve conflicting requirements. Initially our descriptions aren't object-oriented; we add an object perspective after we've described our system more generally. Object concepts will form the kernel of a model of our system's inner workings. But our recipe for analysis looks something like Table 2-1.

Table 2-1 *Analysis includes system definition, system description, and object analysis activities.*

| Responsibility-Driven Analysis | | |
|---|---|---|
| **Phase** | **Activity** | **Results** |
| **System Definition** | Develop high-level system architecture. | Diagram of system boundaries. |
| | | High-level diagrams of technical architecture |
| | | System concepts discussion and diagrams |
| | Identify initial system concepts. | Glossary of terms |
| | Identify system responsibilities. | System perspective and functions |
| | | Usage characteristics |
| | | General constraints, assumptions, and dependencies |
| **Detailed Description** | Specify development environment. | Documentation of existing development frameworks, external programs, APIs, and computer-based tools. |
| | Write text descriptions of the ways users expect to perform their tasks. | A list of the different types of users and external systems that interact with our system: actors |
| | | Free-form text descriptions of the users' tasks: use case narratives |
| | | Text descriptions of concrete usage examples: scenarios and conversations |
| | Analyze special requirements for impact on design. | Strategies for increasing performance, maps to legacy data, plans for handling distributed data and computing, fault tolerance, and reliability |

*Continues*

Table 2-1 *Analysis includes system definition, system description, and object analysis activities. (Cont.)*

| Responsibility-Driven Analysis | | |
|---|---|---|
| **Phase** | **Activity** | **Results** |
| **Detailed Description** *(Cont.)* | Document system dynamics. | Activity diagrams showing constraints between use cases |
| | Show screens and interactions from users' perspective. | Screen specifications<br>Navigation model |
| **Object Analysis** | Identify domain-familiar objects with intuitive sets of responsibilities. | CRC cards that describe object roles and responsibilities<br>A candidate object model |
| | Document additional concepts and terms. | Glossaries defining concepts, descriptions of behavior, and business rules |

Of course, results vary from project to project. Depending on application specifics, certain descriptions may not add value. If your application doesn't interact with users, screen specifications aren't appropriate. To design responsibly, we develop only those descriptions that give us a meaningful perspective. Certain requirements unfold during discussions with stakeholders. They correspond roughly to the users' requirements but include a number of customer or administrator requirements:

- Usage
- Performance
- Configuration
- Authentication
- Concurrency
- Scalability
- Security
- Reliability

We may also uncover these requirements during development and during initial use of early software versions by developers, testers, and beta users. Many requirements and concerns overlap, and different stakeholders often articulate them in various ways. Security may be of utmost concern to users who "don't want credit card information pilfered over the Web," but this is a far less detailed requirement than those of the Web site administrator who speaks as a Web security expert.

In addition to the more obvious requirements that have an appreciable and direct impact on design, other requirements for flexibility, maintainability, extensibility, or reusability can constrain acceptable design solutions, even though they aren't readily glimpsed by considering how our users interact with our software. In many cases, it is these "ilities" that, when ignored, cause a project to fail. As designers, we must absorb requirements and present a design that conforms to their constraints. Of course, no matter how hard you try, you won't identify all the requirements.

## Staging the Production: Design

In design, we construct a model of how our system works. We break the object design process into two major phases: creating an initial design (exploratory work shown in Table 2-2) and then crafting more comprehensive solutions (refinement shown in Table 2-3).

At some point after you've developed an initial exploratory design, you want to break away from designing and start coding. This could occur after a relatively short while, especially if your design is straightforward and you know what needs to be done. Perhaps you want to prove part of your design by implementing a prototype before investing energy designing other parts that rely on that proof of concept being solid. Or you may want to refine your design a bit

Table 2-2 *Exploratory design is focused on producing an initial object model of a system.*

| Exploratory Design | |
|---|---|
| **Activity** | **Results** |
| Associate domain objects with execution-oriented ones. | A CRC model of objects, roles, responsibilities, and collaborators |
| | Sequence or collaboration diagrams |
| | Descriptions of subsystem responsibilities and collaborations |
| Assign responsibilities to objects. | Preliminary class definitions |
| Develop initial collaboration model. | Working prototypes |

The time spent exploring and refining a design, and the amount of design documentation you produce, can vary widely. Our advice: Work on those design activities and results that add value to your project. You don't need to do each and every activity or produce lots of design documents to be successful. Use these activities and results as general guidelines, and tune them to your specific needs.

Table 2-3 *Design refinement includes activities that make a design more predictable, consistent, flexible, and understandable.*

| Design Refinement | |
|---|---|
| **Activity** | **Results** |
| Justify trade-offs. | Documentation of design decisions |
| Distribute application control. | Control styles identified<br>Easy-to-understand patterns of decision making and delegation in the object model |
| Decide static and dynamic visibility relationships between objects. | Refined class definitions and diagrams |
| Revise model to make it more maintainable, flexible, and consistent. | Creation of new object abstractions<br>Revision of object roles, including stereotype blends<br>Simplified, consistent interfaces and patterns of collaboration<br>Specification of classes that realize roles<br>Application of design patterns |
| Document the design clearly. | UML diagrams describing packages, components, subsystem, classes, interaction sequences, collaborations, interfaces<br>Code |
| Formalize the design. | Contracts between system components and key classes |

before starting implementation. Whether you take the time to polish your design a bit more before coding or you adjust your design during implementation, your initial design ideas will change. Most applications are too complex to "design right" the first time. So creating a workable design means revisiting initial assumptions to make sure that your design lives up to stakeholders' expectations. It may also mean spending extra time to design a flexible solution or to enable your design to respond to exceptional conditions.

Design activities—from early explorations to detailed refinements—are the focus of this book. But before we dive into design, let's explore what we need to "see clearly" in order to create an appropriate design.

## "Seeing" from Multiple Perspectives

Each stakeholder in our design process has differing needs and values. Each person will view our work in progress and the emerging application from a unique perspective. Because many of the stakeholders do not speak our native object-oriented tongue, we object designers face two challenges:

- Correctly interpreting stakeholders' concerns and requirements
- Presenting our design work in terms understood by a wide audience

Each participant in our software production has differing criteria for evaluating our software. Their primary concerns and the aspects they value vary with their points of view.

For example, users want to see that they can easily do their jobs using the application. They'll want application controls and processing to be consistent and "feel" natural. A business analyst will want to know that policies, rules, and processes are understood by the design team and clearly supported by our design. A tester wants to see that the actual application matches expected performance and usability objectives. Some stakeholders will care about our design's details, but many will not. All will want assurance that our design addresses their concerns and needs. Let's now take a brief tour through the process and see how we develop a design that meets each stakeholder's specific concerns.

> "Facts are the air of scientists. Without them you can never fly."
>
> —Ivan Pavlov

## WRITING THE SCRIPT: ANALYSIS DESCRIPTIONS

Early in the process, our goal is to understand and reflect important requirements. We turn vague, formative ideas into specifications of what we are to build. Errors in product specification are the most costly because they ripple through all of the downstream activities. So it's important to communicate our software's characteristics in simple, unambiguous language to those who will use it and to others who will keep it running. To understand how our software fits into the immediate environment that it runs on and the extended environment of devices, databases, and external programs that it communicates with, we view our software from several perspectives as shown in Figure 2-5.

What language should we use to describe our system? No one language is common to users, customers, data analysts, developers,

> "There's no sense being precise about something when you don't even know what you're talking about."
>
> —John von Neumann

> "Descriptions are the externally visible medium of thought."
>
> —Michael Jackson

Figure 2-5
*Stakeholders' descriptions of a system reflect their unique perspectives.*

and managers that describes our software adequately. We collect a variety of descriptions using appropriate language and notations. One of our goals is to make clear what is ambiguous, to collect and describe with one voice what our software should be responsible for. We gather various descriptions and reflect these different perspectives in our specifications. We strive to understand where our software "ends," where its external environment "begins," and what functions it should perform. Once we draw these boundaries, we focus on our software's internal workings and the ways it responds to its environment. We develop and use a consistent, common vocabulary for describing the things our software affects, the processes it supports, and its responsibilities to its stakeholders.

Use cases and a user orientation are important, but they don't tell the whole story. A model is a collection of related descriptions. There are various types of models—usage, data, object, state, and process, to name a few.

## Usage Descriptions

Because many of an application's obligations are to its users, we must clarify their understanding. From a user's vantage, there is a boundary around our system that distinguishes the software from the external world. Users' understanding of our software is based on how it supports their tasks. This task-oriented view can be described by a collection of descriptions, or use cases. Use cases are part of a UML model. We break up a large application's specification into use cases, which concisely describe discrete "chunks" of system functionality from this external perspective.

## Actors and Their View of Our System

The Unified Modeling Language defines an actor as some *one* or some *thing* outside the system that interacts with it. These actors tend to be grouped into three different camps:

- Users
- Administrators
- External programs and devices

Actors have two characteristics in common:

- They are external to the application.
- They take initiative, stimulate, and interact with our software.

By organizing our usage descriptions around these actors, we orient the software's responsibilities to each actor's point of view. We eventually will use these descriptions and be guided by the "ilities" that we wish to preserve. But to develop a single object-oriented model, at this stage of development we need different, higher-level descriptions than an object model can provide—descriptions rich with detail, rich with intention, rich with implication and purpose. An object model prescribes only a solution to a problem. This solution leaves unspoken the needs, intentions, and day-to-day concerns of our system's stakeholders.

Objects best describe concepts, or things, their characteristic responsibilities, and interactions.

These rich and detailed descriptions depict usage, points of variability and configuration, and essential system architecture. We identify the groups of people and the external programs and devices that our software interacts with, and we describe how they interact. We note areas where flexibility is needed and variations our software should accommodate. To the best of our ability, we create descriptions that can be understood by those who need to know. If we build object models or code prototypes at this point, it is only to clarify our own understanding of this multitude of requirements. These prototypes can be disposable.

Any expected properties of our software must be apparent from some description. They won't emerge on their own.

## Use Cases

Use cases, introduced by Ivar Jacobson in 1992, are part of UML. Many people use them as a means to describe how a system is to be

A use case is "a behaviorally related sequence of transactions in a dialogue with the system."

—Ivar Jacobson

used. Others quite happily use hierarchical lists of features, simple user stories, or lengthy specifications documents. Use cases are especially valuable for describing an application from an external usage perspective. We use three forms of use case descriptions: simple text *narratives*, *scenarios* consisting of numbered steps, and *conversations* that emphasize the dialog between user and system. Each form of use case description has its particular emphasis.

Use cases can be written at differing levels of detail, depending on their intended audience. We can write high-level overviews and then add detail and describe the sequences of actions and interactions between the user and the program. The forms we choose depends on what we are trying to express.

We may write one or more forms for each use case, depending on the needs of our audience. Typically, we start by writing narratives that present a high-level overview. Then, if appropriate, we can write one or more scenarios or conversations that elaborate this high-level description.

### A Word Processor Example

Consider the use cases we exercised to write this chapter. Our word processor doesn't specifically support book writing; it is a generic document preparation tool. So when we use our word processor, we map our activities onto those tasks supported by our word processor: entering text and revising it. Other tasks are not supported by our word processor: researching, brainstorming, and outlining. Tasks that do map to our application's chunks of functionality include opening a document and creating and editing text.

Our goal is to state the users' tasks at the most meaningful level. Even the simplest high-level tasks become a series of decisions and actions on the part of the user.

Writing is a fairly free-form activity. We mix and match writing tasks in an unpredictable order. Because a word processor is meant to support a wide variety of writing styles, writing is best described with smaller use cases that can be exercised in any order. But meaningful tasks for writing a book are larger; they are composed of various subtasks. Formatting a page is a series of changes to the margins, indentations, headers and footers, and so on. Reorganizing a sequence of paragraphs is a series of cut-and-paste operations. We name use cases and write them from the user's point of view—for example, "Edit Text," "Save a Document to a File," or "Look up Online Help." In these examples, the use case name takes the form "Perform an Action on Some Thing." Here is a use case, written in narrative form, that describes saving a document.

> Documents can be saved in different file formats. When you save a new document, the default file format is used unless another is specified. When a Save Document operation has completed saving an existing document, the file represents accurately the document as displayed to the user upon saving.

Alternatively, we could name and describe use cases from our word processor's perspective. "Open a Document" might be recast as "Open a File and Read It into a Text Buffer." We don't recommend taking the system's point of view. If we do, it gives us an eerie sense of our system peering out at the user, detailing what it is doing.

Our word processor's use cases describe rather small functional chunks. Our rule of thumb is to write use cases that the user finds meaningful. The level of detail also varies. Users might want to see general statements, or excruciating detail, depending on how familiar they are with the task and how complex it is. Despite the variations in the level of abstraction and detail, use case narratives share one common feature: They describe general facilities in a paragraph or two of natural language.

> Although a system-level perspective is important, it isn't particularly relevant to our user. Keep the point of view of the user.

### Scenarios

Whereas use case narratives describe general capabilities, scenarios describe specific paths that a user will take to perform a task. A single use case might be performed a number of different ways. This "Save Document to an HTML File" scenario explains how it varies from its "parent," the "Save Document to a File" use case narrative:

> **Scenario: Save a Document to an HTML File**
>
> 1. The user commands the software to save a file.
>
> 2. The software presents a File Save dialog box, where the directory, filename, and document type can be viewed and modified.
>
> 3. If the file is being saved for the first time and it has not been given a filename by the user, a filename is constructed based on the first line of text in the document and a default file extension.
>
> 4. The user selects HTML document type from the File dialog's options, which replaces the default file extension to ".htm" if needed.
>
> *Continues*

> 5. The user adjusts the filename and the directory location as desired.
>
> 6. The user commands the software to complete the Save Document command.
>
> 7. The software warns the user that formatting information may be lost if the file is saved in HTML format. The user is presented with the option of canceling or continuing the save operation.
>
> 8. The user chooses to save the document in HTML format.
>
> 9. The software saves the document and redisplays the newly reformatted contents. Certain formatting information, such as bullets, indentations, and font choices, may have been altered from their original.

If we need to be more concrete to clarify how a task is to be performed, we write scenarios that describe the actions and information relevant to specific situations. If more detail will be helpful and we want to emphasize the interactions between user and system, we expand narratives into conversations.

### Conversations

Conversations describe the interactions between the user and the software as a *dialog*. Their purpose is to clarify the responsibilities of each: The user, who initiates the dialog, and the software that monitors and responds to the user's actions. The more detailed conversation form allows us to clearly show the application's responses to the actions of the user.

Each conversation has two distinct parts: a column of actions and inputs, and a parallel column of the related software responses. These responses are a first-order listing of the software responses and actions. We designers will use these statements as we design our system and assign responsibilities and actions to a population of software objects.

We develop conversations and scenarios around a course of action, sometimes choosing a single path among many alternatives.

Conversations record rounds of interaction between the user and the system. Each round pairs a sequence of user actions with a sequence of software responsibilities. Rounds can be highly interactive or batch-oriented, depending on the application. For example, a highly interactive round in our word processor might capture and validate every key press, correcting often-mistyped words or signaling the user immediately about an invalid entry. In contrast, the batch-oriented style of Web-based input has you fill out many entry fields and then submit them all at once.

Figure 2-6 shows a conversation for "Save a Document to a File."

This conversation shows details not found in either our use case narrative or our scenario. For example, it shows that our system is working to keep the user informed about all files sharing the same extension as the to-be-saved document. Presumably this is to help the user choose a unique filename.

| User Actions | System Responsibilities |
|---|---|
| Indicate save file. | Display the name of the file to be saved and the current directory contents, including all subdirectories and all files having the same extension as the document to be saved. If saving document for the first time, construct a filename with the extension matching the default document format. |
| Optionally, change directory. | Redisplay contents of directory in dialog box. |
| Optionally, rename file. | Rename file and redisplay filename. |
| Optionally, change document format. | Record document format. Redisplay filename extension to match new format extension conventions. Redisplay directory contents showing files whose extensions match the extension of the file to be saved. |
| Indicate OK to save. | If formatting information will be lost, present notice. Save document to file. Redisplay contents if document format changed. |

Figure 2-6
*A conversation for saving a file lists the user actions and corresponding system responsibilities.*

## Adding Detail

Conversations can be written sparsely or can pack more prose, mimicking talk between old friends.

Designers, like users, need to understand exactly how the software responds to its external environment. The descriptions in conversations and scenarios shape our design work. System responsibilities will be assigned to neighborhoods of objects working in concert to perform various system responsibilities.

Conversation and scenario descriptions need even more detail before most designers can build a working system and most testers can write test cases. What are the conventions for handling errors? What defaults should be assumed? We can describe the following:

- Information supplied by the user and defaults, if any, for missing information
- Constraints that must be checked before critical system actions are performed
- Decision points where the user may change course
- Details of key algorithms
- Timing and content of any significant feedback
- References to related specifications

Descriptions are easier to understand if they are written at a consistent level of detail. We can include details outside the main body of a usage description.

Rather than cram these details into the main body of a use case narrative, scenario, or conversation, we append or reference additional facts, constraints, information, and concerns. By annotating our descriptions with these details, we tie usage descriptions to design constraints and ideas as well as other requirements specifications.

## Alternatives, Annotations, and Other Specifications

Conversations and scenarios benefit from their simplicity and sparseness. However, we may want to capture nit-picky details about how our software carries out its responsibilities. Our software may vary its behavior in response to information supplied by the user or other extenuating conditions. To keep things simple, we separate these details from the body of the conversation or scenario.

## Exceptional Actions

To round out our description, we record deviations from the normal course of events in the "Exceptions" section:

---

***Exceptions***

Attempt to save over an existing file—inform the user and ask him or her to confirm a choice to replace the existing file.

---

Exceptions describe both an atypical condition and its resolution. A resolution can be a short sentence or two if the response is simple. Or it can refer to another conversation or scenario that describes a more complex response. Exceptions describe how our software should react to anticipated conditions. Sometimes our software can react and recover. In this case the user continues the task but on an altered path. At other times, the only response may be to give up and stop forward progress on the user's task.

## Business and Application Policies

Our system's responses often depend on explicit application and business rules. Our software's behavior must reflect policies such as "documents should be storable in different formats." We make pertinent policies explicit by listing them separately:

---

**Policies**

Do not allow a user to save work to a file that another user has open.

If the document is being saved for the first time, construct and suggest a filename based on contents of the first line of text in a document.

---

Our growing understanding of our application often gives us ideas about how the system might be designed. Our guiding principle is "Be opportunistic!" Rather than rigidly compartmentalize our activities and documents into "analysis" or "design," we gather and document information as we encounter it.

*An idea is an opportunity. Don't lose it!*

## Design Notes

We note conditions and conventions that are of interest to the designer in a "Design Notes" section of a use case:

---

**Design Notes**

Document format is indicated by the file's extension. Some formats share the same extension, but information about the actual file format is in the file format descriptor:

- .doc—standard format files of all versions
- .rtf—rich text format
- .txt—plain text files with or without line breaks
- .html—Hypertext Markup Language format

---

## Other Specifications

Screen layouts, window specifications, documentation of existing regulations, constraints on system performance, and references to policy manuals provide even more context. We get even more insights into our software's behavior if we tie these to our usage descriptions. This type of information, although invaluable to designers, also gives other stakeholders an opportunity to see that their concerns are being considered.

## Glossaries

As we write use cases and other descriptions, we try to use consistent terms. By compiling project-specific definitions for frequently used words, phrases, and jargon into a glossary, we clarify and make our specification more consistent:

> Document—A document contains text organized into paragraphs and other bitmap or graphic objects. It is created with the editing tool. Its contents can be modified using various editing commands.
>
> Graphic Object—A graphic object can be visually displayed in a document. A graphic object can be created within the text editor or be imported from other applications and inserted into a document. Depending on its properties the user may be able to resize, scale, or adjust its physical properties.

So far, our descriptions have had little object orientation. Only after we gather descriptions from many perspectives can we make a stab at representing them in a unified form—a candidate object model.

## Conceptual Objects

We want our design to readily translate to an object-oriented programming language. As a first step toward object design, we describe key concepts—a collection of candidate objects. We have crossed into object thinking. Our stakeholders understand these high-level concepts because they directly reflect the core concepts of the domain. But as we progress into even more detailed design activities, our objects will take on more computer-related characteristics and appear even more alien to others.

## Concentrating on the Core

Our goal is to build well-designed software that works according to specifications and can accommodate modest changes. It needs a solid core. This "core" can mean many things:

- Key domain objects, concepts and processes
- Objects implementing complex algorithms
- Technical infrastructure
- Objects managing application tasks
- Custom user interface objects

In our word processing application, those objects that represent parts of a document—objects such as Document, Page, Paragraph, and SpellChecker—form a core. They appeared during initial concept formation.

What you consider to be "core" will depend on the emphasis in your application and what your stake is in its success.

## Document

A document contains text and other visual objects that represent the contents of other applications. Documents are organized as a sequence of document elements, including paragraphs, graphic objects, tables, and other document elements that the user formats and visually arranges on pages.

Candidate objects may or may not survive intact to become part of the application object model.

## Page

A page corresponds to what is visually present on a printed document page. It is composed of paragraphs and other document elements and, optionally, headers and footers consisting of text organized on the top and bottom of each page.

## Paragraph

A paragraph is a document element that consists of text or other graphic objects. A paragraph is created when the user signifies a paragraph break by pressing Enter. Paragraphs have an associated paragraph style that is used to display its contents and control spacing between lines of text in the paragraph.

## Spell Checker

The spell checker verifies that words within the document or a highlighted portion of text are contained in the dictionary that comes with the word processing application or have been added by the user to the user dictionary. The spell checker informs the user about each misspelled word and presents the user with the opportunity to correct, ignore, or add the word to the user dictionary.

If these objects survive candidacy and join the ranks of other newly coined design objects, it means that they represent the application responsibilities in a fashion that supports our design goals.

## CASTING THE CHARACTERS: EXPLORATORY DESIGN

Chapter 3, Finding Objects, presents strategies for identifying and characterizing design objects.

"While most of our mental models are intuitive and largely subconscious, the essence of both science and business is the creation of explicit models, called manifest models, which we can share and discuss."

—Trygve Reenskaug

If analysis is about our application's behaviors, design is about the underlying objects that we derive from them. In design we are laying out and paving the streets that our application does business in. Like a good city planner, a good designer will consider how software will grow and change and what elements are most likely to be the focal points for change.

There is a significant distance between conceptual objects and design objects. Both describe things. However, high-level descriptions ignore details that add heft and definition. This gap rightfully exists. Concepts and system responsibilities form a bridge to the work that remains to be done. In design we create a model of objects that work together to achieve our system's responsibilities.

Designers examine conceptual objects for merit. These conceptual objects are only candidates that may be discarded if they are rejected as unworthy of further consideration. Or they may be incorporated into the design and become important elements of it. In our word processing application, Document proves a worthy design object. It is responsible for knowing and structuring its contents, a collection of Paragraphs organized on Pages. Similarly, a Paragraph is composed of Text, which is formed into Words.

On further examination, Paragraph proves a design gold mine! We can envision Paragraphs to be composed of Text objects and various kinds of nontextual objects representing graphics, drawings, figures, or even elements from external sources. Paragraphs are separated by ParagraphBreak objects. Text is composed of characters that form Word objects that compose Sentence objects.

We glean responsibilities from various descriptions and recast them into well-formed design objects. We add our own inventions to form a more complete, detailed model.

As text is entered, a Parser object forms Text into Words. Words have a document location—a beginning and an ending position—and character contents. Words are composed of characters delimited either by punctuation marks or other nontextual elements. As each Word is formed, it is passed to the SpellChecker object, which checks for correctness.

Often, conceptual objects and early candidates are rich design fodder—being transformed into several objects as design progresses. Less commonly, candidates pass directly from analysis to design, with responsibilities remaining relatively intact. Each object, if it continues in design, will need a clearly stated role and an appropriate set of responsibilities. Most likely, these responsibilities aren't clearly articulated by any earlier description.

Experienced designers, as soon as they hear "requirements," immediately start thinking about objects and their responsibilities. They often quickly conceive of additional responsibilities that round out candidates' behaviors, seemingly taking a leap from rough concept to well-formed candidate. And they invent new concepts and software machinery on-the-fly to fill in the gaps in their object model. Sometimes this leap can appear startling to someone relatively new to object thinking.

For example, as we look further at the SpellChecker, we see that to actually perform its responsibility for knowing correct spellings, we might design it to keep base parts of known words in a SpellingDictionary object and to know rules for pluralization and forming tenses. It is unlikely that the candidate object SpellChecker will survive as a single object. More likely, as design progresses, it will become a community of collaborating objects, perhaps a subsystem.

## CRC Cards

We record preliminary ideas about candidates, whether they are candidate objects or candidate roles, on CRC cards. CRC stands for Candidates, Responsibilities, Collaborators. These index cards are handy, low-tech tools for exploring early design ideas. On the unlined side of the CRC card, we write an informal description of each candidate's purpose and role stereotypes (see Figure 2-7).

Getting more specific, we flip over the CRC card to record its responsibilities for knowing and doing (see Figure 2-8). Responsibilities spell out the information that an object must know and the actions that it must perform. Collaborators are those objects whose responsibilities our object calls upon in the course of fulfilling its own.

Cards work well because they are compact, low-tech, and easy. You move them around and modify or discard them. Because you don't invest a lot of time in them, you can toss a card aside with few regrets if you change your mind. They are places to record your initial ideas and not permanent design artifacts.

Although CRC cards were originally intended to describe classes, their responsibilities, and collaborators, we recommend you look for *candidates* first. Decide on how they are realized as classes later—once you have an idea they'll stick around.

Chapter 4, Responsibilities, discusses how to identify and assign responsibilities to appropriate candidates.

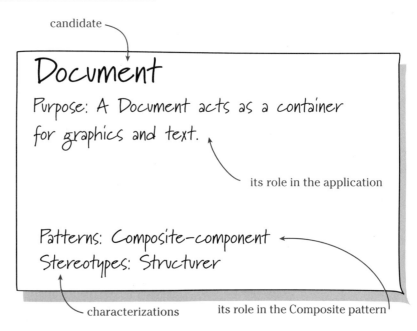

Figure 2-7
*The unlined side of a CRC card characterizes the candidate.*

Because cards are small and not in a computer, you can easily arrange them on a table and view many (perhaps all) of them at the same time. You can pick them up, reorganize them, and lay them out in a new arrangement to amplify a fresh insight. You can leave blank spots to represent gaps in your design.

It is pointless to insist on cards, however. If you work best with sheets of blank paper or yellow legal pads, use them. Use a white board to see the big picture. Describe candidates on Post-it notes, which you can rearrange in an instant (see Figure 2-9).

The obvious conceptual objects that we identify first on CRC cards are only one piece of the puzzle. It is the unintuitive inventions that challenge our creativity. They are the hallmark of a flexible and well-factored program. They are what we look for during design.

Good designers short-circuit the difficult work of invention by adapting proven solutions. They study other designs and reuse their own and others' experience.

## Inventions: Using Patterns

You gain a measurable advantage by knowing where to look for adaptable solutions. One powerful way to increase design skill is to seek out good patterns and learn where and when to apply them.

candidate
collaborators
Document
Knows contents
Knows storage location
Inserts and removes text,
graphics, and other elements
TextFlow
responsibilities

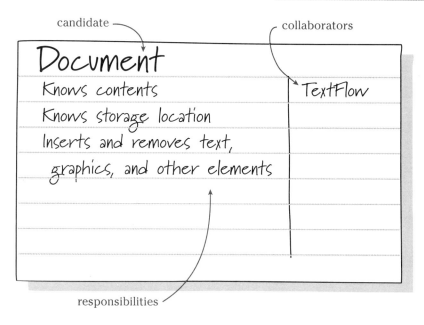

Figure 2-8
*The lined side of a CRC card describes responsibilities and collaborators.*

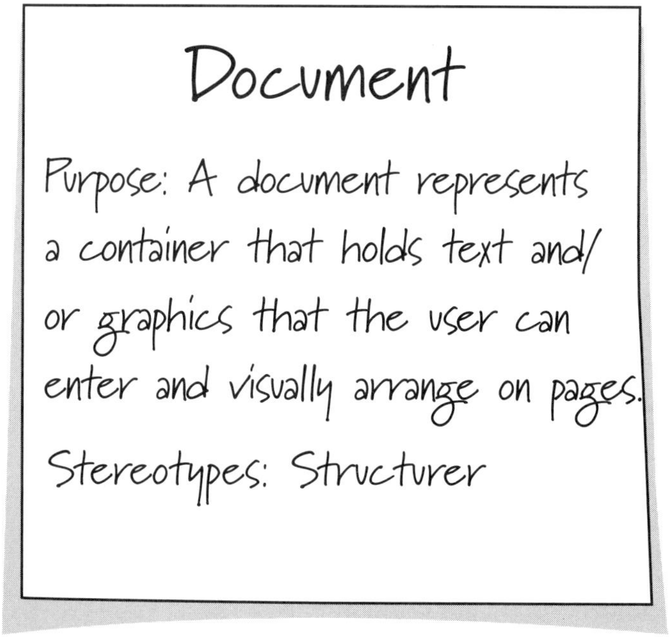

Document
Purpose: A document represents a container that holds text and/or graphics that the user can enter and visually arrange on pages.
Stereotypes: Structurer

Figure 2-9
*Post-it notes are easy, compared to CRC "cards."*

Using solutions that have proven themselves useful in a variety of contexts can help us fill in the gaps in our thinking. These little "whacks on the side of the head" jar us into thinking about solving new problems in proven ways.

There is a key aspect of our word processor that we should study: how it responds to the myriad user actions. The word processor is, quite literally, "responsible" for interpreting requests for editing, inserting, finding, formatting, saving, opening, cutting, copying, pasting, printing, viewing, checking spelling and grammar, and so on.

- How should we perform these actions?
- Each item selected from a menu represents a request for our word processor to take action. How can they be undone?
- Many actions affect a specific portion of the document. How do we keep track of which section to operate on?

The problem of how to exercise control is central to most applications.

For example, a cut action removes highlighted text into a cut buffer, whereas a bold action sets bold emphasis on either the currently highlighted text or, if no text is highlighted, the word containing the current cursor position. Saving a document means writing the document to a specific file.

The Command pattern, described in *Design Patterns: Elements of Reusable Object-Oriented Software*, turns an action into an object. Each specific action can be represented by a distinct object that plays the role of a Command. Using inheritance, these objects can be implemented by classes in an inheritance hierarchy. As described, the Command pattern is very general and must be tailored to fit our word processor application. To use it, we must structure all of our thinking about responsibilities for performing and undoing our many word processing actions into various command objects. What exactly does this mean? How can we fit all actions into the command pattern form?

An experienced designer might recognize the need for the Command pattern almost immediately. A new designer might prototype different ways to solve the problem of providing different types of "command" behavior, before discovering that the Command pattern offers a consistent solution. When you discover that a design patterns is a good fit to your problem, you are leveraging others' design experiences.

We start by declaring that any object playing a Command role has a responsibility for performing a specific action (see Figure 2-10). Undoubtedly, our design will need to have many different kinds of Command objects, and classes that implement them, to model each of the myriad actions our word processor takes. To support "undoing" of each action, each different kind of Command object will be responsible for reversing its action. We will define the responsibilities for each different kind of command. To implement our design, we will construct a superclass Command that declares that all Commands can "execute an action" and can "undo" its effects. Additionally, any Command knows the target of the action. In the word

general responsibilities for knowing

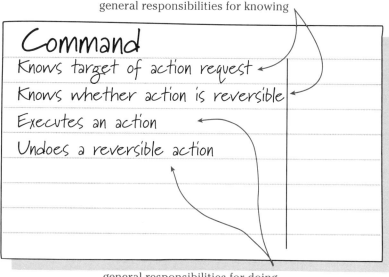

general responsibilities for doing

Figure 2-10
*The Command object responsibilities are stated very generally.*

processor, a Command's target is the portion of the document that it affects.

Each different kind of command object will support all the responsibilities of the Command role—but they will do so in specific ways. For example, executing a SaveCommand means saving the document's contents to a file. Save is not reversible and will never be asked to undo. A SaveCommand object knows that the target of the action is the entire document, and, because it collaborates with the document to fulfill this responsibility, we show Document as a collaborator (see Figure 2-11).

We create a CRC card that shows the responsibilities of each different kind of command object. A PasteCommand fulfills the role of a Command by placing text into a document at the current cursor location, knowing paste is reversible, and cutting it out if asked to undo (see Figure 2-12).

As we specify how each command's responsibilities are delegated, we add responsibilities to the Document CRC card (see Figure 2-13).

Although we applied the Command pattern in this case to illustrate the power of applying a proven solution to our particular design problem, sometimes design is much harder. We must think and rethink our design ideas, bouncing from one card to another, clarifying object

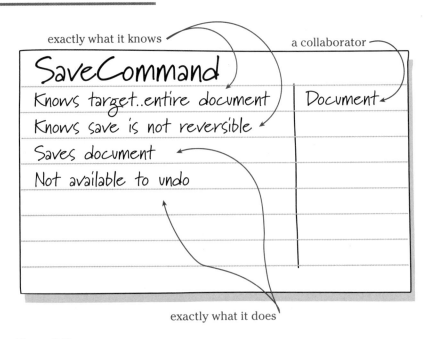

exactly what it knows

a collaborator

**SaveCommand**

| Knows target..entire document | Document |
| Knows save is not reversible | |
| Saves document | |
| Not available to undo | |

exactly what it does

Figure 2-11
*The SaveCommand object responsibilities are more specific statements.*

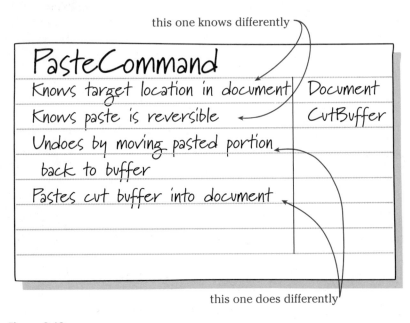

this one knows differently

**PasteCommand**

| Knows target location in document | Document |
| Knows paste is reversible | CutBuffer |
| Undoes by moving pasted portion back to buffer | |
| Pastes cut buffer into document | |

this one does differently

Figure 2-12
*The PasteCommand object responsibilities fulfill the Command responsibilities, too.*

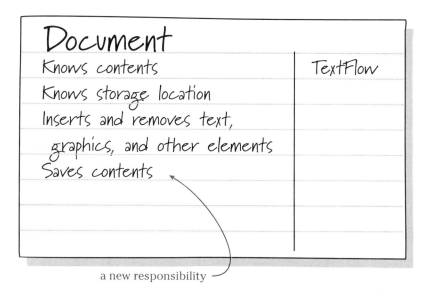

Figure 2-13
*Working out more details, we add responsibilities and collaborations.*

roles, allocating responsibilities, and developing collaborations. Sometimes, as we press forward, solutions aren't readily apparent. Worse yet, when we know more about our design, our earlier solutions may—on further reflection—seem brittle or inappropriate.

In early design, ideas are fluid. It is easy and desirable to make radical changes. We can relocate responsibilities, rearrange collaborations, adjust object roles, and introduce new players without much effort. We gain certainty and conviction by considering options.

## Pursuing a Solution

How should you choose among acceptable design alternatives? Consider this simple strategy:

1. If you don't have any predefined notions, create a solution that seems to work.

2. Explore the limits and strengths of that solution. To hedge your bets, measure at least one alternative against the first solution.

3. Favor a solution that contributes to design consistency.

4. Don't overwork a solution.

5. Fit your solution into known design patterns.

Our primary tool for design is abstraction. It allows us to effectively use encapsulation, inheritance, collaboration, and other object-oriented techniques.

6. Borrow and adapt proven design ideas and archetypes.

7. Be willing to revise earlier decisions when things get ugly.

8. If you don't have the time, don't search for insights. Abstraction or cleverness can't be forced.

## Bouncing Between Ideas and Details

One way to make sure we don't get off track is to constantly test our design with detail. A solution that sounds great in principle can crumble under the weight of detail. We use nitty-gritty descriptions in conversations and scenarios. We challenge our design with extra conditions that occur to us as we dig into details. After modeling at a high level, we spend time working with details. There is a shift in our design work between modeling and abstraction, elaboration and detailing.

We can turn to our descriptions for these details. Revisiting the "Save a Document to a File" conversation, we find many responsibilities that must be assigned to objects (see Figure 2-14). System responsibilities stated in conversations are a great source for finding object responsibilities. When we concentrated on the core design, we purposely ignored these details. To complete our design, we need to sort through system responsibilities and many other details, inventing many design objects and collaborations. To give you a hint at how we assign initial responsibilities, we've noted in parentheses how we made initial assignments of system responsibilities to one or more potential candidates.

Once we've made an initial stab at gleaning responsibilities from conversations and assigning them to objects, we need to construct a more complete solution and weigh its merit against alternatives. We'll answer in detail how any objects supports responsibilities stated at a high level:

- What does it do? How does it contribute to a high-level statement of responsibility?
- How does it collaborate with others that also play a part in supporting this high-level responsibility?
- What does it need to remember?
- What messages does it send to others? In what sequence?
- What are their arguments? What is returned from each request?

We can also use "detail" to help spot abstractions. By looking at all the various commands that one needs in a word processor, you may gain insight into what they have in common and spot the need for some way to unify them.

| User Actions | System Responsibilities |
|---|---|
| Indicate save file. | Present a dialog box that displays the name of the file to be saved and the current directory contents, including all sub-directories and all files having the same extension as document to be saved. (Assign high-level coordination to SaveDialogController, which is directed by SaveCommand).<br><br>If saving document for first time, construct a filename with the extension matching the default document format. (Assign to a new service provider?) |
| Optionally, change directory. | Redisplay contents of directory in dialog box (SaveDialog-Controller collaborating with Directory). |
| Optionally, rename file. | Rename and redisplay filename (SaveDialogController collaborating with Document, which collaborates with File). |
| Optionally, change document format. | Record document format (Document).<br><br>Redisplay filename extension to match new format extension conventions. (Assign to SaveDialogController, which will collaborate with some object that knows the mapping between extensions and document type—possibly a FileManager?)<br><br>Redisplay directory contents, showing files matching to-be-saved file's extension (assign to SaveDialogController). |
| Indicate OK to save. | If formatting information will be lost, present notice (Save-DialogController).<br><br>Save document to file (SaveCommand collaborating with Document).<br><br>Redisplay contents if document format changed (Save-Command collaborating with WordProcessingController). |

Figure 2-14
*System responsibilities are assigned to objects.*

Chapter 7, Describing Collaborations, presents options and advice for documenting key collaborations using both informal techniques and UML diagrams.

We'll design object interactions and further divide their responsibilities. We will create additional design documentation and drawings. We will draw and preserve a few diagrams that depict typical collaborations and show the classes that implement our design. Ultimately, our design will be expressed in code.

## TUNING THE PRODUCTION: DESIGN REFINEMENT

As designers, we play a significant part in realizing a smoothly run production. Exploratory design is only the start. After we mull over initial ideas and explore enough to know where we are headed, we systematically give our design a more thorough consideration. We ask many questions and then make many decisions and adjustments that will have a broad impact:

- What styles of collaborations should predominate?
- How can our design accommodate users' varying needs?
- Where should we build in capability for future extension and modification?
- Can we make our design more consistent, predictable, and easy to comprehend?
- How robust does our software need to be?

A lot of work remains! Strategies for working on and evaluating these details form the heart of this book. Let's briefly touch on some of these activities.

### Determining Collaboration and Control Styles

Chapter 5, Collaborations, discusses how to design objects to work together. Chapter 6, Control Style, presents options for developing consistent patterns of collaboration and application "control centers."

One important decision is how best to allocate control and decision-making responsibilities among collaborators. Control questions crop up in several areas:

- How do we control and coordinate use cases and user-initiated actions?
- What are the architectural constraints on collaboration and control styles?
- Where do we place responsibilities for making decisions?
- How should exception detection and recovery be managed?

Answers to these questions have a huge influence on how responsibilities are distributed across the rest of the model. Our goal is to design consistent, predictable patterns of interactions. Command objects are the locus of control for user actions. With this design choice, a clear pattern for controlling user-directed actions emerges. The Command pattern abstracts what it means to respond to a user action and gives us a recipe for adding new kinds of user-directed action controllers. It should be fairly straightforward to fit new user actions into our existing design by creating new kinds of Command objects.

But there are other places where we will need to ponder what control style is appropriate. Consider spell checking. We must make decisions about how to represent spelling rules and how to detect and report spelling errors. The control of how documents are saved and recovered needs careful design. Developing a style of collaboration and control involves deciding how to distribute control among collaborators as well as deciding on what patterns of collaboration should be repeated. Our options for distributing these command and control responsibilities range from more centralized to more distributed solutions.

## Designing to Support User Variations

A typical word processor supports many different user styles, preferences, and modes of interaction. Numerous features are under the user's direct control, ranging from how a document is displayed to details of how often the document is saved to what spellings are considered "legal." In an application of this sort, how best to support each of the myriad variations will be a predominant design consideration. Our word processor needs to make many tactical decisions as it executes based on current settings and preferences.

Chapter 9, Flexibility, discusses how to design an application so that it "flexes" and supports planned variations. Patterns and implementing designated "hooks" are key to adding flexibility.

## Designing for Flexibility and Extension

Flexibility isn't intrinsic to any design. To gain flexibility, we add appropriate bends and folds to our objects' behaviors that allow for extension and reconfiguration. We start by characterizing the ways our software needs to flex. We briefly describe how a behavior varies, note when this variation should occur, and present enough examples to illustrate the essence of the variation. We write brief descriptions of variations on *hot spot cards* (see Figure 2-15). As with CRC cards, the real estate on a hot spot card is limited. So we record only the essentials.

Once we've characterized how and when our software should flex, we then can employ one or a combination of design techniques: abstraction, classification, composition, inheritance, and parameterization.

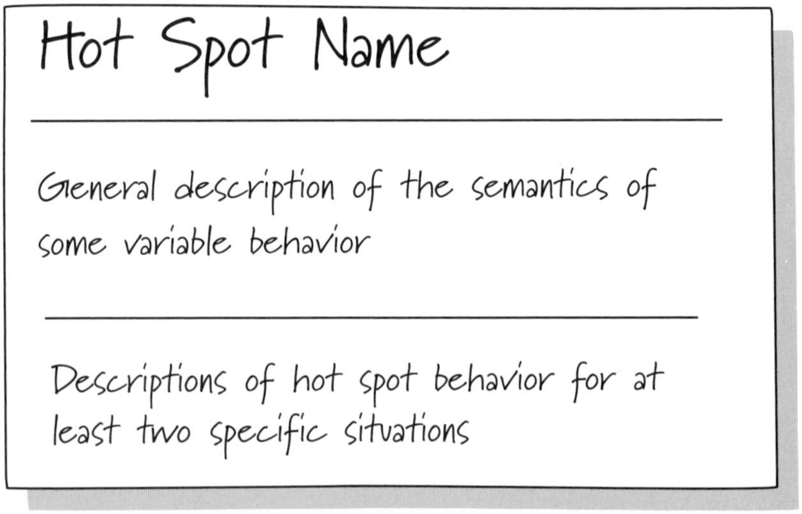

## Hot Spot Name

General description of the semantics of some variable behavior

Descriptions of hot spot behavior for at least two specific situations

Figure 2-15
*The hot spot card describes and demonstrates a variation.*

Our word processor must accommodate many user-specified variations. In addition, we expect to support new features and abilities—new graphics, new document formats, new and more sophisticated grammar checking, and document templates. Our software must be flexible from the start.

There are many techniques we designers use to accommodate planned variations. They range from simple checks on values to much more elaborate schemes. We can configure an object's behavior by passing method parameters. We can design an object to remember information that it can query to decide how it should perform an operation. We can configure an object to vary how it supports a responsibility by having it delegate to a configurable set of service providers. For example, we can add support for a new document format, plug in the appropriate service provider to generate that format when the document is saved, and plug in another to read and interpret it when it is opened.

There isn't one best strategy to accommodate variation. We favor simple solutions that build on each other. We can always add complexity if we need a more accommodating solution. Redesign is big part of sustaining a long-lived production.

## Designing for Reliability

Much complexity in a software design is the result of situations that, although expected, aren't "normal." In the word processing application, there are many opportunities for our user to supply us with incomplete information or to ask the software to do something that isn't exactly in the script.

What happens when we try to save our document over an existing file? How should our software respond to requests to save a document in an exchange format that would lose formatting information? These are the easy ones to handle, and there are many more. What happens when our application doesn't have enough room to execute, or when it discovers a place in a document with uninterpretable data? These are a bit harder to accommodate. Our users expect our application to gracefully recover from those situations if it can, and to politely inform them when it cannot.

We need to design our objects to responsibly and consistently (and to the best of their abilities) react to these exceptions. Designing consistent exception-handling policies and locating them systematically in controllers, service providers, and other "responsible" objects makes the way our software reacts to exceptions more predictable.

Chapter 8, Reliable Collaborations, explores strategies for increasing an application's ability to react to and handle exceptional conditions.

## Making Our Design Predictable, Consistent, and Comprehensible

The essence of a good design is predictability and consistency. We handle our application's complexity by designing consistent solutions. We don't want our design to be startling. So, if we solve one design problem in a particular way, we look for places where the solution might be repeated. Given a complex application, there are an infinite number of designs that will solve it. Many factors contribute to a consistent, comprehensible design:

- Objects are grouped in neighborhoods.
- There are few lines of communication between neighborhoods.
- No one object knows, does, or controls too much.
- Objects perform according to their designated role.
- When one solution is designed, variants will be applied to other parts that are similar.
- There are few patterns of collaboration that repeat throughout the design.

We need to balance a number of forces when we work on developing a consistent, predictable design. There is no recipe. We weigh various design trade-offs and make concerted efforts to be consistent across our design. Sometimes a system architecture or application framework will impose a collaboration and control style on the design. Sometimes using a standard design pattern will help. At other times, we need to discover and adopt a consistent style as we move along.

## SUMMARY

Chapter 10, On Design, explores three different design problems—core, revealing, and the rest—and discusses how best to approach them. If you know the nature of the design problem you are working on, you can be prepared and adjust how you work.

Just as a good cook alters a recipe's ingredients or the order of the instructions, a good designer treats a design method as a guide. Once you are comfortable with the basics, you should feel more comfortable adjusting the dials on the design process—producing what's needed when it is needed, cutting to the essence, and working on the hard problems. With experience you'll learn how to see and describe the problem and then readily design and build objects that model a solution.

Responsibility-Driven Design is suitable for a wide variety of projects because the emphasis is on thinking and creativity. First, guided by the various stakeholders' requirements, we determine how our application should behave. Second, we explore what we know so that we will find out what we don't know. Knowing that designs emerge over time, we create initial design ideas using low-tech tools such as CRC cards that easily let us change our minds or consider different options.

Finally, we turn the lights on the shadowy areas. We pin down what we have fudged. We look for solutions that have proven themselves elsewhere. Our success is directly related to how much opportunity we have seized, how much time for discovery, reflection, and revision we have created, and how satisfied the project's stakeholders are.

## FURTHER READING

Responsibility-Driven Design was first described in a paper by Rebecca Wirfs-Brock and Brian Wilkerson, "Object-Oriented Design: A Responsibility-Driven Approach," presented at the OOPSLA '89 Conference. A year later, the book *Designing Object-Oriented Software*, (Prentice Hall, 1990) authored by Rebecca Wirfs-Brock, Brian Wilkerson, and Lauren Wiener, expanded upon ideas presented in the paper. Since then, the notion of object responsibilities has become commonplace.

Responsibility-driven thinking fits into and complements most development processes and practices. For example, Rational has defined a process called the Rational Unified Process, or RUP. It defines four phases of an iterative/incremental development process: inception, elaboration, construction, and transition. Responsibility-Driven Design principles can be applied during inception and elaboration (what others may consider object design) and certainly should not be forgotten during construction. A good book on RUP is *The Rational Unified Process: An Introduction* (Addison-Wesley, 2000) by Philippe Kruchten.

Agile, adaptable development processes are a popular topic—and Responsibility-Driven Design techniques fit here, too. If you are interested in reading about what makes a development process agile, pick up Jim Highsmith's *Agile Software Development Ecosystems* (Addison-Wesley, 2002). There are several different processes whose authors and proponents classify as being agile. The most written about is Extreme Programming, or XP, which includes just 12 development practices. *Extreme Programming Applied: Playing to Win* (Addison-Wesley, 2001), by Ken Auer and Roy Miller, summarizes Extreme Programming practice and then presents many nuggets of wisdom.

If you are interested in the art and practice of writing good use cases, there are several books we recommend. Ivar Jacobson introduced use cases in his classic book, *Object-Oriented Software Engineering: A Use Case Driven Approach* (Addison-Wesley, 1994). Several authors have put their unique spin on use cases and have made several refinements to Ivar Jacobson's original ideas. The best of the bunch are Alistair Cockburn's *Writing Effective Use Cases* (Addison-Wesley, 2002) and Larry Constantine and Lucy Lockwood's *Software for Use: A Practical Guide to the Models and Methods of Usage-Centered Design* (Addison-Wesley, 1999). Alistair Cockburn's book, an easy read, is packed full of examples and advice on how to fix common use case problems. Larry Constantine and Lucy Lockwood's book isn't strictly just about use cases, although it goes to some length in describing different styles of usage descriptions and their strengths and weaknesses. Their book presents a systematic and thorough approach to developing usable systems and user interfaces, through the development of role models, task models, and content models. Anyone who wants to focus on system usability will find much of value in this book. It is packed with wisdom, great stories, and many practical tools and techniques.

Larry Constantine and Lucy Lockwood introduce the notion of an *essential* use case. It is a structured narrative expressed in the language of the application domain and its users. It describes a user task in a simplified, technology-free and implementation-independent fashion. Because it specifically omits details, it leaves more options for the user interface design.

# Chapter 3

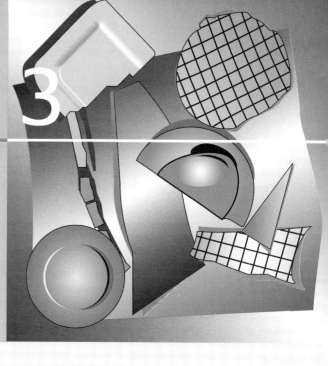

# *Finding Objects*

Joseph Albers could make colors dance or retreat: "I see color as motion . . . To put two colors together side by side really excites me. They breathe together. It's like a pulse beat . . . I like to take a very weak color and make it rich and beautiful by working on its neighbors. I can kill the most brilliant red by putting it with violet. I can make the dullest grey in the world dance by setting it against black." Albers, one of the great graphics artists of the twentieth century, was a master at making visual imagery emerge from form and color. By careful juxtaposition of colors, textures, and shapes, the artist can make images leap off the page. Albers calls this the "1 + 1 = 3" effect. A good design is more than the sum of its parts. A bad design muddles what should be emphasized. Chartjunk—misuse of bold lines and color or addition of pretty stuff that adds no value—shifts attention away from vital information. In graphic design, composition, form, and focus are everything! An object design poses similar challenges. It is strengthened by vivid abstractions and well-formed objects that fit into an overall structure. It can be weakened by glaring inconsistencies or muddled concepts.

A graphics designer enhances important information by layering and separating it, giving focus to the data rather than its container, and by using multiple signals to remove ambiguity.

The abstractions you choose greatly affect your overall design. At the beginning, you have more options. As you look for candidate objects, you create and invent. Each invention colors and constrains your following choices. Initially, it's good to seek important, vivid abstractions—those that represent domain concepts, algorithms, and software mechanisms. Highlight what's important. If you invent too many abstractions, your design can get overly complex. Not enough abstraction, and you'll end up with a sea of flat, lifeless objects.

Your goal is to invent and arrange objects in a pleasing fashion. Your application will be divided into neighborhoods where clusters of objects work toward a common goal. Your design will be shaped by the number and quality of abstractions and by how well they complement one another. Composition, form, and focus are everything.

## A DISCOVERY STRATEGY

Well-formed abstractions and careful attention to how they complement one another have a direct effect on the quality of an object design. This chapter discusses how to find and arrange software objects in an initial object design. The ultimate goal is to develop a practical solution that solves the problem. However, we find that such designs typically are also esthetically pleasing ones.

So let's get to it! Conceiving objects is a highly creative activity, but it isn't very mysterious. Finding good candidate objects isn't a topic that has received a lot of attention. Early object design books, including *Designing Object-Oriented Software*, speak of finding objects by identifying things (noun phrases) written about in a design specification. In hindsight, this approach seems naïve. Today, we don't advocate underlining nouns and simplistically modeling things in the real world. It's much more complicated than that. Finding good objects means identifying abstractions that are part of your application's domain and its execution machinery. Their correspondence to real-world things may be tenuous, at best. Even when modeling domain concepts, you need to look carefully at how those objects fit into your overall application design.

Although software objects aren't just waiting for you to find them, you can identify them somewhat systematically. Although many different factors may be driving your design, there are standard places to search for objects, and you'll find many sources of inspiration. You can use your knowledge of your application domain, your notions about needed application machinery, lessons learned from others, and your past design experience.

Our recipe for finding and assessing candidates has a number of steps:

- Write a brief design story. In it, describe what is important about your application.

- Using this story, identify several major themes that define some central concerns of your application.

- Search for candidate objects that surround and support each theme. Draw on existing resources for inspiration: descriptions of your system's behavior, architecture, performance, and structure.

- Check that these candidates represent key concepts or things that represent your software's view of the world outside its borders.

- Look for candidates that represent additional mechanisms and machinery.

- Name, describe, and characterize each candidate.

- Organize your candidates. Look for natural ways to divide your application into neighborhoods—clusters of objects that are working on a common problem.

- Check for their appropriateness. Test whether they represent reasonable abstractions.

- Defend each candidate's reasons for inclusion.

- When discovery slows, move on to modeling responsibilities and collaborations.

This chapter will cover each of these steps in greater detail. But be aware that you don't always complete each step before moving on to the next. The process of discovery and invention is more fluid than that. Sometimes you perform several steps at the same time. You may discard some candidates and start over if they don't seem to fit in to your emerging design. But if you start by characterizing what is vital to your application's success in a design story, you can then proceed with an organized search for objects that support this core.

At the end of your initial exploration, you will have several handfuls of carefully chosen, justified candidates. Many more will be invented as you proceed. These initial candidates are intentionally chosen to support some key aspect of your system. They will seed the rest of your design. Finding and inventing this first batch of candidates takes careful thought.

## LOOKING FOR OBJECTS AND ROLES, AND THEN CLASSES

The first candidates to look for should represent important things: concepts, machinery, and mechanisms. Typically these kinds of candidates are smart—they do things. They may know things, too, but they perform actions based on what they know. Initially, think very concretely. Abstraction will come later, after you see more concrete

Initially, we recommend you look for candidate roles and objects. Once you have an idea that they'll stick around, make decisions on how they are realized as interfaces and classes.

objects and understand their relationships to others. To start, identify distinct objects that have clear roles. Next, decide what candidates should know and do (their responsibilities) and whom they work with (their collaborators).

Then, thinking more abstractly, you can turn to identifying aspects that are common to a number of candidates. Shift your focus from thinking about objects and their individual roles to deciding what objects have in common. Only after you've made decisions about common responsibilities that are shared by different candidates can you define common roles. We deem our objects and roles candidates until their value has been proven. Only then do we decide how they will be realized as classes and interfaces.

> Abstract and concrete classes are the building blocks we use to specify an implementation. Declaring interfaces is one means to make it more flexible and extensible. A reusable role is best specified as an interface that can be implemented by one or more classes.

When you transition from candidates to classes and interfaces, you have options. You can employ inheritance, abstraction, interfaces, and collaborations to construct a well-factored, flexible design. You will specify abstract and concrete classes as well as interfaces. An *abstract* class provides a partial implementation of responsibilities. It leaves subclasses with the obligation to implement specific responsibilities. A *concrete* class provides a complete implementation. An *interface* specifies responsibilities more precisely as method signatures but leaves their implementation open. Any class can implement an interface, regardless of its position in any class inheritance hierarchy.

## WHY TELL A DESIGN STORY?

We suggest you create a framework for searching for potential candidates by writing a story about your application. After you've done this, the candidates you identify should fall into place and support various aspects of your story. When you state things in your own words, you get to decide what's important. Everybody may have been talking about what your design should do and what will make it great, but you should make a few bold statements of your own. In this design story, identify the things about your application that you know with certainty, as well as things you don't yet know. Rather than being driven by one particular view of your software—whether it be use cases, requirements, architecture, users, or sponsors—pull together all these factors and craft your own description.

Write a rough story—two paragraphs or less is ideal. Don't take a lot of time revising and polishing it. Be quick and to the point. What is notable about your application? What is it supposed to do? How will it support its users? Is it connected to a real-world example that you can study? Have you done something similar? What will make your design a success? What are the most challenging things to work out? What seems clear? What seems ill defined? You need not answer all these questions. Simply write about the critical aspects of your application. If it helps you make your point, draw a rough sketch or two. Focus on the main ideas.

Here are two design stories that were written quickly. The first one rambles. It tells of an online banking application:

If you are a member of a larger design team, write your own story first and then share it with your team. See how your concerns differ from others'. The team can draft a single, unified story, but this isn't necessary. More importantly, identify the important themes in these design stories. Then look for candidates that support these themes.

This application provides Internet access to banking services. It should be easily configured to work for different banks. It should support fast access to banking services for potentially thousands of users at a time. There is a limited number of software resources, such as database connections and connections to backend banking software, that are available. A critical element in the design is the declaration of a common way to call in to different backend banking systems and a reliable means of sharing scarce resources. We will define a common set of banking transactions and a framework that will call into banking-specific code that "plugs into" the standard layer implementing the details. The rest of our software will only interface with the bank-independent service layer.

We've developed a prototype implementation of this layer and have configured it to work for two different banks. Although it is still a prototype, we understand how to write a common banking service layer. Lately, our bank has been busy acquiring other banks and integrating their software. We've been through three system conversions in the past year. We want to focus on making this service layer easy to implement and test. At the heart of our system is the ability to rapidly configure our application to work for different backends and to put a different pretty face on each. This includes customizing screen layouts, messages, and banner text. The online banking functions are fairly simple: Customers register to use the online banking services and then log in and access their accounts to make payments, view account balances and transaction histories, and transfer funds. This is straightforward, easy to implement. There is added complexity. Customers record information and notes about each online transaction. This extra information will be maintained by our application in its own database because preexisting bank software has no way to store it. We want a customer to view human-readable information, not ancient bank software detailed transaction records. When a customer asks to view an account's transaction history we'll have to merge this data with records supplied from the backend software. Multiple users can access a customer's accounts, each with potentially different access rights. Certain users might have no access to sensitive accounts. A company executive might view only account balances, whereas a clerk in the accounts payable department could make payments and a comptroller might be able to transfer funds between accounts.

This next, more focused, story is about a Web-based game. It describes new design challenges as well as, to us, familiar territory:

This game playing application supports an Internet variant of chess called Kriegspiel. Kriegspiel is a chess version of the popular game Battleship. The novelty is that players make moves not knowing where their opponent's pieces are located. Our immediate concern is how to distribute responsibilities among major software components. In this distributed application, we need to consider time lags and limited communication bandwidth between architectural components. We also need to consider the unpredictability of Internet communications. Each player interacts with our application via a Web browser. Hundreds of games can be played simultaneously. A user logs in and requests to play a game with another. If no one is available, the user can elect to play a game with the computer. We will need to design our software to play a credible game of Kriegspiel as well as referee games played by humans. A game can be suspended and resumed. From our computer gaming experience, we know that computerized games generally have player input directives, rules about legal actions, some representation of the current state of the game, and animations. In this application, our animations are simple and not a major concern. It is worth stating how Kriegspiel is played, although our application won't mimic the real-world game. We will draw design ideas from this description.

In the game of Kriegspiel, three boards and sets of chessmen are used. There is a referee, whose chess set is in the center, with two players seated back-to-back, each at his own board. Each player moves his own chessmen, and the referee duplicates each move on his own board. The referee tells a player when his attempted move is impossible. Each player tries to guess what move his opponent is making. When a player completes a legal move, the referee announces, "Black (or White) has moved." When a player tries an illegal move, the referee waves his hand to prevent it but does not let the opponent know. When a move results in a capture, the referee announces, "Black (or White) captures on (the rank, file, long or short diagonal)" and removes the captured piece from the board of the player who lost it. A player may ask, "Any?" and be told by the referee if he has a possible capture with a pawn. That's the only question he is permitted. Having asked the question he must try at least one pawn capture before making a different move. To summarize, players make moves, ask "Any?," suspend or resume a game, claim a draw, or concede.

Let's contrast what we can glean from each story and then sketch out our candidate search strategies. The underlying requirement for the online banking system is flexibility. Functionality, implementation, and information need to be configurable. The application will maintain additional user-supplied information and construct account history from online and other banking transactions.

Our strategy for identifying candidates for this application will be to focus initially on modeling concepts that represent online banking services, the common interface to backend banking systems, and accounts. We should have objects that are responsible for performing banking functions and storing application-specific information about online transactions. Because we are building a multiuser online system, we also need objects that are responsible for managing access to limited resources such as the database and backend banking system connections. The key themes in the banking story are

- Modeling online banking services
- Flexibly configuring behavior
- Sharing scarce software resources among thousands of users
- Supporting different views of accounts and access privileges

The Kriegspiel application, even though it too is an Internet application, has fundamentally different drivers. As with any gaming application, we need to take a step back from our vivid real-world reference of the physical board game and ponder what mechanisms and inventions are needed by a computerized game. This is always a major design challenge with gaming applications. It is one we are familiar with from past experience. Our goal in designing Internet Kriegspiel isn't to simulate the real world but instead to construct a model that represents what is needed to run a computerized game. Choosing the right abstractions to represent the game and moves will be critical. We also need to consider how running over the Internet will impact our design. This will affect how we divide the work between application components. Finally, we'll need to implement a semi-intelligent computerized game player—something that is smart enough to play a decent game against a human opponent. Our central concerns for Internet Kriegspiel:

- Game modeling
- Computer playing a game
- Partitioning responsibilities across distributed components

## SEARCH STRATEGIES

Once you have identified major themes, you can use them as sources of inspiration. Make educated guesses about the kinds of inventions that you will need based on the nature of your application and the things that are critical to it. Candidates generally represent the following:

- The work your system performs
- Things directly affected by or connected to the application (other software, physical machinery, hardware devices)
- Information that flows through your software
- Decision making, control, and coordination activities
- Structures and groups of objects
- Representations of real-world things the application needs to know something about

We guide our search from these perspectives. The kinds of inventions we seek are closely related to the role stereotypes.

If an application's central mission boils down to computation, look to populate it with objects playing the role of service providers that calculate, compute, transform, and figure. You will likely invent objects that represent algorithms or operations along with objects that control work processes. If your application's major activity is to assemble and move information from one place to another, identify candidates that model this information as objects along with others to coordinate their movement. If your application connects with other systems, invent external interfacers that form these connections. Most designs need objects that control or coordinate the work of others. Depending on the complexity of the control, this design decision may or may not be a prominent one. If your application needs to sort through, organize, and make connections between related objects, structurers need to be identified. There are relatively direct links between the kinds of objects you look for and the nature of the work your software carries out.

> The best way to evaluate potential candidates that represent external things is to shift perspective. Climb into your software and look out at the world. Take your application's viewpoint. Ask what you need to know about your users, the systems you connect to, and things out there that you affect.

As you look for candidates one question to ask is, "How much does our software need to know about things in the external and virtual worlds it is connected to?" At the borders, model connections to other systems as interfacer objects. You may include in your design objects that represent these other software systems. These service providers will be called upon by other parts of the application. But when should you model things that are outside a computer, such as your software's users? If it is only their actions that matter and not whom they are, leave them out of the design. Users' actions can be conveyed via user interface objects (objects charged with translating user requests and information to other parts of the system). There is no need to know who is pushing your application's buttons! On the other hand, if whom users are makes your software behave differently, include some representation of them as a candidate. Some knowledge of its users (and objects to represent that knowledge) is needed if your software bases any decisions on whom it interacts with. For example, if different users have different access rights to accounts or if the ability to resume a game requires knowledge of whom the players are, then some representation of these users should be part of the design.

Tables 3-1 and 3-2 outline our search strategies for our two applications. Although we consider each perspective, typically only one or two are relevant to any particular theme. If we find that a particular perspective does not yield any insights, we move on. For each theme, we briefly summarize the perspectives that yielded insights and the kinds of candidates we are looking for.

Table 3-1 *The initial search for online banking application candidates is based on exploring four themes.*

| Theme | Perspective | Candidates That Specifically Support. . . |
|-------|-------------|-------------------------------------------|
| Online banking functions | The work our system performs | Performing financial transactions, querying accounts |
| | Things our software affects | Accounts, backend banking system transactions |
| | Information that flows through our software | Information about transactions, account balances, transaction amounts, account history, payments |
| | Representations of real-world things | Customers, users, and the accounts they access |

*Continues*

Table 3-1  *The initial search for online banking application candidates is based on exploring four themes. (Cont.)*

| Theme | Perspective | Candidates That Specifically Support. . . |
|---|---|---|
| Flexibly configuring behavior | Things our software affects | A common interface to back-end systems |
| | Information that flows through our software | Configurable display of Web page banners, text, messages, and account formats |
| Sharing scarce resources | Structures and groups of objects | Managing limited connections to backend systems and our online banking application database |
| Different views of and access to accounts | The work our system performs | Restricting users' views of and ability to perform banking transactions that modify account balances |
| | Decision making, coordination, and control | Prohibiting access to accounts unless user has specific privileges |

Table 3-2  *The initial search for Kriegspiel application candidates is based on the themes of game modeling, intelligent computerized game playing, and distributed games.*

| Theme | Perspective | Candidates That Specifically Support. . . |
|---|---|---|
| Game modeling | The work our system performs | Assigning players to games, refereeing, storing and resuming suspended games, playing a game, determining the legality of a move, determining the outcome of a move, displaying the state of each player's board |
| | Information that flows through our software | Information about moves and player requests |

Table 3-2 *The initial search for Kriegspiel application candidates is based on the themes of game modeling, intelligent computerized game playing, and distributed games. (Cont.)*

| Theme | Perspective | Candidates That Specifically Support. . . |
|-------|-------------|-------------------------------------------|
| Game modeling *(Cont.)* | Representations of real-world things | Players and their actions |
|  | Structures and groups of objects | Managing saved games, the various games, game pieces, and their locations on a game board |
| Computer playing a game | The work our system performs | Playing a game with a user |
|  | Decision making, control, and coordination | Determining a reasonable move to make based on the current view of the game (which should be just as limited as any human player's view) |
| Partitioning responsibilities across distributed components | Decision making, control, and coordination | Communicating a player request to the referee and game state between players, detecting whether a player is still connected |
|  | Information that flows through our software | Player moves, updated boards, and game state |

We will identify candidates that support the relevant perspectives. Sometimes candidates leap right out of the page from our brief descriptions; are Player and PlayerAction good candidates based on the fact that we need to have candidates that support our game's real-world view of "players and their actions"? Highly likely. At other times, we must speculate about exactly how our software might work in order to come up with candidates; perhaps there should be a BankingServicesConnectionManager that manages BankingServicesConnections or a DatabaseConnectionManager to manage DatabaseConnections that are scarce resources? Often, different themes and perspectives reiterate and reinforce the need for certain kinds of candidates. This is good. It builds confidence in the relevance a particular candidate has to our application. At other times, ideas do not come so quickly, and we must think more deeply to come up with potential candidates.

We won't find all the key candidates in this first pass; nor will our initial ideas about our candidates remain fixed. Our notions change as we give candidates further definition. The initial candidates that we come up with will seed our design. So it is particularly important to give each candidate a strong name that suggests its role and purpose. So before we continue searching for candidates, let's explore what it takes to find useful names.

## WHAT'S IN A NAME?

"...the relation of thought to word is not a thing but a process ... Thought is not merely expressed in words; it comes into existence through them. Every thought tends to connect something with something else, to establish a relationship between things. Every thought moves, grows and develops, fulfills a function, solves a problem."

—Lev Vygotsky

Good names increase design energy and momentum. You can build on a good name. When the name of a software object is spoken, designers infer something about an object's role and responsibilities. That's why grizzled object designers say, "Choose names carefully." A well-formed name creates a link to past experience and common practice. Meaning comes along with any name, whether we like it or not. Our brains are wired to find connections to things we already know. So the key to giving an object a good name is to make its name fit with what you already know while giving a spin on what it should be doing. Most names fit into a system of names. Different naming schemes coexist, even within a single application. There isn't one universal naming system.

***Qualify generic names.*** One scheme for naming things that are special cases of a more generic concept is to tack on to the generic name a description of that special case.

> A Calendar represents a system of dates and time at a particular location. GregorianCalendar extends the Calendar class. Following convention, we could invent JulianCalendar or ChineseCalendar classes. Others familiar with this scheme could make educated guesses about how their implementations would differ from GregorianCalendar.

***Include only the most revealing and salient facts in a name.*** The downside of any descriptive scheme is that names can become lengthy. Don't name every distinguishing characteristic of an object; hide details that might change or should not be known by other objects.

> Should people really have to care that they are using a Millisecond-TimerAccurateWithinPlusOrMinusTwoMilliseconds, or will Timer suffice? Detailed design decisions should not be revealed unless they are unlikely to change and they have a known impact on the object's users. Exposing implementation details makes them hard to change.

Consider the Singleton pattern described in the *Design Patterns* book. This pattern ensures that a class has only one instance with a global point of access. We could name every concept that applies this pattern a MumbleMumbleSingleton. Following our guideline, we recommend against this. Singleton is a distinction that is more important to a class implementer than to a client who uses a singleton. Give names that will be meaningful to those who will be using the candidate, not those who will be implementing it. If someone using your candidate must know the details of its implementation, you have likely missed an opportunity to do a better job of abstraction. One possible exception to this rule is to append Singleton to a class name when it is crucial for its users to know this.

***Give service providers "worker" names.*** Another English language naming convention is to end job titles with "er." Service provider objects are "workers," "doers," "movers," and "shakers." If you can find a "worker name," it can be a powerful clue to the object's role.

> Many Java service providers follow this "worker" naming scheme. Some examples are StringTokenizer, SystemClassLoader, and AppletViewer.

If a worker-type name doesn't sound right, another convention is to append Service to a name. In the CORBA framework, this is a common convention—for example, TransactionService, NamingService, and so on.

***Look for additional objects to complement an object whose name implies broad responsibilities.*** Sometimes a candidate represents a broad concern; sometimes its focus is more narrow. If you come across a name that implies a large set of responsibilities, check whether you've misnamed a candidate. It could be that your candidate should have a narrower focus. Or it might mean that you have uncovered a broad concept that needs to be expanded. Looking for objects that round out or complement a broad name can lead to a family of related concepts—and a family of related candidates. Many times we need both specific and general concepts in our design. The more generic named thing will define responsibilities that each specific candidate has in common.

> An object named AccountingService likely performs some accounting function. The name AccountingService isn't specific. We cannot infer information about the kinds of accounting services it performs by looking only at its name. Either AccountingService is responsible for performing every type of accounting function in our application, or it represents an abstraction that other concrete accounting service objects will expand upon. If this is so, we'd expect additional candidates, each with a more specific name such as BalanceInquiryService, PaymentService, or FundsTransferService. These more specifically named candidates would support specific accounting activities.

Forming an abstraction by looking at two specific cases might work, but comparing and contrasting three or four cases is even better. The more closely related concepts you can compare and contrast in order to identify what they have in common, the better.

Highlight a general concept with more specific candidates. If you can think of at least three different special cases, keep both the general concept and specific ones. If later on, you find that these more specific candidates don't share any responsibilities in common, the more abstract concept can always be discarded. However, if you have simply assigned a candidate a name that is too generic, by all means rename it.

> If your candidate could represent historical records of many other things, better to leave it with a more generic name, History, instead. If you intend to model transaction history, rename your candidate TransactionHistory. You decide how specific you want to be.

Therein lies the art of naming: choosing names that convey enough meaning while not being overly restrictive. Leave open possibilities for giving a candidate as much responsibility as it can handle, and for using it in different situations with minor tweaks. It certainly is a more powerful design when a candidate can fit into several different situations. The alternative—having a different kind of object for each different case—is workable, but not nearly so elegant.

***Choose a name that does not limit behavior.*** Don't limit a candidate's potential by choosing a name that implies too narrow a range of actions. Given the choice, pick a name that lets an object take on more responsibility.

> Consider two alternatives for a candidate: Account or AccountRecord. Each could name an object that maintains customer information. From common knowledge we know one meaning of record is "information or facts set down in writing." An AccountRecord isn't likely to have more than information holding responsibilities if we fit its role to conventional usage of this name. The name Account, however, leaves open the possibility for more responsibilities. An Account object could make informed decisions on the information it represents. It sounds livelier and more active than AccountRecord.

***Choose a name that lasts for a candidate's lifetime.*** Just as it seems funny to hear a 90-year old called "Junior," it's a mistake to name a candidate for its earliest responsibilities, ignoring what else it may do later on. And don't be content to stay with the first name you give a candidate if its work changes.

> An object that defines responsibilities for initializing an application and then monitoring for external events signaling shutdown or re-initialization, is better named ApplicationCoordinator than ApplicationInitializer. ApplicationInitializer doesn't imply having ongoing responsibilities after the application is up and running. ApplicationCoordinator is a better name because its more general meaning encompasses more responsibilities.

***Choose a name that fits your current design context.*** When you choose names, select ones that fit your current design surroundings. Otherwise, your candidates' names may sound strange. What sounds reasonable in an accounting application may seem jarring in an engineering application.

> A seasoned Smalltalker tried hard to set aside his biases when he started working with Java. Although he expected Java classes to have totally different responsibilities, he was surprised to find the Java Dictionary class to be abstract. In Smalltalk, Dictionary objects are created and used frequently.

Our thoughts shape our words, and our words influence our thoughts. Names subtly shape our ideas about our candidate's expected behaviors.

Shed your past biases when they don't fit your current situation.

***Do not overload names.*** Unlike spoken language, where words often have multiple meanings, object names should have only one meaning. It isn't good form to have two different types of Account objects with radically different roles that coexist in the same application. Some object-oriented programming languages let you assign the same name to different classes but then force you to uniquely qualify a name when you reference a particular class in code. In Java, for example, classes from different packages can have the same name. In order to uniquely designate a specific one, its name must be qualified by the name of the package where it is defined.

> A Java designer can define classes with the same name, each residing in a different package. You should do so only if one package is designed as a replacement for another.

Names of things that can simultaneously coexist within a single application should be given different names. Don't overload a name. Programmers have only one context—the running application—in which to interpret names. They already have enough to think about without adding yet another source of confusion. Compilers are good at automatically applying the correct qualification to a name. Humans aren't!

***Eliminate name conflicts by adding an adjective.*** Sometimes the best names are already chosen. Still, you need to name your candidate. By adding a descriptive phrase to a name, you can come up with a unique name.

> The candidate TransactionProperties might be a reasonable name for a candidate whose preferred name conflicts with the preexisting Java class named Properties.

A word of caution: If your candidate has a radically different meaning, don't co-opt a familiar name. Follow convention. Designers familiar with existing names will expect your candidate to fit in and work similarly.

***Eliminate conflicts by choosing a name with a similar meaning.*** Sometimes, your best bet is to look for a synonym. Each synonym has a slightly different shade of meaning, so finding a satisfactory name may be hard.

> The synonyms for Property, a class defined in the Java libraries, include these words: characteristic, attribute, quality, feature, and trait. Although "attribute" or "feature" might work, "characteristic" seems stuffy, and "quality" seems strained.

***Choose names that are readily understood.*** A name shouldn't be too terse. Don't encode meaning or cut corners to save keystrokes. If you want others to get a sense of an object's role without having to dig into how it works, give it a descriptive name. A name can be descriptive without being overly long.

If your problem domain has well-known and understood abbreviations—such as USD in banking, or Mhz or Gbyte in technology—it is reasonable to include these in a candidate's name.

> "Acct" is too cryptic. "Account" is better.

## DESCRIBING CANDIDATES

We judge an object by how well its name suits its role and how well its role suits its situation. Stereotyping a candidate's role provides a handy means for quickly creating an image about an object's intended use. When you find a candidate, name it and then characterize it as fitting one or more stereotypes. Each candidate could be a service provider, controller, coordinator, structurer, information holder, or interfacer. To be even more specific, you may want to distinguish between three different types of interfacers: *user interfacers* (objects that interface with users), *external interfacers* (objects that interface between your application and others) or *intersystem interfacers* (objects that bridge different parts of an application).

To be more explicit with your intentions, you can distinguish whether an object is designed to be passive and just hold on to related information (an information holder), or whether you expect it take a more active role in managing and maintaining that information (an information provider). If these finer distinctions seem too subtle, don't fret about them. Don't worry about giving an object the "right" stereotype. If your application is populated with objects that don't seem to fit these predefined stereotypes, come up with your own stereotypes. Stereotyping is intended to help get you started thinking about your candidates, not to bog you down.

If you aren't sure about the role your candidate will play, make an educated guess. Use its stereotype as a guide to build a simple definition. In that definition, explain what your candidate might do and list any traits that distinguish it from others. Write this brief definition on the unlined side of a CRC card (see Figure 3-1).

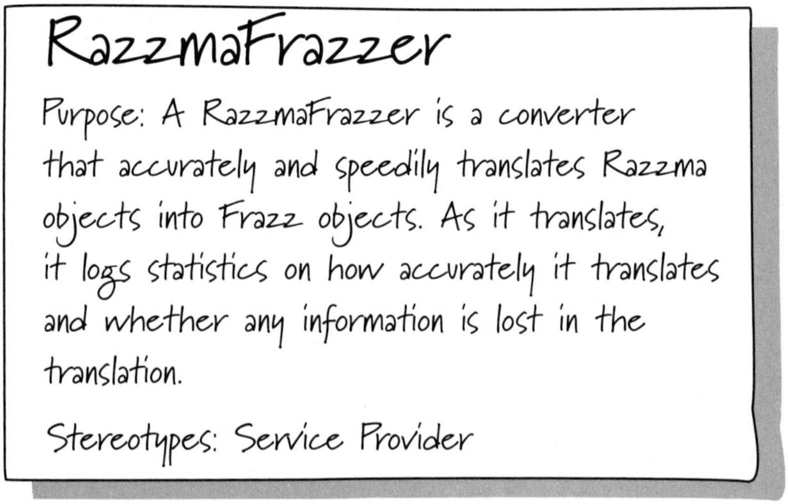

**RazzmaFrazzer**

Purpose: A RazzmaFrazzer is a converter that accurately and speedily translates Razzma objects into Frazz objects. As it translates, it logs statistics on how accurately it translates and whether any information is lost in the translation.

Stereotypes: Service Provider

Figure 3-1

*The unlined side of a CRC card is used to describe an object's purpose and stereotypes. In this case, a RazzmaFrazzer has only one stereotype.*

More generally, a pattern to follow when describing an object is as follows:

> An object is a type of thing that does and knows certain things. Briefly, say what those things are. Then mention one or more interesting facts about the object, perhaps a detail about what it does or knows or who it works with, just to provide more context.

Service providers, controllers, and coordinators are distinguished by what they do. Here's a simple way to describe these stereotypes:

> A service provider (or controller or coordinator) is some kind of thing that does some kind of work. Briefly, describe this work. Then mention something about what is important or interesting about the work it performs or whom it interacts with.

If you are working on your own, you may feel less of an urge to write down these thoughts. After all, you know what you mean! Even so, it still can be helpful to jot down an abbreviated thought. You don't want to forget what was so important about that darned Razzma-Frazzer by next Friday. Similarly, if you are working in a team, others likely won't know what's important about a candidate unless you tell them. Any description you can write about a candidate's purpose and what you expect it to do will help.

Consider this definition:

> A compiler is "a program that translates source code into machine language."

Contrast it with this slightly abbreviated definition:

> "A compiler translates source code into machine language."

The two definitions are nearly identical. The first adds that a compiler is a software program. This seems nit-picky—as software designers, we all know that compilers are programs. But the first definition provides just enough context so that someone not on our same wavelength can relate a compiler to other computer programs. Whenever you can relate something to a widely understood concept (such as a computer program), its meaning will be clearer to all.

If you and your fellow designers eat, sleep, and breathe design 24 hours a day, a lot may remain unspoken and unwritten. You understand one another because you think alike. However, if there's ever a question or disagreement about what a candidate is, it could be that you are making different assumptions. To make intentions clear, add enough detail to remove any doubt; then expect to have a discussion about whose ideas are better. Describe both what a candidate is and what it is not. Relate it to what's familiar.

We provide even more context by giving examples of how a candidate will be used and a general discussion of its duties. This is particularly important when you are describing a role that can be assumed and extended by several different objects.

> A FinancialTransaction represents a single accounting transaction performed by our online banking application. Successful transactions result in updates to a customer's accounts. Specific FinancialTransactions communicate with the banking systems to perform the actual work. Examples are FundsTransferTransaction and MakePaymentTransaction.

***If a common meaning suits a candidate, use it to form a
basic definition.*** Don't invent jargon for invention's sake. In the
case of alternative definitions, choose one that most closely matches
your application's themes. Start with a standard meaning, if it fits.
Then describe what makes that object unique within your application.

The American Heritage Dictionary has six definitions for *account:*

1. A narrative or record of events

2. A reason given for a particular action

3. A formal banking, brokerage, or business relationship established to provide for regular services, dealings, and other financial transactions

4. A precise list or enumeration of financial transactions

5. Money deposited for checking, savings, or brokerage use

6. A customer having a business or credit relationship with a firm

It isn't too much of a stretch to conceive of different candidates that
reflect each of these definitions. In our online banking application,
accounts most likely represent money (definition 5). Rules that govern access to and use of funds are important. Different types of
accounts have different rules. Although it is conceivable that an
account could also be "a precise list of financial transactions" (definition 4), we reject that usage as being too far off the mark. People in
the banking business think about accounts as money, assets, or liabilities and not as a list of transactions. In the same fashion, we
reject definition 6. It doesn't specifically mention assets. We easily
reject definitions 1 and 2 as describing something very different from
our notion of accounts in banking. In banking, accounts represent
money. We choose definition 5 because it is the most central concept
to the world of banking:

> An account is a record of money deposited at the bank for checking,
> savings, or other purposes.

***Add application-specific facts to generic definitions.*** The
preceding definition is OK, but it is too general for online banking. In
the online banking application, users can perform certain transactions and view their balances and transaction histories. We add
these application specifics to our original description:

> An account is a record of money deposited at the bank for checking, savings, or other purposes. In the online banking system customers can access accounts to transfer funds, view account balances and transaction historical data, or make payments. A customer may have several bank accounts.

The more focused a candidate is, the better. Of course, a candidate may be suited to more than one use. Objects can be designed to fit into more than one application. A framework operates in many different contexts. A utilitarian object can be used in many cases. If you want your candidate to have a broader use, make this intent clear by writing the expected usage on the CRC card.

***Distinguish candidates by how they behave in your application.*** If distinctions seem blurry in the world outside your software, it is especially important to clarify your software objects' roles. Even if you can distinguish between a customer and an account, you still need to decide whether it is worth having two candidates or to have one merged idea. (Don't expect the business experts to help make this decision. It is a purely "technical" modeling one.) A candidate that reflects something meaningful in the world outside your application's borders may not be valuable to your design.

Let's look at the sixth definition of account:

> "An account is a customer having a business or credit relationship with a firm."

What is the difference between a customer and an account? Are they the same? If we had chosen this definition, would we need both customer and account objects in our banking application?

When you discover overlapping candidates, refine their roles and make distinctions. Discard a candidate or merge it with another when its purpose seems too narrow (and could easily be subsumed by another candidate). When in doubt, keep both.

> For both Customer and Account to survive candidacy and stick in a design, their roles must be distinct and add value to the application. We could conceive of a Customer as a structurer that manages one or more Account objects. And, in the online banking application, one or more users can be associated with a Customer. For example, the customer "Joe's Trucking" might have four authorized users, each with different privileges and access rights to different accounts. Another option would be to give an Account responsibility for knowing the customer and users. We could then eliminate Customer. We decide to include both Customer and Account in our design because giving those responsibilities to Account objects doesn't seem appropriate—we can envision customers and users sticking around even when their accounts are closed (and perhaps new accounts are opened). So customers are somewhat independent of accounts.

During exploratory design, expect a certain degree of ambiguity. You can always weed out undistinguished candidates when you find they don't add any value. Put question marks by candidates that need more definition. A candidate is just that—a *potential* contributor.

## CHARACTERIZING CANDIDATES

Before eliminating any possibility, consider how a candidate might work and how it relates to others. It is best to consider a candidate in a larger context. We can characterize candidates according to their

- Work habits
- Relationships with others
- Common obligations
- Location within an application architecture
- Abstraction level

To explore a candidate's work habits, ask, "What does it do, and how does it fit in?" Take one point of view—from the outside looking in. This is the same view a peer or client would take. Speculate about what services it might offer or how it might affect others. Think about these things, but don't assign responsibilities just yet. Ask whether the object is self-contained, working on its own initiative, or directed by others. Will it be constantly busy? Or will it need to be prodded into action? Is it an important, central character, or is it somewhere on the periphery? Ask what each candidate might do and be. If you haven't any idea, dig in and look for its potential value. If you are undecided, spend a few minutes speculating how it might fit into its neighborhood and about the nature of its role:

> We think of an Account as an information holder. So we do not think of it adjusting its balance on its own—it is probably changed by outside requests (both online banking transactions and other account activity). An Account knows its balance and transaction history. An account doesn't manage its customer, so it doesn't have much of a structuring role, but it is associated with its customers (does it need to know its customer, or does its customer know about it?). It isn't obvious how backend banking transactions that affect an account's status will be controlled (will an Account be involved in delegating this work or not?) —so we are uncertain how much work it will actually do. We'll defer thinking through these issues until we develop a more detailed blueprint for our application's control architecture.

## CONNECTING CANDIDATES

Given its limited space, what you can say on a CRC card will be brief. But CRC cards are much more than a compact space to record design ideas. They are real and tangible. You can pick up a card and talk about it as if it were the object itself, forgetting that the card "stands in" for a "real" object. You can use CRC cards to explore what candidates are and how they relate to others. You can move a card closer to any collaborators. You can poke at them, making as many connections and distinctions as you can. You can pick them up and lay out a new arrangement that amplifies a fresh insight, looking for patterns and similarities and differences. Which objects do similar things? Put them in a pile. Which objects are part of a neighborhood working on part of the problem? Move them closer. Get a sense of how your candidates fit and relate. Some useful ways to cluster candidates are as follows:

CRC cards, as invented by Ward Cunningham and Kent Beck, were originally used to teach object-oriented concepts. They have far broader applicability than as teaching aids. They can help you think about and link candidates.

- By application layer
- By use case
- By stereotype role
- By neighborhood
- By abstraction level
- By application theme

There is no standard way to fill out or use CRC cards. Several books have been written on the "art" and "practice" of CRC card modeling. David Bellin and Susan Suchman Simone's *The CRC Card Book* (Addison-Wesley, 1997) talks much about the process and people aspects of CRC cards. In Nancy Wilkinson's *Using CRC Cards: An Informal Approach to Object-Oriented Development* (SIGS, 1995), a CRC model for a library application is worked out and its translation to a C++ implementation is described.

Figure out what works best for you. Use CRC cards to express your ideas. Jot down initial ideas on the unlined side: At the very minimum, record a candidate's name, a brief description, and its role stereotypes (see Figure 3-2). That's mainly what you're initially looking for. Later you'll get more specific.

But you can also note things of interest: Does a candidate play a role in a well-known design pattern? Name that pattern and the candidate's role in it. Is it intended to fit into a narrow context, or, if carefully designed, might it be used in different applications? Note anything unusual and worth remembering. Is it an important abstraction? Put a big star by its name. As shown in Figure 3-3, use CRC cards to express what you think is important to know about a candidate.

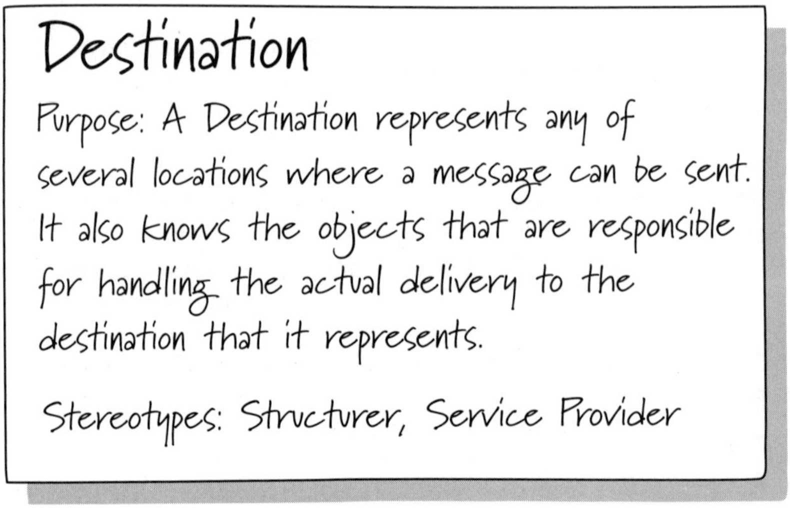

> **Destination**
>
> Purpose: A Destination represents any of several locations where a message can be sent. It also knows the objects that are responsible for handling the actual delivery to the destination that it represents.
>
> Stereotypes: Structurer, Service Provider

Figure 3-2
*The purpose of a candidate is recorded on the unlined side of a CRC card.*

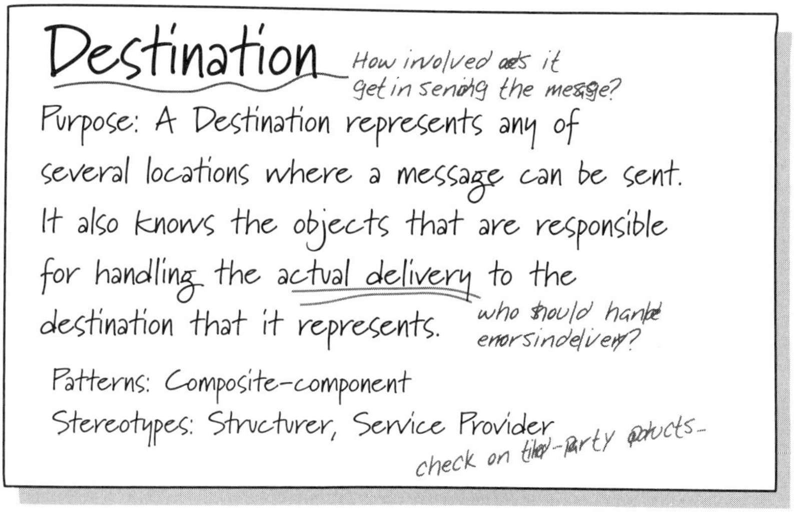

Figure 3-3
*You can add scribbles, questions, and comments to a CRC card to help you remember key points.*

## LOOKING FOR COMMON GROUND

Earlier, we suggested that you make sharp distinctions between candidates. If you couldn't find enough differences, we recommended that you merge candidates that have overlapping roles. Now we suggest that you take another, closer look at your candidates. This time you want to see what your candidates have in common. You should always be on the lookout for common roles and responsibilities that candidates share. If you can identify what candidates have in common, you can consciously make your design more consistent by recognizing these common aspects and making them evident. You can identify a common category that objects fit into. You can define a common role that all objects in a category play. Shared responsibilities can be defined and unified in interfaces. Objects that collaborate with them can ignore any differences and treat them alike. Furthermore, a class can be defined to implement shared responsibilities that make up a shared role, guaranteeing that the implementation of classes that inherit these implemented responsibilities works consistently.

You are likely to find several ways to organize your candidates. Some will be more meaningful than others. Each one that seems useful will likely contribute to your design's clarity. The more you can identify what objects have in common, the more opportunities you have to make things consistent. Eventually you may define several new roles that describe commonly shared responsibilities. Your initial cut at this won't be your last. Keep looking for what objects have in common and for ways to exploit commonalities to simplify your design.

**Common behavior could also imply the need for another candidate that is the supplier of that shared behavior.**

***Look for powerful abstractions and common roles.*** Things in the real world do not directly translate to good software objects! Form candidates with an eye toward gaining some economy of expression. Carefully consider which abstractions belong in your object design.

> In our Kriegspiel game, there are various actions that a player can perform: "propose a move," "ask whether a pawn can capture in a move," "suspend a game," and so on. It's a pretty safe bet that we have a different candidate for each action: ProposeAMove, Suspend-AGame, and so on. Proposing a move seems quite distinct from suspending a game. A harder question is whether we should define PlayerAction as a common role shared by each of these action-oriented candidates. If we can write a good definition for Player-Action, we should do so and define a role that is shared by all player action candidates. There seem to be several things common to all actions (such as who is making the request and how long it is active). Eventually, if we find enough common behavior for PlayerAction, it will be realized in our detailed design as a common interface supported by different kinds of PlayerAction objects. We may define a superclass that defines responsibilities common to specific player action subclasses. Or common behavior might imply the need for another candidate that is the supplier of that shared behavior.

***Look for the right level of abstraction to include in your design.*** Finding the right level of abstraction for candidates takes practice and experimentation. You may have made too many distinctions and created too many candidates—a dull design that works but is tedious. At the end of the day, discard candidates that add no value, whether they are too abstract or too concrete. Having too many candidates with only very minor variations doesn't make a good design. Identify candidates that potentially can be used in multiple scenarios.

Certain actions affect the position of pieces on a board. Should we have different candidates for each piece's potential types of moves? Not likely. This solution is tedious and offers no design economy. If you can cover more ground with a more abstract representation of something, do so. A single candidate can always be configured to behave differently under different situations. Objects encapsulate information that they can use to decide how to behave. The Propose-AMove candidate can easily represent all moves suggested by any chess piece. This single candidate will know what piece is being moved and its proposed position.

**Discard candidates if they can be replaced by a shared role.** To find common ground, you need to let go of the little details that make objects different in order to find more powerful concepts that can simplify your design.

What do books, CDs, and calendars have in common? If you are a business selling these items over the Internet, they have a lot in common. Sure, they are different, too. Books likely belong to their own category of items that can be searched and browsed. But all these kind of things share much in common. They all have a description (both visual and text), a set of classifications or search categories they belong to, an author, an availability, a price, and a discounted price. It sounds as if their common aspects are more important, from the Web application's perspective, than their differences. This suggests that all these different kinds of things could be represented by a single candidate, InventoryItem, that knows what kind of thing it is and the categories it belongs to.

Purely and simply, you gloss over minor differences. You don't need to include different candidates for each category of thing. In fact, those distinctions may not be as important to your software as they are to those who buy and use the items.

When you are shopping for items, you may be thinking of how they are used—books are read, calendars hung on a wall, and CDs played—but those distinctions are not important if you are designing software to sell them. Sure, you want to allow for your software to recognize what category something belongs to. You want to list all books together. But you probably want to categorize things in the same subcategory, whether or not they are the same kind of thing. Books about jazz and jazz CDs are in the "jazz items" category.

Only if objects in different categories behave differently in your software do you need to keep different categories as distinct candidates. The real test of whether a category adds value to a design is whether it can define common responsibilities for things that belong to it.

***Blur distinctions.*** There are times when both concrete candidates and their shared role add value to a design. There are times when they do not. If you clearly see that candidates that share a common role have significantly different behavior, then keep them. Test whether the distinctions you have made are really necessary.

> What value is there in including different kinds of bank accounts, such as checking or savings accounts in our online banking application? Checking accounts, savings accounts, and money market accounts have different rates of interest, account numbering schemes, and daily account draw limits. But these distinctions aren't important to our online banking application. We pass transactions to the banking software to handle and let them adjust account balances. In fact, because our application is designed to support different banks, each with its own account numbering scheme, a distinction made on account type (checking or savings) isn't meaningful. Our application doesn't calculate interest. So we choose to include only BankAccount as a candidate. If we were designing backend banking software that calculated interest, our decision would be different.

## DEFEND CANDIDATES AND LOOK FOR OTHERS

For a candidate to stay in the running, you should be able to state why it is worth keeping, along with any ideas you want to explore:

Marvin Minsky theorizes about the many agents working at different levels during problem solving. Most people don't forget that they are packing a suitcase to go on a trip when they stop to fill a toiletry bag. Side excursions are a normal part of problem solving.

> "A user accesses accounts to transfer funds, make payments, or view transaction history." In the next breath you can add, "Accounts contain information that enables a customer to perform financial transactions. Accounts know how to describe themselves; they know and adjust their balance; they are affected by different financial transactions; they know their transaction history. Are there any other candidates we should be identifying to support accounts in their role?"

By taking short side excursions to look for more candidates, you will come back with a better sense of whether you are on target. You can find more candidates by looking for ways to support and complement the ones you've already found:

Potential candidates that complement and support Account:

AccountHistory—A record of transactions against an account

FinancialTransaction—An operation applied to one or more accounts. A service provider could represent each type of transaction that affects an account. There are multiple types of transactions that we support with our online banking application. What's the difference between a transaction that affects an account's balance, and an inquiry into some aspect of an account such as its balance, history, or activation status? How should we model each inquiry?

Searching can go on for quite a while if you are full of ideas. Stop when you feel you are looking too far afield. You need enough candidates so that you can compare and contrast them and to seed your further design work. There isn't any magic number. The more you know about a problem, the more candidates you are likely to invent in a first pass. Fifty candidates may seem like a lot, but it's not an unreasonable number. Twenty is OK, too. You find candidates in bursts as you consider your design's themes. It's pretty common for candidates to support more than one theme. All this means is that your objects fit into and support more than one central concern.

Stop brainstorming candidates when you run out of energy. Then review how these candidates might collectively support the responsibilities implied by a theme. When you think you have enough candidates, review them once more for their merit.

Keep any candidate and put it on the "A" list, for acceptable, when you can

- Give it a good name
- Define it
- Stereotype it
- See that it might be used in support of a particular use case
- See that it is an important architectural element
- Assign it one or two initial responsibilities
- Understand how other objects view it
- See that it is important
- Differentiate it from similar candidates

You are always free to decide all your candidates stink, toss them, and start over. At the beginning this is cheap and relatively painless. Defend candidates on their merits, and don't protect them from close scrutiny.

Discard a candidate when it

- Has responsibilities that overlap with those of other candidates that you like better
- Seems vague
- Appears to be outside your system's boundaries
- Doesn't add value
- Seems insignificant or too clever or too much for what you need to accomplish

You may still be uncertain about some candidates. Put these on the "D," or deferred, list to revisit later. For now, keep them in the running. The best way to make more progress is to design how these objects will work together. The very next step we'll take is to assign each candidate specific responsibilities. And during that activity, we will come up with more candidates and reshape those we've already found.

## SUMMARY

You can approach the finding of objects somewhat systematically. Establish a framework for searching for candidates by writing a story about your application. In this story, write about the important aspects of your application. The candidates you identify should support various aspects of your story. You can use CRC cards to record your preliminary ideas about these candidates. CRC stands for candidates, responsibilities, collaborators.

Candidates generally represent work performed by your software, things your software affects, information, control and decision making, ways to structure and arrange groups of objects, and representations of things in the world that your software needs to know something about.

Good names for candidates are important. Choose them with care. Choose names that fit within a consistent naming scheme and aren't too limiting or overly specific. Once you've named and described each candidate's purpose, you can compare and contrast the candidates. For a candidate to stay in the running, you should be able to defend why it is worth keeping.

But your initial ideas are just educated guesses about the kinds of objects that you will need based on the nature of our application and the things that are critical to it. The real test of each candidate's worth will be when you can assign it specific responsibilities and design it to collaborate with others.

## FURTHER READING

Timothy Budd, in *An Introduction to Object-Oriented Programming* (Addison-Wesley, 2002), presents a thoughtful discussion of abstraction and object-oriented design. Another source of inspiration is Martin Fowler's *Analysis Patterns: Reusable Object Models* (Addison-Wesley, 1996). This book reveals how a good modeler and analyst thinks through issues and comes up with useful abstractions.

# Chapter 4

# *Responsibilities*

Christopher Alexander states, "Form is part of the world over which we have control, and which we decide to shape while leaving the rest of the world as it is." The measure of a design's goodness is how well the form fits into its context. When we shape an object's responsibilities, we are inventing a form that should fit smoothly into its environment. We have the luxury of shaping both form and context when we distribute responsibilities among collaborators.

A careful designer considers several divisions, identifies those that provide fruitful distinctions, and then designs the form.

The rightness of a form, according to Alexander, depends on how effortlessly it contacts with its environment. To make informed decisions about an object's responsibilities, we should divide form and context across several dimensions and consider several aspects of the problem. Looking at several possible divisions of form (that which we can shape and make whole) and context (that which we cannot control) sheds light on the problem. You should consider what the real problem is before you design a solution.

But how many dimensions of a design problem *should* you consider? Too much digression, and you never finish. Not enough exploration, and you hack out a solution while potentially missing a significant opportunity. You need to strike a proper balance. There's a lot to be gained by taking *quick* side excursions from time to time. It is easier to reshuffle responsibilities on cards than it is to rewrite thousands of lines of code. Consider some alternatives before you spend a lot of time building the wrong solution.

## WHAT ARE RESPONSIBILITIES?

Responsibilities are general statements about software objects. They include three major items:

- The actions an object performs
- The knowledge an object maintains
- Major decisions an object makes that affect others

Physical objects, unlike our intelligent software objects, typically do work or hold on to things or information. A phone book is a physical object but it takes no action. A thermostat exists, and it makes decisions and sends control signals. A teakettle exists, but it does little more than act as a reservoir (and occasionally whistles to send a signal). Physical objects usually don't make informed decisions. However, a dog is man's best friend and companion and does many different things on its own behalf. Our software objects lie somewhere between these extremes: They aren't sentient beings, but they can be more or less lively, depending on what responsibilities we give them.

Let's consider the design of a simple physical object. Alexander, in *Notes on Synthesis and Form,* asks what the right form is for a kettle. A teakettle holds water that can be heated until boiling. People safely pick it up when it is filled with boiling water and pour a cup of tea. And, if we follow convention, a teakettle signals us by whistling when the water boils. We can rephrase these characteristics as general responsibilities:

- Pour contents without spilling or splashing
- Hold water that can be heated until boiling
- Notify when water boils
- Offers a convenient means for carrying in a safe manner

How do we know whether we've got these right? Sure, some designers shamelessly redraw boundaries between the form they are working on and the context within which it exists. Overzealous framework designers we've known come to mind. If you think "outside the box," you can always change the boundary between a form and its context. You can claim that it is not the kettle that needs to be designed, but the method of heating water. Then the kettle becomes part of the context, and the stove or heating appliance becomes the form under consideration. In this case, lateral thinking might lead to innovation—an "instant hot" unit that heats tap water as it flows through it. We walk a fine line when we invent design solutions. If we are clever in redrawing the boundaries of the problem, we may come up with a novel solution. But we also risk creating unnecessary complexity instead of following a more straightforward path.

The key is to know when to push on redefining the problem and when to push on defining a solution. In this chapter we explore the art of finding, defining, and assigning object responsibilities . . . and striking a balance between thinking through alternatives and making reasonable responsibility assignments.

## WHERE DO RESPONSIBILITIES COME FROM?

Our strategy for assigning responsibilities to objects is very simple: Cover areas that have big impacts. Look for actions to be performed and information that needs to be maintained or created. You can glean information from several sources: Perhaps you have a specification of your software's usage; you may have written some use cases; or you may know of additional requirements or desired characteristics of your software. Responsibilities emerge from these sources and from ideas about how your software machinery should work.

You will need to reformulate demands and characteristics and software descriptions into responsibility statements. If statements seem too broad to be assigned to individual objects, create smaller duties that can be. These smaller subresponsibilities collectively add up to

> "Do not try to design objects to have all the conceivable behavior shown in the real world. Rather, make software objects only as smart as the application needs them to be and no smarter."
>
> —Jon Kern

> Responsibilities aren't just there waiting for us. Ouch, I've bumped into a responsibility, better assign it to one of my candidates! How to optimally distribute individual responsibilities between objects is often the most difficult problem in object design.

Activities for identifying responsibilities fall into one of three categories: finding them from external descriptions, inventing, and adding details.

larger ones. Formulating and assigning responsibilities to objects involves inspiration, invention, and translation of constraints and general descriptions into specific responsibilities. Assigning responsibilities to objects gives them shape and form. Once you make initial responsibility assignments, you should test whether they are well formed. Let's consider several activities for forming responsibilities. We do the following:

- Identify system responsibilities stated or implied in use cases
- Plug inherent gaps in use cases and other system descriptions with additional lower-level responsibilities
- Tease out additional system behavior from themes and software stories
- Follow "what if. . . then. . . and how?" chains of reasoning
- Identify stereotypical responsibilities to match stereotypical roles
- Search each candidate's deeper nature
- Identify responsibilities to support relationships and dependencies between candidates
- Identify responsibilities associated with objects' major "life events"
- Identify technical responsibilities that need to be assumed by objects to fit into a specific software environment

***Responsibilities come from statements or implications of system behavior found in use cases.*** There is a gap between use case descriptions and object responsibilities. Responsibilities are general statements about what an object knows, does, or decides. Use case descriptions are statements about our *system's* behavior and how actors interact with it. Use cases describe our software from the perspective of an outside observer. They don't tell how something is accomplished. Use cases provide a rough idea of how our system will work and the tasks involved. As designers we bridge this gap by transforming descriptions found in use cases into explicit statements about actions, information, or decision-making responsibilities. This is a three-step process:

- Identify things the system does and information it manages.
- Restate these as responsibilities.
- Break them down into smaller parts if necessary, and assign them to appropriate objects.

Consider this narrative that describes how a university student registers for courses. It leaves out a lot of details (such as how the user interface is laid out and the specific rules that affect registration), which we presume are found elsewhere:

---

### *Use Case: Register Online For Classes*

A student can register online for classes by filling out and submitting an online registration form for approval. While filling out the registration form, a student can browse the course schedules and cross-listed courses, audit degree requirements, and update personal and financial aid information. The student can also access the Wait-list Class and Drop Class functions.

Each course on a student's schedule has the following information: grading option, term, course title, section number, and class number. Although not prohibited from adding courses with time conflicts, a student should be made aware of any potential problems when building a schedule. When a proposed schedule is submitted for approval, it will be checked for conformance to all of the rules that the university specifies for course load, prerequisites, and required approvals. The system should notify the students of full classes and allow students to add themselves to the wait list for a particular class. In some cases, exceptions to the rules can be requested (such as time conflicts or overload of credit), but these actions are performed separately. Once students have received confirmation of an approved course schedule, they are considered registered for the term.

---

Depending on how much detail is included in a use case, it can be more or less difficult to find statements about our software's behavior. Use cases aren't packed with actions or behaviors that are readily ascribed to individual objects. However, even from this high-level narrative we can glean these responsibilities and in parentheses suggest some ideas about how they might be dealt with:

---

Generate and display an online registration form. (Something needs to know the structure of a registration form and the details of how it is displayed.)

Provide feedback as the student enters course selections about conflicts or problems. (Something needs to check that the student can sign up for a course, given the student's academic standing, and then there is a UI component that displays feedback.)

*Continues*

---

Provide capabilities for browsing, auditing degree requirements, updating personal and financial information. (Browsing sounds like a large responsibility involving several objects. Auditing degree requirements seems complex. We don't know how much work is involved in comparing a student's transcript and major against required courses. This needs further investigation. Updating personal and financial information seems specific. It will involve objects with responsibilities for displaying and editing this information.)

Provide capabilities for wait listing and dropping classes. (These two functions will likely involve several objects: Something needs to coordinate both tasks, update the waiting list, and adjust the student's schedule.)

Validate that each course in a schedule meets constraints such as pre-requisites, approvals, etc. (Sounds like a specific task that could be assigned to a StudentSchedule object.)

Notify the student of approved course selections (Notification seems like a subresponsibility that could be assigned to the same object who has responsibility for coordinating the work of schedule validation and reports the results to the user. The means of notification will likely involve instantiating and using objects from pre-existing UI components)

Notify the student of conflicts and allow him to resolve them (Again, notification seems like a responsibility of an object responsible for coordinating the registration task; other objects will likely be involved in the resolution of conflicts.)

By intent, use cases leave out design details. They are descriptive, not prescriptive. They tell a story. Use cases are descriptions that we use as general guides as we build our design. Use case scenarios describe step-by-step sequences. Supposedly they include more detail than an overview. Let's see what additional responsibilities we can glean from this scenario:

> ### Use Case Scenario: Register Online For Classes
>
> 1. Student pulls up the registration form and identifies self.
> 2. System verifies that student is allowed to register at this time.
> 3. Student enters the following for each course: course number, section number, and grading option.
> 4. Student submits course schedule for approval.

> 5. System verifies that the student meets credit load policies and course prerequisites and that none of the requested courses are full.
>
> 6. System returns approved courses in proposed schedule for confirmation.
>
> 7. Student confirms schedule.
>
> 8. System adds student to each class roster and returns confirmation of successful registration.

We find a few additional responsibilities that are more specific:

> Check that the student is eligible to register. (From step 2. Probably can be assigned to an object that coordinates the registration activity.)
>
> Add student to course rosters. (From step 8. Seems pretty specific. Some object will undoubtedly coordinate registration and ask the course roster to be updated.)
>
> Display confirmation of registration. (From step 8. Again, UI elements are involved, and something that coordinates the work.)
>
> Validate that each course in a schedule meets constraints such as prerequisites, approvals, etc. (Sounds like a specific task that could be assigned to a StudentSchedule object.)
>
> Notify the student of approved course selections. (Notification seems like a subresponsibility that could be assigned to the same object that responsibility for coordinating the work of schedule validation and reports the results to the user. This will likely involve instantiating and using preexisting UI components.)
>
> Notify the student of conflicts and allow him or her to resolve them. (Again, notification seems like a responsibility of an object responsible for coordinating the registration task; other objects will likely be involved in the resolution of conflicts.)

Most of these statements only hint at part of the work that needs to be done. They tell that confirmations are displayed, but not that they should be constructed by formatting specific registration information. They don't define acceptable responses to errors. They don't tell which system responsibilities interact. They don't tell what actions will be complex, nor do they specify timing constraints. Use cases describe the general nature of our work. We must shape all the details.

*Additional responsibilities come from plugging inherent gaps in use case and other system descriptions.* To gain confidence in your design, you must dig deeper into the nature of the problem and ask questions. Just by looking at our list of responsibilities we can come up with questions leading to more responsibilities. Here are a few:

---

How are course prerequisites specified? They may be part of a course description that our system can check, or they may be a relationship between courses, or a course may be responsible for knowing its prerequisites.

What states does a student's schedule go through? A student can build a schedule, submit it for validation, and confirm it. But what happens when things go wrong or problems are detected? When is a student really finished with his or her schedule? What different responsibilities does a student schedule have depending on what state it is in?

What happens when a student submits a schedule to be validated? Are the slots in the class reserved after each course is validated? How long does it take or should it take for prerequisites to be validated? What happens in exceptional cases?

Does registering happen in "real time," or does the student receive notification after work is carried out behind the scenes?

How much help should the system give to a student when things go wrong? Is notification of problems enough, or should the system provide support for remedying problems?

---

The sooner you ask and get answers to specific questions that will shape your system's behavior, the better. The answers will guide your thinking as you discover more detailed software responsibilities.

Use cases rarely describe aspects of control, coordination, error detection, visual display, timing, or synchronization. Designers must figure out these details. You can push forward with assigning responsibilities, even with many questions left answered. Tag those questions that will have the biggest impact. If you envision a range of possible answers and guess at those that are most likely to have the most impact, you can know where to push for answers.

Take two approaches: Identify responsibilities as well as unresolved questions. Continue to work on what you do know. Identify questions that are most likely to significantly impact your design. Once you get answers, you undoubtedly will refine your design. You won't know how comprehensive your solution needs to be until you get some answers.

Defer the specific design of control and coordination responsibilities until you make choices about how to distribute decision making and control responsibilities. Test your collaboration model with both "happy path" and more complicated scenarios. For now, collect and assign as many specific responsibilities as you can.

Design, and the assignment of responsibilities, is iterative. You make an initial pass at pinning down responsibilities, and then you rework your ideas as you come to know more about your objects and their interactions.

### *Responsibilities come from themes and design stories.*
Earlier, we recommended that you write a brief story that describes the key ideas behind your software. This design story kept you focused on what's important and stimulated your thinking about appropriate candidates. You can return to this story to extract some responsibilities. Let's reconsider the Internet banking story. Phrases that require system action are bold:

---

This application provides Internet access to banking services. It should be easily **configured to work for different banks**. A critical element in the design is the declaration of **a common way to call in to different backend banking systems**. We will define a common set of banking transactions and a framework that will call into banking-specific code that "plugs into" the standard layer implementing the details. The rest of our software will interface only with the bank-independent service layer.

We've developed a prototype implementation of this layer and have configured it to work for two different banks. Although it is still a prototype, we understand how to write a common banking service layer. Lately, our bank has been busy acquiring other banks and integrating their software. We've been through three system conversions in the past year. We want to focus on making this service layer easy to implement and test. At the heart of our system is the ability to rapidly configure our application to work for different backends and to put a different pretty face on each. This includes **customizing screen layouts, messages, and banner text**. The **online banking functions** are fairly simple: Customers **register to use the online banking services** and then **log in and access their accounts to make payments, view account balances and transaction histories, and transfer funds**. This

*Continues*

---

is straightforward and easy to implement. There is added complexity. Customers **record information and notes about each online transaction**. This **extra information will be maintained** by our application in its own database, because preexisting bank software has no way to store it. We want a customer to view human-readable information, not ancient bank software detailed transaction records. When a customer asks to **view an account's transaction history** we'll have to **merge this data with records supplied from the backend software**. Multiple users can access a customer's accounts, each with potentially **different access rights**. Certain users might have no access to sensitive accounts. A company executive might only view account balances, whereas a clerk in the accounts payable department could make payments and a comptroller might be able to transfer funds between accounts.

The more specific the responsibility, the easier it is to assign. Broad statements need to be broken down into smaller activities that can be assigned to one or more objects.

Because of the story's brevity, the responsibilities we find reflect only the highlights. This story mentions maintaining transaction-specific information but doesn't describe anything about registering for online banking. We search for responsibilities that support something the story emphasizes. We summarize these responsibilities and note where they lead us:

- Know a specific bank's configuration of supported features, default languages, and so on (will lead to designing objects with responsibilities for knowing a bank's configurable parameters and options).
- Translate common service requests to standard backend bank calls (will lead to designing service providers that handle these requests).
- Translate results from backend API calls into standard results (will lead to responsibilities assigned to interfacers between the common service layer and backend bank systems).
- Manage configurable banners, customized screen layouts, and user messages (will lead to the design of customization responsibilities and design of external resources).
- Perform financial transactions (will lead to designing objects that perform individual transactions).
- Record information and transaction notes in the database (will cause us to design transaction records and a means for storing them in our database).

- Merge notes with bank transaction records (will lead to specific responsibilities for assembling transaction summaries from notes and merging them with backend bank data).
- Display and format account histories and current balances (will lead to UI objects, objects that represent account history, and responsibilities for coordinating their display).
- Manage users and their access rights to accounts (will lead to responsibilities for knowing and changing access rights—perhaps directly associated with customers and users).
- Manage connections to the database and the backend banking services (leads to specific responsibilities for various connection and connection managing objects).

We can assign responsibilities for managing connections to specific connection managers. Financial transactions will be performed by the coordinated work of many objects, each with specific responsibilities. To assign responsibilities for performing transactions, we need to consider the details of each transaction in turn. Each transaction will require a different sequence of work steps, although some may be in common (for instance, all transactions are logged along with user-specific notes in the system's database).

***Responsibilities come from following "what if. . . and then. . . and how?" chains of reasoning.*** To gain even more insight, you need to consider how various requirements may impact your design. This involves more heavy mental lifting than our other responsibility sources. In this case, you don't start with a specific task such as "make a loan payment" or specific action such as "verify credit load." Instead, you need to lay a path from a high-level goal, such as "the software should be offline only during routine maintenance," to a series of actions or activities that achieve it. Only then can you make statements about what the system needs to specifically do as a consequence. Once you've come up with these specific conclusions, you can formulate specific responsibilities.

Coming up with a plan to solve a familiar problem is trivial. We're talking about something much harder—reasoning about an unfamiliar problem and a solution at the same time. This involves making an initial assessment and then following that to some logical conclusions.

We can think of many situations when we've chased design implications. Most involved short, solo excursions. Individuals thought through the problem and followed their instincts. As a group we might have kicked around the nature of the problem before the individuals went away and thought through the problem. Reasoning toward a solution seems to be an individual activity or one taken on by a small team of like-minded souls.

Here is one example that shows how thinking about a design constraint led to a new understanding and additional responsibilities. Our online banking application had a design constraint: it needed to recover from component failure. If a component went down or became unavailable, our system had to keep working and bring up another copy of a component. Our timeline for researching solutions was extremely short.

Len Lutomski, our distributed system expert, quickly assessed that the weakest link in our architecture was the name server. As the registry for distributed components, if this server failed, the entire "memory" was lost of how connections could be made to services. If this component failed, the entire system went down. This led Len to conclude that the name servers needed additional responsibilities for publishing location information changes, and that we needed additional shadow name servers standing in reserve, ready to be tapped into service if the leading name server failed. In his own words, here is how Len came to a workable solution:

> . . . [the solution] was dictated by the need to get something up fast, and by my desire to begin by isolating the problems of fault-tolerance from the problems of developing support for service groups. Early moves made on these grounds constrained the possible future developments, just as though it was a game of chess.
>
> My separation between the fault-tolerance part and the service groups part was developed prior to a clean understanding of the problem space . . . I was operating off the intuition that naming contexts should be naming contexts and not something else, and the sense that the fault-tolerance would not be trivial . . . in a good design the notions of a service group, a naming service, and of fault-tolerance and state-replication, would be both orthogonal and simply composed . . . If I had had the time, I think I could have put in another level of abstraction . . .

**The key to solving design problems quickly and adequately is to stick to your principles while you follow your hunches.**

Often your initial design will not be as simple or as elegant or as complete as you'd like. You don't have time to make many wrong moves. On the online banking project, the designer followed these principles: Keep concerns separate, and don't intermix responsibilities. Each object or component should do its job simply and well.

Following his initial line of reasoning led him to very specific responsibilities. His objects weren't up to his high standards, but they did the job.

***Responsibilities naturally arise from an object's stereotypical roles.*** Whether an object primarily "knows things," "does things," or "controls and decides" is based on its role stereotype. Exploring an object's character will lead to an initial set of responsibilities.

Information holders answer questions. They are responsible for maintaining facts that support these questions. When assigning responsibilities to an information holder, ask, "What do other objects or parts of the system want to ask?" Restate these queries as responsibilities for "knowing." Look for specific information that fits each candidate's role. Each information holder should support a coherent, related set of responsibilities. Secondarily, ask, "What else does this information holder need to know or do in order to carry out its public obligations?" These will be private responsibilities it undertakes to carry out its public duties.

When designing a service provider, ask, "What requests should it handle?" Then turn around and state these as responsibilities for "doing" or "performing" specific services. Similarly, structurers should have responsibilities for maintaining relationships between other objects and for answering questions about them. Interfacers will have specific duties for translating information and requests from one part of the system to another (and translating between different levels of abstraction). Coordinators have specific duties for managing cooperative work. Controllers should be responsible for fielding important events and also directing the work of others.

***Look for private responsibilities that are necessary to support public responsibilities.*** Even as you make general statements of responsibilities, you may think about how your objects might accomplish them. When should you focus on these details? As a matter of principle, concentrate first on what an object does for others. Once you've arranged these core, publicly visible responsibilities, reach for additional private responsibilities that support them.

Up to this point, we have been looking outwardly at descriptions of our system's behavior, its main themes, and its challenging requirements. The following activities shift our focus from external descriptions to stereotypical views of objects within their software environment.

Our early attempts at characterizing our candidates naturally leads to ascribing to them certain responsibilities. We can find more if we dig deeper.

Consider a BankAccount object designed for the online banking application. It is a simple information holder. It has these public responsibilities:

- Maintaining its current balance
- Knowing recent transaction history
- Knowing a displayable representation of itself (an abbreviated account number)

The fact that it needs to know a unique account identifier (used when using the backend bank transaction services) and a currency (for representing balances and transactions) is incidental to clients that use its public responsibilities. These responsibilities contribute to fulfilling its public duties but aren't directly visible to clients.

Nailing these supporting responsibilities means the difference between a workable design and failure. We live and die by these details! Although they are as important to our design as any publicly visible responsibilities, don't get bogged down in them too soon.

Record responsibilities as you think of them. Make sure you are comfortable with your object's role in its community before you work out many details. If you know these details, you can record them. What's the best way to do this? Should you get more specific with your responsibility statements, or are there other options?

Consider another example from the online bank: the design of an ErrorMessage object. This object holds onto specific error information and can translate errors into text in multiple languages. It is a pretty smart information holder. The request "Please translate this error into a human-readable message!" becomes a responsibility to "construct an error message." This high-level statement doesn't reveal how messages are formatted into different languages.

We could refine our initial responsibility "construct an error message" to read, "construct error message in a specified language." Adding "format messages with specific error parameters" is even more specific. However, we can also revise our object's purpose to be, "An ErrorMessage represents a specific error condition in the system that can be displayed in a form readily understood by end users. User-readable messages are constructed from language-specific templates and include details about the specific error." If we do this, the general statement "construct an error message" doesn't need to be overloaded with these details. We choose this option, leaving the responsibility stated simply and expanding the purpose instead.

Earlier, we mentioned that responsibilities are recorded on CRC cards along with a statement of purpose and a list of collaborators. Given the limited space on the CRC cards, you should use this real estate wisely. Make responsibility statements as brief as possible. Convey necessary information by reworking and revising all parts of your object's description. Don't pack everything into responsibilities. Record details in ways that let you remember them without creating clutter.

***Responsibilities come from examining relationships between candidates.*** Examining relationships between candidates can identify additional responsibilities. Objects can be related in complex ways: "composed of," "uses," "owns," "knows about," and "has" have very imprecise meanings in the English language. However, objects we tag as "structurers" nearly always have responsibilities for "maintaining" or "managing" objects they organize, whether we think of them as being "composed of," "owning," "knowing," or "aggregating" those objects.

UML has two very precise ways of modeling complex object structures: as composition or aggregation relations. Elements of a composite are stable, existing together over time; aggregates have somewhat looser ties. These are very precise distinctions that don't give us a clue as to responsibilities! What we want to determine is what related object is responsible for knowing and doing on behalf of that relation.

> We say an object "has" another when it needs to exhibit some property related to having that object. Does a meeting have attendees? Yes. If so, what do we know about the meeting? Answer: the number of attendees. This begs the question, should we give a meeting responsibility for knowing the attendees, or the attendees responsibility for knowing their meetings, or both? Viewing a meeting as "representing a gathering of attendees at a location for a specific agenda" (a structuring role), we assign a Meeting object responsibility for knowing all these things. Attendees don't seem to have much responsibility on behalf of their relationship to a meeting, and they shouldn't! Attendees may keep a calendar (another relationship between the attendee and a calendar object) that notes meetings to which they have been invited. We speak of "having a meeting" to go to, but that isn't fundamental to our behavior.

When an object plays the role of a structurer, it organizes groups of objects. Because of this role, it likely has responsibilities for answering questions about the things it knows of. To make specific responsibility assessments, we need to understand why a structurer exists and how its responsibilities change as its composition changes.

***Responsibilities may be associated with important events during an object's lifetime.*** Some objects' responsibilities are largely shaped by how they react. These objects are spurred to action by specific events. Controllers and coordinators fit this profile: most of the work they do is in response to stimulus they interpret.

In the online banking application, a UserSession object was responsible for coordinating user requests. It waited for requests it could delegate to others. Most of its responsibilities were tied to these requests and the passage of time:

- Know the users and their accounts
- Time user session activity
- Handle user requests by delegating them to appropriate service providers
- Report results back to the users
- Maintain a session summary

Like clockwork, whenever a user request was received, the UserSession object would spring to action. It would instantiate the appropriate service provider, ask it to do its work, report its results, and then idle, waiting to be spurred by another request or the passage of time. If too much time elapsed before a request was received, it would drop the user session.

---

A mark of skilled designers who use a specific software environment is that they know about all the responsibilities that can be customized.

---

Not all objects are so externally driven. Some react to internal changes. When an object is created and when it is no longer used are common places to find responsibilities for gracefully entering and leaving the scene. In most object-oriented languages, objects are notified of their impending exit with a "finalize" notice, allowing them to release resources before leaving.

***Responsibilities may be assumed when an object fits into its technical environment.*** The responsibilities we have identified up to this point have been in support of required system behavior. We mention this source last because it yields responsibilities of a different nature: those required for an object to fit into its software context. As a designer, you don't invent these responsibilities but you must understand their implications. Quite simply, your objects won't function properly unless they take on these *implementation-specific* responsibilities.

Let's look at a Java class library example. Object is the name of the root class in the inheritance hierarchy. All classes are subclasses of Object, and thus all objects "get for free" implementations of responsibilities defined by Object. The Object class provides reasonable default implementations of these responsibilities. Some are expected to be overridden.

---

Inheritance provides a mechanism for letting a form be customized in specified ways to fit with its environment: Superclasses can provide default implementations of responsibilities that can be freely overridden or extended by subclasses.

---

To be compared to others of its kind or stored in a structurer, classes must support two responsibilities: answer whether one object is equal to another, and produce a value that can be used as an index into a structure that will store the object. Many more responsibilities *could* be redefined.

Implementation-specific responsibilities shouldn't be your first concern. But if you know where your objects are headed, plan for them.

## STRATEGIES FOR ASSIGNING RESPONSIBILITIES

We've presented you ways to search for responsibilities. Although all responsibilities are necessary, they are not of equal significance. It's best to spend time and energy assigning responsibilities to those candidates who will have the most dramatic effects.

Although some objects may be central, they may not have interesting responsibilities. They may be important to begin with, but their importance quickly fades. Consider objects that are responsible for handing out work assignments to others. Although they are important, after they make work assignments they don't have much to do. Others may have intricate responsibilities that, although called on infrequently, are of critical importance. These objects need to be well designed for our application to be credible.

As you think through your design, what seems important may shift. Take a broad pass over the key aspects of your design and those important objects before assigning more detailed responsibilities.

Several points determine an object's stature and relevance:

- What position does it play in the application architecture? (Objects that bridge between layers or coordinate others' work have important responsibilities that knit our system together.)

- How visible is it to its surrounding neighbors? How visible is it to others outside its immediate neighborhood? (Visible objects may be important.)

- Is it a central concept in the domain? (Objects that model the real world or that represent the work of our system can be important.)

- Are its services complex? (Complex responsibilities take time to pin down and may impact others.)

- Does it make many decisions that affect others in its community? (If so, understanding these decision-making responsibilities is key to understanding how others will be affected.)

- How many steps away from key decision makers is it? (The farther away, the less likely it is to be a central player.)

- Does it structure and manage relationships between others? (This is important to know when you follow paths that lead to information and other objects' services.)
- How many others use and are aware of its services? (This is an indicator of relevancy but not importance.)

Look for high-impact objects, and assign them responsibilities that make them fit with their context. While you assign responsibilities to individuals, these assignments will impact close neighbors. A responsibility given to one object lessens the work of others. One division of labor may mean additional collaborations; another, fewer. No object is ever designed in isolation. When deciding what an object's primary obligations are, ask the following:

- What does each object offer as services to others? What information does it provide to others? (These are its public responsibilities.)
- What actions does it take in support of these public responsibilities? (These are its private responsibilities.)

## Recording Responsibilities

Keep a working list of unassigned responsibilities. Periodically work at assigning them to existing or new candidates. Keep a running list of unassigned responsibilities so that they don't have to stop and figure out everything at once.

As we stated earlier, we create a CRC card for each candidate (see Figure 4-1). When you do this, write the name of each candidate on the cards, one per card. On the unlined side of the card, state the candidate's purpose and stereotypes. Note anything else you think may be important to remember about that candidate: questions, concerns, or ideas.

On the lined side, again write the name of the candidate (see Figure 4-2). Draw a horizontal line that divides the card into two uneven parts: responsibilities on the left, and collaborators on the right.

Although you can write responsibilities directly on cards, sometimes you don't know where a responsibility should be located. If that's the case, try to capture the responsibility first and then assign it to the appropriate candidate later. Individual responsibilities can be written on Post-it notes that can be allocated to a candidate in one quick motion (see Figure 4-3). Unassigned responsibilities can be piled in a cluster, waiting assignment.

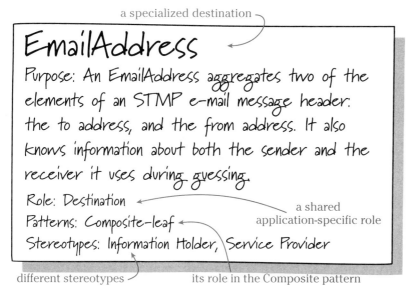

Figure 4-1
*The unlined side of a CRC card is for listing the candidate's name, purpose,*
*stereotypes, and other important notes.*

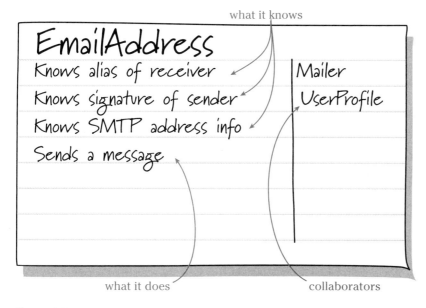

Figure 4-2
*The lined side of a CRC card is divided roughly two-thirds for responsibilities*
*and one-third for collaborators.*

Notify administrator of messages that cannot be sent

If you insist on using a computer, don't be lulled into thinking your candidates are well formed because typed responsibilities look neater. At this stage, exploring options should be fun, easy, and low-cost.

Figure 4-3
*Write unassigned responsibilities on Post-it notes that can be "assigned" when you identify the appropriate candidate.*

## Making Initial Assignments

Choose those objects you deem central players and concentrate on them first. Expect to work on more than one object at a time. Here are some ways to select a cluster of candidates to work on. We expect that you'll march through your candidates several times, tackling one group at a time:

- Candidates that represent domain concepts
- Candidates that participate in a certain use case
- Candidates that support an application theme
- Candidates that interface to the outside world

Make broad, encompassing general statements of responsibilities. Don't express responsibilities as individual attributes or operations.

Look for responsibilities that fit each candidate's primary role. A well-formed responsibility is a high-level statement of what an object knows or does.

***To start, state responsibilities generally.*** Responsibilities are best stated at a level above individual attributes or operations. Don't get overly specific in your statements. A statement of responsibility, if worded generally, can encompass many specific requests. There may be 10 ways to ask for tax calculations that are covered by the statement "Calculate all taxes based on locale." There isn't enough room on a CRC card to record very many details. These lower-level details belong in an information model or some other, more precise description. Use CRC cards for high-level descriptions.

> For example, say a Customer object has a name. That name may comprise a first name, surname, middle name, and maiden name; there may be aliases or nicknames. Don't state each of these as individual responsibilities. Write one general statement that covers all cases: Say that a Customer "knows its name and preferred ways of being addressed." Don't say that a Customer "knows first name," "knows last name," "knows nickname," "knows title,"and so on. Besides overflowing the card, this is far too much detail.

If you are worried you'll forget details, jot down hints on the card that will help you remember them as you work: "knows its name and preferred ways of being addressed (e.g., title, nicknames, etc.)". Space on cards is limited, so use it wisely.

***Find the right level of description.*** How many responsibilities do you need to shape an object's character? Responsibilities can be tersely worded or slightly more descriptive. It's a matter of personal and team style. You can be more or less brief, just as long as you and your teammates understand one another.

> The more broadly you state responsibilities, the fewer statements you need.

Your statements of responsibilities should be understandable with only a small amount of context setting. Let's look at the responsibilities for the Model-View-Controller roles as presented in the book *Pattern-Oriented Software Architecture* (John Wiley, 1996), or POSA to see how they are worded.

> The Model-View-Controller framework was first introduced in the Smalltalk-80 programming environment. MVC divides an application into three areas: the Model, which represents something in the domain; a View that displays information to the user; and a Controller, which receives input, usually as events. Events are translated to service requests to either the model or view. An application can be constructed with many different objects playing model, view or controller roles. To be displayed in a View and manipulated via a Controller, an application-specific object needs to assume the responsibilities of a Model object. One Model object can be displayed in multiple views.

Let's now look at statements of responsibilities for each of these roles:

---

***Model***

- Represents an application-specific object that can be changed or viewed
- Registers dependent views and controllers
- Notifies dependent components about changes in state

***View***

- Creates and initializes its associated controller
- Displays information to the user
- Implements the update procedure
- Retrieves displayable information from the model

***Controller***

- Accepts user input as events
- Translates events to service requests for the model or to display requests for the view
- Implements the update procedure, if required

---

These responsibility statements are fairly broad. They don't state the details of update notification, how or what kind of information is displayed, or the patterns of collaboration between these roles. Responsibility statements in POSA are chattier than those found in *Designing Object-Oriented Software* (DOOS) (Rebecca, Wirfs-Brock, Prentice Hall, 1990), the earliest book in which responsibilities were extensively used. Here is an example from it:

---

Here are how the responsibilities of a Document (a kind of model that holds onto the contents of an editable document) and a Display Frame (a view on a portion of a document) were stated:

***Document***

- Access and modify elements
- Change the attributes of the elements
- Copy portions of itself
- Maintain the style of the first page
- Knows its views
- Knows its target

---

- Knows its name
- Inform views of changes

### DisplayFrame

- Displays itself
- Composes itself
- Knows its contents
- Knows its bounding box

The POSA descriptions are complete statements; the DOOS responsibilities are terse, and more specific. Model-View-Controller responsibilities are more broadly stated because they describe roles that can be taken on and adapted by application-specific objects. The responsibilities of a Model are general; in contrast, the responsibilities of a Document (which assumes the role of a Model) are specific to its distinct purpose. We expect objects, such as Document and Display-Frame, to be explained more concretely than generalized roles. This brings up an important consideration. The more concretely you've been thinking about your design, the more likely you are to make specific responsibility statements.

> When describing a general role that can be assumed by many different kinds of objects, you can't get very specific. The more general a concept, the more general its responsibilities. The more specific a concept, the more specific its duties.

***Use strong descriptions.*** An object can seem ill defined if its responsibilities seem hazy. Behind a wall of vagueness can lie details that should not be ignored. Avoid weakly stated responsibilities if you can find stronger, more explicit descriptions.

Daryl Kulak and Eamonn Guiney, in their book *Use Cases: Requirements in Context* (Addison-Wesley, 2000), caution against giving use cases weak names. They suggest that more concrete verbs make for less vague use case names. If you use weak verbs, it may be because you are unsure of exactly what your use case should accomplish. The same principle applies to naming responsibilities for actions. The more strongly you can state a responsibility, the less you are fudging. In Table 4-1, contrast the stronger verbs with the weaker ones.

Table 4-1 *Use strong verbs to state responsibilities.*

| Strong Verbs | Weak Verbs |
| --- | --- |
| remove, merge, calculate, credit, register, debit, activate | organize, record, find, process, maintain, list, accept |

Of course, there are always exceptions to the rule. A weak-sounding phrase may have specific meaning in a certain context. In this case, don't look for a stronger term. *Listing a property* has a very specific meaning in the real estate business: It means to put a property on the market for sale.

***Be opportunistic.*** Thinking about one object leads to thinking about others. When considering an object's public responsibilities, you think about why its clients need to call on these services and what they are ultimately responsible for accomplishing. When you look at a single responsibility, you think about how it might be accomplished. This shift of focus is good (as well as hard to avoid). You test the fit of an object to its context by looking at both its use and its effects on others. If you hop around too much, however, you might leave an object before you have a firm grasp of its responsibilities. To avoid this, take a first pass at an object's major responsibilities before moving too far away from it.

***Decide how an object will divide or share the work of a large or complex responsibility.*** An object has three options for fulfilling any responsibility. It can either

- Do all the work itself
- Ask others for help doing portions of the work (collaborate with others)
- Delegate the entire request to a helper object

When you're faced with a complex job, ask whether an object is up to this responsibility or whether it is taking on too much. A responsibility that is too complex to be implemented by a single object essentially introduces a new sub design problem. You need to design a set of objects that will collaborate to implement this complex responsibility. These objects will have roles and responsibilities that contribute to the implementation of the larger responsibility.

At this point we're not asking you to make detailed decisions about how to design specific collaborations between these objects, only that you think through your options for assigning subresponsibilities. If a responsibility seems too big for one object, speculate on how you might break that responsibility into smaller logical chunks. These can be given as work assignments to other objects. Pursuing this line of thinking may lead you to new candidates with smaller, more tightly focused roles.

***Make sure an object isn't doing too much.*** If you find an object with a long laundry list of responsibilities, this could indicate one of two problems: Either you are stating its responsibilities in too much detail, or it is taking on too much. It is easy to rewrite responsibilities at a higher level.

However, if your object is too busy, consider splitting it into several smaller ones that will work together on the problem. Expect these objects to collaborate with one another. Although it may require more study before you obtain an overall understanding of this new system of objects, distributing the work among a number of objects allows each object to know about relatively fewer things. It results in a system that is more flexible and easier to modify.

***Keep behavior with related information.*** If an object is responsible for maintaining certain information, it is logical to assign it responsibilities for performing any operations on that information. This makes the object smarter; not only does it know things, but also it can do things with what it knows. Conversely, if an object requires certain information to do its job, it is logical (other things being equal) to assign it the responsibility for maintaining that information. In this way, if the information changes, no update messages need to be sent between objects.

> In banking, Account objects can have more or less behavior. By giving them responsibilities for knowing the rules of adjusting their balances, we turn them from simple information holders to hybrid information holder/service providers. If these resposibilities were assigned to some controller object, such as a FundsTransferTransaction object, it would mean separating the rules for changing account balances from the Accounts themselves.

***Distribute system intelligence.*** A system can be thought of as having a certain amount of intelligence. The sum of a system's intelligence is what it knows, the actions it can perform, and the impact it has on other systems and its users. Given their roles within a system, some objects can be viewed as being relatively "smart," whereas others seem less so. An object incorporates more or less intelligence according to how much it knows or can do and how many other objects it affects. For example, structuring objects such as sets or arrays are usually not viewed as particularly intelligent: They store and retrieve objects but have relatively little impact on

An extreme example of a "big object doing too much" would be a design in which a single object implemented all responsibilities of an application. This is obviously a poorly factored design!

the objects they store or any other parts of the system. Other structurers can be more intelligent. They have responsibilities not only for maintaining their contents but also for answering questions about them collectively.

Objects with responsibilities for controlling activity can be more or less intelligent, depending on how much work they delegate and how much they know about the work of those they manage. Guard against the tendency to make controllers too intelligent. We prefer to give the collaborating objects as much responsibility as they can handle. The more intelligent controllers are, the less intelligent are those that surround them. If you place too much responsibility in a controller, you lose design flexibility. Our goal isn't to evenly distribute intelligence but to give objects those responsibilities they can handle.

> Our decision to make Account objects know the rules for adjusting their balances lets us design a FundsTransferTransaction control object that is concerned only with coordinating the transfer, handling errors, and reporting results.

***Keep information about one thing in one place.*** In general, meeting the responsibility for maintaining specific information is easier if that information isn't shared. Sharing implies a duplication that can lead to inconsistency. Part of making software easier to maintain is eliminating potential discrepancies. If more than one object must know the same information to perform an action, three possible solutions exist:

- A new object could be created with the responsibility for being the sole repository of this information. This information holder would be shared among those who have a "need to know."

- It may be that the information "fits" with the existing responsibilities of one of the existing objects. In that case, it could assume the added responsibility of maintaining the information. Others could request this information when they need it.

- It may be appropriate to collapse various objects that require the same information into a single object. This means encapsulating the behavior that requires the information into a single object and obliterating the distinction between the collapsed objects. Sometimes we go overboard, factoring out responsibilities into roles that are too small. In that case it is better to pull them back into a single, more responsible object.

> Just because a customer's name appears on an invoice doesn't mean that the Invoice should "know the customer name." When it comes time to print, it can "know the customer" and collaborate with it by asking for the name.

***Make an object's responsibilities coherent.*** They should all relate in some way to the overall role of the object. An object as a whole should be the sum of its responsibilities. These responsibilities should complement one another. Everything an object knows or does should contribute to its purpose or fit into your design model.

***Restrict an object's responsibilities to a single domain.*** Meilir Page-Jones in *Fundamentals of Object-Oriented Design in UML* (Addison-Wesley, 1999) introduces a way of dividing a software system (and the objects that live within it) into domains. Domains are Page-Jones's way of dividing the machinery of an application into different contexts. According to Page-Jones, objects that live in lower domains shouldn't have responsibilities that tie them to objects in a higher domain. The more you tie objects in a lower domain to a higher one, the harder it is to reuse them in different contexts.

> If certain responsibilities seem unrelated, they need to be reassigned. Especially insidious are responsibilities that seem slightly tangential to an object's purpose.

Page-Jones's divisions (from higher to lower level domains) are as follows:

- Application: objects valuable for one application
- Business: objects valuable for one industry or company
- Architectural: objects valuable for one implementation architecture
- Foundation: objects valuable across all business and architectures

Foundation objects are further divided into three categories or subdomains:

- Fundamental: objects so basic that many programming languages include them as primitive data types, such as integers or reals
- Structural: objects that organize others, such as sets, collections, hashtables, or queues
- Semantic objects: objects that represent basic concepts with specific meaning, such as date, time, or money

To test whether two different objects are in the same domain, ask, "Can one object be built without any knowledge of the other?" If so, these two objects aren't likely to be in the same domain. But there are still places where you could tangle domains if you aren't careful—for example, when you need to convert from one type of object to another.

> Where should you place responsibilities for converting a temperature reading into a measurement or from one geometric shape to another? Measurements are readings (of temperatures, among other things) recorded at a particular time and for a particular instrument and location. A Temperature represents a degree of heat or cold on a definite scale. We can envision Temperatures existing without Measurements, so Temperatures are in a lower domain. It is OK for Measurements to have the responsibility for "knowing their temperature." But don't give Temperatures the ability to convert to higher life forms. This doesn't overburden Temperatures with higher-level duties. If you follow this advice, Temperatures can readily be used in other contexts. If they did know about Measurements, you'd have to drag along Measurements to any new context.

***Avoid taking on nonessential responsibilities.*** Avoid diluting an object's purpose by having it take on responsibilities that aren't central to its main purpose. Taking on responsibilities is easy to do, especially when you're deciding who should be responsible for maintaining a relationship. The obvious first answer is to make one or the other, or both, related objects be responsible.

> Consider adding the responsibility to a Person object to know how many dogs it owns. If we're building an application that handles dog show registrations, this might be reasonable. But if our Person could own cats, birds, gerbils, treasury bills, automobiles, life insurance policies, and so on, we could quickly pile on responsibilities for "knowing" all these things. This multiowner Person isn't useful in any other context because it is encumbered with a variety of responsibilities and links to all those other objects. The Person object becomes the pathway to these other objects and tends to pile on responsibility after responsibility after responsibility. In one design we reviewed, a Person object had more than 500 methods (and way too many responsibilities)! A better solution is to factor those responsibilities that aren't intrinsic to a Person into distinct objects.

---

*Sidebar (left margin):*

Typically you are not free to add responsibilities to foundation libraries. They come from the vendor with all kinds of warnings and prohibitions. You are prevented from tinkering with them. But you may be able to extend these classes by creating new subclasses.

---

Reuse isn't our only concern. For maintenance reasons, clear intent is paramount: Objects shouldn't take on responsibilities that go above and beyond their specific purpose. When an object does "favors" for others, its role becomes obscured.

The easy first answer isn't always the best. Each new responsibility needs to be considered carefully. It is easy to "slip one in" as an easy solution and avoid thinking through the consequences. An object that has a lot of links to others will be harder to maintain and move to a new context.

Consider creating a new object that is responsible for structuring the relation between people and dogs, another for people and valued property, and so on. Each of these new objects knows of a specific relationship. Instead of one big object knowing many others, the net result is a few simpler objects, each knowing some specific relationship. This is one way to "straddle" objects in separate domains. It results in a trimmer Person, unburdened with responsibilities that aren't intrinsic to its nature. Of course, this, too, can be carried to extremes. Too many objects with responsibilities to "glue" others together can also make a design brittle and hard to understand. Decide what relations are intrinsic to an object in the context of your application and which are not. Assign responsibilities for maintaining nonessential relations to new structurers.

***Don't overlap responsibilities.*** Sometimes you aren't sure which object should check, guarantee, or ensure that things are done the right way. Who should ultimately be responsible? If you want a robust system, you must make your objects and neighborhoods resistant to careless mistakes and errors.

Should you make the client check before it calls on the services of another? Should you give service providers responsibilities for checking that their requests are properly formed? If you're not sure whom the clients are or under what situations a responsibility will be carried out, you might be inclined to put in safety checks everywhere.

> If we followed this strategy in the design of physical objects and systems, we would design teakettles with responsibilities for notifying when their contents boil, we'd give monitors responsibility for checking water contents of the teakettle, we'd ask the person who filled the teakettle to determine whether the kettle is boiling, and we'd put safeguards into a stove burner so that when it detects the kettle whistling for a period of time, it'd reduce its temperature.

This line of reasoning leads to overly zealous objects, all of them fretting about the state of the system. It can be extremely costly to maintain such a complex system of objects. You are better off developing

Even if you are building only one application, avoid big, fat objects. There are always reasonable alternatives. Instead of burdening either object in a relationship, consider creating a new object that is responsible for structuring the relation.

a simple, consistent strategy for checking and recovering, and sticking with that. Not everyone needs to be involved or "share in an important responsibility."

If you want an object to be impervious to malicious requests, give it responsibilities for detecting and deflecting them. Once you've given an object that responsibility, design its clients to be more cavalier; they need only react to bounced requests, not prevent them. We will return to this topic when we design collaborations. But for now, consider that when you give one object a responsibility, you are potentially relieving the workload of another. It isn't necessary to build in overlapping responsibilities unless your system explicitly demands redundancy.

## Getting Unstuck

Even with the best of intentions, you can spin your wheels, unable to come up with convincing responsibility assignments. Relax and take a deep cleansing breath. Here are some common "sticky problems" and ways to move beyond them.

***Problem: You have a big responsibility that doesn't seem to belong to any candidate.*** Who *should* be responsible for solving world peace or ending world hunger? There aren't simple answers because these are extremely broad problems. If you really wanted to tackle world peace or hunger, you'd have to break these enormous problems into smaller factors that, if solved, might contribute to lessening friction or reducing hunger. Divide a big problem into smaller problems, and solve those.

Big software responsibilities can seem equally daunting to those tasked with solving them. What object should be responsible for "interacting with the user" or "performing business functions" or "managing resources" or "doing the work"? If a responsibility seems too big or too vague, break it into smaller, more specific ones that can be assigned to individual objects. Treat the "big responsibility" as a problem statement and reiterate through identifying specific objects with smaller responsibilities that add up to the larger responsibility.

***Problem: You don't know what to do with a vague responsibility.*** If you can't get more concrete, perhaps you are trying to add precision to a statement that is so general that you can't get any traction. You don't know enough to break it down into subparts.

Before you can design a solution, you may need further definition from someone who knows more about the problem than you do. It's always fair to ask, "Can you be more specific about what you mean by performing business functions?" If you are lucky, your statement may not really be a problem at all. You may already have assigned specific responsibilities that are subsumed by a broad unapproachable statement.

> "Interacting with the user" may simply not be something you have to deal with if you know where responsibilities for "redisplay up-to-date chart information on a periodic basis," "know chart viewing parameters," and "perform request to . . .," "calculate . . .," "display archived charts . . .," responsibilities are covered. If so, relax. You've assigned specific responsibilities; your job is finished.

***Problem: You can't decide between one of several likely candidates.*** Sometimes it isn't obvious which candidate should be assigned a specific responsibility. When you're choosing which of several objects to assign a responsibility, ask, "What are all my options for assignment? If I choose this possibility, what does that imply for its surrounding neighbors?" If you have trouble assigning a particular responsibility, the solution is simple: Make an arbitrary assignment and walk through the system to see how it feels. There isn't necessarily a single "right" answer. Don't get in a jam thinking that you must optimally solve the problem or that there is only one optimal assignment. There may be several, or none.

Assign a responsibility to one object, and then follow through with how this affects others. If it seems reasonable, stick with it. Feel free to play out several options before making a final decision. You can always change your mind. Assignments will be revised and adjusted as you get deeper into design.

> Should a Session be responsible for timing itself, or should the SessionManager do so? There may be reasons for both alternatives. The SessionManager could adjust the session times based on overall system performance. Well, each Session could react to changing system performance characteristics by querying the SessionManager before deciding to time out. Well, sure. Both seem workable. How can you decide?

You can try several different approaches to distributing responsibilities. Look at how different responsibility assignments impact objects in the neighborhood.

***Problem: You have trouble assigning a specific responsibility.*** You may get stuck on a responsibility that seems to be reasonably stated but has nowhere to go. This could mean that you are covering new territory and may need to invent a new candidate. Great! This is progress. Or it could be that even though the responsibility is specific, your existing candidates' responsibilities are stated at a higher level of detail. If so, remember that responsibilities are general statements; what you think of as a specific responsibility you have trouble assigning may actually be an implementation detail that doesn't really belong on a CRC card. If so, save it for later.

Responsibilities do not dictate any specific implementation. When we say that an object maintains certain knowledge, we aren't stating that it stores it directly as data.

**Problem: *You are worried about how a responsibility is actually going to be accomplished.*** You've stated responsibilities generally, but you have nagging doubts. How will each object carry out its duties? Are you concerned because you suspect that something is missing? If so, follow your instincts and figure that out. Are you a stickler for details? Until you see running code, you never believe a design will work. If so, relax. Your design isn't finished quite yet. And it will change as you design collaborations, too. Once you are comfortable with how you've arranged responsibilities among a set of collaborators, then you can pin down responsibilities to a specific implementation. A responsibility for maintaining knowledge could mean that

- The object holds on to the fact directly.
- It could derive it from other information sources.
- When asked, it turns around and collaborates with another that can compute (and is responsible for reporting the results to others).

At this point, all your options are open. Stating that a Monetary-Transaction "knows its applicable taxes" could mean that it stores its taxes directly in variables or that, when asked, it turns around and delegates this request to a tax calculator object that does all the work. We don't have to decide these things just yet. In fact, until we know our candidates and all the dimensions of the problem better, we don't know enough to make informed decisions about how "knowing" responsibilities are best implemented.

## IMPLEMENTING OBJECTS AND RESPONSIBILITIES

Sure, we're fudging a bit. We have written responsibilities on index cards, but we haven't yet decided on an implementation—although we may have a pretty good idea. So far, we have identified candidate objects or roles (or both). We have also characterized our objects and stereotyped their role. We have made no implementation decisions. This shift between objects and their possible implementation in classes and interface specifications is an important one. When you make this shift, you have options. There isn't necessarily a one-to-one correspondence between a candidate and a class.

## An Object Can Play Multiple Roles

Let's review how objects and roles are related. This will help us specify implementation classes and interfaces. An object can take on one or more different roles. We distinguish roles as being one of the following:

- Primary: comprising of responsibilities that clearly define an object's main purpose and its character
- Secondary: comprising of responsibilities that are incidental to an object's purpose but necessary for it to fit into its environment of technical libraries, frameworks, and application-specific conventions

When you make the transition from candidates to an implementation specification, you will create abstract and concrete classes that implement your objects' responsibilities. An abstract class provides a partial implementation. It leaves its subclasses with the obligation to implement specific responsibilities. A concrete class provides a complete implementation. You are also likely to specify interfaces for responsibilities that can be implemented by different classes. An interface specifies method signatures without specifying an implementation. It defines the vocabulary clients use to invoke responsibilities, regardless of their implementation.

> Abstract and concrete classes are the building blocks we use to specify an implementation. Declaring interfaces is one means to make it more flexible and extensible.

Implicit in the declaration of an interface is the design idea that a single role can be carried out by several types of objects, regardless of their implementation. When you suspect that a role might be played by different kinds of objects, declare an interface. Do so even if you intend to implement a number of classes belonging to the same inheritance hierarchy. This makes it clear that your abstract and concrete classes are just one possible implementation and that others may be declared in the future without being constrained to a specific ancestry. It makes clients who use objects that support this interface more flexible, too. They needn't know about specific classes in order to use objects that share a common role declared in an interface.

> Certain object-oriented languages, such as C++ or Smalltalk, do not support the construct of an interface. For these languages, you are likely to declare the common methods in a class that can be inherited from, in lieu of defining a common interface.

An object *can* have multiple roles. But if you've kept your candidates on the narrow path, each most likely represents only one role. Each is what it is and does what it does. The mapping from candidate to implementation is straightforward: You define a class to implement each candidate that supports a single primary role.

Following this guideline, we'd declare a BankAccount class to implement our BankAccount candidate, with these responsibilities:

- Maintain its balance
- Know its customer
- Know its unique ID
- Know recent transaction history
- Know a printable representation of its ID

The BankAccount class may pick up additional implementation responsibilities to fit into its software context. If we implement a BankAccount class in the Enterprise Java Beans framework, our BankAccount might take on the responsibilities required of EntityBeans:

- Know its context
- Initialize itself
- Retrieve and store itself from a database
- Activate/passivate itself when asked to by the container

These are declared in the `EntityBean` interface that our BankAccount class implements.We also might alter our class's name from Bank-Account to BankAccountBean, just to make it clear that it fits into the J2EE framework.

The roles an object can play can be framework- and technology-based or domain-specific. Interfaces can also be domain-specific or technology-based abstractions. For example, if we wanted to push a bank account object in another, domain-specific direction, we might declare it to be a FinancialAsset. A FinancialAsset is a role that represents something held by the bank that has a projected and current valuation. CertificatesOfDeposit and MoneyMarket Accounts are other examples of FinancialAssets. We could declare our Bank-Account candidate to assume this secondary role and adjust its implementation accordingly.

---

To sharpen your role modeling skills, go to your favorite class libraries and reverse-engineer some interfaces and classes into one or more roles, each with clusters of responsibilities.

A class implements responsibilities that are intrinsic to the roles its objects play (see Figures 4-4 and 4-5). These can be application-specific or technical. Consider technical roles after you're confidant about your application-specific design and have decided on an implementation strategy.

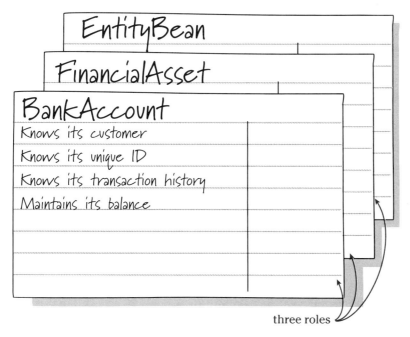

Figure 4-4
*A BankAccount candidate is the sum of its one primary and multiple secondary roles.*

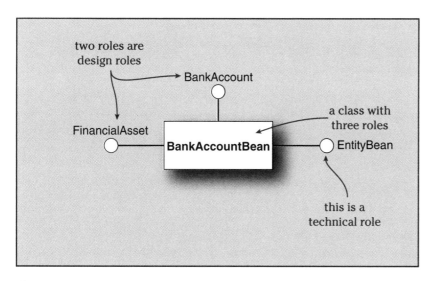

Figure 4-5
*The* BankAccountBean *class represents three roles.*

### Designing Methods and Signatures That Support Responsibilities

Objects may know and do similar things, but because they do them differently, they require different interfaces and implementations. When you look for what is in common, you need to look below the surface. You want to discriminate among that which is in common and will be implemented identically, that which is common but requires a different implementation, and that which appears to be in common but isn't.

Sharpen your focus and ask, "Are these really the same responsibility? Do they mean the same to clients?" Let's look at a simple example to see how responsibilities that seem common might be implemented.

---

Consider these two candidates and their responsibilities:

**_Rectangle_**

- Knows how to draw itself
- Knows its dimensions

**_Circle_**

- Knows how to draw itself
- Knows its dimensions

We expect circles and rectangles and other graphic shapes to be asked to draw in the same way (their clients can draw them interchangeably if this is the case, even though the way they draw themselves differs). But what about their dimensions? A circle can be described by its radius; a rectangle, by its width and height. Both kinds of objects know their dimensions. But they have different ways of defining them. We expect clients to change and inquire about them differently. Circle and rectangle will have distinct methods that implement this responsibility.

We could restate each responsibility to be explicit: A rectangle "knows its width and height," or a circle "knows its radius." But we won't. As a natural consequence of getting more precise, you create different interfaces and implementations. Instead of patching up cards with this new precision, leave this to detailed design and to class and interface specifications. At one level of abstraction, circles and rectangles do share a common responsibility to "know their dimensions." Because they do so differently, different classes will implement them.

---

## TESTING YOUR CANDIDATES' QUALITY

Responsibilities are general statements that describe software objects and the actions they take, the information they manage, and the decisions they make. When you spread responsibilities around among object neighborhoods, make sure that each object keeps to its task and doesn't demand too much or take on responsibilities better assigned to others. The quality of a form can be tested by how well it fits into its context.

Here are some ways to test whether an object is well formed:

- Does it stick to its purpose?
- Are its responsibilities clearly stated?
- Do its responsibilities match its role?
- Is it of value to other objects in its neighborhood?

It is relatively easy to remedy one object's flaws and make it a better fit. If you have created an all-knowing, all-doing object with too many responsibilities, carve it up into several cooperating ones. If an object is responsible for maintaining information, reassign it the responsibility for performing any operations on that information. If you've dispersed responsibilities, consider consolidating them.

It is somewhat more difficult to adjust the responsibilities of several objects. If you have scattered related information across several objects, you may want to integrate this information in a single object. When you design a software application, you are inventing systems of objects. Not only should each fit with its software context, but also objects within natural partitions should work well together. You are bringing communities of objects into existence.

The quality of a design can be proved only by how well it stands up to its complex requirements over time. Some designs are better than others. If every part is connected, then it is hard to limit the effects of change. So it is better to isolate parts—to identify subsystems of objects—and establish patterns of communication between them. Each subpart should have a coherent role; obligations shouldn't spill across different areas. This speaks to the heart of encapsulation, which states that like things belong together.

Although each object has a distinct part to play, object neighborhoods collectively take on larger, related responsibilities. They, too, have larger roles to play in the application. They, too, should be coherent wholes. You need to consciously organize and design how objects in different parts of your system interact. In Chapter 5 we discuss how to develop a model of objects and their collaborations.

## SUMMARY

Objects do things, know things, and make decisions. In this sense, they are responsible. Their responsibilities come from your ideas about how your software machinery should work. Objects shouldn't do too much or too little. They should stay in character. A good test of whether an object is well formed is that its responsibilities form a cohesive unit. Does it stick to its purpose? Are its responsibilities clearly stated? Do they match its role?

Whether an object primarily knows things, does things, or controls and decides is based on its role stereotype. Exploring an object's character will lead to an initial set of responsibilities. Information holders answer questions and are responsible for maintaining specific information. Coordinators have specific duties for managing cooperative work. Service providers field requests from others. Requests can be restated as responsibilities for performing specific services.

To come up with responsibilities, you will need to reformulate software descriptions into responsibility statements. This process can be more or less direct. Most of the time you will need to get more specific and concrete to identify responsibilities that can be assigned to individual objects. When responsibility statements seem too broad, create smaller duties that fit with an object's role. As you find and assign responsibilities, you will make choices about how individual objects contribute to the overall working of your application. Although each object has a distinct part to play, it fulfills its responsibilities by interacting with others. So your model won't be complete until you understand how objects collaborate.

## FURTHER READING

If you haven't read Christopher Alexander's *Notes on the Synthesis of Form* (Harvard University Press, 1970), you are missing out on one of the early works of the architect who inspired the software pattern inventors. Alexander's book has nuggets of wisdom for those who are consciously designing complex systems made out of things with interdependent parts, whether they be software or physical structures.

Donald Norman's *The Design of Everyday Things* (Basic Books, 2002) contains many examples of poorly designed physical objects—VCRs, doors, refrigerators—and discussions of how to improve them. It's a matter of paying careful attention to the design of interfaces and appropriate feedback in response to users' actions. It doesn't matter how many nifty features an object has if people can't figure out how to use them! This book is a great source of inspiration for software designers, too, who also need to pay careful attention to their objects' interfaces, side effects, and responses.

Meilir Page-Jones, in *Fundamentals of Object-Oriented Design in UML* (Addison-Wesley, 1999), talks about good design using terminology we've never encountered anywhere else. His book contains lots of good advice. If you want to know more about cohesion, encumbrances, and valuable design principles, read this book. Be prepared to increase your vocabulary and to enjoy Meilir's unique wit and wisdom.

Craig Larman, in *Applying UML and Patterns* (Prentice Hall, 2001), devotes two chapters to the discussion of principles to use when assigning responsibilities to objects. He defines several patterns for identifying and assigning well-formed responsibilities.

# Chapter 5

## *Collaborations*

**C**hristopher Alexander suggests that we solve a design problem in "the least arbitrary manner possible." If we do so, we avoid misfits between form and context. So let's not be cavalier about how our objects cooperate! Software objects are connected through interactions and shared responsibilities. If we design simple, consistent communications, our solution won't be arbitrary. Our design will be more adaptable if parts can be changed without effects rippling throughout the system. A complex software system becomes manageable when responsibilities are partitioned and organized and when collaborations follow predictable patterns.

## WHAT IS OBJECT COLLABORATION?

Collaborations are requests from one object to another. One object calls on, or collaborates with, another because it needs something. The two objects work in concert to fulfill larger responsibilities. Designing collaborations forces us to consider objects as cooperating partners and not as isolated individuals.

> Collaborate: To work together, especially in a joint intellectual effort.
> —*The American Heritage Dictionary*

Until this point in our design, any discussion of "this object doing this" and "that object doing that" has been predicated on the notion that our objects will have information or services within reach at the precise moment when they need them. As execution flows around our object model, however, necessary connections between collaborators need to somehow come and go. Our model is incomplete until we describe how our objects interact and how they connect. The collaboration model will describe the dynamic behavior of "how" and "when" and "with whom."

As we organize objects into neighborhoods with collective responsibilities, we need to carefully arrange how objects within a neighborhood collaborate to fulfill their larger responsibilities. We also decide how objects outside a neighborhood will interact with services that the neighborhood offers. As a side benefit of this effort, we should be able to modify parts of our systems without changes rippling throughout the entire system. A well-designed object-oriented application should absorb a certain amount of change without buckling.

Designing roles and responsibilities lays out a floor plan; deciding on collaborations adds the wiring and the plumbing.

### Preparing for Collaboration

Object-oriented design is fundamentally different from procedural design. Objects are structured in a network and not a hierarchy. Procedures separate data from behavior, whereas objects blend them. The line between these two technologies can get blurry, though. What about a powerful object that is surrounded by simple information-holder objects? The all-capable object pauses occasionally to get data from its minions, but otherwise, it doesn't collaborate or delegate work to anybody. It holds all the logic. Where is the information hiding? The encapsulation?

A more object-oriented design is organized into neighborhoods, each having a distinctive character and specialized responsibilities. Within each neighborhood, each object has a role to play and knows which of its neighbors to ask for help. Responsibilities are shared among neighbors. Paths of collaborations are established within and between neighborhoods. Some objects reach outside their communities for help. Others stay put, do a well-defined job, and demand little of others. The architecture of an application dictates certain patterns of communication. Preexisting components or frameworks impose their preferred styles of interaction. Our collaboration model must incorporate our inventions into any preexisting fabric.

> Using an object-oriented language promotes, but does not guarantee object-oriented thinking. It is how objects are defined and how they interact that determines whether a design solution is object-oriented.

An object design evolves through iterations that adjust both its behavior and its support structure. Objects, roles, and responsibilities evolve. Responsibilities shift as we discover better ways to balance the workload among collaborators. We rearrange interactions as we discover preferred ways to communicate. Frequent paths become more efficient; standard ways of accomplishing work become routine. Patterns of collaboration!

## Recording Candidate Collaborations

Early in exploratory design, when our objects, responsibilities, and collaborations represent initial guesses, we are building a candidate model. Candidates come and go, responsibilities move from one object to another, and collaborations shift. As long as we are building a candidate model, we jot down our thoughts on CRC cards. They are as dynamic as our thinking. Only when we have evidence that our objects, responsibilities, and collaborations are "right" do we document them with more formal tools, or write some code. With that in mind, how do you write collaborations on CRC cards?

> CRC cards are informal tools we use to capture rough ideas about collaborations. Details of specific message sequences and interactions with specific objects are best shown with collaboration or sequence diagrams.

Responsibilities fill up most of the space. Because a collaborator may be asked to fulfill several responsibilities, we mention it once, regardless of how many times it is used. When it comes time to write code, we certainly need to know more. But now it's enough to say that the object is a collaborator and list it on the right side of the card. If you want to be more specific, you can draw a line from one responsibility to each collaborator it uses (see Figure 5-1).

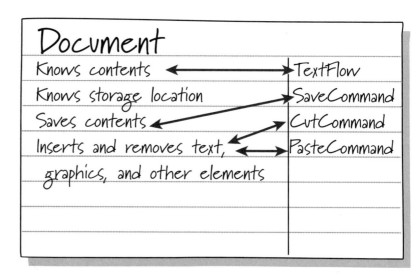

Figure 5-1
*Responsibilities can be connected to their collaborators.*

Don't clutter a card with obvious or uninteresting collaborations. An object can always use its own information or services, so don't bother to list it as a collaborator. If you need two or more objects playing the same role, record the role only once. Similarly, if an object plays two roles, then we should list both, each on a separate CRC card. We list potential collaborations between objects playing roles and not each individual collaborator.

Avoid recording low-level decisions. If an object's role is to hold information, we typically don't list the objects it uses from a standard class library to store information (such as numbers or strings or arrays) unless they are particularly unusual choices. Leave that as an implementation detail.

## THE DESIGN STORY FOR THE SPEAK FOR ME SOFTWARE

As a source of design ideas and examples throughout this book, we will consider the design of software that enables a person with severe limitations to communicate with others. Here is the Speak for Me design story.

---

### The Speak for Me Software

Our user is paralyzed and blind and cannot speak. Confined to a hospital bed, she is "locked in," unable to communicate by any means other than blinking her eyes to indicate "yes" or "no." Speak for Me allows her to spell and send messages. The software speaks the alphabet to her, using a small motion sensor to monitor for the eye blinks that she uses to select the letters that she wants. After she selects each letter, it speaks "space" to her, which she selects to end a word. If the partially spelled word is longer than one letter, the system attempts to guess what she is spelling, using a variety of contextual and linguistic rules for guessing. If it finds an appropriate word to guess, it speaks it and watches to see whether she selects it. If she does, it appends the entire word to her message and begins a new word, presenting the letters from the beginning of the alphabet again.

When she finishes a message and wants to tell the computer what to do with it, she spells one of the software's special *command words*. There are commands for ending the current sentence ("ES"), sending the message to different places ("SM"), displaying the message on the screen ("DM"), holding the message for later ("HM"), and so on. Most of the available commands operate on the *current* message— the one that she has just finished constructing. A few other commands do not require a current message. For example, when she wishes to read e-mail, she starts the idling software with an eye-blink and builds just one word: the command for reading e-mail: ("RE"). Or she might spell the command for calling for help ("CH"). When the software recognizes any of these special command words, it executes the command's corresponding behavior.

---

## COLLABORATION OPTIONS

Some objects collaborate a lot; others, little. Some objects offer help to many others; other objects are used infrequently. An object's frequency and patterns of collaboration will depend on what its responsibilities are and how it carries them out. We may design an object to gather information and then make a decision, or we may decide that it should delegate the decision making to a neighbor that already has the information. Either choice results in collaboration. Another object might be designed to perform all of its own responsibilities. As it gets big and clumsy, we might delegate part of its work to

An object that has grown too big might be split in two, and what were the responsibilities of a single object become a collaboration between the two.

others. After we've reassigned responsibilities to others, we'll have to form collaborations between these smaller, more focused objects.

Often, objects are designed to fit together as an ensemble. Their roles and responsibilities are designed at the same time. A responsibility exists in one object because it plays a role that supports another. Without its collaborator, we couldn't conceive of a reason for it to exist.

> In Speak for Me, how are Letters and Words spoken? They know their textual and spoken representation, but it is probably inappropriate for them to also speak. They need to collaborate with another object, a Presenter.

The fact that a helper turns around and delegates the entire task to one or more subspecialists isn't of any concern to the requester. If we hide from an object's users the details of how it accomplishes its responsibilities, we have the flexibility of changing how it accomplishes its work without impacting those who use it.

> The Presenter may do everything, or it may wrap a native code text-to-speech library and pass the text along again. Letters and Words know about the Presenter's public responsibilities but not how it actually speaks.

Other collaborations are much looser. Relationships between objects offering services are established on-the-fly. After a connection is made, requests flow. In these designs, who actually provides the service is less important than how to ask for help.

> In the online banking application, a component logs in to the domain server by sending a request to the UserSessionManager. The UserSessionManager, after verifying the user's password, creates and returns a UserSession object. The UserSession object is responsible for handling all subsequent requests for service until a logout request is received or too much time elapses.

Objects that work in the same neighborhoods communicate more freely with one another than do long-distance collaborators. In a close-knit neighborhood, the cost of communications is rarely a factor. The collaboration can be more chatty and collegial; objects can exchange information without worrying much about communications overhead. Crosstown collaborators—those objects working together while located in different processes—need to consider the cost of collaborations. These collaborations definitely dictate fewer, more powerful communiqués; requests and information are carefully planned, communications are typically packaged into large, meaningful chunks, and the cost of sending and receiving information becomes a significant design consideration. Even if cost were not a factor, we would still limit the collaborations between neighborhoods in order to decouple their responsibilities.

If you are traveling to a distant location to conduct business, you take care to make sure the trip is worthwhile. You agree on an agenda, pack what you need, and prepare for contingencies. The same is true for communication between long-distance collaborators.

## Who's In Control?

Control strategies have a strong influence on how responsibilities are distributed. As we consider alternatives, we seek ways to distribute control between objects. We prefer a model with moderately intelligent, collaborating objects over one that concentrates intelligence in only a few. Decisions about where to place responsibilities for controlling execution are central to our design work. The choices that we make as we consider the control aspects occur at several levels:

Control is decision making and selection of paths through the software.

- How do we control and coordinate application tasks?
- Where do we place responsibilities for making domain-specific decisions (rules)?
- How should we manage unusual conditions (the design of exception detection and recovery)?

As we develop a collaboration model, we need to develop a dominant pattern for distributing the flow of control and sequencing of actions among collaborating objects. An object may incorporate more or less intelligence according to how much it knows or does and how many other classes or objects it affects.

## How Much Should Objects Trust One Another?

Objects are designed to collaborate with their neighbors. But who their neighbors are impacts how willing they are to loan out their data and how tightly they lock their doors and windows. Can collaborators be trusted? There is another definition of collaboration:

> Collaborate: 1. To work together, especially in a joint intellectual effort. **2. To cooperate treasonably, as with an enemy occupation force.**
> —*The American Heritage Dictionary*

These two very different views of collaboration lead to two extremes. The first definition is collegial: working together toward a common goal. When one object asks collaborators for help, it expects that they will carry out its wishes. There are no hidden surprises. The second definition is a bit startling and has serious implications. If the object's collaborators can't be trusted to do the right thing, you must build in extra safeguards:

- If you don't want information to change, you send a copy.

- If you don't want an object to get out of whack, you make it read-only by eliminating any features that can modify it. It becomes idiot-proof.

- If you can't afford for things to go wrong, after calling on others for help you double-check to see that things were performed correctly.

Eiffel was the first object-oriented language to let programmers define preconditions that must be true before a body of code executes, and postconditions and invariants that must be true after a body of code executes. Writing assertions that can be checked during program execution adds teeth to object contracts.

All these tactics add a lot of defensive behavior just to collaborate! This often results in duplicated responsibilities for error checking. There's more chance of introducing errors in code when the checking logic needs to by updated in several places. If you don't want to always be on the defensive, you can get more formal, especially when you need to establish a high degree of trust between disparate parts of a system. You can use *object contracts* to spell out explicitly how objects are designed to interact. Without saying how these things are accomplished, contracts show who uses which responsibilities (client contracts) and declare under what conditions these responsibilities are called on (conditions-of-use guarantees) and what marks they leave when they are finished (aftereffect guarantees). Write contracts when you want to be absolutely clear about expected usage and side effects of use.

All collaborations—whether among close partners, among different parts of an application, or among components separated by time or space or communication overhead—require thought. It isn't enough to design a path for collaboration. Collaborations should be effective and should preserve any natural separations between responsible parties. Objects passed along with requests tie collaborators to one another. Inconsistencies can occur if the overall plan for the ways information is to be used and maintained is uncertain to either party.

What does it really mean for an object to be untrustworthy? And if objects can't be trusted, how did they get that way? Were they built by a treasonous developer? Or a third-party saboteur? Not likely. "Treason" rarely occurs. Instead, when an object can't be trusted it is usually the result of a simple failure to communicate design intentions:

- Failure to specify clearly what the object will do. An object may seem to promise one thing while actually doing another quite effectively. It may not document that it changes data that is passed to it or that the values that it returns can be outside an expected range. This information cannot be declared in an interface. We can only hope that the designer documented it somewhere that is within our reach, in a contract stating what is affected.

- Failure to clearly state how the object should be used. A collaborator may require special initialization—either of its own state or of others surrounding it—before it is called on. Again, these types of constraints won't be published in an interface. Yet if we don't set up its environment correctly before we use an object, things can break. The conditions required for correct operation can be declared in a contract. But perhaps the documentation overstated what an object actually does, and you believed it.

- Failure to fulfill the object's promises. Bugs! Errors in logic! The only way an object can avoid these is to refuse to collaborate with any unknown source and implement all the behaviors itself. Unfortunately, no contract can prevent coding bugs, and contracts cannot specify everything you need to know in order to avoid problems.

In general, those objects that we design to work in the same neighborhoods can be designed with a high degree of trust. It is those objects that we pick up from other sources and use that we must be wary of. When we use services provided by preexisting class libraries or components, our objects must fit with and use the services that are provided. How much trust we place in these objects and components depends on how well their designers convey how to use them and how carefully we conform to their constraints. When we don't know much about our collaborators, we make our objects as autonomous as possible. And when they ask for help, they must do what they can to ensure that their intentions are fulfilled.

## STRATEGIES FOR IDENTIFYING COLLABORATIONS

Experienced designers spot and document many collaborations as they distribute responsibilities. Their candidates are linked from the start. Of course, there will be gaps in any preliminary model. Designers fill these gaps by demonstrating how collaborations are enabled and by testing that they are well formed.

Our strategy for giving shape and form to our collaborations model is very simple: Focus on areas that have big impacts. Instead of concentrating on individual objects, we focus on how candidates work together to perform complex, coordinated actions. Initially, our goal is to link individual responsibilities to collaborators. Next, we take a pass at solving more complex scenarios. We explore collaborations using low-tech tools: CRC cards and rough sketches on white boards. We simulate collaborations by tossing around Koosh balls and making rough sketches.

But before we get locked into any solution, we explore alternative ways for objects to collaborate. We look for ways to simplify and streamline communications. Our goal is to create a workable solution that fits our design constraints and values. We approach finding collaborations from several angles. Each reveals different insights. We do the following:

- Look at an individual object's stereotype. We can think about collaborations based on the nature of each object. We ask, based on its stereotype, what an object needs from its neighbors and what it offers them. Whom does it need help from? Whom does it help?

- Look at individual responsibilities. At the next level of detail, we make initial decisions about how an object carries out any responsibility. As we do so, we look for collaborators. If there are objects that are needed to fulfill specific aspects of a responsibility, we add them as collaborators.

- Design the details of a complex responsibility. If a responsibility seems large or complex, we decide how it can be broken into smaller parts. As we divide complex responsibilities into smaller ones, we assign them to appropriate objects. These objects will be involved in a collaborative effort.

- Design collaborations for a specific use case or event. We can design how a grouping of objects cooperate to fulfill a use case or, at a lower level, how they respond to a specific event. As we do so, we make decisions about how objects will work together.

- Look for ways to organize communications. As we think about each object's position in the application architecture and natural arrangements for collaborators, we may find that patterns of communications can and should be stylized.

- Look for ways to simplify. After we've established several paths of communication, we can look for places where collaborations seem complex or tedious. Are too many objects talking to one another? Can we consolidate many low-level communications?

We now turn to examining each of these strategies in detail. Although we have arranged these strategies from simple to complex, we don't necessarily march down this list in order. During design, we often back up and revisit initial decisions, especially as we gain further insights. We comb over our entire design once in awhile, just to get our bearings and see whether we're still on track. Our goal is to end up with a collaboration model that adheres to a consistent style, not an arbitrary one.

Once we are convinced that our objects fit together and work to support a larger set of responsibilities, we get more precise. We pin down how objects become aware of their collaborators and design message sequences, arguments, and return values.

## Looking at an Individual Object's Role: Stereotypes Imply Collaborations

The roles an object plays imply certain kinds of collaborations. We consider both how an object typically fulfills its responsibilities and how it is used by others.

Stereotype roles give clues as to collaboration needs. Service providers and controllers need information. Coordinators and interfacers need services. Structurers organize others.

### Information Holders

When an object is an information holder, it is primarily responsible for knowing facts. Typically, it won't collaborate much with other objects except to acquire any information it is responsible for knowing. After it acquires its information, it may not need to ask for it again. Sometimes, even gathering its information is someone else's responsibility. An information holder can be created fully formed and populated with what it needs to know. Its only real responsibility, then, is to hold on to and keep its information consistent.

However, there are always exceptions to these general tendencies. Information holders can always answer questions by turning around or finding out information from others. They represent to the world that they know a fact when, indeed, they know it only by referring to a helper that is hidden from others' view. Sometimes, information holders can be charged with additional responsibility for making their information persist. Or they can compute instead of only holding on to uninterpreted facts. Each of these design considerations implies certain responsibilities and collaborations. Ask these questions of an information holder:

- Where does its information come from? Does the object create it or ask for it or get told about it? (Whomever it asks will be a collaborator.) Who knows the information in the first place?

- Is any information derived? Who is responsible for calculating the derived information? Does the object do the calculation itself or just hold on to the result? (If another object does the work or holds on to other knowledge, it will be a collaborator.)

- Do the ways that the object derives its facts vary? How are the variations represented?

- Does the information persist? Who handles the persistence?

- Is information cached and refreshed when its sources change? When does it need to be updated? How is this coordinated? (There will be some collaboration in order to keep information in sync with other sources.)

- Does any information need to be converted to another form that the requester wants? If so, who does this conversion? (If another object helps with conversion of "raw" information, it will be a collaborator.)

> A transaction record in online banking is built by gathering information at the UI and passing it to a service provider that stores it in a transaction record. The only collaborations that the transaction record itself uses are persistent storage services to put itself onto disk.

Don't assume that a responsibility for knowing some fact means that an object holds on to that information. It can always turn around and get information from another object that knows it.

### Structurers

Most applications organize and structure information and group objects in different ways. Objects need to be pooled, collected, and managed. Objects that are responsible for structuring and organizing must get the things they structure from somewhere. The objects they organize may come into being through collaborations with other objects that are responsible for connecting to databases or devices outside the software. Look for those collaborations. Or objects being structured can be built up and added to the structurer as the application executes. Responsibilities for retrieving, matching, and updating the structured information are also places to look for collaborations. Some of the same questions we ask of information holders also apply to structurers:

- Where do the objects that are structured come from? Does the structurer create them, ask for them, or get told about them?

- How are the objects processed? Does the structurer process the objects that it structures, or does another object "visit" them?

- Does the structurer (or the objects it structures) persist? Who handles the persistence?

- How are objects held by a structurer accessed? Is the way a structurer organizes and relates objects hidden? Or is it visible to outsiders that collaborate with the structurer? Do other objects know of this organization and visit?

- Is the structurer responsible for answering cumulative questions about what it structures? Does it do so itself, or does it call on others to tabulate information?

Some objects have responsibilities for maintaining complex relationships. These, too, are structuring roles. These structurers aren't responsible for maintaining pools of like objects but instead are responsible for managing connections and constraints among related things. Each relationship generally implies one or more collaborations. A structurer has visibility of other objects because it needs to know about them for a reason. Similarly, an object being structured may need to know its structurer (but this is much less common).

The rules surrounding permanence and connectivity between structurers and their parts is rarely simple or straightforward. Debating whether a structuring object is a composition or an aggregation can sometimes be a wasted effort. The important point is that composition and aggregation are special cases. Many structurers don't fit neatly into a compositional or an aggregational role. Networks of objects often coexist with complex interrelationships, responsibilities, and collaborations. Trying to sort out their interdependencies is what is important. To get to the crux of the matter, ask these questions of objects that structure and relate others:

> The Unified Modeling Language lets us denote two interesting structural relations: *composition* and *aggregation*. An aggregation consists of an object that represents a whole (a structurer) that has responsibility for managing its parts (objects that are related only through the aggregation). The UML notion of a composition relationship implies a further restriction: Parts in a composition cannot exist independently of the whole.

- Why does the relationship between a structurer and those objects it structures exist? Who needs to know about each other, and why?

- What responsibilities are implied by the connections between a structurer and the objects it structures? Is it responsible for knowing about the objects and answering questions about them? Does it delegate requests to them? Is a structurer responsible for knowing how the objects it structures are related?

- Does the structurer represent new, emergent properties of the group of objects?

- Sometimes an object that is organized by a structurer needs to turn around and collaborate with it. An object that knows its structurer should do so for a specific reason. Does the object tell the structurer when something about it has changed? Or does it need to delegate the responsibility to its structurer when it receives a request that it can't handle?

- Is a structurer responsible for maintaining certain limits or constraints on the objects it structures? If so, how does it come to know about these constraints and know when objects are to be removed?

> In the online banking application, several structurers are involved: Customers know about BankAccounts and Users. BankAccounts know about their Customers. Visibility of Accounts can be restricted among Users. Each of these structuring relationships implies responsibilities for limiting or organizing the views of related objects and specific collaborations.

### Service-Providers

Responsibilities that require specialized skill or computation can be organized into service-providing roles. Sometimes the member of a family of service providers are designed together, each member providing a slightly different means of accomplishing a specific task. This leads us to ask the following:

- Who has the information that a service provider uses? Does the service provider get told, or must it ask another?

- Are services configurable? Who has the configuration information? How will the service be configured?

- Is any part of a responsibility prone to change? Will it evolve as the application matures? Should a responsibility that belongs to one object be removed and isolated in a separate service provider for this reason?

- Does the application require different forms of the same service? How do the services vary, and who is responsible for each?

> Each transaction in the online banking application is responsible for recording information about the transaction on permanent storage. If a transaction is responsible for logging its actions, it could do it itself or ask another object. The decision depends on how much is involved in logging and how narrowly you define the transaction's responsibilities.

## Controllers

Objects that make decisions and direct the actions of others are controllers. They always collaborate with others for two reasons: to gather the information in order to make decisions and to call on others to act. Their focus typically is on decision making and not on performing subsequent actions. Their ultimate responsibility for accomplishing actions is often passed to others that have more specific responsibilities for part of a larger task that the controller manages. This leads us to ask the following:

The distinction between controller and coordinator is a matter of degree. Controllers figure things out and take action; coordinators are generally told what to do and make few, if any, decisions.

- Who knows the information that a controller uses to make the decisions? How does the controller find out what it needs to know?

- How much of the actions resulting from decisions is the controller responsible for? Whom does it delegate responsibilities to if it doesn't take direct action? (The objects taking these reponsibilities will be collaborators.)

- Is the decision making complex enough to warrant sharing the responsibility? (If so, the objects sharing the responsibility will be collaborators.)

- Are there events or intermediate results that the controlling object will have to track and respond to?

> When a user chooses Save when editing a document in a word processor, the software must make several decisions before saving the file. It decides what format to save the document in (HTML, text, PDF, etc.), whether or not to invent a name for the file, and the rules for naming it. The object that is monitoring the user's actions will either be directly responsible for these decisions or will share the decision making among its collaborators.

## Coordinators

A coordinator, like a structurer, holds connections to other objects. But their purposes differ. A coordinator is focused on managing the actions of a group of workers, whereas a structurer manages a grouping of objects and presents a coherent view of them to others.

Coordinators exist solely to pass along information and call on others to act. Their focus is on holding connections between objects and forwarding information and requests to them. Their job is to facilitate communication and the work of others. We can find the collaborations related to a coordinator by asking the following:

- How does a coordinator delegate work or pass along requests?

- How does a coordinator inform others of things to do or changes in state?

- How does a coordinator come to know about those objects that it delegates to? Do they need to know about the coordinator?

> If an object listening to the user's actions simply delegates a series of requests to those objects around it, it is passing on the responsibilities for making the decisions. It may ask an object for the document format and then ask another object for the name. These collaborators know the rules for formatting and naming. The coordinator is responsible only for delegating the work to others.

## Interfacers

Interfacers provide bridges between naturally disjoint parts. They can act as a bridge between users and our software (user interfacers), between objects in other neighborhoods (internal interfacers), or between our application and outside services and programs (external interfacers). Each type of interfacer has its own collaboration profile.

User interfacers transmit user requests for action or display information that can be updated. User interfacers typically collaborate only with objects in other non-UI parts of the application to signal events or changes in the information they display. Ask these questions of a user interfacer:

- How does a user interfacer let others know about user actions, gestures, and changes in information it maintains?

- What other objects, in other parts of the application, does a user interfacer know about?

- How many states does it track and notify others about?

- How do other objects tell a user interfacer they want to know about certain events or state changes?

> When a user clicks a button labeled Close, a standard message is sent to an object that has been assigned responsibilities for listening and responding to this event. The path of communication between the user interfacer and the event handler it notifies is established when the UI object is created and configured for display.

Internal interfacers provide outsiders a limited view into an object neighborhood. They serve as the "storefront" to services offered to outsiders. They convey requests to objects hidden from view. An internal interfacer collaborates by delegating external requests to objects in its neighborhood. Whom it collaborates with and how it does so depend on how transparently it packages the services it offers. To determine collaborations, ask:

- How does an internal interfacer collaborate with objects in the part of the application it hides from others' view?

- How does it come to know about the objects that really offer the services it provides?

- Does it simply delegate requests, or does it need to collaborate with others to translate "external speak" to "internal speak"?

> In the online banking application, each component has a Session-Manager object that can create specific Session objects that provide services to other components. The WebServer component interacts with only two objects in the DomainServer: the UserSessionManager, and a UserSession that the manager creates. The UserSessionManager initially handles all requests from the WebServer component by creating the appropriate UserSession service provider and then delegating the work to it. When the specific service is completed, the UserSession reports the results directly to the WebServer. Only the UserSessionManager and UserSession are visible to outsiders; individual service providers in the DomainServer component are hidden.

External interfacers usually do not collaborate with many other application objects. They may delegate to service providers the responsibility to format or convert information that they push or pull from their external partners, but mostly they just encapsulate non-object-oriented APIs. Who collaborates with them is much more interesting than whom they collaborate with. But there are a few questions to ask about their responsibilities that may lead to identifying some interesting collaborators:

- Will the external interfacer have to convert the data into an object form? Does it make sense to separate the conversion from the interfacing?
- How does the external interfacer connect to the outside? Are the connections limitless? Does another object manage a pool of connections?
- What will the interfacer do if it can't make the connection or if it detects errors? Who will handle the problem?

> In a telco integration application, which coordinates the processing of service orders across multiple preexisting systems, each integrated system has its own kind of adapter object. An adapter is responsible for translating generic service requests into one or more specific API calls. A request to the BillingSystemAdapter, "Add a Product to a Customer's billing account," for example, translated into multiple calls to the billing system. Both requests and information had to be translated to the appropriate format. The BillingSystemAdapter reported any errors in processing but left the resolution of problems to others.

## Looking at Individual Responsibilities: They Imply Collaborations

Object responsibilities come in three flavors: knowing, doing, and deciding. These responsibilities usually overlap and interact. To do something, an object might need to know certain information; to make a decision, an object might need to know certain other information; to know something, an object might need to do something. When we look at individual responsibilities, we are trying to decide what is needed to actually carry out a particular responsibility. Our goal is to determine obvious connections between necessary collaborators. As we make these decisions, we have many options to explore.

Conceptually, an object may have a responsibility for knowing a fact, but it holds on to a grouping of more primitive objects it uses to represent that knowledge. Objects that have public responsibilities for knowing can decide to hold on to and yield information directly or to translate from one internally known form to an externally presentable one.

There are three primary reasons why we don't give objects free access to all others: information hiding, abstraction, and adaptability. If every object had visibility of every other, then changes to any single object's design would impact many, many others. Selectively revealing things through interfaces creates a barrier between collaborators. We have a choice in how we represent things an object is responsible for knowing. We can design a higher-level view of information instead of presenting a smorgasbord of raw data for public consumption. This technique lets us change low-level details of how an object actually knows something without impacting any of its clients.

To form the next guess, Speak for Me's Guesser object collaborates with several smaller, more focused guesser objects. Each is responsible for looking at the current Message and making a guess. The LetterGuesser object knows the rules for guessing a next letter, and the WordGuesser uses different rules to guess a word. These objects, in turn, hide the actual sources of data that they are using. Because these data sources are hidden from the Guesser, they can change their data sources on-the-fly. For example, the LetterGuesser can switch from an EnglishAlphabet to a SpanishAlphabet (which loads a different data file) without affecting the Guesser that calls on it.

An object's responsibilities are often based on information that it asks others about. For example, an object that computes a corporation's annual taxes needs access to many different pieces of information: tax tables, income categories, deduction rules, and so on (see Figure 5-2). Further analysis of this responsibility reveals many sub-responsibilities. Responsibilities often depend on information, the information itself may need to be computed, and decisions are always based on information. We must study an object's responsibilities, looking for necessary collaborations it should make to acquire missing information or ask for help.

When we assign an object a responsibility, we are taking only the first step. Fulfilling its responsibility may involve collaboration with a number of other neighbors, each with more specific responsibilities for knowing or doing.

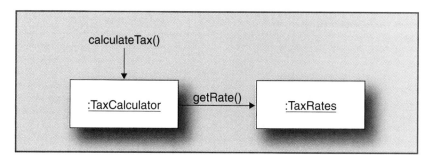

Figure 5-2
*TaxCalculator collaborates with TaxRates to compute tax.*

> If an object is responsible for calculating taxes but does not know the tax rates, it must either take on that responsibility or get the tax rate from another object. Someone must know the tax rate. We choose to assign this responsibility to a TaxRates object whose knowledge is used by the TaxCalculator.

## Designing the Details of a Complex Responsibility

If a responsibility seems large or complicated, a rough sketch of the collaborations isn't enough. Instead, we dig deeper into its design and partition its subresponsibilities into collaborators. We do this by dividing these subresponsibilities into two parts:

- The major steps of the responsibility (subordinate responsibilities)
- A responsibility for sequencing the execution of the subordinate responsibilities (sequencing responsibility)

The sequencing responsibility will call on the subordinate responsibilities. In this part of the design, spend time identifying the major steps. Write these down, but don't assign them to objects just yet. One complex responsibility can easily be rewritten as 5–10 subresponsibilities. The trick is to keep each of these responsibilities at the same level of precision and abstraction.

> Calculating annual corporate taxes, if we are to be more precise, really means
>
> - Calculating applicable municipality taxes
> - Itemizing income, expenses, and allowable state or provincial tax deductions
> - Calculating applicable state or provincial taxes
> - Itemizing income, expenses, and allowable federal tax deductions
> - Calculating applicable federal taxes

We can assign subordinate responsibilities to the object itself (if it fits with its role and current set of responsibilities) or to others (including new ones not yet discovered).

> Part of making any tax calculation involves looking up tax rates. Earlier, we decided to assign this knowing responsibility to the TaxRates object and decided that the TaxCalculator would collaborate with the TaxRates object to find the tax rate used in tax calculations. We initially separate the responsibility for knowing from doing for two reasons: It allows us to update TaxRates independently of their use, and it keeps any tax calculation object focused on computing.

Each time you assign subparts of a complex responsibility, you are faced with this decision: Where should subordinate responsibilities be allocated? If the subresponsibilities seem to fit and belong together, keep them with the initial object. If they don't seem to fit with the original object, look for opportunities. Don't be content to pile them into the original object. You might invent a new object, and right away you have a cohesive set of responsibilities for it. Or you might place them in a near neighbor (increasing its responsibilities while still keeping it in character).

> We choose to assign the responsibilities for calculating taxes, as we break it down further, to new and separate SpecializedTaxCalculators, each responsible for a particular tax jurisdiction. Each is responsible for knowing how to itemize income, expenses, and deductions. These individual calculators are coordinated by an overall TaxCalculator. Similarly, we model deductions or expenses as separate service providers, which know how to calculate their amounts based on information that we supply them and the tax rules that they have access to.

Sometimes you just don't know who should have a subordinate responsibility. It could belong with the complex responsibility, but it seems slightly out of character. As a last resort, you can always put it there. However, if you don't know just yet who should have that responsibility, put it on an "unassigned" list and move on. Use this list to jog your design thoughts later, after you've made progress in other areas.

## Designing Collaborations for a Specific Task

Starting with a specific use case or event, our goal is to design a candidate collaboration model that supports it. The first goal is to develop a "big picture": a sketch of the objects, their responsibilities, and their interactions. After we have the general sense of things, we can pick out an important or seemingly troublesome area and dive into designing a small neighborhood of objects that does only that one part. The goal of designing collaborations for a specific task is to answer some key questions:

- What services are being invoked between collaborators? What is the sequence of the work? Who is in control at any one time? How do objects work together?
- How and when are the objects created?
- How long and how often do they need to see each other?
- Where are the branches in the logic? Where are the decision points?
- Do the decision makers have what they need? Where will the information that they need come from?
- What information holders are passed around? Are we passing objects or simple data? Are any of them passed everywhere?

After we've answered these questions we will have a good idea of how work is divided among collaborators and a good sense of which objects are busy and active. But this beginning-to-end-of-a-task view isn't a complete picture. Many objects are likely to support more than one task and accrue additional responsibilities. After we've designed these, we are likely to refine our initial design, splitting roles into two or more objects, collapsing multiple roles into one, simplifying collaborations, and applying the tools of object orientation: patterns, generalization, polymorphism, and information hiding. All the while, we will push toward a well-thought-out, justifiable design.

## Identifying Applicable Patterns

Design patterns can help us assign and arrange responsibilities and organize collaborations. If we recognize that a particular pattern might be a good way to factor a shared responsibility among collaborators, then we don't have to invent a complete solution. Instead, we adapt a pattern to our particular needs.

To leverage design patterns, you need to know several things. You need to know how to read pattern descriptions and where to look for them. Before incorporating a pattern, you need to know how to weigh the consequences of applying it:

- Does it change your objects' roles and responsibilities in ways that improve your design?

- Does it make your design more adaptable? Is this needed, or is it overkill for the problem you are solving?

- What are some viable alternatives?

- What does the pattern do to your design's complexity or clarity? Is it a good choice?

Finally, you need to be able to adapt the generic solution offered by a design pattern to your specific situation. To do this, you need to be facile at applying the fundamental object technology that underlies all design patterns: use of messages between collaborators, composition, polymorphism, and inheritance.

Certain patterns in the *Design Patterns* book (Erich Gamma et al., Addison-Wesley, 1995) are particularly worth studying. Composite, Facade, State, Strategy, Mediator, Flyweight, Builder, Observer, and Visitor are patterns we've applied in many situations. Each is worthy of imprinting in your design solution space. If we haven't mentioned one of your favorites, don't feel slighted. Sure, we could list all 23, but we wanted to prune this list to 10 or fewer, just to keep those who aren't pattern-savvy from feeling overwhelmed.

Patterns describe ways to organize and arrange responsibilities. They aren't a substitute for thinking. You must consider the consequences and then decide whether a pattern fits with and improves your design.

> If you know only the 23 patterns described in the original pattern book written by Erich Gamma and his colleagues, you are missing out on a lot of other wisdom.

> Two roles are defined within the Composite pattern: a leaf and a composite. A composite can structure other objects, whereas a leaf does not. The Composite pattern is an aggregation of objects, each supporting common responsibilities in addition to the ability to add and remove itself from the structure.

---

A mailing list can hold individual e-mail addresses and other mailing lists. For example, the "Party" mailing list might contain the "Work" and "Personal" lists, along with any number of individual addresses. The recursive nature of this structure brings to mind the Composite pattern from the *Design Patterns* book. The intention of the Composite pattern is to simplify the processing of a structure's elements. If the mailing lists or e-mail addresses have similar responsibilities, then the Composite pattern gives us a standard way to add elements to a composite and to ask them to perform tasks. Individual addresses and mailing lists are both types of Destination objects that can send messages. An object that wants to send mail need not care which type of destination it has. It simply tells it to send the message. The MailingList reacts by iterating across its contents, asking each Destination it holds to send the message. Eventually, the contents of all of the MailingLists have been exhausted and each of the e-mail addresses has actually sent the message.

## Identifying How Architecture Influences Collaborations

An object's position in an architecture also may have implications about its potential collaborations. In a strictly layered architecture, objects in one layer talk mostly to other objects in the same or adjacent layers. Messages flow between layers, but the range of communication is limited. Other architectures support very stylized means of communications. In several distributed system frameworks, components that provide services register with a ServiceBroker (see Figure 5-3). Components needing remote services request them from a ServiceBroker. They may then communicate directly with the remote

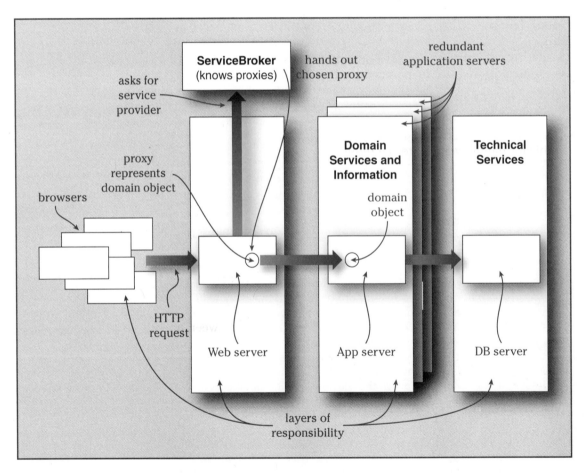

Figure 5-3
*Distributed systems often use a service broker to find collaborators.*

service provider or speak through a Proxy, which has responsibilities for forwarding requests to a remote service and handling the communications synchronization.

## Solving Problems in Collaborations

Collaborations should be simple and powerful. Objects that are designed to work together should have an easy style of communication. Here are some common problems and some simple ideas for streamlining and simplifying them.

***Too many connections from outside to objects within a neighborhood.*** A common design goal is to minimize dependencies between different parts of the system. Exposing all of a neighborhood's objects defeats this purpose. Instead of having lots of objects visible, we can construct portals to services that remain hidden. The Facade pattern introduces a single intermediary (called a facade) between clients and services offered by a neighborhood. A facade is an internal interfacer with a restricted set of responsibilities. This single point of entry takes on responsibilities for

- Knowing which objects inside the neighborhood are responsible for handling any external request

- Delegating requests to appropriate objects

Interfacers can be more or less intelligent, depending on how much responsibility you give them. Typically a facade doesn't make complex decisions about whom should receive a request, nor does it translate requests into sequences of delegated actions.

The idea of a facade is fairly simple: create a single point of contact instead of exposing the interfaces of several objects (see Figure 5-4). Outsiders can speak to the facade and don't know who is actually fulfilling a request. Objects within the neighborhood don't have to change to work with a facade. Instead of receiving requests directly from outsiders, they receive requests forwarded by the facade. They remain oblivious of whom it is that calls them to action.

Applying the Facade pattern promotes a looser coupling between a neighborhood and its clients (see Figure 5-5). Because only one object (the facade) is used, designers are freer to change how things work without impacting clients.

***Many low-level messages.*** Sometimes an object packages its responsibilities into actions that are too small. Sending a flurry of messages may add up to a bigger action, but the client must describe what it wants as tiny steps. If you find a client issuing a stream of messages, ask whether any of these requests can be bundled into higher-level ones. The use of fewer, more powerful messages is often

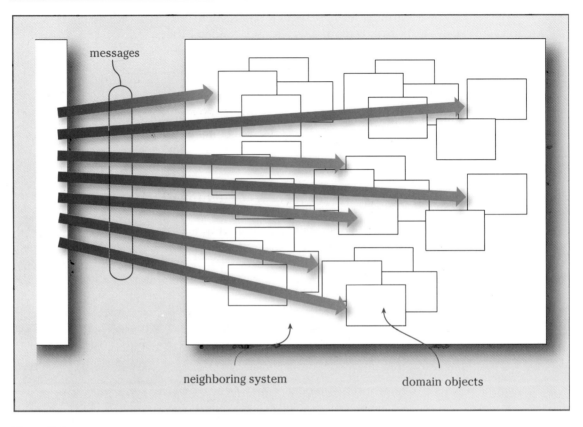

Figure 5-4
*Without a facade, client objects must know about the objects in the neighboring system.*

an improvement. Instead of setting up a service provider's state through a series of messages, offer a higher-level request that uses reasonable defaults. This removes the burden of establishing the right context before using its services from all but the most sophisticated clients.

Code should rarely, if ever, explicitly check an object's type. If you find yourself writing code that checks type and then branches, it indicates that responsibilities are misplaced and need refactoring.

***Too many branches and choices.*** Communications get overly complex when many paths are possible and the rules for determining which path to follow are complicated. You know you have potential problems when code that implements a responsibility is filled with checks of object types and conditions. This makes collaboration paths difficult to follow. To fix this, you may need to change both the client's code and the interfaces of collaborators. The goal is to

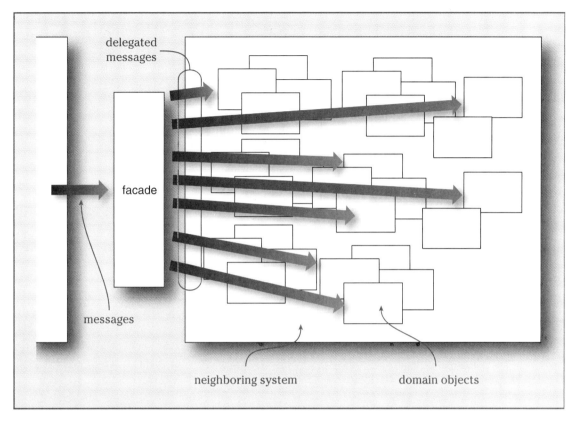

Figure 5-5
*The Facade pattern centralizes the interface to a neighborhood's services.*

simplify what any client needs to know in order to collaborate. If collaborators' interfaces are similar but not identical, perhaps they can be made more consistent. If argument types are being checked to determine which collaborator to use, this too, is a sign that decision making may be in the wrong place. Not all complexity can be removed simply by readjusting interfaces and redistributing decisions. Sometimes, things are just complicated and irregular. But be on the lookout for ways to simplify and make collaborations more consistent and thereby improve your design's clarity.

The Double Dispatch pattern is one example of how conditional checking based on object type can be eliminated. In Figure 5-6, decisions are made based on checking an object's type.

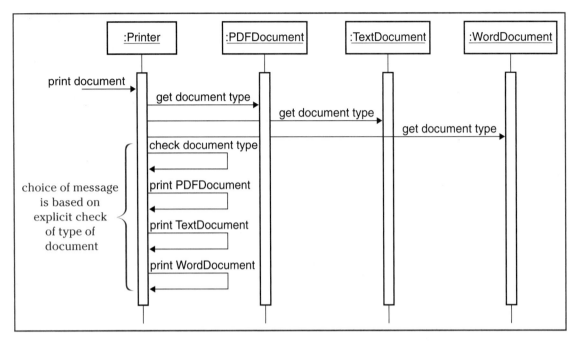

Figure 5-6
*Before the Double Dispatch pattern is applied, these objects are basing their actions on type checking.*

In the Double Dispatch pattern, a common request is issued to receivers, who turn around and call the right method. This eliminates checks for object type in the caller (see Figure 5-7).

## SIMULATING COLLABORATIONS

Why simulate? What collaborations do you simulate? What are the end products of a simulation? This section offers guidance on planning and running a simulation, outlines what you can hope to accomplish, and describes the changes and additions you will likely make to your design.

You can quickly find errors and omissions in your model by simulating the messaging between objects. It helps you to find new objects (you will likely have to invent objects with responsibilities for controlling the flow of work or responding to events), to discard ill-conceived objects, and to elaborate any vague responsibilities, and it results in responsibilities shifting from one object to another. All this without writing a line of code! Simulating with low-tech tools is also a good way to surface and handle missing or ambiguous requirements.

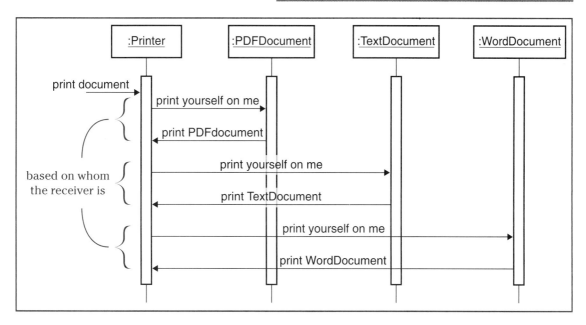

Figure 5-7
*The Double Dispatch pattern eliminates type checks.*

The basic idea of simulating a collaboration is simple, but there are several subtleties to pay attention to. Given that your goal is to develop an optimal collaborations model, how do you balance the trade-offs in one decision or another? Although there are no hard-and-fast rules, the following guidelines should get you started.

## Planning a Simulation

It is all too easy to gloss over little details when you work with CRC cards only. Simulating collaborations will force you to look more closely at your design. Running a simulation forces you to consider how one object gains visibility of a collaborator, why one object is communicating with another, or whether a collaboration sequence is too simplistic or too complex.

Whether you are working in a design team or developing a design on your own, it is useful to review your collaboration model with others.

***Role-play the hard parts first.*** Not everything is worth simulating. The roles-and-responsibilities model usually reveals specific areas of the model that will be difficult to design or areas where your understanding of the design is very rough. Identify these areas, and put them on the agenda for exploration. They may be whole use cases or key events that exercise the core of your system. Simulation may involve modeling your application's response to specific actions, or there may be specific parts of your application's machinery that you want to investigate. When you choose one of the areas to simulate, identify exactly what it is you are trying to understand.

***Set a goal for the simulation.*** It is best to decide what it is you are trying to accomplish *before running the simulation*. Here are some possible objectives:

- Developing a simple, consistent collaboration style
- Testing or proving your ideas
- Identifying what you know and don't know
- Exploring the details of a small area
- Studying the coordination and control
- Refining an already working collaborations model
- Finding logical partitions (object neighborhoods)
- Identifying and rewriting responsibilities

> We aren't simulating to "prove" anything—at least, not in the mathematical sense. We are developing a model that handles the external events and actions well.

The way you conduct simulations changes according to what you are trying to accomplish. A well-defined goal—such as "Test the pattern of interactions that act to control this use case" or "Explore alternative ways to diagnose a disease"—has an implicit statement of which objects will be involved and for which details are best left out.

***Set the boundaries.*** Based on your goal for the simulation, decide up front where you will stop—which objects and responsibilities you will invoke and which ones you won't. Sometimes it is clear that a particular responsibility is at a different level of detail from those of the others that you are simulating. If a piece of the system's actions can be isolated because it doesn't depend on the other objects that you are studying, defer it. Focus on the particular area as stated in your objectives for the simulation.

***Assign candidates to team members.*** One way to get everyone involved is to role-play a simulation. People playing the role of objects? You bet! Each role player should be assigned at least one object. Estimate how active each object will be. Dole them out so that there is a fairly even distribution of message senders and receivers. Sometimes an object will be a center of activity, a hub. Whoever has that one should have little or nothing else to do. If a CRC card shows no collaborators, then the person playing that role won't collaborate with others. That person only handles requests but never calls on others for help. Try to have everyone role-play at least one object that will collaborate with another. Otherwise, team members won't feel involved.

**Simulate use cases.** Scenarios or conversations, with their step-by-step descriptions, are a good place to start. They outline exactly what the system is responsible for and when it takes specific action. When the user does this, what objects will answer? How will they fulfill the system's responsibilities at that point? What other actions of the system lie hidden? How does a scenario start? What actions and collaborations must be carried out to fulfill the actor's goal? We may have waved our hands in the early design, but simulating the exact response to the users' actions will iron out the wrinkles in our candidate model. Start at the beginning of the use case, and make sure you can get to the end.

Use cases divide an application's responsibilities, as seen from a user's point of view. Simulating the object collaborations involved in each is a good way to verify (and find) collaborations.

**Invent controllers if you need them.** Your candidate objects usually don't include controllers, at least not initially. It is at this time that you need to identify new objects that monitor events and react by delegating work to others, objects that manage the flow of interaction between objects to accomplish a sequence of action, and objects with control or coordination responsibilities. If you are simulating a use case, invent at least one object that monitors the user and delegates to the objects that do the work. You will often find that you need several more, but you can start simply with one. When a controller seems to be doing too much work, study it independently. Try to break up its work and distribute it among collaborations in a neighborhood. Make the object delegate more to others and become less involved.

**Test one area at a time.** Any task that the software can be asked to do is a candidate for role-playing. These tasks range from entire use cases to specific computations buried deep in the software. If you want to demonstrate the high-level decision making and coordination architecture, ignore the details of the objects that are beneath the surface.

In Speak for Me, the presentation of letters must be synchronized with the user's actions for selecting them. There are only five or six objects involved in that: the Presenter, the Selector, the Message-Builder, the Timer, the Message, and the Guesser. We first work with that small set to design the basic control strategy. Then, to test at a more detailed level, we simulate what the Guesser does when you ask it for the next guess, or what the Message does when you tell it to add a letter to itself. We first pinpoint the fundamental collaborations between these key objects before exploring further. We design one small set of collaborations at a time.

***Test for what you don't know.*** If you don't think that role-playing a collaboration will reveal any new information, don't do it. It is those complicated or interesting collaborations that you have glossed over that need to be explored. Simulating lets you draw and redraw alternative collaboration sequences and run through alternatives, always looking for better ways to distribute object responsibilities.

***Limit the time spent simulating.*** If you spend more than an hour or so simulating any collaboration, either you are covering too much detail or too many variations, your scope is too large, you are doing too much design work during simulation, or your team isn't sticking to the main point.

## Running a Simulation

The goal of running a simulation is to make sure your model hangs together and makes sense. Do collaborations seem reasonable? Are responsibilities correctly stated? Can you make it all the way through to accomplishing a specific goal? Are there better ways of collaborating? Do responsibilities need to be reassigned? Have parts of the design been ignored or slighted? As you run a simulation, you will be checking all of these things.

***Start with an event.*** Begin by determining what event starts the action. A user makes a selection, types in some data, or signals a choice. A timer signals that time is up, or a port signals that a piece of data has arrived—whatever. Ignore the details of any interface objects. Know that they exist and notify some other object of the user's intentions or external events. What you are interested in is which objects in your model are responsible for handling these events and what chain of collaborations is involved afterward. When an event occurs, ask these questions:

- What object should be informed of the event? Is there a CRC card that describes the object? If not, make one. Does its role fit the current situation? If not, change the role or choose a different object card.

- What responsibility will we ask the responding object to fulfill? Is the responsibility listed on its card? If not, write it down.

- Who will it collaborate with to fulfill the responsibility? Will it do the work itself or call on others?

Express the event as an intention and not as a button click or countdown timer time-out: "The user chooses to save a file" rather than "The user selects Save File from the menu." Express it as a "time for next guess" event and not an operating system process. All you care about is that something specific happened.

Now make your objects take responsibility for processing the event. Follow the action and record the sequence of collaborations. As seen in Figure 5-8, you can toss a lightweight ball (we prefer a Koosh ball) to simulate messaging between objects. Tossing a ball gets everyone kinetically involved. If you don't want to be so active, you can still simulate collaborations. Point at a card of a collaborator. It may

Figure 5-8
*Rebecca, Alan, and friends run a simulation.*

seem silly, but making connections between collaborators is important. Move a card toward its collaborator. Draw lines between collaborators. If you can't explain interactions, then you have found a gap in your design.

***Stay at the same conceptual level.*** First, develop a breadth-first, high-level view of key object interactions, tracing object collaborations at the same conceptual level (or one step lower) in the design. Then explore the depths of individual areas, elaborating and subdividing roles and object responsibilities (see the "Test one area at a time" guideline in the preceding section). Modeling candidates at widely differing conceptual levels makes simulation much more difficult. It requires you to switch gears and think differently.

If you were analyzing a painting, your best strategy would be to consider the composition separately from how the oils were mixed.

***Follow the simulation closely.*** Watch both how the messages flow among objects (if you are tossing a Koosh ball, see how it travels) and how the cards represent responsibilities and collaborators. There is a tendency to become occupied with the mechanics of the simulation at the expense of the critical thinking. Dig in! As the ball is tossed around or collaborators are pointed at, keep checking that the collaborations and responsibilities on the cards are in sync with what is happening. If you spot an omission or inconsistency, stop to correct it, either on the cards or in the simulation. If you see an alternative that simplifies the collaborations, try it out. And pin it down!

As we simulate the run-time behavior, we inevitably discover gaps and inconsistencies in the model.

***Think critically.*** Be a skeptic. When someone responds to a message, ask, "What information did the object need to do be able to do that?" If you didn't see the information gathered explicitly through another collaboration, the object must have known the information itself. Is that one of its responsibilities? If not, what other object should it ask? Is that collaboration written down on the object's card? If not, get it down.

If you see someone send a message, ask, "Where did the connection from the sender to the receiver get made?" There are only a handful of possible ways that an object can hold a reference to another: It has it in a variable, it received it in a method parameter, it got it as a return from a message it sent, it created it on-the-fly, or it referred to a widely visible object. It must be one of these. Defer this questioning until you work out most of the collaborations, but then address it. This is not something you want to leave undecided.

***Sketch the collaborations.*** Lay out the object neighborhood and design the paths of the communications. You can place CRC cards on big sheets of paper and draw thick lines to represent general paths of collaboration. Or you can redraw objects on white boards and draw collaboration lines between them. Some teams may want to get more formal and draw UML sequence diagrams. Whatever you do, connect the collaborators. After you've laid out the paths, check out the sequence of their collaborations.

How many objects does any one object collaborate with? Communications create dependencies. Are there any traffic hubs? These create objects that tend to be bloated with responsibilities. Do any objects flow through the system and make themselves visible to everybody? Pay special attention to these. A change to their public responsibilities will have an impact on their neighbors across the system.

**Write down what you don't know.** Don't try to decide everything during one simulation. When you encounter a gap in the collaborations model, write it down and go on. If you can't decide which object should be doing something or who should be collaborated with, start a list of questions and responsibilities that you need to consider later.

**Rewrite candidate cards.** When an object receives a message, the role player should check the object's CRC card to verify that one of the responsibilities covers the message's intent. If you shift responsibilities from one object to another, sometimes the responsibility should be reworded. Instead of doing a task itself, an object may be delegating it to another. It may be ultimately responsible for getting the task done but is collaborating with another to get a bigger job done. Be sure to keep things straight. As you revise your design during a simulation, write new cards for your objects and take care to phrase responsibilities correctly and to keep collaborations up-to-date.

> Our initial cut at the roles and responsibilities is mostly educated guesses. They make sense because they mirror our notion of what the objects are. Often they have real-world features. But as we look for better collaborations, the objects expand their responsibilities and become better software objects.

## DESIGNING GOOD COLLABORATIONS

There are no hard-and-fast rules for designing collaborations. Our goal is to design consistent, nonarbitrary communications. We want to keep things simple and reduce unnecessary coupling between objects. There are no rules that will lead to the ultimate design. Here are some guidelines, however, that we find useful.

**Don't pass around primitive data types.** If you find yourself passing text and numbers around among collaborators, ask yourself what

"... use small objects for small tasks, such as money classes that combine number and currency, ranges with an upper and a lower, and special strings such as telephone numbers and ZIP codes."

—Martin Fowler

that text and those numbers represent. Words? Money? OrderQuantities? Are you really communicating at the right level? You may have overlooked some simple concepts when inventing your first set of candidates. It is best to use high-level representations of these things during design. When it's time to implement them, you may choose to use simple data types, but you may also find that a Money object is a sensible place to put responsibilities that you had overlooked: Who should convert from one currency to another? You can't do that with a float! Using these placeholder objects gives you places to put new responsibilities that you encounter later. Give these information holders names, and get them on the cards.

***Keep the big picture in mind.*** Are there a lot of requests made of a particular object? Or do any seem to be the primary delegator? Are too many of the decisions or actions taking place in one object? Is it possible to shift its responsibilities around to make it less of an authority? Do any of the objects seem to know about lots of other objects? Are there any areas of the collaboration where more than the usual hand-waving is going on?

***Watch for collaboration patterns.*** Some of the collaborations will look familiar. They may fit a pattern that you recognize, or they may be similar to something that you have already done. If you use a consistent collaboration style and keep the collaborations simple, you'll find that you have more confidence in your model—without simulating every scenario—because you have seen a similar pattern of collaboration that already works.

## The Law of Demeter: A Case Study

The best design is one that satisfies its requirements without being overly complex or inconsistent. Inconsistencies make a design hard to change or comprehend. Making a design more flexible often increases its complexity. Many times one design is tossed in favor of a less elegant, but more justifiable, one. The point is that design always involves trade-offs, and we are giving you the tools necessary to adequately consider design trade-offs. Others contend that there may be "laws" of object design that, if followed, will always lead to a good design. This is not so. Consider the Law of Demeter.

The Law of Demeter was proposed by Karl Leiberherr and other researchers as a style to follow for designing collaborations. When first proposed, this law caused a stir in the object community because it limits permissible collaborations. "Only talk to your immediate friends" is its credo. A more general formulation of this

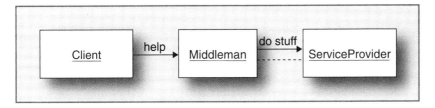

Figure 5-9
*The Law of Demeter minimizes object visibilities.*

law is that each object should have only limited knowledge about others. It should use only objects "closely related" to it. A strict form of the law suggests that collaborators should be used in very limited ways. It is worth exploring some of the finer points to see the impact of this approach on a design.

The Law of Demeter says that if one object needs to request a service of another object's subpart, it should never do so directly (see Figure 5-9). It is considered bad design to dig into a structurer to retrieve and use a subcomponent. The more a potential collaborator knows how to "dig out" internal structures of an object, the more dependent it is on that deep structure. The design is more brittle. It is OK to request a service of an object, but if you knowingly request one of its structural subparts and then request a service of that subpart, you've violated the Law of Demeter (see Figure 5-10). It supports the notion that structural details should be concealed from collaborators. Instead of asking an object for something it knows and then turning around and asking a second object for something it knows and then turning around and asking a third object to do something, requesters should make their requests only to the enclosing

It is hard to call anything in software design a law. Unlike the physical world, software machinery doesn't have to obey physical laws, nor are we issued a citation if we break one. The intention of the Law of Demeter was to indirectly couple objects. We are more comfortable thinking of it as a design guideline.

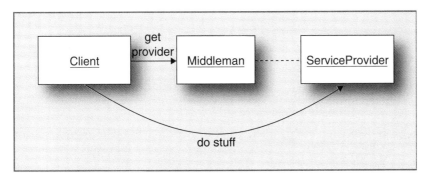

Figure 5-10
*These collaborations don't follow the Law of Demeter.*

object. That structurer should then turn around and take responsibility for propagating this request to all of its subparts. This sounds reasonable. Why give a potential collaborator the extra burden of traversing long networks to get what it needs?

However, this technique becomes of questionable design value when there aren't so many visibility links to chase. If we strictly adhere to the law, instead of asking an account object for its transaction history and then asking the transaction history object for its most recent item, a client should ask the account for its most recent transaction history item. This places the extra burden on the account for knowing more detail about its history (rather than just holding a reference to the history object that is responsible for knowing these details).

More formally, the Law of Demeter states that an object should call on the services only of the following kinds of objects:

- Itself

- Any objects passed to it as parameters

- Any objects it creates

- Any objects it stores references to that are its own subparts

Although following the Law of Demeter may increase the maintainability and adaptability of a design, it also has the effect of forcing structurers to have additional responsibilities for propagating requests to their subparts. Structurers, in turn, must know more about the abilities of the objects they structure. This may not always be a good design choice. The law makes the trade-off of hiding structural details at the expense of adding to structurers' responsibilities.

Our recommendations for designing collaborations are not so strict. They are intended to limit visibility and avoid unnecessary coupling. They are not laws to follow, but guidelines. This means that you as the designer need to exercise judgment and critical thinking to choose which parts of your design should be hidden (and changeable) and which parts should be revealed to clients. We suggest that you observe these principles:

- Establish a collaboration reference when needed. Discard it when it is no longer needed.

- Store a reference to a collaborator if it is used repeatedly or when you discover that it is expensive to re-create or reestablish the connection to the collaborator.

- Give structurers added responsibilities to navigate to their parts and subparts when the way a structurer is organized is considered a private detail that should be hidden.

- If it is more important to get the right service than to get a specific object to perform the service, ask for help indirectly.

The goal of all this is to develop a collaboration model in which object roles are clear and simple, responsibilities fit with roles, and the number of objects seen by any one object are few and well chosen. Simulating with low-tech tools lays the foundations for refinement. After we have demonstrated that fundamental collaborations work, we can always simplify, expand, compress, and make things more consistent.

## MAKING COLLABORATIONS POSSIBLE

Objects can collaborate only if the classes that implement them make it possible. We can use CRC cards and Koosh balls to simulate the collaborations, but to enable collaborations among objects, we must design their classes to support them. A collaboration has two sides. The behavioral side is the most obvious; objects call on each other for help. UML sequence and collaboration diagrams demonstrate this flow of control, action, and information much more precisely than do CRC cards or white board sketches. We will turn to these means of documenting our design soon enough. But to make these calls in the first place, the calling objects must have references to their helpers. This underlying structural side of an object must show the following:

- How many other objects it will need to know

- How it will refer to them

- How long it should hold their references

A collaborations model is not complete until we have decided how each and every collaboration will be possible. This level of detail is very hard to figure out and even harder to show on any UML diagram. Often, a class diagram shows only the static, compile-time associations among the objects. Not only are we talking about these connections, but we also are considering run-time associations that are enabled by these static declarations—references that enable dynamic connections that may come and go or may be created and find permanent homes.

Limiting visibility to other objects and limiting deep knowledge about how something does its job on your behalf are good design principles to follow. Following this advice results in fewer dependencies among objects.

Collaborators on CRC cards will show up as references to variables, arguments, or return types. Or they may be established by code that connects objects via events or object creation. But by one means or another, all objects that collaborate must be made aware of those objects that they use. The more any one object knows about others, the more dependent it is on the context provided by those collaborators. An object that is bound to many collaborators must live in close proximity to them or reach out to other neighborhoods where those services exist. The less an object knows about and relies on others, the more neighborhoods it will fit into. This creates a conflict:

> **Autonomy versus Collaboration**: To collaborate with others, an object needs to know its neighbors. Collaboration is good. To be reusable, an object should be as independent as possible. Collaboration creates dependencies. What's a designer to do?

The most successful design makes reasonable connections between collaborators. We try to make decisions about collaborators that limit unnecessary dependencies.

## Guidelines for Making Connections

When implementing a design, the programmer will discover any hand-waving about object associations done by the designer. There is a harsh reality to designing collaborations:

> To collaborate with another, an object must have a reference to it.

Every call from one object to another must be supported by some practice that establishes the communication path from one to the other. These associations may be long-term, composition relations or sporadic and on-demand. Follow these guidelines when you design collaborations.

***Get a collaborator when you need it.*** Modern languages accommodate only a few schemes for associating objects:

- Create a collaborator and then ask it for help.
- Pass a helper as an argument to a request. The receiver will use it as a collaborator.
- Grab an object reference that is returned from an earlier collaboration.

***Hold on to a collaborator if it is used repeatedly.*** Creating a helper on-the-fly is appropriate when help is needed to fulfill a specific responsibility. If there is too much overhead in creating a new helper repeatedly, or if the same helper can be reused to fulfill different responsibilities, you can cache a reference and use it repeatedly. Choosing a caching strategy depends on the frequency of use and the cost of creation. These are low-level concerns. As a first approximation, an object can always create a helper when needed. If and when the cost of creation becomes an issue, then maintaining a reference to a helper in its internal stores (instance and class variables) is always a viable alternative:

- If an object needs its own collaborator, store a reference to the collaborator in one of the object's private instance variables.

- If all the instances of a class need the same collaborator, hold it in a private class variable. This makes it visible to all the instances of the class.

- If different kinds of objects need the same collaborator, store a reference to the collaborator in the object-oriented version of a global variable: a public class variable. In this way, any object that can see the class can use the collaborator.

A collaborations model describes what objects any given object associates with, what requests it makes of them, when it does so, and how much it trusts them to help carry out its purpose.

If an object is created when needed and then is forgotten when the responsibility is completed, the helper is a use-once throwaway. This may be appropriate. However, if you have the luxury of designing the object and its collaborators at the same time, it can be useful to give the helper more intelligence. If it isn't disposable, it can remember and adapt to repeated requests. If you design the helper to stick around, you can gain leverage by having it adapt to repeated use.

***Ask for help by service name and not class name.*** An object can always create and use a service provider directly. But there are ways to ask for help that aren't so direct. They usually increase a design's flexibility. Instead of creating the object we need, we can ask another known object (a service broker) to give us the right kind of help, based on the kind of help we need. This gives us the option to design the service broker in a variety of ways. And it gives us the freedom to change who provides the implementation of a service or how that service provider is managed without impacting any object that needs the service. When you need the flexibility, introduce an intermediary instead of directly creating a helper (see Figure 5-11).

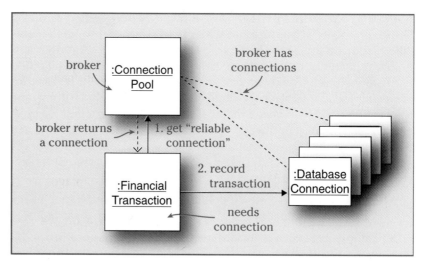

Figure 5-11

*A broker's role is to provide collaborators to other objects.*

The difficulty in designing
exception-safe software isn't
in pinpointing where an
exception gets thrown, or in
determining who eventually
handles it. The real problem
is in designing all the
intermediate collaborations
so that they leave the system
in a reasonable state and
allow the exception handler to
do its job.

## Designing Reliable Collaborations

It is easy to design objects to work under perfect conditions. It is much harder to design for exceptional conditions. In general, making one object more adept at handling its own problems relieves the burden of doing so from those that collaborate with it. At the very least, if a responsibility completes only partially because of an error, the object should make its best attempts to leave any resources it obtained in a consistent state. In general, if an object detects an error during the middle of its performance, it should tidy up after itself.

> A method in the middle of a long collaboration sequence opens a file and normally closes it. On error, it takes care to close the file. This makes it a more responsible citizen.

Leaving things in a consistent state shifts the burden to clients to figure out how to recover—something they may not always be equipped to do.

If a side effect of a neighbor's action could result in catastrophe, sometimes an object will want full control over its holdings. If an object is to be used in many different environments or if it will travel around a distributed network and is designed to work under adverse conditions, it must raise its guard. We use a simple strategy to prevent an object from breaking: Hide the object behind a limited interface. By narrowing its responsibilities, we let an object restrict the ways that others can affect it.

> As shown in Figure 5-12, a Web browser can't possibly anticipate who its neighbors (applets) will be, so it doesn't trust them. It protects itself and its operating system resources from malicious objects by accepting only a few simple messages.

In an ideal world, the browser would offer many more services to the applets. As developers, we would be able to leave images and sounds—and not just text cookies—on the client machines.

Therein lies the rub. As we narrow the services we provide, we can make objects more reliable, but we offer fewer services and less flexibility to our neighbors. It is one of the many compromises that we make.

## WHEN ARE WE FINISHED?

Object design is devoted to creating an arrangement of responsibilities among collaborators. Identifying roles defines the participants; assigning responsibilities distributes the work. Designing

Figure 5-12
*When you use Java applets, visibility and access to system resources is restricted.*

collaborations connects the workers. As we design collaborations, we readjust and reorganize the roles and responsibilities to make a better fit between any given participant's needs and abilities. We factor responsibilities and design reliable communications.

There are many sources of raw material for building a collaborations model:

- Use cases
- Events
- Themes derived from application stories
- Real-world views of the domain
- Patterns
- Architectural styles

Designing collaborations will ground any hand-waving that we did earlier. Browsing (and thinking about!) responsibilities gives a broad dynamic view. Analyzing the possible factorings of subresponsibilities among cooperating objects and carefully simulating how our objects interact will fill in many details. Thinking carefully through visibility, trust, and reliability issues completes even more of the picture. Although we've simulated collaborations, we are still short of implementing them.

But this invites a question: When is a collaboration model good enough? It is good enough when it demonstrates that objects interact in consistent ways and that any natural divisions in a system are preserved. Move on to more detailed work when your objects, their responsibilities, and their collaborations are no longer candidates; when they fit together in nonarbitrary ways; and when you have located the hard places and explored options for solving them as simply as you can. At this point, you could rightfully declare that you are finished with exploratory design and ready to move on—either to refinement or to a first implementation.

Developing a collaboration model has taken us a big step forward. However, more precision can be added, and many more decisions must be made. Roles and objects will need to be mapped to their implementation as interfaces and classes. Decisions will be made about which relations between collaborators should be static and which should be fixed. Hooks may be added to the design to support variation, and extra behaviors to support more reliable collaborations. Whether you make time to refine your design before you start coding or refine your ideas after you've been coding for a while, an exploratory design model still lacks many details. In reality, design continues during coding, testing, bug fixing, and code refactoring.

## SUMMARY

Collaborations are requests from one object to another. One object calls on, or collaborates with, another because it needs help. Some objects collaborate a lot; others, little. Some objects offer help to many others; others are used infrequently. An object's frequency and patterns of collaboration depend on what its responsibilities are and how it carries them out.

To develop a collaboration model, you need to focus on how candidates work together to perform complex, coordinated actions. Initially your goal should be to link individual responsibilities to collaborators. Responsibilities usually overlap and interact. To do something, an object might need to know certain information, which it might get by asking a collaborator. To make a decision, an object might need to know certain other information that it asks another object about.

When you have a rough idea of how objects call on one another for help, you can take a pass at solving more complex scenarios. You can quickly find errors and omissions in your collaboration model by simulating the messaging between objects. Pick an area of your design to simulate. Start by asking, What gets things rolling? When an event starts the simulation, what object should be informed of the event? What responsibility will you ask it to fulfill? Who will it collaborate with to fulfill this responsibility? Follow a chain of collaborations from beginning to end. Explore alternatives for how objects might work together.

Your goal is to develop a collaboration model in which object roles are clear and simple, responsibilities fit with roles, and the number of objects seen by any one object are few and well chosen. After you have demonstrated that fundamental collaborations work, you can always simplify, expand, compress, and make things more consistent.

## FURTHER READING

Earlier we mentioned that you should look further than *Design Patterns* (Addison-Wesley, 1995) by Erich Gamma and his colleagues for design patterns. A rich source for design pattern information is the patterns home page: http://www.hillside.net/patterns/. The many *Pattern Languages of Program Design* conferences are another rich source. There are four volumes in the PLoP series published by Addison-Wesley:

- *Pattern Languages of Program Design* (James O. Coplien and Douglas C. Schmidt, 1995)
- *Pattern Languages of Program Design 2* (John M. Vlissides et al., 1996)
- *Pattern Languages of Program Design 3* (Robert C. Martin et al., 1998)
- *Pattern Languages of Program Design 4* (Neil Harrison et al., 2000)

In addition to these books, online PLoP conference proceedings have even more patterns. Check out http://st-www.cs.uiuc.edu/~plop/.

"How Designs Differ," by Rebecca Wirfs-Brock, analyzes two designs for the same problem. This paper explores how control architecture and level of communication between controllers and the objects they control can have a major impact on a design. An online version of the paper can be found at www.wirfs-brock.com.

# Chapter 6

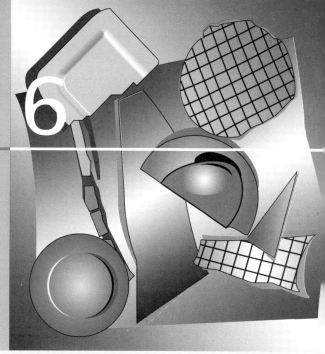

## Control Style

**D**ouglas Hofstadter challenged his colleagues and friends to translate "A une Damoyselle malade," a poem originally written in French, into any other language, maintaining seven properties of the original:

1. The poem is 28 lines long.

2. Each line consists of three syllables.

3. Each line's main stress falls on its final syllable.

4. The poem is a string of rhyming couplets: AA, BB, CC, etc.

5. Midway, the tone changes from formal ("vous") to informal ("tu").

6. The poem's opening line is echoed precisely at the very bottom.

7. The poet puts his own name directly into his poem.

*From* Le Ton beau de Marot *by Diuglass Hofstader. Copyright © 1997 by Basic Books, a member of Perseus Books, L.L.C. Reprinted with permission of Basic Books, a member of Perseus Books, L.L.C.*

Hofstadter and his friends penned more than 100 translations, each with a unique style and twist. For many of the same reasons, "translating" requirements into a software design results in wide variation. Given a complex software problem, there are many ways to solve it. But fortunately, there are only a few options for distributing control responsibilities—and developing a control style.

## WHAT IS CONTROL STYLE?

Writers express style with their choice of words, punctuation marks, breathers, emphasis devices, phrases, lists, clauses, and sentences. Their style evolves from a combination of many factors. Finding a pattern and following a style make a piece consistent. It's important to find a style and stick with it.

Translators of poems or works of fiction have an even tougher job. Not only must they decide on a style and the constraints they will honor, but also they constantly make micro-decisions as they work. How will they address new constraints they discover? How will they deal with concepts or ideas that aren't easily translated? How liberally or literally should each thought or idea be translated? How much of their own style and experience should they bring to the translation?

"I suspect that the welcoming of constraints is, at bottom, the deepest secret of creativity."

—Douglas Hofstadter

Software design shares similarities with translation. There are many constraints on a solution. We loosely translate requirements into a design. But there is much room for originality and creativity. In no way is translation from requirements to design direct or straightforward. Even a simple design problem has many good solutions. It is important to develop a sense of style and, when possible, to stick with it.

> Conceptual integrity is an attribute of a quality design. It implies that a limited number of design "forms" are used and that they are used uniformly.
> —*Alan Davis*

Many things contribute to a design style: your choice of objects, their names, the kinds of responsibilities they have, and their patterns of collaboration. Deciding on and developing a consistent *control style* is one of the most important decisions a designer makes. In this chapter we explore how to consistently design *control centers*—places where objects charged with controlling and coordinating reside.

## CONTROL STYLE OPTIONS

Although design variations may seem limitless, it's fortunate that there are only a few control styles to pick from. Control style choices affect the way intelligence is distributed among objects charged with controlling others' actions—controllers and coordinators—and those under their control.

A control style can be centralized, delegated, or dispersed. But there is a continuum of solutions: One design can be said to be more centralized or delegated than another. Within this continuum, this chapter will primarily explore the first two styles: centralized and delegated.

If you adopt a *centralized* control style, you place major decision-making responsibilities in only a few objects—those stereotyped as controllers. These decisions can be simple or complex, but with centralized control, most objects that are used by controllers are devoid of any significant decision-making responsibilities. They do their job, but generally they are told by the controller how to do it.

A variation of a centralized control style is one in which decision-making responsibilities are assigned to several controllers, each working on a small part of the overall control. Control is factored among a group of objects whose actions are coordinated—a *clustered* control style.

If you choose a *delegated* control style, you make concerted efforts to delegate decisions, not only to other, smaller controllers within a control center but also to objects having other responsibilities. Decisions made by controllers will be limited to deciding what should be done. Following this style, objects with control responsibilities tend to coordinate rather than control every action.

Choosing a *dispersed* control style means distributing decision-making responsibilities across many objects involved in a task. In fact, when you spread actions across a large population of objects, it can be hard to locate where a control center is—and harder yet to discern who's responsible for making major decisions. Every object has a piece of the action, and all decisions have been reduced to very small ones.

As shown in Figure 6-1, most control designs fit within a band of solutions ranging from centralized (but not overly so) to delegated (but not totally dispersed).

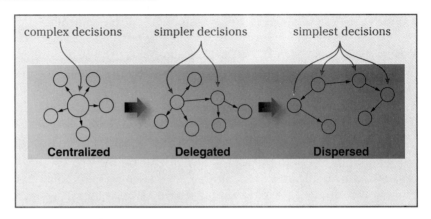

complex decisions        simpler decisions        simplest decisions

**Centralized**          **Delegated**            **Dispersed**

Figure 6-1
*Control styles lie along a continuum.*

## MAKING TRADE-OFFS

There are a number of forces to balance when you choose a control style. If you make controllers take more responsibility for setting up and monitoring activities, the objects under their control need not be so clever. If you make them let go of the little details, the objects under their control must take care of them. Responsibilities and workloads shift according to the choices you make.

Many decisions contribute to the design of a control style: How smart should objects with control responsibilities be? How will responsibilities be factored between controlling objects and others? Will work be divided among several controllers working together, or will it be concentrated in a single controller? What paths of collaboration will exist among controllers and objects under their control? How much will controllers decide? How much will they push out to others? These decisions are interrelated. Developing a control style means working on several aspects of a design at once.

### Centralizing Control

With centralized control, generally one object (the controller) makes most of the important decisions. It may do so by collaborating with other objects, by querying information they maintain, or by using a combination of techniques.

Decisions may be delegated, but most often it is the controller that figures out what to do next. Responsibilities are delegated; after all, the controller isn't doing everything! But typically the controller asks others to perform simple, isolated responsibilities that are pulled together by the controller.

There is one very good reason for centralizing control: You can quickly locate control decisions. Decision-making logic is concentrated in controllers, making it easy to find. If decisions are regular and simple, you can use a state model to drive the controller's decisions.

On the other hand, plenty can go wrong if you don't counteract certain tendencies.

***Control logic can get overly complex.*** Controlling code can get complicated. Determining what to do next may end up as a nest of if-then-else-otherwise-until-unless code. Overly complex code with lots of branching doesn't always go hand in hand with centralized control, but it is something to watch for. There are techniques for refactoring code to make it simpler. If decisions are based on ranges or related facts, you can make them easy to read and more testable by factoring them into helper methods that provide yes or no answers. Or you can design helper methods implemented by the controller to return partial answers to a series of decision-making questions, ordered according to their expected frequency of selection.

***Controllers can become dependent on information holders' contents.*** This is a big problem. Centralizing control and decision making means that other objects tend to do little work. Rather than being asked to do something significant, they are poked and prodded by simple, transparent accessor methods. Information is moved in and out of them by the controller. The controller may depend on details that should be hidden from it.

***Objects can become coupled indirectly through the actions of their controller.*** Any change to the surrounding objects ripples throughout the controller and those objects it controls. If one object is queried for information that is then copied by the controller into another, these two objects are coupled—even if they don't collaborate. If one object changes the way it manages information, it will affect both the controller and the other controlled object.

*The only interesting work is done in the controller.* Responsibilities can get sucked into a controlling object, leaving collaborators with very minor roles and not much to do. One smart controller plus many small controlled objects with minor responsibilities means that only the controller object is of any real interest.

## Delegating Control

A delegated control style passes some of the decision making and much of the action to objects surrounding a control center. Each neighboring object has a significant role to play. Delegating responsibility for control reaps several very important rewards.

*Delegating coordinators tend to know about fewer objects than dominating controllers.* With a delegated control style, objects surrounding the control center both know and do things. Objects surrounding the coordinator take on more responsibility, leaving the coordinator with a simpler task and, typically, fewer objects to manage.

*Dialogs are higher-level.* Collaborations between a coordinator and the objects it coordinates are typically higher-level requests for work and not simple requests to store or retrieve data. Communications are more abstract and more powerful. Instead of asking objects to do small chores or divulge small bits of information, coordinators typically delegate larger-grained requests.

*Changes typically affect fewer objects.* With more objects making decisions and taking on responsibilities, each worker has a well-defined role and a smaller number of different kinds of objects to collaborate with. Consequently, changing one responsibility will have a limited impact.

*It is easier to divide design work among team members.* With more objects having interesting responsibilities, challenging work can be distributed among several designers. With centralized control—and responsibilities concentrated into a single control center—there is less interesting design work on the periphery. With delegated control, there still are control centers to be designed, but the workload among objects (and designers) can be more evenly distributed.

Of course, there are pitfalls.

***Too much distribution of responsibility can lead to weak objects and weak collaborations.*** Carried to extremes, a delegated control style results in objects that neither do nor know enough or that collaborate awkwardly. Look for these characteristics of weak factorings:

- Small service-provider objects that are used by a single client. They have been factored out of their controller and instead should be merged into the controller as helper methods.

- Complicated collaborations between delegator and delegates. This can happen when not enough context is passed along with a delegated request.

- Lots of collaborations but not much work getting done.

## The Limits of Control Decisions

Our preferred style, given that it suits the problem and meets other constraints, is a delegated control style. We prefer a design in which no one object knows or does too much. But there are times when we must adapt to an existing control style rather than invent one to our liking. Most frameworks force designers to work with a particular set of collaborations and initial distribution of responsibilities. Framework designers make choices that predefine certain collaborations and lead to certain control styles.

When you use a framework, it is best to go with the flow and adopt its control style. For example, control style in stand-alone, interactive Java applications is dictated by patterns of collaboration with the user interface library. When designing a control center that handles user interface events, you typically distribute control among many listeners. Each listener, after registering with its widget, is responsible for responding to events raised by that widget—a controller per widget distribution of control.

> Most frameworks dictate a particular control style. You plug your objects in to an existing control structure. Control has been designed by the framework author.

But the Java Swing framework stops short of telling you how to design how a listener handles a particular event (see Figure 6-2). After all, frameworks don't make every choice for you! When a user pokes at a widget, it turns around and notifies its listener. It's up to you to decide what the listener does next and how. You could design it to delegate responsibilities to others under its control, or to make most decisions and do the work itself. Your listener could be a coordinator or a controller. You could have either a centralized or a delegated control style, depending on how many responsibilities you give each listener.

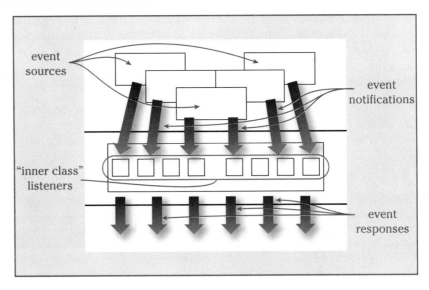

Figure 6-2
*Java Swing uses distributed control among listeners.*

Most designers who use this framework tend to separate responsibilities for interpreting events from responsibilities for performing domain-specific actions. Each listener is typically designed to delegate work to one or more objects in the domain layer. This is a conscious design choice. It makes good design sense to separate knowing what to do from knowing how to do it. Separating these responsibilities into different objects keeps listeners focused on interpreting and reacting to UI events. It also permits domain-specific responsibilities to be invoked from several different listeners.

Instead of going with a one controller per widget design, nothing prevents us from hooking up one big listener to several widgets. This listener would have to react to many widgets' events. But to do so, it would have to take on the added responsibility of deciphering what a particular event meant. A clicked event from one button means a certain thing, whereas a clicked event from another button means something else. As seen in Figure 6-3, creating a big listener can even tighten the coupling between it and the user interface, especially if the listener must collaborate with UI widgets to determine who said what in order to figure out what to do.

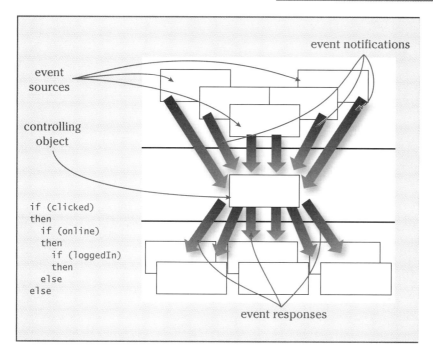

Figure 6-3
*Centralized control can lead to concentrated decision making.*

Lest we dismiss centralized control too quickly, there are advantages to locating control decisions into a single controller. The single controller holds connections to collaborators, so if its context changes, it is a simple matter for it to refresh and readjust connections to objects under its control (see Figure 6-4).

However, when we follow the natural style dictated by the Swing framework, there is a direct relation between each listener and its corresponding widget. So each listener knows what to do without deciphering what the event means. Control is dispersed among the listening objects in the application services layer whose actions may need to be coordinated. This control style variation might be characterized as *many small related controllers.*

Often, controllers working in tandem need to be synchronized. Clicking on an item in a list may mean populating another widget with

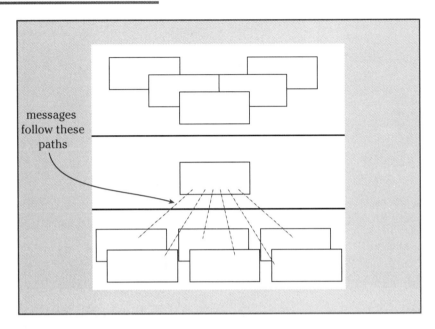

Figure 6-4
*Centralized control collects connections to the domain.*

contents extracted from an object in the domain layer associated with the list item. The identity of this domain object may need to be passed to one or more controllers, which need to know whom to talk to whenever their events fire. Coordination can get quite complex.

Taking an even closer look, we can see that many decisions are involved in designing related controllers: Who sets up and gives each controller visibility to the objects it needs? How should these connections be maintained? When an event affects several controllers, who should notify them? Are they all listening to the same event, or does one controller take the lead and inform the others? How will actions be synchronized and connections to domain objects be maintained?

By distributing control among related controllers, we eliminate one design problem—how to interpret many widgets' events—and swap it for two others: the need to coordinate actions and synchronize connections to collaborators (see Figure 6-5).

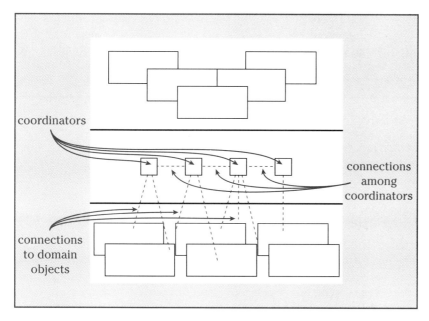

Figure 6-5
*Distributed control requires distributed connections and synchronization among interrelated controllers.*

## Developing Control Centers

In all but the simplest applications, you will have multiple control centers to design. A control center is a place in an application where a consistent pattern of collaboration needs to exist. Control design is important in the control of

- User-initiated events
- Complex processes
- The work within a specific object neighborhood
- External software under your application's control

After you've identified those control centers, pick one, decide on a control style you think is appropriate, and then work on specific responsibilities and patterns of collaboration. Get down to details.

Because control centers that aren't identified as important tend to accrue responsibilities until they are unmanageable, it is important to really determine how much each will need to know or do, and how many other kinds of objects it affects.

What does it really take to fulfill control and decision-making responsibilities? How much work will objects in the control center do? How much work will those they collaborate with do? How complex are their responsibilities? Explore your options. Try one distribution of responsibilities to see whether your control center turns out as you anticipated. You may want to back up and reconsider an alternative distribution of responsibilities.

***Don't try to use the same style everywhere.*** Develop a control style suited to each control situation. Pick a centralized style when you want to localize decisions in a single controller. Choose a delegated style when you want to delegate work to objects that are more specialized. Several control styles can happily coexist in a single application. Not all control centers need to have the same style. Although similar use cases often share similar control style designs, control style within various neighborhoods varies widely. Control styles for control centers handling critical events or complex processes may be quite different; it all depends on what's right for a particular area of your design and how diligently you pursue a consistent style.

Developing a control style for a control center means deciding the following:

- How decisions should be made
- Who should make them
- Whether decisions should be delegated
- What patterns of delegation should be established and repeated

Be aware of the cumulative effect of design decisions. The more control centers you've designed, the more difficult it may be to fit a new style in with established styles.

There are many valid reasons to choose one style over another. But as a general guideline, it's best to design collaborations so that like things work similarly. For example, use cases with the same kinds of user interactions might share a similar control style even if the participating objects differ. This will bring consistency, predictability, and an overarching style to your entire design.

## A CASE STUDY: CONTROL STYLE FOR EXTERNAL USER EVENTS

In a layered architecture, application-specific control is usually located in an architectural layer that sits between the presentation layer and the domain layer. Objects in this application services layer receive and interpret events passed from interfacer objects located in the presentation layer. Messages are sent from the presentation layer to objects in the application services layer. They then react to user events and coordinate the invocation of related software actions (see Figure 6-6).

To demonstrate the main feature of this software, take a look at Figure 6-7, the "*Speak for Me*" use case for building a message.

To start, we invent a single object that is responsible for responding to user events and controlling the subsequent action of the "Build a Message" use case. We name this object MessageBuilder. It must interpret two events: one from the presentation layer when the user selects something that has been spoken, and another from the timer, signaling that time has elapsed without her selecting something. We initially assign this controller three responsibilities, as shown in Figure 6-8.

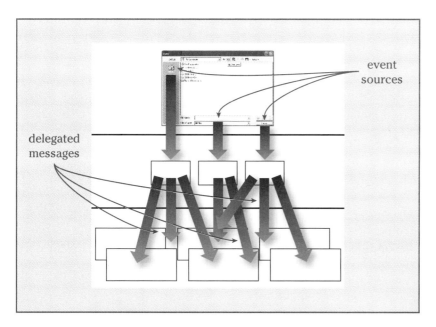

Figure 6-6
*Responses to UI events are delegated by controllers and coordinators.*

| Actor Actions | System Responsibilities |
|---|---|
| Click to start software speaking | Start building a message |
| Repeat until. . . | |
| Optionally, click to select letter | Determine what to speak (letter, word, sentence, or space):<br>   Speak letter<br><br>Add letter to word |
| Optionally, click to select space | Speak space<br><br>Add working word to end of sentence<br>Start new word |
| Optionally, click to select word | Speak word<br><br>Add word to end of sentence<br>Start new word |
| Optionally, click to select sentence | Speak sentence<br><br>Add sentence to end of message<br>Start new sentence, start new word |
| . . .a command is issued | |
| | Process command (a separate use case) |

Figure 6-7
*This use case conversation describes the user's interactions with the system as she builds a message.*

We know that the MessageBuilder has the overall responsibility for handling these events, but we don't yet know how much work it will take on itself or delegate to others (see Figure 6-9). We'd like to see how much work is involved and, if things get overly complex for the MessageBuilder, develop a delegated control style.

## Centralizing Control in the MessageBuilder

With such a simple user interface, one might think that one controller should be responsible for receiving notifications as well as responding to them:

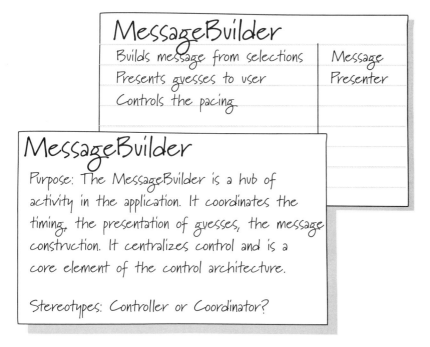

Figure 6-8
*The MessageBuilder's stereotype depends on how this object interacts with surrounding collaborators to perform its role.*

- When the timer ticks, the MessageBuilder will select the best thing to present next: a letter, a space, a word, and so on. This depends on the state of the message and what has been previously presented.

- When the user makes a selection, the MessageBuilder will update the message with the selection. How it does this depends on what the user selected.

The MessageBuilder's response to the user's selection of what was spoken depends on many different conditions. As the user builds the message, the software tries to guess each word (only one word guess for each letter that she chooses) as it sees more letters. It matches the partial constructions against complete words in an online vocabulary. Special rules apply to the beginning of a word. In what is called

It is not necessarily the number of different events that makes control complex. It can also be the number of differing responses to the same event.

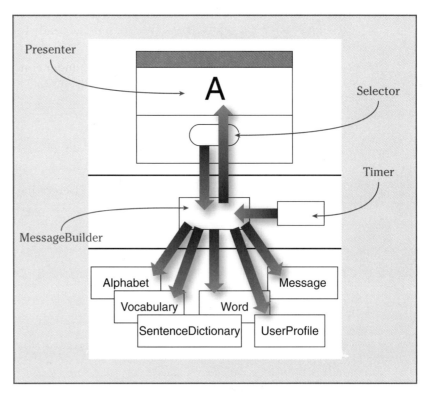

Figure 6-9
*The MessageBuilder listens for events and delegates work to others.*

the onset of the word, there are only a few letters that may follow the first letter. This consonant co-occurrence provides the software with a relatively simple way to predict the second and third letters of a word, given the first letter, or first and second letters, respectively.

Reacting to the selection event involves two subresponsibilities (and numerous decisions):

1. What action must be performed when the user makes a selection?

   - Is the user at the very beginning? If so, she has just clicked to start the application. Do nothing except set up to handle her first real selection.

   - Did she just now select a letter? Add it to the word under construction.

- Did she just end a word by choosing a space? Add the word under construction to the message, and get ready to build a new word.

- Did she just choose a word? Clear out the word under construction and append the chosen word to the message.

- Did she just hear and choose an entire sentence? Replace the sentence under construction with the one she chose.

2. Depending on the contents of the message, what should be presented to the user?

- Did the user just now start building a message? Determine the first letter in the alphabetic (A to Z) or frequency (E to Z) sequence.

- Did she just select a letter? Give her a "space" ("space" acts as the end-of-word).

- Did she just end a word by choosing a space? Check to see whether the word under construction is a command. If it is not, then start over with the letters in the chosen alphabetic sequence.

- Are there two letters in the latest word construction? If so, ask the Vocabulary for any guesses.

- Are there at least two words in the latest sentence? If so, get any sentences that match from the SentenceDictionary.

- If the SentenceDictionary and the Vocabulary both have something to guess, choose the best one and present that to her.

Initially, reacting to these events might have seemed simple. But it's not. If we keep all these decisions inside the MessageBuilder, the code quickly becomes complex. The simplified code below demonstrates the kind of checking necessary to control the presentation and selection of the user's choices. For brevity, only portions of this class are shown. Where something is not shown, we will make note of the fact.

```
class MessageBuilder {
    // Holds the letters, words, and sentences
    private Message message = new Message();
```

*Continues*

```
// The source of the letters
private Alphabet alphabet = new Alphabet();
… declarations for vocabulary, sentenceDictionary missing
// The last thing presented to the user (letter, etc.)
private Object lastPresented = null;
// The output device for a blind person.
private Presenter presenter = new Speaker();
// Controls when the user hears "space"
… Note: This state variable could easily be replaced with
… more state objects.
private boolean spacePresented = false;

public void handleSelection( ) {
    … The code for handling Commands, Words, and Sentences is not shown.
    … If you did, you would make a type check for each type of selection.
    … Furthermore, you wouldn't admit to having written it.
    if (lastPresented instanceOf Letter) {
        if (((Letter)lastPresented).getValue() == ' ') {
            // The user completed spelling a word, so end the current word
            // and start a new one
            getMessage().endLastWord();
        }
        else {
            // She didn't end the word with a space, so add her selected
            // letter and continue, starting with a space
            getMessage().addLetter((Letter) lastPresented);
            spacePresented = false;
        }
        // Reset the alphabet back to the start of the letter sequence
        alphabet.reset();
    }
    … And on and on. Three increasingly complex if/then blocks would
    … follow to handle the user's selections of Words, Sentences,
    … and Commands.
}

public void handleTimeout(){
    … This code doesn't show suspending or presenting Words,
    … Commands, or Sentences. It illustrates only how the user handles
    … the first two letters of a word.
    // This is a call to a private method that checks the length of the
    // last word in the message. If the word has no letters in it, it
    // returns true.
    if (this.gettingFirstLetter()) {
        // While getting the first letter, present only letters
        nextLetter = alphabet.nextLetter();
        getPresenter().presentLetter((Letter)lastPresented);
    }
    // This is true when the last word in the message has exactly
    // one letter.
    if (this.gettingSecondLetter()) {
        // While getting the second letter, present only letters and
        // spaces
        if (!spacePresented) {
            // If we haven't already offered the user a space, do it now.
            // Then, present the sequence of letters. Present the space
            // only once.
            lastPresented = new Letter(' ');
            getPresenter().presentLetter((Letter)lastPresented);
            spacePresented = true;
        }
```

```
        else {
        // The space has been presented for this sequence, so present
        // only the letters in sequence until the user selects one.
        lastPresented = alphabet.nextLetter();
        getPresenter().presentLetter((Letter)lastPresented);
    }
    … Code for suspending, handling Words, Commands, and Sentences
    … is not shown
  }
}
… other MessageBuilder methods
}
```

Work on understanding the complexity of the decisions that need to be made. If you fudge on this, your design will end up with black holes of complexity that will be difficult to implement.

## Refactoring Decision Making into Small Controllers

The MessageBuilder must know a lot in order to handle a selection or timer event. Its correct responses are based on the state of the message being constructed as well as what has been already spoken. When an object seems burdened with complex decisions based on state, you can simplify its processing by distributing state-specific actions to other objects. The State pattern explicitly addresses moving decisions from an object into a number of smaller decision makers working directly on its behalf. If we adopt the State pattern, we'll end up with a clustered control style. Each small decision maker will assume responsibility for responding to the events that the controller is handling given a particular state the controller is in, explaining the name State pattern.

> Don't be misled by the number of events that need to be processed. The number of events does not equate to complexity.

**Name:** State Pattern

**Problem:** How to design an object to alter its behavior when its internal state changes.

**Context:** Sometimes you need to make complex decisions about what to do based on the current state of an object. An object's state can be represented by a number of different objects that collectively represent what state the object is in. The object must change its behavior at run time depending on that state.

*Continues*

**Forces:** Complex, multipart conditional expressions are often used to decide what action to take. But this can result in code that is hard to maintain.

**Solution:** Instead of writing code that specifically checks what state an object is in before deciding how to react, design one new class for each possible state the object can be in. Reassign responsibilities for handling events to each state object. Delegate all responsibilities to the state objects, and pass in whatever context they need to do their work. It is the responsibility of each state object to know specifically what should be done. Typically, in addition to handling state-specific responses, each state object also knows what the next state should be after completing its response.

**Consequences:** The State pattern puts all behavior associated with each particular state into distinct objects. New states and transitions can be easily added by defining new state classes. The State pattern does have some drawbacks. It distributes behavior for different states across several state classes and is less compact than a single class. But such distribution is actually good if there are many states, something that would otherwise necessitate large conditional statements.

Controllers and coordinators make decisions, but to different degrees. A coordinator decides whom to pass the buck to, whereas a controller retains control, enlisting others under close supervision.

The states in the State pattern come from identifying the sets of different responses to the same events.

Although you have applied a pattern, you still must make choices about the distribution of responsibilities. Instead of the state object knowing what the next state is, the controller could take on this responsibility. Just make sure that one or the other makes this decision.

The first step in using the State pattern is to analyze and enumerate the conditions that cause different responses. For example, in Speak for Me, the state diagram in Figure 6-10 shows the states the MessageBuilder goes through as it constructs a message. States are distinguished by how the MessageBuilder responds to the timer ticks or the user selections.

After we decide to use the State pattern, it is a simple matter to assign the responsibilities for each state to a different object (see Figure 6-11). Each state has its own object to handle the responses! We end up with seven states, seven different kinds of objects, and seven pairs of responses to timer ticks and user selections.

Because they must be able to fulfill the same responsibilities but they have different implementations, we can implement seven concrete state classes, as shown in Figure 6-12.

With this new control style design, when the MessageBuilder is notified about an event it makes no decisions whatsoever. It simply delegates the responsibility to whatever state object is currently plugged

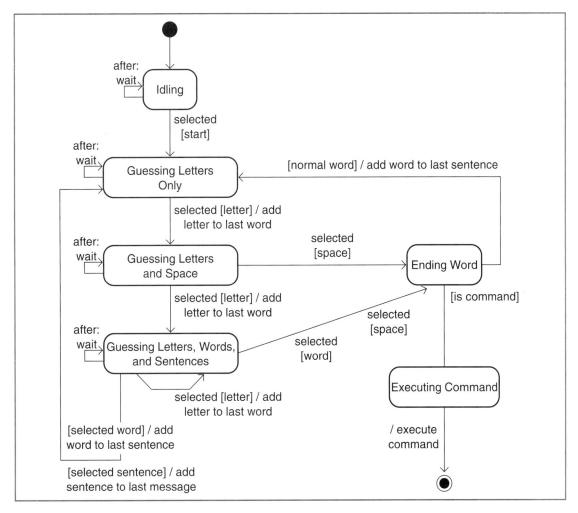

Figure 6-10
*Speak for Me has many states that determine what the event responses will be.*

in and is responsible for handling events given the current state. That state object is responsible for responding to events based on current conditions, instantiating the next state object, and plugging it in to its coordinator.

The order in which the state objects are plugged in mirrors the transitions that appear in the state diagram. Together, the state objects collectively handle all the conditions that can occur. Each state object makes two decisions on behalf of the MessageBuilder: what to

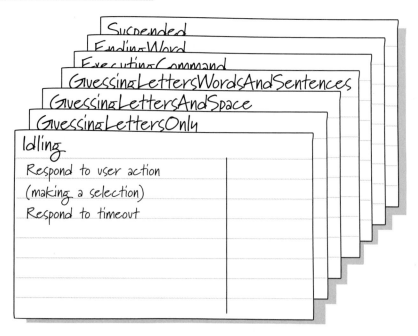

Figure 6-11
*Each state becomes an object.*

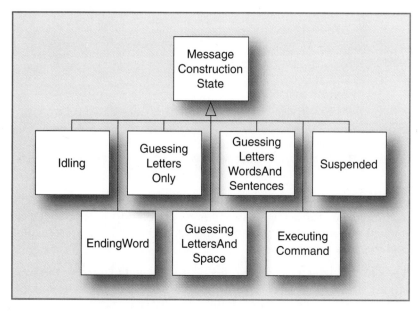

Figure 6-12
*The State classes form an inheritance hierarchy.*

do with the selection, and what to do with a timer event. Because each state object represents one branch of the current state of the message building process, each object's methods are a bit simpler than the original MessageBuilder code. Each is simpler to understand. Let's look at several classes' methods to see how relatively simple each one is.

The Idling class handles the timer and user events with its two methods. Its only responsibility is to handle message construction:

```
class Idling extends MessageConstructionState {
// This class is used when the user has not signaled to start building
// a message. The clock is ticking, but the software does nothing in
// response.

    public MessageConstructionState handleTimeout(MessageBuilder builder){
        // The clock is ticking, but because we are idling, do nothing, but
        // stay in the same state.
        return this;
    }

    public MessageConstructionState handleSelection(MessageBuilder builder){
        // The user signaled to start building a message.
        // Transition to the next state, the one that will handle presenting
        // and selecting the first letter of a word.
        return new GuessingLettersOnly();
    }
}
```

The GuessingLettersOnly state class is simple too. It is responsible for presenting only letters to the user and, because the user can only select letters, only adding them to the Message:

```
class GuessingLettersOnly extends MessageConstructionState {
// This class is used when the last word in the message is empty (the user
// has started the software but hasn't selected a letter yet).

    public MessageConstructionState handleTimeout(MessageBuilder builder) {
        // User is at the beginning of a word. Present only letters.
        Letter nextLetter = alphabet.nextLetter();
        … code for handling end-of-alphabet (suspend) missing
        // Record that this letter was just presented to the user.
        // If she signals before we present a different one, this one
        // will be added to the message.
        builder.setLastPresented(nextLetter);
        builder.getPresenter().presentLetter(nextLetter);
        // Stay in the same state.
        return this;
    }
}
```

*Continues*

```
public MessageConstructionState handleSelection(MessageBuilder builder) {
    // Only letters are being presented to the user, so we know exactly
    // what to do: it must be a letter that the user selected, so add it to
    // the message, reset the sequence of letters to the beginning, and
    // start getting the next letter (but offer the user a space first).
    Letter letter = (Letter) builder.getLastPresented();
    builder.getMessage().addLetter(letter);
    builder.getAlphabet().reset();
    // We have to present a space after each selection from now on, so
    // transition to the state that behaves that way.
    return new GuessingLettersAndSpace();
}
```

GuessingLettersAndSpace is responsible for deciding when to present a space instead of a letter. Even this decision could be eliminated by creating a MessageConstructionState subclass to handle this condition:

```
class GuessingLettersAndSpace extends MessageConstructionState {
    // This class is used when the last word in the message has exactly one
    // letter. Under this condition, each letter selection is followed by a
    // space. The user selects the space to terminate the word.
    // This static variable is visible to all of the instances of the class.
    // They use it to know whether a space should be presented. It could
    // be eliminated by creating a MessageConstructionState class
    // that handled the condition of not yet having presented
    // the space (PresentingSpace).
    private static boolean spacePresented = false;

    public MessageConstructionState handleTimeout(MessageBuilder builder) {
        // The user has chosen exactly one letter. Offer a space to allow
        // the user to terminate the word even if it has only one letter
        // (such as "I"), and if the user doesn't select it, present the
        // letters in sequence.
        … The code for handling the case when the user doesn't select a
        … letter or a space (otherwise known as suspending) is not shown.
        Letter nextLetter = null;
        if (!spacePresented){
            // If the space hasn't yet been presented, choose it for
            // presentation to the user.
            nextLetter = new Letter(' ');
            spacePresented = true;
        }
        else {
            // The user didn't select the space when it was presented, so
            // fetch the next letter in the sequence.
            nextLetter = alphabet.nextLetter();
        }
        // Present the space or the letter to the user.
        builder.setPresented(nextLetter);
        builder.getPresenter().presentLetter(nextLetter);
        return this;
    }
}
```

```
public MessageConstructionState handleSelection(MessageBuilder builder) {
    // The user could only have selected a space or letter
    State newState = null;
    Letter lastLetter = (Letter) builder.getLastPresented();
    if (lastLetter.getValue() == ' ') {
        // If the user selected the space, it means she has finished
        // building the word.
        builder.getMessage().endLastWord();
        // Start getting the first letter of a new word.
        newState = new GuessingLettersOnly();
    }
    else {
        // The user chose a letter. Add it to the word under construction.
        builder.getMessage().addLetter(lastLetter);
        builder.getAlphabet().reset();
        … The GuessingLettersWordsAndSentences class that will handle
        … presenting letters and guessing words and sentences is not
        … shown.
        // Now we have two letters in the word under construction.
        // Begin guessing words and sentences along with the letters.
        newState = new GuessingLettersWordsAndSentences();
    }
    // We are either going on to guess words and sentences or are
    // getting the first letter of a new word.
    return newState;
}
}
```

Simplicity comes from having two relatively straightforward methods implemented by each `MessageConstructionState` class. Very cool.

As shown in Figure 6-13, the State pattern is one way of divvying control responsibilities—pushing them out to a cluster of decision makers. It does make the MessageBuilder more manageable and state management systematic, but is it really the solution we want? The State pattern removes responsibilities for deciding what to do from the MessageBuilder. But it still leaves decision making in objects that are located within the control center located in the application control layer—a clustered control style and not a delegated one.

If a particular pattern improves your design, you may jump on it without considering other options. Applying any pattern may have benefits. But there are also consequences. The most important one is very subtle:

> Choosing a pattern means that you are not designing a solution of your own.

The State pattern works well if all the states are discrete and detectable, and the transitions between them are deterministic. This is not always the case. For example, a book in a library can be in multiple states at the same time: for example, checked-in and lost.

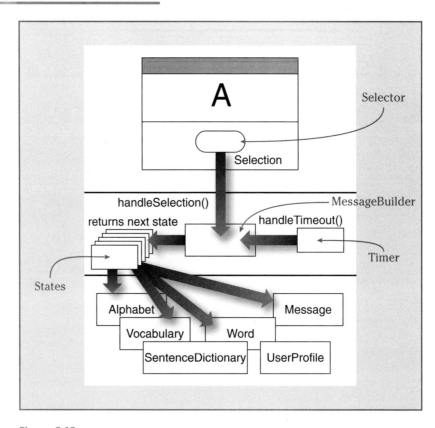

Figure 6-13
*The MessageBuilder delegates responses to its state objects.*

What if there is an elegant solution waiting just around the bend? You will never get there if you put on pattern blinders! Patterns are built on the tenets of object orientation. If a pattern doesn't suit your style, use basic strategies—abstraction, encapsulation, classification, inheritance, polymorphism, and information hiding—and stick to your design goals.

Adopting a pattern limits your options for distributing responsibilities to others. Responsibilities fulfilled by objects in a pattern are responsibilities that might have been assigned elsewhere but weren't. There may be other solutions with a different distribution of responsibilities that are better suited to your design goals. If you leap on a pattern without thinking things through, you may be applying a solution to a well-known problem but still not have solved the problem in a way that matches your control style goals.

## Refactoring Decision Making into State Methods within the MessageBuilder

A state machine is an obvious control choice for our message building task. But instead of factoring state-based responsibilities into different state objects, we could keep track of the current state within the MessageBuilder and redesign its handleSelection() method to invoke its own action methods based on its current state. Instead of delegating state-based behavior to state objects, the MessageBuilder would now comprise several smaller methods, one for each unique state in our state model. We might prefer this design over the State pattern if we needed to support slightly different state-based behavior. We could implement a subclass of the MessageBuilder that overrode a couple of methods in order to implement different idling or guessing behaviors.

## Abstracting Away Decisions

But to truly adopt a delegated control style, we need to remove decisions from the control center and place them in domain objects. How can we make our control style delegated? Let's shelve the State pattern and state-based solutions for now and go back to the drawing board. Let's try really hard to push responsibilities out of the MessageBuilder. What if we reassigned the responsibility for constructing a message to those objects that the user selects? Instead of making that the MessageBuilder's responsibility, why not make Letter, Word, and Sentence objects responsible? If a Letter is selected, it should append itself to the last word in the message. A Word should add itself to the last Sentence in the Message, replacing the last Word in the Sentence. Given that each selected object knows what kind of thing it is, it can add itself to the message without making any decisions whatsoever!

In this new design, the MessageBuilder simply accepts the selection from the presentation layer, whatever it is, and delegates to the selected object the responsibility for adding itself to the Message (see Figure 6-14). The MessageBuilder treats all selected objects alike. When the Letter is asked to add itself to the message, it turns around and asks the argument (the Message) to add "this" letter. How the letter is added to the Message is completely hidden inside the Message, where it should be.

To make this work, all the kinds of objects the user selects must share a common role and implement the same interface. The user is presented with guesses that she can select. When she does so, these guesses are added to the Message she is building. Let's define a Guess role that Letters, Words, and Sentences have in common as shown in Figures 6-15 and 6-16. By doing so, we delegate work to Guess objects and eliminate decisions (what to do with a guess) from the controller.

When you discover a new role, create a CRC card for it, and note on the unlined side any candidate that plays the role (the fact that it does).

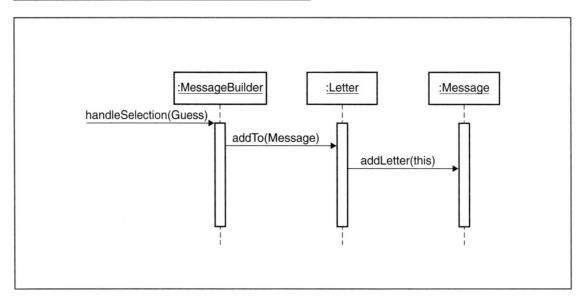

**Figure 6-14**
*Polymorphism and the Double Dispatch minimize concerns about object type.*

**Figure 6-15**
*The role of Guess is shared by Letters, Words, and Sentences.*

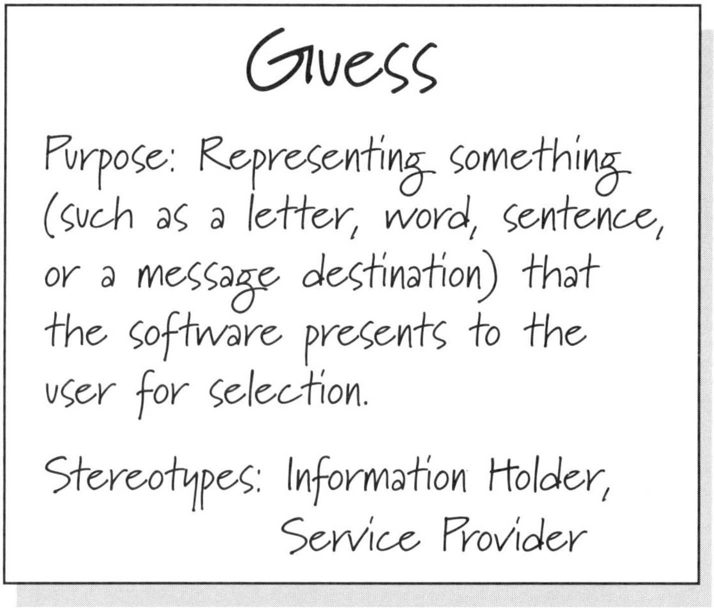

> # Guess
>
> Purpose: Representing something (such as a letter, word, sentence, or a message destination) that the software presents to the user for selection.
>
> Stereotypes: Information Holder, Service Provider

Figure 6-16
*Guesses are responsible for adding themselves to a Message.*

This solution demonstrates some fundamental design principles:

- Abstraction. Without the new role, Guess, we have nothing to represent the "sameness" of the different kinds of objects that can be selected by the user.

- Responsibility. So far, a Guess has only one responsibility: adding itself to a Message. But we now have a place to hang other responsibilities if we need to. Of course, any new responsibilities will have to make sense for all objects that share this common role.

- Inheritance. All objects that play the role of Guess may be implemented by different classes in a common hierarchy. Or we are free to define a common interface for a Guess role that is implemented by different classes, whether in the same inheritance hierarchy or not. It's too early to tell. Regardless, each different kind of Guess will implement all Guess responsibilities.

- Polymorphism. This is key. By assigning the responsibility for adding themselves to a message to Guess objects, we have reduced the complexity of our controller. This is a much more extensible and maintainable solution.

> In Java, abstract, interchangeable parts can be implemented by an abstract class or an interface. When they share common behavior, use an abstract class. When they simply share a role, use an interface.

MessageBuilder code for handling a selected Guess is reduced to a single line that looks something like this:

```
selection.addTo(message);
```

When an instance of `Letter` receives the `addTo(Message msg)` message, it turns around and asks the `Message` to add it:

```
msg.addLetter(this) // ask the Message to add the Letter
```

When an instance of `Word` receives the `addTo(Message msg)` message, it requests the `Message` to add it:

```
msg.addWord(this) // ask the Message to add the Word
```

With this design choice, the decision making has been removed from the MessageBuilder and reassigned to each particular kind of Guess. And each guess knows just what to do without making any decisions whatsoever!

## Delegating More Responsibility

The purpose of this section is to demonstrate how a "decision" is changed into a strategy and how varying the identity of an object can eliminate conditional "decisions."

The MessageBuilder must come up with a new Guess every timer tick. As we've seen, this behavior is pretty complex. If the Message-Builder doesn't delegate guessing, it will have to evaluate the current state of the message and any local state that it keeps track of, find all the possible matches that it has to choose from, and decide which possibility is best. It must query all the dictionaries that hold the different kinds of guesses and get the best guess given the current state of the message under construction: the Alphabet, the Vocabulary, and the SentenceDictionary. Lots of work, lots of collaborators, lots of connections and low-level information-gathering. Whew!

When you see a controller deciding which of many low-level objects to call upon, it's a good idea to move this complexity outside the controller and into other objects—even if you have to invent them. If you follow this strategy, objects with control responsibilities will have narrower coordination responsibilities. As a result, you may end up with more objects, but each one will be more focused.

Because determining the appropriate guess to present to the user is not related to controlling message building, it is a cleaner solution to wrap up all this guessing machinery and put it in a new object: a Guesser. The Guesser will access the current state of the Message and various dictionaries (Alphabet, Vocabulary, SentenceDictionary). From the MessageBuilder's perspective it will simply serve up a best guess every time it is asked for one. With this final design decision, the MessageBuilder remains dedicated to coordinating actions. The complex guessing machinery is wrapped inside the Guesser (see Figures 6-17 and 6-18).

As a side effect of both this decision and the previous one, the MessageBuilder truly has become a simple coordinator . . . and we have designed a delegated control style for the "Build a message" task.

## Designing the Control Style for the Guessing Neighborhood

Pushing out the responsibility for providing the best guess to the Guesser doesn't mean we're finished designing. We still have work to do. Let's shift our attention from the MessageBuilder control center to the neighborhood consisting of the Guesser and various dictionaries. Earlier, we nixed adopting the State pattern. But we are always on the lookout for patterns that clarify our design. A pattern that

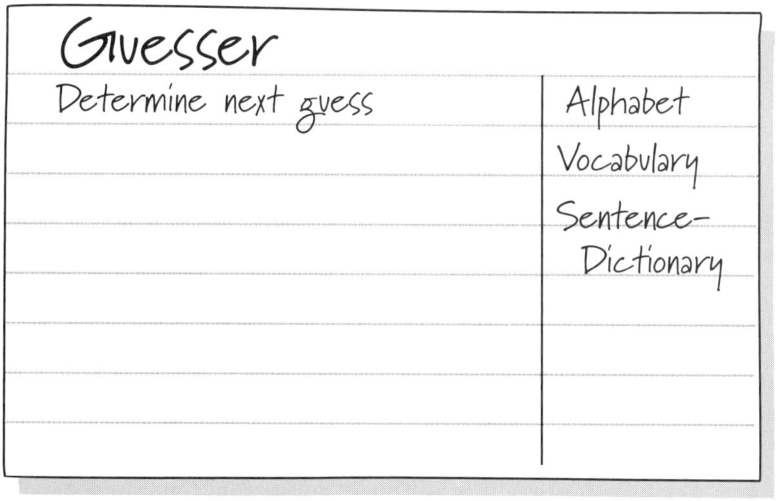

Figure 6-17
*The Guesser determines the next guess to present to the user.*

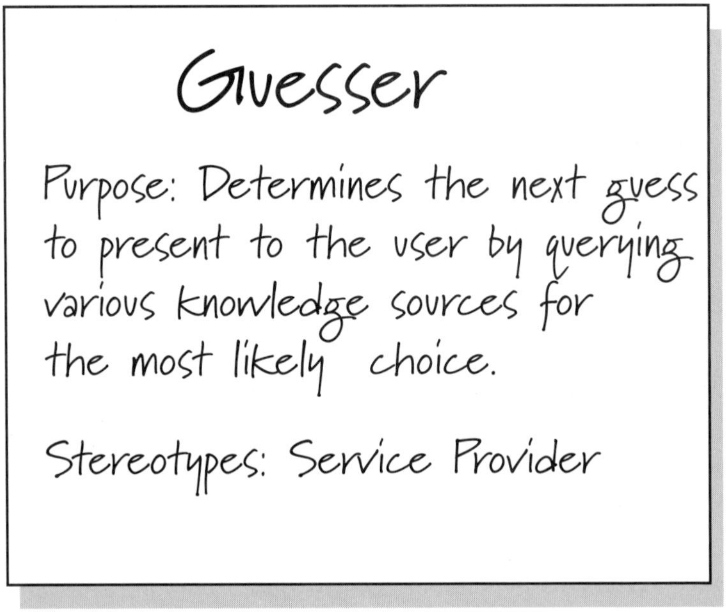

**Guesser**

Purpose: Determines the next guess to present to the user by querying various knowledge sources for the most likely choice.

Stereotypes: Service Provider

Figure 6-18
*The Guesser collaborates with several sources to determine the best guess.*

seems to fit this best guess problem is the Blackboard pattern described in *Pattern-Oriented Software Architecture*. It is an architectural pattern that is useful when the answer is a best guess. It is realized by three roles: a Blackboard, one or more KnowledgeSources, and a Control (see Figure 6-19).

To come up with a result (in our situation, a guess), processing is done in cycles. During each cycle, the Control asks several KnowledgeSource objects to evaluate information in a common store (the Blackboard). Each KnowledgeSource determines how relevant its rules are to the information on the Blackboard and makes a correspondingly low or high bid. The Control simply looks at all of the KnowledgeSources' bids and chooses the highest. The chosen object then updates the information on the Blackboard according to its rules, and the cycle begins again. This repeats until the Control decides that the Blackboard contains an answer that none of the KnowledgeSources can improve upon.

The Control is not making many decisions, and any one Knowledge-Source has a small portion of the rules governing the program's execution. It is a delegated control strategy devoted to the control of guessing an answer to a problem. The Blackboard pattern provides a basic architecture for distributing responsibilities among three roles.

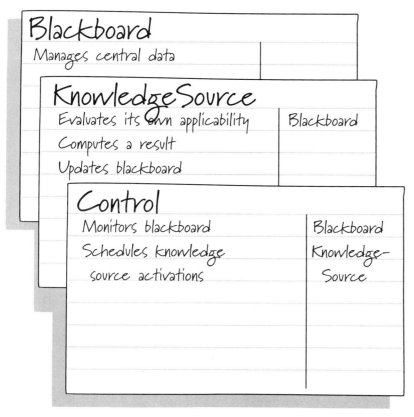

Figure 6-19
*The blackboard architecture uses three object roles.*

We will use it to guide our invention: a control object, several objects to embody the knowledge and rules, and a shared information holder to hold the answer as it evolves. In any given cycle, the Guesser has several possible guesses: a Letter when there is nothing better, a Space if there is at least one letter in the last word and it hasn't been guessed during this cycle, a Word if the last word in the Message is long enough and there are some matches, and the same for the Sentence. Also, the Guesser needs some way to represent that there are no more guesses possible, not even any more letters. Where should we put these rules? We should put them as close as we can to the objects that they apply to!

That means putting the rules and their evaluation into various dictionaries that hold Guesses. Matching the Blackboard pattern's roles to our design objects, the Guesser plays the role of Control, GuessDictionaries are KnowledgeSources, and the Message is the Blackboard they all query (see Figure 6-20).

Each GuessDictionary is asked by the Guesser to check the Message and make a bid. The Guesser looks at all the GuessDictionaries' Bids, selects the Guess from the highest Bid, and returns it to the Message-Builder as the best guess. Decisions made by the Guesser are limited to evaluating and choosing the highest bid. The real intelligence is distributed among the dictionaries.

Instead of adding their results directly to the Blackboard, each KnowledgeSource instead returns its bid to the Guesser. In our design, a Bid knows its value and its proposed Guess. You notice that we've slightly modified the Blackboard's roles and responsibilities as we adapted this pattern to our design. We've done so because the Guesser's responsibility isn't to update the Message directly. Instead, it needs to return the best guess when asked so that the guess can be

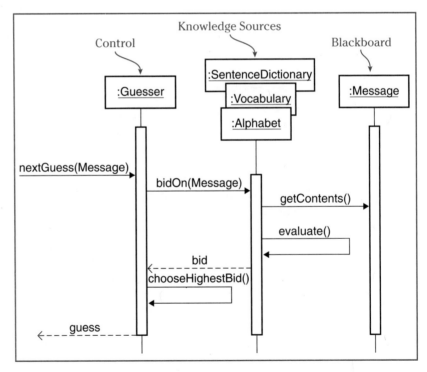

Figure 6-20
*Guessing uses a Blackboard architecture.*

presented to the user. Only when the user selects a Guess will the MessageBuilder add her selected Guess to the message. We've had to adapt the general roles and collaborations described by the Blackboard pattern to suit our specific design situation.

The final design of the MessageBuilder is now pretty simple. We've really pushed out most of the work to objects that the Message-Builder collaborates with (see Figure 6-21). When it hears the timer tick, the MessageBuilder passes the current Message to the Guesser and asks it for the next guess. It gets back a Letter, Word, or Sentence, but it doesn't know exactly what kind of thing it is. It only knows that it is a Guess. So it gives the Guess to the Presenter, which voices it to the user. If she selects it, the MessageBuilder is notified, and the MessageBuilder asks this Guess, whatever it is, to add itself to the Message.

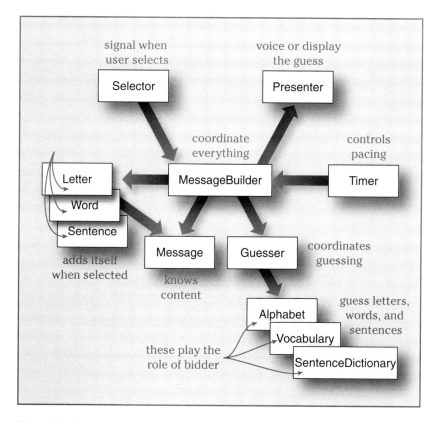

Figure 6-21
*The Build a Message control center, delegates to the Guesser, Guess, and Message.*

The MessageBuilder is a pure coordinator. This approach is quite different from our initial one. Control and decision making have been removed from the MessageBuilder. But where have they gone? Actually, we've given responsibilities to objects that the MessageBuilder collaborates with. And in the process, we've defined away the need for complex decisions based on explicit states maintained by the MessageBuilder. The MessageBuilder simply coordinates guessing and adds guesses to the Message—but it does so by delegating. Dictionaries will have to know some things about the current state of the message in order to offer a bid, but those decisions are localized and pretty simple, too. Decisions that before rested with the MessageBuilder are now accomplished as a side effect of choosing the highest bid, presenting it to the user, and having her Guesses add themselves to the Message. Because each different Guess knows how to add itself to a Message, the decision on how to update a message has been replaced with explicit responsibilities of Guess objects for doing the right thing when asked.

## Designing a Similar Control Center: Can We Be Consistent?

You can't always repeat collaboration patterns. By their nature, some design problems don't lend themselves to regular, consistent solutions. Sometimes, collaborations are prickly, and the rough edges in the problem will be reflected in the solution.

When you develop a simple and effective control architecture for a given system task, you instinctively try to fit similar tasks to the same style. However, some applications aren't regular and consistent; each use case is slightly different, so no common pattern for designing a use case controller emerges, no matter how hard you push. If objects and their patterns of collaboration are too dissimilar, don't try to fit them into the same mold. However, if things seem similar enough—if the objects involved and the patterns of collaboration are close—you might be able to refactor responsibilities and readjust collaborations to make them more similar than they might initially appear. You won't know until you try hard to see how similar things are.

Can the objects involved in the "Send a Message" use case fit the same roles and use the same collaboration patterns established by objects in "Build a Message"? Or do we need an entirely different control style? Let's compare the candidates involved in each use case and see what's alike and what's different. Here are the objects involved in "Build a Message":

- In the presentation layer:

    — Presenter—voices the guesses to the user
    — Selector—notifies the MessageBuilder of user actions

- In the application services layer:

  — Timer—controls the pacing of the presentation of guesses

  — Guesser—serves up the best guess

  — MessageBuilder—coordinates the events and responses

- In the domain layer:

  — Guess—when selected, adds itself to the Message

  — Letter, Word, Sentence—all play the role of a Guess

  — GuessDictionary—makes a best guess based on the Message

  — Alphabet, Vocabulary, SentenceDictionary—all play the role of a GuessDictionary

  — Bid—associates a bid value with a particular Guess

  — Message—structures the series of selections

The "Build a Message" task ends when the user spells the "send the message" command (the two-letter word SE). Then a new task and a new group of objects take over. When the software recognizes SE as a command word, it needs to build the community of objects: objects to coordinate the activities of building the list of destinations and, when the addressing is complete, to send the message to those destinations (see Figure 6-22).

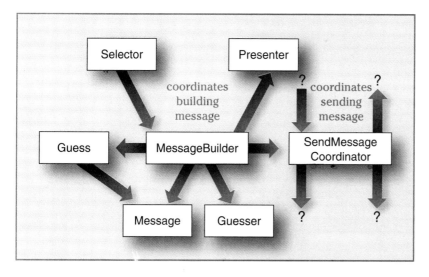

Figure 6-22

*Control transfers from one control center to another. We'd like to design related control centers to work in a similar fashion.*

Again, as an initial placeholder in our design, we invent a control center (and a control object, the SendMessageCoordinator) to monitor the user's actions and to coordinate the presentation of the addresses. If we can, we'd like it to follow a delegated style (see Figure 6-23).

As this controller fetches destinations from the business layer's AddressBook and presents it to the user, the user chooses what she hears. Here is the initial list of candidates involved:

- In the presentation layer:

    — Presenter—voices the destinations to the user

    — Selector—notifies the SendMessageController of address selections

- In the application services layer:

    — Timer—controls the pacing of the presentation of destinations

    — SendMessageCoordinator—controls activities in building a destination list and sending the message

- In the domain layer:

    — AddressBook—knows all the possible destinations

    — EmailAddress—knows a recipient's user name and domain

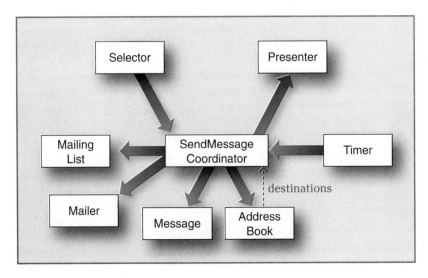

Figure 6-23
*Send a Message control is more centralized than the Build a Message control center design.*

— NetworkNode—knows a machine's network address

— DisplayScreen—knows the computer screen

— PagerAddress—knows a network address of a pager

— MailingList—structures the destinations that the user selects

— Message—knows the text to be sent

When the user makes her selections, the user interface signals our new controller and passes it the objects that correspond to her selections: the EmailAddresses, MailingLists, and so on. The controller then delegates to the MailingList the task of holding her selections. When she indicates that she is finished, the controller passes the MailingList and the Message to the Mailer for delivery.

We would like the pattern of collaboration to be consistent with those in "Build a Message." We can make a few simple checks to evaluate whether we can achieve a similar control design.

***When you're designing a control center, check to see whether the candidates involved are the same as those in a similar one.*** If so, there is a possibility that the pattern of collaborations can be made to look alike. The messages may be different, but the paths between the objects might be the same. But if any of the objects involved are playing more than one role, the collaboration patterns may be too different.

In the "Build a Message" task, the following objects are involved: Selector, Timer, MessageBuilder, Guesser, Presenter, Message, Guess, Letter, Word, Sentence, various Dictionaries, and Bid.

"Send a Message" uses Selector, Timer, SendMessageCoordinator, Presenter, Message, EmailAddress, NetworkNode, DisplayScreen, PagerAddress, MailingList, and AddressBook. Some of the previous objects are here, but some key objects are missing: the Guesser, the Guess, and all the various kinds of objects that play the role of a Guess.

There are similar coordination and control responsibilities: The SendMessageCoordinator must build a list of destinations and then send the message to them; the MessageBuilder must build a message. The collaborations between the presentation layer and the controllers looks identical, but the domain objects are entirely different. If objects that at first glance appear to be different are playing the same role, we might still make the control design mimic the style that we adopted earlier.

***Check whether responsibilities for actions are separate from responsibilities for information.*** When the doing is located in one or very few objects and the knowing is done by many others, control is centralized. The object that performs the actions will be constantly asking for the information that it needs.

As it currently stands, our "Send a Message" use case has only one area of activity: the SendMessageController. The other objects involved are simple structurers, information holders, or service providers. In contrast, the control center for "Build a Message" has spread responsibilities for constructing the message across the various Guess objects, and for guessing among the GuessDictionaries. Currently, there is none of that blending of action and information in the "Send a Message" domain objects.

***Check to see whether the stereotypes involved are similar.*** If so, there is a possibility that they will fit into the other collaboration's control architecture. But if one style uses lots of hybrids and while the other uses purer (and simpler) stereotypes, it will take redistribution of responsibilities to make it fit.

In our "Build a Message" use case control architecture, we had the following stereotypes:

- Timer—service provider
- Presenter—interfacer
- Selector—interfacer
- MessageBuilder—coordinator
- Guesser—service provider
- Guess—information holder/service provider
- Letter—information holder/service provider
- Word—information holder/service provider
- Sentence—information holder/service provider
- Message—structurer/service provider

Do the objects involved in "Send a Message" have similar roles? Or do we need an entirely different control style for this new part of the system? Our first stab at a candidate model resulted in these objects and stereotypes:

- Timer—service provider
- Presenter—interfacer

- Selector—interfacer
- SendMessageCoordinator—controller
- AddressBook—structurer
- EmailAddress—information holder
- NetworkNode—information holder
- DisplayScreen—interfacer
- PagerAddress—information holder
- Mailer—service provider
- MailingList—structurer

The stereotypes of objects involved in "Send a Message" reflect a concentration of action in the Mailer and the SendMessageCoordinator.

***When the roles are similar but not the same, look for common abstractions.*** Objects that appear to be different are sometimes similar in essential ways if we look for what they do in common. By expressing different responsibilities more generally, we can unify disjoint responsibilities and use a common pattern of interaction.

Taking all these tips into consideration, we look to

- Refactor the responsibilities out of the control center into domain objects to form smarter, hybrid stereotypes
- Use many of the same roles in our new collaboration
- Condense and unify the responsibilities and collaboration patterns

First, let's shift responsibilities for action out of the SendMessage-Coordinator to the information holders. In addition to representing an addressable location, we give each one the responsibility for doing something: adding its addressing information to the message. We also define a common role, a Destination, shared by all. A Destination represents all the different kinds of locations where Messages can be sent. The Message has a new responsibility too: knowing where it will be sent.

Next, let's see if we can find any abstraction that would simplify the collaborations and make it more like the control style for building a message. The most obvious abstraction missing is the notion of a Guesser and a Guess. Can we incorporate this idea into this part of the design? Yes, if we shift our perspective on the EmailAddress, NetworkNode, DisplayScreen, PagerAddress, and MailingList objects.

They, too, are kinds of guesses that the software presents to the user. Once she selects them, they are added to the list of addresses the message will be sent to. Furthermore, another Guesser could easily serve up Destination guesses. Voila! If we take this leap at unifying Destinations with Guesses that can be added to messages, our design can evolve toward the same delegated style.

In both cases, information holders have additional responsibilities. Letters, Words, and Sentences add themselves to a Message. Similarly, EmailAddresses, NeworkNodes, PagerAddresses, Display-Screens, and MailingLists add their corresponding destination to the Message. They are hybrid information holder/service providers. The "Send a Message" control center now resembles the distribution of responsibilities in the "Build a Message" use case (see Figure 6-24).

Unifying a responsibility can mean making a more general statement of that responsibility.

When the user finishes addressing the Message, the SendMessage Coordinator can delegate all responsibility for delivering the Message to the Mailer. The Mailer will in turn collaborate with the Message and its various Destinations to send the Message.

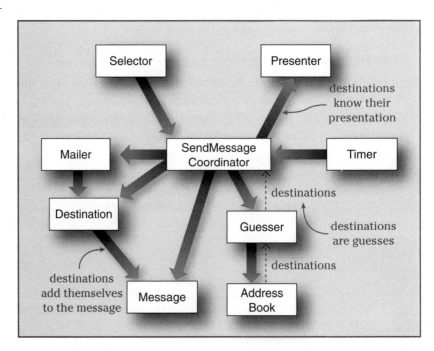

Figure 6-24
*Objects outside the control center take on more responsibility when we make the Send a Message control center similar to the Build a Message control center.*

## SUMMARY

Developing a control style means deciding how objects assigned responsibilities for controlling action within a control center—objects stereotyped as controllers or coordinators—interact with and direct others' actions. Adopting a particular style narrows your choices. Repeating it makes your design consistent. Control style is governed by how decision making and control behaviors are distributed. Control styles come in three major forms with several variations. Decisions can be

- Centralized
- Delegated to objects outside the control center
- Spread across many objects with no obvious centers of control

When you design collaborations, look for important control centers and choose the best control style for each. If you are trying to be consistent, make similar things work alike. The clarity and simplicity of your design depend on your ability to refactor responsibilities, invent roles, and define common patterns of collaboration so that like things work in similar ways.

Often, the decisions made by a controller depend on information and services provided by objects in its surrounding neighborhood. So the neighborhoods must be designed accordingly to provide the right information and take appropriate action.

We suggest that you select a control style suited to the task at hand. Choose centralized control when the decisions are few, simple, and related to a single task. Delegate control when the work or decision making can be broken into smaller subresponsibilities and when each subresponsibility has clearly different semantics or requires a different context. Look for ways to use patterns to simplify your design choices, as long as they match your design goals. The State pattern removes decisions into separate state objects, simplifying the design of a controller and creating a clustered control center. As you develop decision makers and their collaborators, strive to create a design having moderately intelligent, collaborating objects.

Designing a control center takes time and effort. You many not get it right the first time, especially if you don't know beforehand which responsibilities will require complex decisions. Designing a delegated control style generally requires careful thought and effort. But the payoffs are worth it, especially when the problem is complex.

The most startling result may be that decision making can be eliminated simply by making objects responsible for doing the right thing,
based on what kind of thing they are. Polymorphism really simplifies
a design!

# Chapter 7

## Describing Collaborations

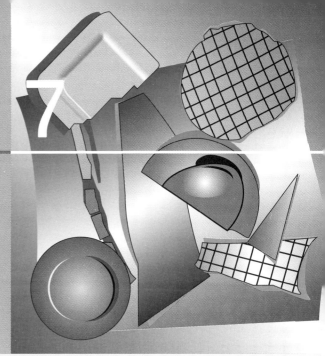

Francis Galton, a 19th century geneticist, remarked, "It often happens that after being hard at work, and having arrived at results that are perfectly clear and satisfactory to myself, when I try to express them . . . I feel that I must begin by putting myself upon quite another intellectual plane. I have to translate my thoughts into a language that does not run very evenly with them." We, too, experience a shift when we move from informal CRC card modeling to more formal descriptions of collaborations and interaction sequences. Sometimes we need to paint a broad picture of collaborators; at other times we need to offer quite exact explanations. When our models get more detailed, we must change our level of abstraction. We're presenting a more concrete view of our design.

## TELLING COLLABORATION STORIES

As you design the way objects collaborate, you will draw many rough sketches. You won't keep much of this white board art, but sometimes you tidy things up, make your collaborations presentable, and show them to others. You want to explain how things work—to describe the interplay of objects as they collectively accomplish system responsibilities. You need to tell a story.

During early design, collaboration stories are less precise and more evocative. You may have started with CRC cards and now want to design specific interactions. So you run through a few scenarios, role-playing some fairly intricate collaborations with your teammates. Afterward, your team asks you to draw diagrams to illustrate the design. How much detail should you include? A lot of things were mentioned during role-playing, and not all of them seem to fit neatly on a diagram. Are there things you should definitely highlight? Should certain things be left out?

The further along you are, the more you know. So you can show and describe more things—if it's appropriate. You can retell a simple collaboration story, embellishing certain parts while leaving others understated.

Maybe you want to tell how your design supports key use cases. After people get the gist of these, they should be able extrapolate. There must be a way to condense information and present it so that your readers don't get overwhelmed. How can you avoid creating lots of very similar diagrams?

Perhaps you drew diagrams that illustrated "happy path" scenarios. But people want to know how exceptional conditions are handled. What happens when happy paths aren't followed? Your colleagues won't really believe that your design works until you show them. Should you add these exception-handling details to your initial drawings, or draw new ones? Is there some way to explain how exceptional conditions are handled without drawing lots of new diagrams or adding complexity to existing ones?

Perhaps you want to explain to newcomers the key aspects of your design—the subsystems, their responsibilities, and general patterns of collaboration. You also want to introduce some important objects and put them through their paces. So you explain your CRC card model and draw several sequence diagrams that illustrate a few typical collaborations. But there's more that you'd like to explain. Is there a way to explain some alternatives you considered and rejected without describing them in any great depth?

A story can be more or less involved, depending on what needs to be said and how complex the interactions are. The best way to communicate any aspect of a collaboration depends on what you want to emphasize.

## A STRATEGY FOR DEVELOPING A COLLABORATION STORY

As you can see, your intent in presenting any story varies widely. Sometimes you want to show things; many times you also want to briefly explain them. Mostly, you want to get your ideas across effectively and compactly. You don't want to leave out the important points or lose people in too many details. A story is meaningful if it tells people what they want to know in a form they can easily digest. Often, multiple forms are needed; no one picture, diagram, or written description tells all.

One tool that should be part of your design and storytelling repertoire is UML. UML, or the Unified Modeling Language, is an industry-standard visual language for describing object designs. In UML, several different diagrams can be drawn. We won't cover UML in any great depth because that is the subject of other books. We will, however, touch on those parts of it that are useful to illustrate collaborations. Specifically, we'll explain how to describe collaboration relationships and specific interaction sequences. We'll discuss how to draw subsystems, collaboration diagrams, sequence diagrams, and collaborations. With these diagrams you can show collaborations at different levels of abstraction and in greater or lesser detail.

The Unified Modeling Language describes standard diagramming notations and their meaning. The UML symbols and diagrams are readily understood. UML is a visual language for describing designs; it is up to you to use it effectively.

Before you launch into developing your story, briefly consider what you'd like to accomplish. Here is a basic plan for developing any collaboration story:

- Establish its scope, depth, and tone.
- List the items you want it to cover.
- Decide how detailed your explanations should be.
- Choose the appropriate forms for telling your story.
- Tell it, draw it, describe it.
- Organize your story.
- Revise, clarify, and expand as needed.

Be sure you know what you are trying to communicate and who needs to understand your story. Establish the appropriate scope, depth, and tone of your story as well as point to places that deserve special emphasis. You will make more informed decisions as you craft your story if you know your reasons for telling it.

## ESTABLISHING SCOPE, DEPTH, AND TONE

Your scope—how much or how little territory you cover and how comprehensively you cover it—depends on your goals. Many stories have a narrow scope and limited depth. Perhaps you need to explain how your design supports a use case or to illustrate some collaborations. Often, stories are dashed off quickly to impart knowledge or get reactions. Their tone is informative but brief. Explanations (if offered at all) are intentionally sketchy. After all, you are around to answer questions. The focus is on illustrating collaborations and not on explaining them at any length. Stories that need to be understood without your helpful presence likely require some minimal written explanation in addition to one or more drawings.

> After a role-playing session, you decide to draw collaboration diagrams to illustrate each scenario you discussed. Because you didn't get to designing message signatures, you just draw collaboration diagrams with message names and returned values (where they matter). You list the issues and ideas that were brought up, too.

The tone of any story can be adjusted to be more or less formal, authoritative, precise, comprehensive, and instructive. It is up to you to set the tone by adjusting it along several dimensions.

You can always adjust your story's tone and broaden or narrow its scope. At first, your goal may be to get buy-in. You present issues and options along with your collaborations. After you've nailed down answers, you illustrate and explain instead of merely propose and question. You go into slightly more depth. At other times, you *are* writing for the record and want to be as precise as you can. But you don't want to overwhelm your readers with details.

Diagram choices, as well as word choices, help set the tone. Sequence diagrams are more formal than collaborations diagrams. Both serve a nearly identical purpose. There are times when informality is preferred, especially when you want to throw out a rough idea for comment and review. At other times more formal presentations are in order. But don't think that every part of your story needs to be told in the same way or to the same depth. CRC cards are informal, but they convey information about an object's role and responsibilities that cannot be found on either sequence or collaboration diagrams. Diagrams as well as cards are valuable parts of a collaboration story. CRC cards informally state what an object knows and does. These responsibilities can be hard to infer from looking at more formal method signatures on class diagrams.

Formal and informal descriptions and diagrams all have a place in a collaboration story. Precision does not go hand in hand with formality.

Sequence and collaboration diagrams can be drawn with differing degrees of precision. It is perfectly "legal" to leave messages unlabeled or to get highly exact and show message signatures, return values, branches, and looping, all dressed up with accurate timing marks. Your story can be more or less formal, precise, or comprehensive—depending on your goals.

## LISTING WHAT YOU WILL COVER

If your story is a comprehensive one, there will be many things to say. Even a simple story may have several points. List everything that comes to mind, whether it is big or small or it overlaps with something already on your list. Don't be concerned with how items on your list relate. Also, list things you want to exclude from discussion.

For example, if you are illustrating a specific use case, you may want to explain only a happy path scenario—what actions take place when nothing goes wrong. Even so, consider how much you want to tell and what the main points are.

---

### Key Points for "Make a Payment" Collaboration

- Use a sequence diagram—keep it simple (not a lot of adornments).
- Point out calls to backend banking system that could be bottlenecks.
- Start with a well-formed request (don't explain UI details).
- Relate the diagram to the "Make a Payment" use case.

---

Don't worry about how to organize your story or the items on your list until you've written a large part of it. Perhaps you need to develop several subplots, explain each one, and then weave them together. Even if your story is short and sweet, you won't know the best way to present it until you've gotten it down. Worry about organization after your content is in place.

## DECIDING ON THE LEVEL OF DETAIL

The same story can be told in different levels of detail. Your choice of level (or levels) should be based on how much you know about a collaboration and how much you want to reveal. There are at least these different views of a collaboration:

- A bird's-eye view of system components and subsystems showing the overall architecture and general collaboration paths
- A view showing only participants in some collaboration (and omitting all interaction)
- A sequence of interactions among collaborators
- An in-depth view that explains how objects interact under exceptional conditions or that goes into more details
- A focused view that ignores some aspects in order to concentrate on specific collaborators and their interactions
- An implementation view
- A generalized view that illustrates how to adapt a collaboration

After you've decided what to tell, plot the best way to tell it.

## Showing a Bird's-Eye View

In UML, a package can organize any arrangement of design elements—from a set of classes to everything designed to support a number of use cases. When labeled with a fork or <<subsystem>> designation, a package represents a subsystem.

You don't have to stick to describing collaborations among individual objects. At the highest level, you can show how a system is organized into subsystems and illustrate their collaborations. A subsystem in UML looks like a file folder with either a fork symbol or the word *subsystem* enclosed in double angle brackets (see Figure 7-1). The file folder symbol is called a *package* symbol. It can be used to designate a subsystem. To say that one subsystem depends on another (shown by a dashed line with an open arrow pointing to the dependent) means that the dependent likely uses services defined by that subsystem.

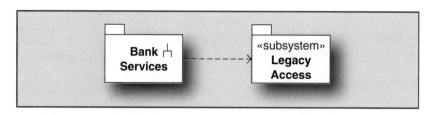

Figure 7-1
*The UML package symbol can be used to represent subsystems. A dependency is drawn as a dashed line ending with a stick arrow.*

Paths of communication between subsystems can be shown more or less precisely. For example, you can illustrate precisely which interfaces are offered by each subsystem and which clients use them. An interface symbol can be drawn rather imprecisely as a lollipop figure (a circle attached to a line), or more precisely as a box with two compartments (see Figure 7-2).

Even if you're looking at a system from 30,000 feet, you can choose from among several degrees of precision to describe subsystem collaborations. If you've just begun, you may choose to show only general paths of collaboration. At a more detailed level, you can enumerate the operations supported by each subsystem interface (see Figure 7-3). You can always revise drawings and add interfaces after they've been designed.

If you wish you can explain even more about how a subsystem is designed. You can draw a subsystem that is divided into three compartments. These compartments describe interfaces and explain how they are realized by classes within the subsystem (see Figure 7-4). Most of the time you don't need to be so precise.

## Showing Collaborators Only

You may want to include a high-level explanation of your objects' responsibilities and collaborators in your story, so use CRC cards. You can transfer these cards to a high-level design document. But what next? Sometimes, looking at specific message sequences gets in the way of seeing the potential pathways between collaborators. To highlight these pathways, you can illustrate your CRC cards with a

How many diagrams you draw and how precisely you draw them should be based on your project's goals and design process. Use diagrams to communicate ideas. Diagrams hastily drawn on white boards are likely to be less precise than those drawn in a tool. Consider how much information your intended audience really needs to see before adding it.

If you want to paint collaborations with broad brush strokes, stop short of describing specific messages between objects or identifying classes. Instead, emphasize paths of communication between key collaborators.

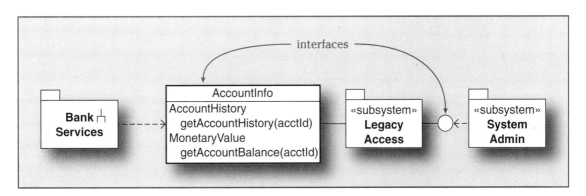

Figure 7-2
*Interfaces can be drawn showing more or less detail.*

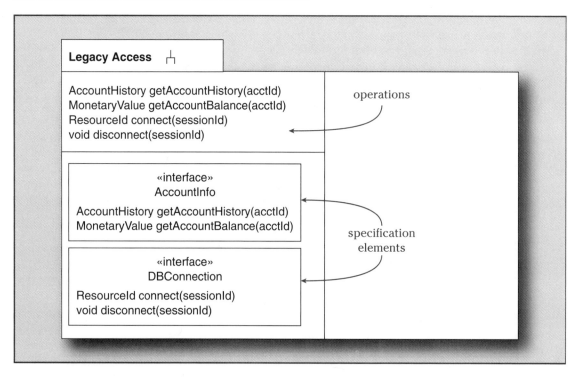

Figure 7-3
*A subsystem symbol can be divided into compartments. Publicly accessible operations and interfaces can be defined.*

simple UML collaboration diagram. In its simplest form, a collaboration diagram includes only objects and their collaboration relationships (see Figure 7-5).

A straight line, called a link, establishes a relationship between two collaborators. One thing that isn't apparent from the simple drawing in Figure 7-5 is who is collaborating with whom. Are two linked objects both sending messages to each other? Most likely not. Probably the collaboration is only one-way. To make this perfectly clear, you can put a visibility arrow at the end of the link pointing to a collaborator that is seen by the object that uses its services (see Figure 7-6).

Extra precision can illuminate, but it can be constraining, too. If you add visibility arrows to some links, people will expect them everywhere. But what if you don't yet know who is collaborating with whom? If you don't know something, don't specify it. You can always redraw any diagram to reflect current reality. If you decide that two

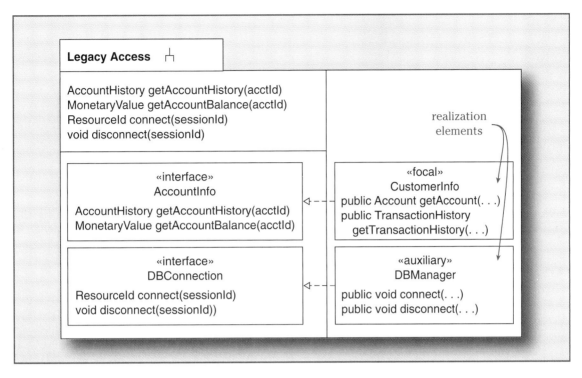

Figure 7-4
*A subsystem's interfaces can be mapped to their realization. Not all classes are shown.*

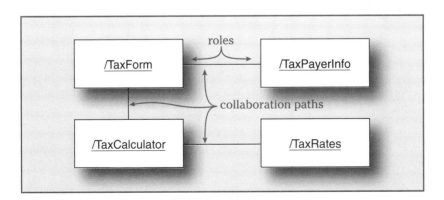

Figure 7-5
*A simple UML collaboration diagram shows roles and collaboration paths.*

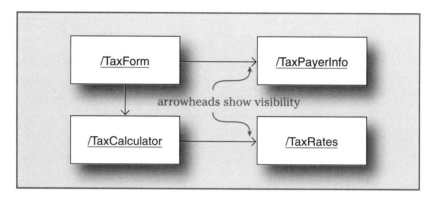

Figure 7-6
*The collaboration diagram can be drawn to show object visibility.*

objects are co-collaborators, you can draw arrows on both ends of a link. But don't feel compelled to add these details just because UML lets you.

The degree of precision you use on a diagram should be a conscious choice. Even if you do know who is collaborating with whom, you need not specify it diagrammatically. After all, this isn't your only means of explanation. A collaboration diagram can include more or less detail and still be accurate (but less precise). People will probably understand your collaborations without this extra precision.

Even collaborators can be labeled more or less precisely. You can distinguish between a role and an object. The way you do so is subtle: The name of a role is preceded by a backslash character ("/"); the name of an object is not (see Figure 7-7). You can both name an object and identify its role.

Should you wish to be even more precise, you can specify the class that implements the object or role (see Figure 7-8). You designate the class by following its role and instance name with a colon and class name (":" class name).

Of course, this may be far more precision than you need. If you've created a role that can be assumed by objects belonging to different classes, you have no need to ever specify its class. Or if you've determined a role but haven't yet mapped it to its implementation, designating its class is premature.

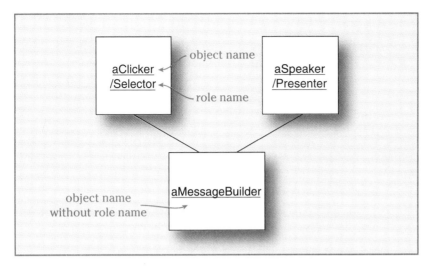

Figure 7-7
*You can specify both role names and object names on a collaboration diagram.*

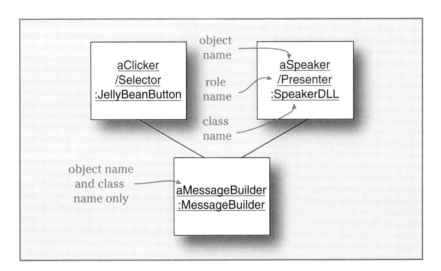

Figure 7-8
*Collaborations can show object names, role names, and class names.*

## Showing a Sequence of Interactions Among Collaborators

Sequence diagrams and collaboration diagrams can show roughly the same things, and many tools let you transform from one form to another without losing information. Which form you choose is a matter of style and emphasis.

A collaboration diagram, drawn with an appropriate degree of precision, sets the stage for illustrating subsequent interactions. These specific interactions can be illustrated either with another, more elaborate collaboration diagram or with a sequence diagram. To show sequence, you can add lines with arrows next to collaboration links on a collaboration diagram (see Figure 7-9). Each line represents a specific message between two collaborators. The arrow points from client to collaborator. Sequence is indicated by numbers that label message names. If you want to show a different sequence, you draw another collaboration diagram.

As an alternative, you can use a sequence diagram (see Figure 7-10). It, too, can be used to illustrate a specific interaction. Objects are located along the top. Their lifelines are drawn as a vertical line. Instance creation and destruction can be shown. When an instance is created, its lifeline appears; when it is destroyed, it terminates. Messages are drawn as lines with arrows, similar to those on the collaboration diagram. But they are not numbered. Sequence simply proceeds from top to bottom.

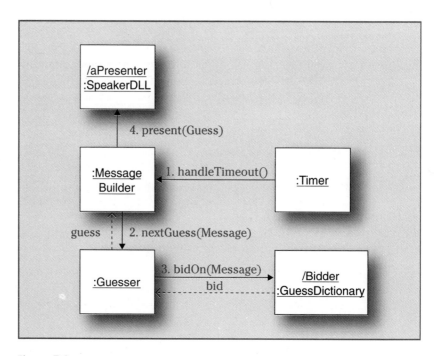

Figure 7-9
*A UML collaboration diagram emphasizes relations among objects.*

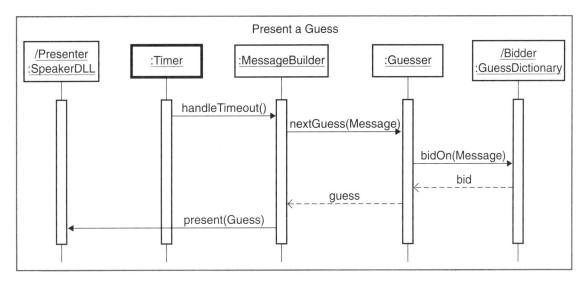

Figure 7-10
*A UML sequence diagram emphasizes the sequencing of messages.*

## Showing an In-Depth View

Numerous things can be shown in an interaction sequence: branching, object creation, destruction, iteration, asynchronous communication, active objects (those that represent a flow of control), even recursion. If you need to visually represent complex interactions, you can get very elaborate.

If an interaction involves complex decisions, you can dress up a diagram to explain alternative paths (see Figure 7-11). Instead of marching along in strict sequence, flow proceeds along a chosen path. Expressions, called guard expressions and enclosed within brackets, specify which path will be taken. A guard is an expression that must evaluate to true before the message can be sent. UML doesn't specify the language for guard expressions, so you are free to use plain text, mathematical expression, or even pseudo-code.

In an application in which timing constraints must be met, sequence diagrams can be annotated with timing marks, event identifiers, and timing expressions (see Figure 7-12). To draw a timing mark that describes how much time has elapsed, you draw a vertical bar with a time value expression. A timing expression, like a guard condition, can be written more or less informally. If events that invoke a message are added to a diagram, timing expressions can use them.

"Sequence diagrams aren't depictions of precise execution semantics; they are statements of desired communications under a limited set of conditions which may never occur in a normal running program."

—David Harel

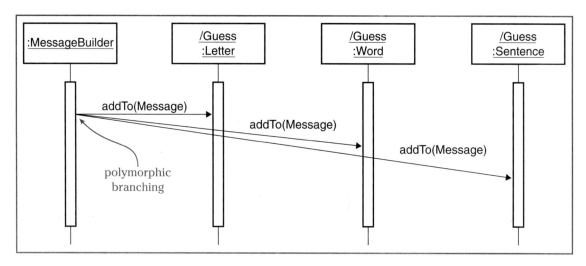

Figure 7-11
*A UML sequence diagram can show polymorphic messaging.*

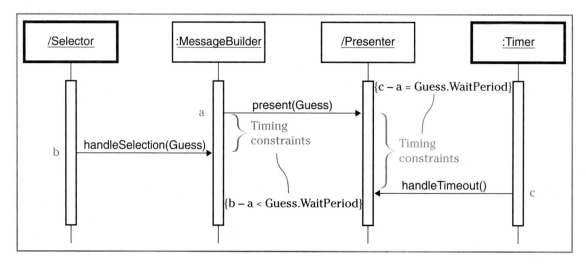

Figure 7-12
*You can add timing constraints to a sequence diagram.*

A *concurrent* application has more than one flow of control—that is, more than one set of interactions can be happening logically at once. You can describe interactions for a concurrent application using only these few additional UML constructs: active objects, asynchronous messages, and broadcast messages (see Figure 7-13). In UML, a

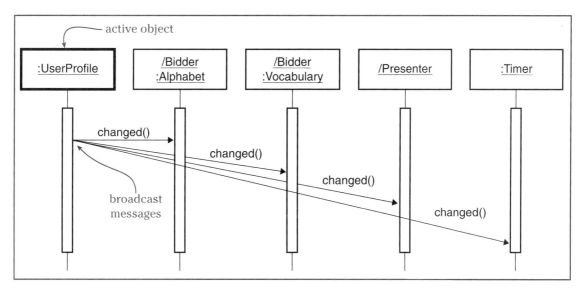

Figure 7-13
*Sequence diagrams can highlight active objects and show message broadcasting.*

class can be designated as being active. An active class is a class whose instances are active objects. When an instance of an active class is created, its associated flow of control starts, too. When the instance is destroyed, its flow of control terminates. An active class can create instances that are either heavyweight (processes) or lighter weight (threads). A process represents a flow that executes concurrently with other processes, whereas a thread executes concurrently with other threads in the same process. In a system with both active and inactive objects, both kinds of objects communicate with one another. In UML diagrams, an active object is drawn with a bold border. Messages can be sent asynchronously or can be broadcast to a number of objects.

> "Building a system that encompasses multiple flows of control is hard. Not only do you have to decide how best to divide work across concurrent active objects . . . you also have to devise the right mechanisms for communication and synchronization . . . . For that reason, it helps to visualize the way these flows interact."
>
> —Grady Booch

## Showing a Focused Interaction

At times, it is desirable to treat part of the system as a black box whose contents are purposely hidden. This technique lets you focus on a part that is of particular interest that you want to describe. Perhaps you want to show how user actions stimulate some part of your design into action. In this case, you remove most UI details, ignore the myriad objects in a screen, and assume that those necessary objects can be assembled and play their interfacer roles. Yes, you are removing a lot of detail. This detail will have to be dealt with fairly soon. But you don't want to explain those objects if your story is trying to emphasize what happens *after* the user clicks the Save button.

> To remove detail about UI interactions, ignore individual keystrokes, button clicks, or what happens when the cursor moves in and out of focus. You can represent requests as being UI-independent, if you like. Instead of notification of button click events in a particular messaging protocol defined by a particular UI implementation, they can be logically shown as requests to "make a payment" or "view account history" or "save a file."
>
> When you draw a sequence diagram with this focus, you aren't really lying about the UI. Instead, you are abstracting away its details so that you can concentrate on what happens when your system receives notification of an important UI event. Even if your design must update the UI, these details, too, can be summarized with a message at the same level of abstraction: "present confirmation" or "present account history" or "return control to the user."
>
> UI details are elided for a reason. You are confident that you can construct a lower-level model of the UI using an arrangement of objects (even though this can be quite a lot of work). But this is not the focus of your collaboration story (see Figure 7-14).

## Showing an Implementation View

If you are documenting something that is already implemented, you want to be very accurate; what you see on a diagram is precisely what has been coded. But even so, your diagrams include fewer details than are found in code. Diagrams are not executable specifications. As a consequence, unless you explicitly label it, it will be impossible to tell whether a diagram illustrates a proposed or a working solution. Make this perfectly clear in your diagram's title. And include specific facts—message signatures, significant return values, branches, and interaction. But don't show everything. It is up to you to decide what deserves emphasis in a diagram. There's always code to read.

## Showing How to Adapt a Collaboration

You may have designed collaborators to be configurable—to be adapted by replacing one collaborator with another, by setting

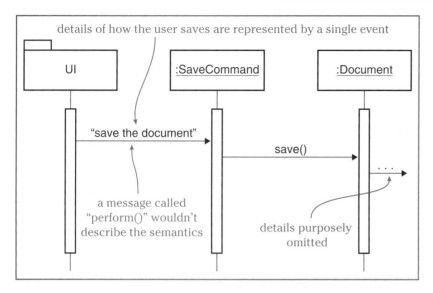

Figure 7-14
*A user event from the UI subsystem starts the collaboration.*

certain conditions or parameters, or by plugging in new objects to complement existing ones. To explain how to adapt a collaboration, you really need to explain three things: how the current design works, which aspects are adaptable, and how to make these adaptations.

Start by concretely explaining how your design works. After you've done this, explain how to adapt your design. If your adaptation is simple, you can use the techniques we've already presented. You can also provide a simple step-by-step description of how to make an adaptation.

---

### To Add a New Kind of Guess

1. Define a class that implements the Guess interface. This type of object must know contents, formatted for both display and speech, know how long to wait before continuing with another guess, and be able to add itself to a message. Specifically, it must implement these methods:

```
public String displayableText()
public String speakableText()
public String getContent()
public Duration waitTime()
void addTo(Message m)
```

*Continues*

---

> 2. Define a class that implements the Bidder interface. This type
> of object will contain all of the corresponding Guess objects
> and determine which is most relevant to the current message.
> Then wrap up the chosen Guess and the numeric bid value in a
> Bid object. Specifically, it must implement
>
> ```
> Bid bidOn(Message m)
> ```

To emphasize objects and collaborations that are adaptable on a diagram, use notes to tag places where new collaborators could be plugged in (see Figure 7-15).

You may have developed a pattern of collaborating roles instead of collaborating objects. Instead of being adapted, this collaboration must be *adopted* (or instantiated) by designing multiple objects that fill these specific roles and plug into a stylized collaboration architecture. To communicate how a generalizable collaboration works, at the very least you must describe each role and discuss its specific responsibilities and collaborations. Of course, there is much more to describing a full-blown pattern than what we outline here.

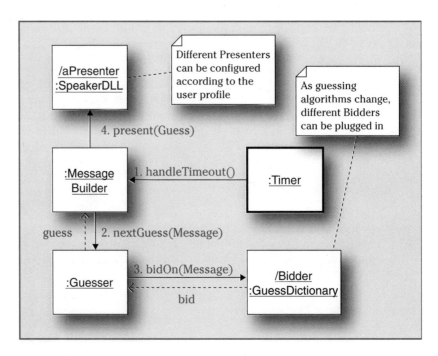

Figure 7-15
*Notes can show where collaborators are configurable.*

You can use a UML drawing, called a collaboration, to illustrate a generalizable grouping of collaborating roles (see Figure 7-16). Dashed lines are drawn from the named collaboration to each participant. Lines are labeled with role names.

This drawing is very similar to a high-level collaboration diagram but serves a narrower purpose. You can illustrate how a particular implementation plugs in and realizes the collaboration by showing how specific classes generalize the roles in the collaboration (see Figure 7-17).

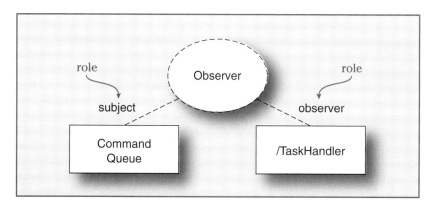

Figure 7-16
*The Observer pattern has two roles: a subject and an observer.*

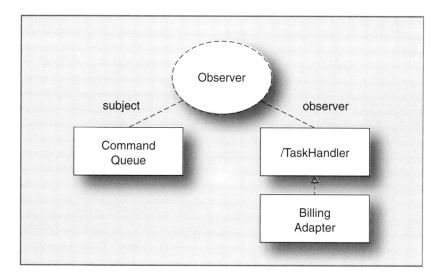

Figure 7-17
*A collaboration diagram can show objects that realize the Observer pattern roles.*

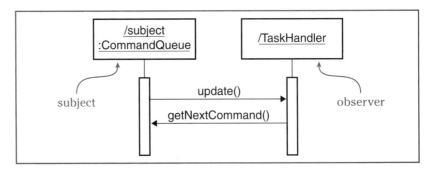

Figure 7-18
*Observer role interactions can be shown in a sequence diagram.*

You can identify roles (not just objects and their classes) on a sequence or collaboration diagram, too (see Figure 7-18). Thus, it is simple to explicitly illustrate how roles in a collaboration interact.

## Where UML Diagrams Fall Short

There is only so much you can piece together by studying a sequence diagram. Looking at one is like observing a butterfly in flight. You can see what flowers the butterfly visits and in what order, but you won't know why it chooses to visit one flower over another or how it affects a flower. Unless there is some other explanation, you won't know the effect a message has on the object receiving it.

Still, the best way to "see" isn't always with a diagram. Consider complex algorithms. It's hard enough to figure out that sorting is going on by reading a sequence diagram, let alone discriminate the key aspects of the algorithm. A sequence of messages doesn't illustrate any side effects. So you can't see what happens when an object is added to a hashtable or when a buffer overflows. And unless you add explicit annotations, you won't know what conditions cause branching, iteration, or the successful completion of the algorithm. Algorithmic details are better expressed in words, pseudo-code, real code, a BNF-grammar, a state machine diagram, decision tables, or pictures that identify and illustrate the important aspects and characteristics of the algorithm (see Figures 7-19 through 7-23). This doesn't mean that you shouldn't draw a sequence diagram; it just won't explain these algorithmic details.

The algorithm for bubble sort consists of two nested loops. The inner loop traverses the array, comparing adjacent entries and swapping them if appropriate, while the outer loop causes the inner loop to make repeated passes. After the first pass, the largest element is guaranteed to be at the end of the array; after the second pass, the second largest element is in position, and so on. That is why the upper bound in the inner loop decreases with each pass; we don't have to revisit the end of the array.

Figure 7-19
*Text is often the best way to describe something.*

Consider the array 42,56,13,23

Let's start sorting.

**42,56**,13,23  no swap

42,**56,13**,23  swap

42,13,**56,23**  swap—end of 1st pass outer loop

**42,13**,23,56  swap

13,**42,23**,56  swap—end of 2nd pass outer loop

**13,23**,42,56  no swap—end of 3rd pass, sorted

Figure 7-20
*Visualizing the bubble at work demonstrates the algorithm clearly.*

Bubble Sort Code

```
class BubbleSorter
{
    void sort(int a[])
    {
        for (int i = a.length; --i>=0 ) {
            boolean swapped = false;
            for (int j = 0; j<i; j++ ) {
                if (a[j] > a[j+1]) {
                    int T = a[j];
                    a[j] = a[j+1];
                    a[j+1] = T;
                    swapped = true;
                }
            if (!swapped) return;
        }
    }
}
```

Figure 7-21
*Code makes the bubble sort algorithm clear . . . to a programmer.*

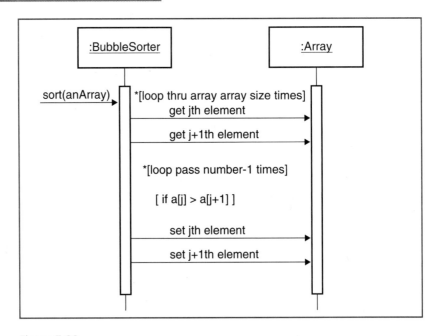

Figure 7-22
*A sequence diagram is not the best tool for documenting the bubble sort algorithm.*

Every message on a sequence diagram has equal visual significance. Nothing stands out as special unless you add a note or guard expression or write some commentary. What appears to be a recurring pattern may not be. Although the collaboration paths look identical, the messages vary. So, for example, if you want to emphasize how exceptions to a happy path scenario are handled, a table can be an extremely useful addition to your story (see Table 7-1). You can use a row in a table to describe specific information about each exception: a general description, where it is detected, and how it is resolved. You can even highlight, perhaps by shading their row, those exceptions that aren't recoverable.

Explaining these things on a sequence diagram alone would be difficult, if not impossible.

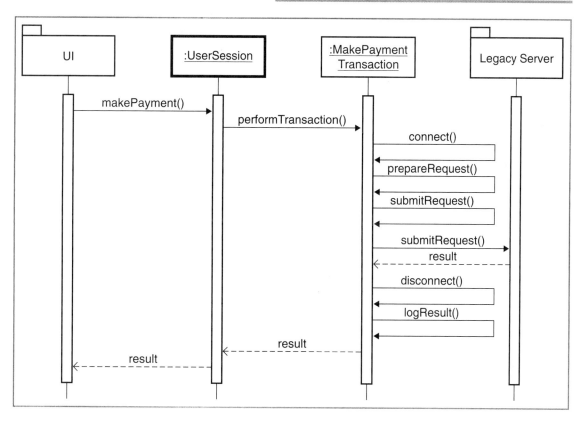

Figure 7-23
*Sequence diagrams are best used to show happy path interactions.*

Table 7-1 *A table explains online banking transaction exceptions and their impacts on the system and its users.*

| Exception or Error | Recovery Action | Effect on User |
|---|---|---|
| Connection is dropped between UI and domain server after transaction request is issued. | Transaction continues to completion. Instead of notifying user of status, transaction is just logged. User will be notified of recent (unviewed) transaction results on next login. | User session is terminated. User could've caused this by closing browser, or the system could have failed. Users will be notified of transaction status the next time they access the system. |
| Failure to write results of successful transaction to domain server log. | Administrator is alerted via console and e-mail alerts. Transaction information is temporarily logged to alternative source. If connections cannot be reestablished, the system restricts users to read only and account maintenance requests until transaction logging is reestablished. | Users can see an unlogged transaction in transaction history constructed from backend banking query but won't have it embellished with any notes they may have entered. |
| Connection dropped between domain server and backend bank access layer after request is issued. | Attempt to reestablish connection. If this fails after a configurable number of retries, transaction results are logged as "pending" and the user is informed that the system is momentarily unavailable . . . check in later. When connections are reestablished, status is acquired and logged. Further logins are prevented until backend access is reestablished. | User will be logged off with a notice that system is temporarily unavailable and will learn of transaction status on next login. |
| Backend banking request fails. | Error condition reported to user. Transaction fails. Failed transaction is logged. | User receives error notification but can continue using online services. |

## CHOOSING THE APPROPRIATE FORM

Drawings you created using a tool have a certain polish. They appear solid and finished; a design illustrated with them must be good, right? But they aren't the only way to communicate. Illustrations, charts, written explanations, tables, and CRC cards all have a place (see Table 7-2). Common sense tells us that any diagram should show less detail than can be found in code, and any written explanation should offer something more than can be found on CRC cards. This still leaves a lot of leeway.

Consider what you want your readers to learn by studying a particular collaboration story. Then decide how best to tell each part. Base your decisions on several factors: where you are in design, what you want to communicate, and which tools and how much time you have available. If you are just beginning, your collaboration stories probably aren't very elaborate. The further along you are, the more likely you are to include more detail.

To tell stories that have impact and present insights, you'll need to develop a wide range of expression that includes words, charts, CRC cards, UML diagrams, and other illustrations.

Table 7-2 *Many collaboration representations and options are available.*

| Goal | Simple Representation | Options |
|------|----------------------|---------|
| Describe responsibilities and collaborators. | Use CRC cards. | Transfer information on cards to a document. |
| Show collaboration relationships among objects. | Draw a simple collaboration diagram. | Add visibility links to make explicit who collaborates with whom. |
| Show paths of collaboration among subsystems. | Draw a subsystem diagram with dependencies. | To be more precise, add subsystem interfaces. |
| Illustrate an interaction sequence. | Draw a collaboration diagram. | To be more formal, draw a sequence diagram.<br><br>To explain how objects are affected, add a running commentary.<br><br>To explain interactions among subsystems, treat them as "big objects" and describe messages between them. |

*Continues*

Table 7-2 *Many collaboration representations and options are available. (Cont.)*

| Goal | Simple Representation | Options |
|------|----------------------|---------|
| Explain complex algorithms. | Create a visual animation or storyboard. | Pseudo-code.<br><br>Draw an interaction diagram and annotate it with information that explains branches and choices and makes algorithmic details more evident. |
| Describe detailed interactions. | Use either a collaboration or a sequence diagram. | Add timing marks, guards, branches, loops, recursive calls, and notes to the diagram.<br><br>Include a running commentary. |
| Describe design alternatives. | Write a brief description of alternatives and rationale for options chosen. | Additional sequence or collaboration diagrams that illustrate key alternatives. |
| Describe how to reconfigure a collaboration. | Define a collaboration.<br><br>Define responsibilities of configurable objects.<br><br>Draw a typical interaction sequence. On it, identify where configurable alternates can be plugged in. | Write a recipe describing a step-by-step procedure for configuring a collaboration.<br><br>Include examples or sample code. |

## TELL IT, DRAW IT, DESCRIBE IT: GUIDELINES

Joe Molloy, a graphics design teacher, says that writing and drawing use parallel strategies. Although your goal is probably not to become a talented writer or visual artist, you can apply Strunk and White's advice to describing *and* illustrating your collaboration stories.

Theodore Strunk and E.B. White wrote *The Elements Style* in 1935. Since then, countless writers have turned to this slim book for straightforward advice. Strunk and White's words ring true for software designers, too. Form, presentation, and content matter. The following guidelines for describing collaborations are based on the principles outlined in Strunk and White's book.

***Do not overwrite.*** Sure, you can keep written explanations brief and to the point, but what about drawings? If a picture is worth 1,000 words, are 10 pictures worth 10,000 words? Certainly not. Consider each drawing's purpose. Your goal should not be to use every UML feature in a diagram. Instead, draw at the level of detail your audience needs. If collaborations are similar, show a typical case first and then note how remaining ones differ. Draw representative interactions. Consider your readers' attention span as well as what you want to communicate.

***Do not overstate.*** Any explanation can include more or less information. Our advice: Don't tell more than what you believe at any given point in your design. Don't dress up a collaboration story with speculation. If you know only general paths of collaboration, don't show specific messages. If you know specific messages but not the arguments, don't invent arguments just to fill in the blanks. Be as specific as you can, but don't state more than you will feel comfortable defending in a review.

***Omit needless words.*** Stop short of telling everything. Keep your explanations to the point. There are ways to avoid clutter in technical writing. We mention a few particularly relevant techniques. Don't start a discussion with metatext—text that describes the text that follows. Don't pile on extra words or invent jargon; use simple language. Don't blindly fill in the blanks of a heavy-handed template; say what you want to say, and stop.

But how can you keep drawings simple without oversimplifying them? Too much clutter on a diagram will cause your readers to tune out, just as too many words will. Visual equivalents of needless words include the following:

- Values returned from message sends
- Internal algorithmic details
- Details of caching and lazy initialization
- Object creation and destruction

Sometimes, these details are important. If so, take exception to our guideline. Most of the time, however, they just add clutter. Show return values only when they affect or alter the message flow. Or, if you can't see how one object could possibly collaborate with another, perhaps show that it was returned earlier.

Omit details of how objects do low-level tasks. Stop short of explaining how preexisting objects work. Describe only how they are used by objects of your design; do not show their collaborations (unless they interact with your objects). Don't describe collaborations with primitive data types unless you really are trying to explain how a collection or string is used. These are probably implementation details.

A collaboration story, just like refactored code, improves whenever it is reworked for clarity.

**Revise and rewrite.** If people don't understand what you are saying, rewrite. If people don't understand a diagram, redraw it. If certain people want to see some things and others do not, draw two versions: an abridged one and an unabridged one. Sometimes, the same story needs to be told slightly differently to different audiences.

> A designer drew two views showing the same collaboration between subsystems. One view omitted the interface details, and the other included them. Developers who were going to use these subsystems' services wanted to know which interfaces to use. Developers who wanted to understand how their parts of the system were activated didn't want to see these details. It was simple enough to draw the same collaboration both ways. So that's what the designer did.

If a diagram becomes too complex, you can break it into smaller subdiagrams. UML lets you draw a dangling message arrow on one diagram (meaning that details aren't shown there) that can lead to a hanging message arrow in another diagram (see Figures 7-24a and 7-24b). To explain how these diagrams are linked, you'll need to add a note.

If a diagram is too simple, add missing details. But think before you pile them on. What was misunderstood? Was some internal detail unclear? If so, perhaps it is better explained in another form. Maybe your readers should be reading code to get these details. Attach an explanatory note instead of adding several low-level collaborators. These low-level messages might make the diagram too busy and might cause important collaborations to become lost in these new details.

When you're drawing rough sketches on a white board, use whatever form seems to fit your style (and the degree of precision you are striving for). White board collaboration drawings can be converted to any standard drawing format when they are redrawn in a tool.

**Do not affect a breezy manner.** Don't fudge on details. Are CRC cards too breezy? They are if you want to explain an interaction sequence. In that case, CRC cards don't go far enough. You are being breezy if you intentionally leave things understated, undrawn, or unexplained because you cannot be bothered or because you don't know the answer.

Just because things are hard to communicate or take time to draw, don't leave them unexplained. If you need to illustrate and explain things, too, don't worry about being redundant. Repeatedly stating things in a slightly different fashion adds emphasis. Condense your work only after you've clearly spelled things out. (See the earlier quideline on revising and rewriting.)

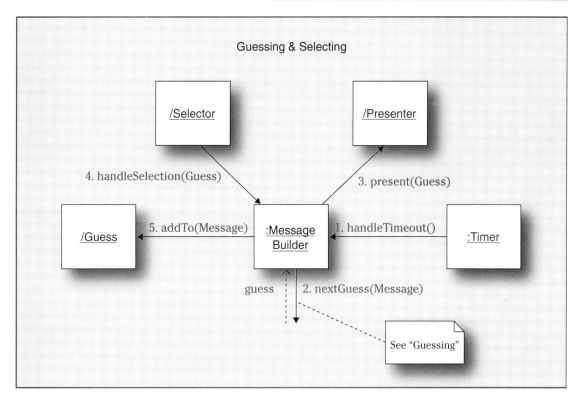

Figure 7-24a
*Dangling arrows can be used to link two diagrams.*

Don't arbitrarily limit your diagrams to a single page or to 10 or fewer objects. Stick with your story. You may have difficulty reproducing a large diagram drawn with a CASE tool on paper or on a Web page. But worry about that later. Get it down first, and then figure out how to present it.

***Be clear.*** If you choose the right form of expression, your collaborations will be more understandable. To emphasize message order, use a sequence diagram. Annotate it to show timing, branching, looping, return values, and many other things—if these things bring clarity to your design. If they cause confusion, perhaps you need to explain things, too. Add a running commentary alongside a sequence diagram, tool permitting, or write commentary in a text editor.

When you want to arrange collaborators in a pleasing fashion, choose a collaboration diagram. Emphasize which objects are important by

If you are focusing on interactions between domain objects, stick to a description of their interactions. Don't explain how database connections are established in order to store and retrieve them. This may be interesting, but why are you talking about this now?

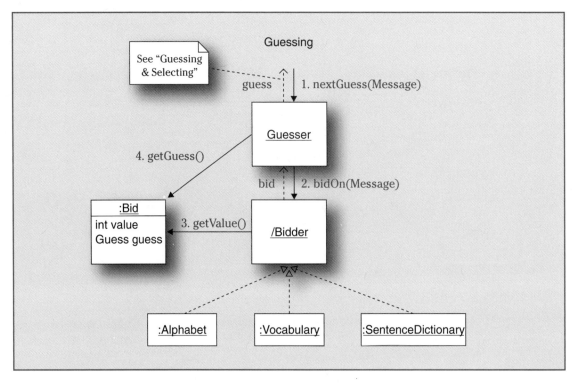

Figure 7-24b
*Hanging arrows can also be used to link two diagrams.*

placing them in the center. Place a controller in the middle to emphasize the delegation to objects surrounding it. Messages radiate from
it like spokes on a wheel. Put a coordinator in the middle and
arrange its collaborators around it (see Figure 7-25).

Or you can organize objects according to their position in a layered
architecture. This approach will let you see that messages follow a
layered communication pattern: flowing either between objects in a
given layer or from an object within a given layer to objects in adjacent layers. Whatever your strategy, try to arrange collaborators so
that people won't have to hunt for the next message in sequence.

To improve legibility, you can limit the number of objects and messages on a diagram. An interaction will be more understandable
when it shows a limited number of messages (25 or fewer) between a
limited number of participants (10 objects or fewer) with nominal
branching.

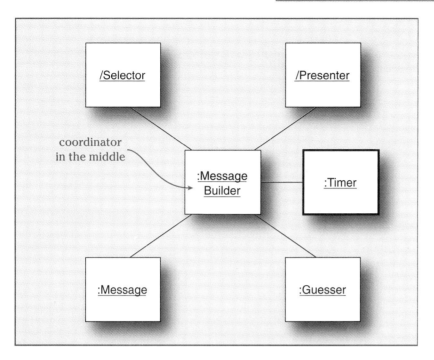

Figure 7-25
*A coordinator is surrounded by the things it delegates to or receives requests from.*

**Make sure the reader knows who is speaking.** Sticking to a single point of view is equivalent to speaking in one voice. If you are telling a story from one perspective, stick to that storyline. If you are explaining how subsystems collaborate, don't drop down two levels of detail and show objects inside those subsystems collaborating with objects from a standard library. Do not shift between outside and inside views. Present internal subsystem details in another diagram. To explain things, you often have to dive in and explain how some things work at the next level of detail. But if you do so, don't inadvertently raise more questions than answers or detract from your main point. So if your intent is to show how a complex responsibility is divided among collaborators, show which helper methods are invoked. But stop there. Don't show how the helper methods work unless these details are relevant to your story. And after you've burrowed down two or three levels or have moved to the side to follow a distant collaborator, it can be easy to get lost.

"The first rule of style is to have something to say. The second rule of style is to control yourself when, by chance, you have two things to say; say first one, then the other, not both at the same time."

— George Polya

This is a distraction—ignore it!

Don't change your voice or add new voices to your discussion. Parenthetical comments and notes are often spoken with a different voice and tone. When you point things out too often, people stop reading. Too many parenthetical comments, cautionary notes in text, or even notes on diagrams convince your readers that you speak hesitantly.

> Anticipating questions that would be asked at a presentation, a designer included answers (parenthetically enclosed) in running commentary about a high-level interaction. (She chose to parenthesize this side commentary so as to not detract from the main flow.) These parenthetical comments (even with the best of intentions) were quite distracting and impossible to skip over. (They might include something of interest, so you just had to read them. But it turns out they weren't of general interest. They included only details that some folks might question.) After she removed the parenthetical comments, the commentary was surprisingly easy to read.

Use these devices only when you really have something important to say and you want it to stand out.

> NOTE: This is really, really important!! Keep notes to 2% or less of what you are saying, unless you like writing stuff that nobody reads.

## ORGANIZING YOUR WORK

The best way to present a story isn't likely to be the same way it was developed. Consider which topics belong together and which ones deserve special emphasis. Ideally, closely related information belongs together. But when you're explaining collaborations, it can be hard to structure information. Everything is interconnected! Should you explain your objects, before describing their collaborations? Should you present an overview before going into details? Should you present details first, and then explain the principles behind them, or vice versa? What if you are telling your story to people who have different interests and backgrounds?

## Adding Emphasis

You can consciously attempt to emphasize or deemphasize certain parts of your story. Certain things gain prominence, whether you like it or not, merely by their position or their appearance. You need to be aware of these factors so that you can give aspects of your story proper emphasis. Here are some ways to increase emphasis:

- Put something first. Things that appear first have more emphasis. That's why we recommend that you orient your readers first before plunging into your collaboration story. It's also why we relegate topics that aren't central to an appendix.

- Highlight something. In UML, active objects are drawn with bold lines.

- Surround text with white space.

   **Surrounding an example with white space and making text bold give it double emphasis.**

- Give something more space. If explanations are lengthier, are they necessarily more important and deserving of extra emphasis? No. But they will have it. If the name of one object is longer than another's and your tool draws a larger shape, the longer-named object will gain emphasis.

- Place something in the center. Attention is drawn to objects in the middle of a collaboration diagram.

- Make a bulleted list.

- Refer to something many times. If you talk about some object or some collaboration pattern or some subsystem in many different places, it will be emphasized.

- Restate things in different forms. Showing exceptional paths as well as describing them in a table increases their emphasis. Adding a running commentary to an interaction reemphasizes the actions.

> "Emphasis is a way of distinguishing the two percent of the content that is most important from the remaining ninety-eight percent."
>
> —Ben Kovitz

> If explanations are too lengthy, they can put your reader to sleep. Giving an inconsequential item too much space causes readers to tune out and ignore whatever follows.

## Unfolding Your Story

There are ways to begin simply and then lead to more interesting or intricate views. Landscape architects use the principle of progressive realization to design linked scenes. They design views that purposely conceal things that are revealed only as you move through the landscape. The idea is to move the viewer to the desired destination in gradual, interesting steps. Something new and interesting is around every corner! John Simonds, in his book *Landscape Architecture*, states, "A view should be totally revealed in its fullest impact only from that position in the plan where this is most desirable." Each view is intriguing in its own right. And each new view contains new surprises. With progressive realization, pleasure builds in anticipation of what's around the corner.

You, too, can set up your readers to comprehend things more deeply as they move through your collaboration landscape. Your collaboration stories will benefit from pacing, emphasis, and progressive realization techniques.

> When you're telling a high-level collaboration story, stick to the main points. Present it as if it were a news flash. Your audience will want to scan the headlines before deciding to read further. So grab their attention. Present the fundamentals first: who the players are, what is important about them, and how their collaborations work. Reveal only enough to keep readers engaged. After they've read this overview, direct them to more detailed explanations. After explaining typical cases, give your readers options to veer off in one of several directions: to a more detailed view, to exceptional conditions, to alternatives.

## Understanding What's Fundamental

Even if you try very hard, you can't avoid forward references. If an object collaborates with another—and you haven't yet read a description of that second object's role and responsibilities—you can only guess at why it is being used.

Ben Kovitz, in *Practical Software Requirements,* admits that achieving an ideal sequence—in which every explanation precedes its use in any description that follows—is difficult, if not impossible. Present your stories in a way that builds interest and momentum instead of worrying about eliminating forward references. Even if you could manage to organize your story so that fundamentals were presented first, it could make for a very dull presentation.

Readers' interests and backgrounds differ. Some may know more than others and don't want to be bored by a review of things they know. Others may be looking for specific facts. Still others may want to know only the punchline. There are many reasons to tell a story in one way or another. If you know that some readers may lack fundamentals and while others are not patient enough to wade through them, you'll have to choose which things come first. Things that are only moderately interesting, or are background material, can always be relegated to an appendix.

Deciding whether some information is more fundamental than other information can be tricky. These heuristics, based on Ben Kovitz's work, are equally applicable to collaboration stories as to software requirements:

- Information not within your power to choose or change is more fundamental than those things that are under your control. So descriptions of a problem (which is not something you are likely to alter) should generally come before solutions (which are your own creation). This means that use cases are more fundamental than the collaboration diagrams that illustrate them.

- Things are more fundamental than relations between them, their attributes, and their actions. So ideally, you would want to understand objects, their responsibilities, and their purpose before understanding their collaborative relationships or how they participate in specific interaction sequences.

- The normal case is more fundamental than exceptional cases. A happy path collaboration is more fundamental than an exceptional path-filled collaboration. If you want to explain both, you should separate the two.

## Putting It All Together

So can you emphasize new material while building a story's energy and momentum? And when and where should you present fundamental information? With progressive realization, each step along the way presents something new. New things, *if they are different enough from what has already been seen*, are looked on with fresh interest. Your new perceptions are colored by memories—past impressions shape new ones—and your overall impressions accumulate. That's how a story can build to a dramatic conclusion: It lays down the important parts and then presents new material in novel, interesting ways.

Be aware of monotony setting in. After four or five nearly identical drawings, attention wavers. If you want to keep your readers' attention, shift their focus by inserting commentary that explicitly calls out some details or explains what's different in the next diagram. Or point out that the next five diagrams are similar and all but the most eager readers can skim them in good conscience. You can't always spice up your stories. After all, there are only so many ways to draw sequence diagrams.

Progressive realization works if your readers want to follow your lead and you lead them where they want to go. Those who are seeking specific facts won't sit still for very much nonsense. To help them search for facts, include an index or a section that answers frequently asked questions (FAQs). There are many different ways to put together a story. Pick one and make it work. You needn't present fundamentals first. Important things that need emphasis should be stated first. Pointers to supplementary information can always satisfy the needs and curiosity of those lacking fundamental knowledge.

## PRESERVING STORIES

Preserving stories requires commitment to a written and drawn design record. We offer you this thought on why you should go to this effort: Do you really want to explain your design over and over again, or have people make gratuitous changes that break your design? If not, preserve some key collaboration stories even after the code is released. After the code is working, detailed design drawings become less valued by those maintaining the code. They rarely look outside their code browsers for inspiration. But design discussions and explanations can increase in value, especially if they tell things that cannot be inferred from the code. So focus on preserving things that will have value and impact over time.

Collaboration ideas will change as you get closer to a working implementation. You can spend a lot of time spinning your wheels revising collaborations diagrams every time you make a slight change. Avoid this—even if you are using the ultimate power design drawing tool.

Some important collaboration stories are likely to become part of your permanent design record. It is these that you want to keep up-to-date. It's important to distinguish between working and archival documents. But after you've pushed further along in design, the early stories that you preserved can seem naïve. They need retelling to keep their currency. However, you don't want to constantly retell and redraw as you redesign and recode. Yet you don't want stories to get hopelessly outdated.

We offer this simple preservation strategy: Whenever you significantly readjust your design, update your collaboration stories. Changing a message or one of its arguments probably isn't significant. Adjusting what several objects do (or don't do) probably is. Revise a story whenever responsibilities shift among collaborators or newly invented objects become central to the story.

## SUMMARY

As you design how objects collaborate, you will draw many rough sketches. As you work out details, you may want to describe and diagram specific interactions. Maybe you want to show how your design supports key use cases or explain tricky exception-handling logic. In each case, you need to tell a collaboration story.

The best way to communicate a collaboration story depends on what you want to emphasize. How much detail you show should be based on how much you know about a collaboration and how much you want to reveal. Sometimes you want to show things; many times you also want to briefly explain them. Mostly, you want to get your ideas across effectively and compactly.

You can use UML diagrams to describe collaboration relationships and specific interaction sequences. Using UML, you can show collaborations at different levels of detail. But sometimes the best way to explain your design isn't with a diagram. For example, algorithmic details are better expressed in words, pseudo-code, real code, a state machine diagram, or decision tables.

Some important collaboration stories are worthy of being part of your permanent design record. Use these stories to explain your design to others. Preserving these collaboration stories requires some commitment. Unless you are using a roundtrip-engineering tool, changing detailed design diagrams to reflect actual code can be difficult. We recommend that you update important stories when you significantly readjust your design.

## FURTHER READING

Ben Kovitz's book, *Practical Software Requirements: A Manual of Content and Style* (Manning, 1998), is about writing software requirements. But parts of this book are priceless for all those who want to improve their technical communications. The chapters on organization, clear writing, and small details are worth the price of the book.

Bruce Powel Douglass, in *Real-Time UML: Developing Efficient Objects for Embedded Systems* (Addison-Wesley, 1999), has packed a lot of good advice on how to design as well as describe real-time systems. If you need to design, describe, or define systems with active objects, hard timing constraints, and complex state-based models, there's a wealth of material in this book.

"Use Case Maps can express the causal flow of responsibilities, even without an underlying structure of components. Afterwards, the same UCM scenario can be placed on top of different such structures, allowing one to evaluate different architectural alternatives. . . . People working directly at the level of message sequence diagrams tend to make many (premature) decisions."

—Daniel Amyot

There are ways to illustrate collaborations other than those we've explored in this chapter. Ray Buhr, a professor at the University of Ottawa, invented the *use case map*. Don't confuse use case maps with use cases. The two things are totally different. Use case maps can be drawn to tie together related responsibilities that are invoked as a result of a specific chain of events so they can be used to illustrate use cases.

A thorough explanation of use case maps can be found by browsing the Web site www.usecasemaps.org, which is devoted to promoting the use and understanding of use case maps. A good explanation of use case maps can be found in the chapter Understanding Macroscopic Behavior Patterns in *Building Application Frameworks: Object-Oriented Foundations of Framework Design* (Mohamed Fayed, ed., John Wiley, 1999).

# Chapter 8

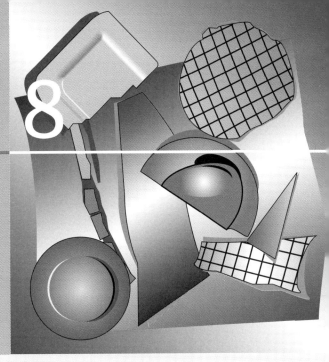

# *Reliable Collaborations*

**H**enry Petroski, structural engineer and historian, talks of the need to understand the consequences of failure: "The consequences of structural failure in nuclear plants are so great that extraordinary redundancies and large safety margins are incorporated into the designs. At the other extreme, the frailty of such disposable structures as shoelaces and light bulbs, whose failure is of little consequence, is accepted as a reasonable trade-off for an inexpensive product. For most in-between parts or structures, the choices are not so obvious. No designers want their structures to fail, and no structure is deliberately under designed when safety is an issue. Yet designer, client, and user must inevitably confront the unpleasant questions of 'How much redundancy is enough?' and 'What cost is too great?'" As software designers, we too must make our software machinery hold up under its anticipated use.

## UNDERSTANDING THE CONSEQUENCES OF FAILURE

Software need not be impervious to failure. But it shouldn't break easily. A large part of software design involves building our software to accommodate situations that, although unlikely, still must be dealt with. What if the user mistypes information? How should the software react? What if items a customer wants aren't available? Even if the consequences of not delivering exactly what the customer wants are not catastrophic, this situation must be dealt with reasonably—in ways that are acceptable to the customer and the business. When information is mistyped, why not notify the users and let them reenter it? Not enough stock on hand? Again, ask the users to cancel or modify their order. Software should detect problems and then engage the user in fixing them!

But what if a user is unable to guide the software? Shouting "stack overflow!" or "network unavailable!" won't be helpful to the disabled user of Speak for Me. "Punch in the gut" error messages are unacceptable in that design. It should handle many exceptional conditions and keep running without involving the user.

There is an enormous difference between making software more reliable and user-attentive, on the one hand, and designing it to recover from severe failures on the other hand. Fault-tolerant design incorporates extraordinary measures to ensure that the system works despite failure:

> Telephone switching equipment is extremely complex and yet must be very reliable. Redundancies are built into the hardware and the software. Complicated mechanisms are designed to log and recover from many different faults and error conditions. If a hardware component breaks, a redundant piece of equipment is provisioned to take its place. The software keeps the system running under anticipated failure conditions without losing a beat.

The more serious the consequences of failure, the more effort you must take to design in reliability. Alistair Cockburn, in *Agile Software Development* (Addison-Wesley, 2001), recommends that the time you spend designing for reliability fit with your project's size and criticality. He suggests four levels of criticality:

- **Loss of comfort.** When the software breaks, there is little impact. Most shareware falls into this category.

- Loss of discretionary monies. When the software breaks, it costs. Usually there are workarounds, but failures still impact people, their quality of work, and businesses' effectiveness. Many IT applications fall into this category, as do applications that affect a business's customers. If a customer gets overcharged because of a billing miscalculation, this doesn't cause the business severe harm. Usually the problem gets fixed, one way or the other, when the customer calls up and complains!

- Loss of essential monies. On the other hand, some systems are critical. At this level of criticality, it is no longer possible to correct the mistake with simple workarounds. The cost of fixing a fault is prohibitive and would severely tax the business.

- Loss of life. If the software fails, people could get injured or harmed. People who design air traffic control systems, space shuttle control software, pacemakers, or antilocking brake control software spend a lot of time analyzing how to keep the system working under extreme operating conditions.

The greater the software's criticality, the more justification there is for spending time to design it to work reliably. Even if it is not a matter of life and death, other factors may drive you to design for reliability:

- Software that runs unattended for long periods may operate under fluctuating conditions. Exceptional conditions in its "normal" operating environment shouldn't cause it to break.

- Often, software that glues larger systems together must check for errors in inputs and must work in spite of communications glitches.

- Components designed to plug in and work without human intervention need to detect problems in their operating environment and run under many different conditions. Otherwise, "plug and play" wouldn't work.

- Consumer products need to work, period. Their success in the marketplace depends on high reliability.

When you've gauged how reliable your software needs to be, you'll need to consider key collaborations and look for ways to make them more reliable. As you dig deep into design and implementation, you will uncover many ways your software might break. But let's get real! It is up to us designers to decide what appropriate measures to take, to propose solutions, and to work out reasoned compromises—but extraordinary measures aren't always necessary.

## INCREASING YOUR SYSTEM'S RELIABILITY

"At an architectural level, the basic patterns, policies, and collaborations for exception handling need to be established early, because it is awkward to insert exception handling as an after thought."

—Craig Larman

Reliability concerns crop up throughout development. But once you have decided on the basic architecture of your system, have assigned responsibilities to objects, and have designed collaborations, you can take a closer look at making specific collaborations more reliable—by designing objects to detect and recover from exceptional conditions.

We suggest you start by characterizing the different types of collaborations in your existing design. This will give you a sense of where you need to focus efforts on improving objects and designing them to be more resilient. Then identify key collaborations that you want to make more reliable.

Consider conducting an "environmental impact study" on the existing or proposed architectural environment where your system may live— is it a software-friendly fit?

After you've characterized your system's patterns of collaborations and prioritized your work, you need to get very specific:

- List the exceptions and errors cases you want your design to accommodate.

- Decide on reasonable exception-handling and error recovery strategies to employ.

- Try out several design alternatives and see how responsibilities shift among collaborators. Settle on a solution that represents a best compromise.

- Define additional responsibilities for detecting exceptions and obligations of other objects for resolving them if that is part of your solution.

- Look at your design for holes, unnecessary complexity, and consistency.

A system is only as reliable as its weakest link. So it makes little sense to design one very reliable object surrounded by brittle collaborators, or to make one peripheral task very reliable while leaving several central ones poorly designed. The system as a whole needs to be designed for reliability, piece by piece.

## DETERMINING WHERE COLLABORATIONS CAN BE TRUSTED

One way to get a handle on how collaborations can be improved is to carve your software into regions where trusted communications occur. Generally, objects located within the same *trust region* can communicate collegially, although they may still encounter exceptions and errors as they perform their duties. Within a system there are several cases to consider:

- Collaborations among objects that interface to the user and the rest of the system
- Collaborations among objects within the system and objects that interface with external systems
- Collaborations among objects outside a neighborhood and objects inside a neighborhood
- Collaborations among objects in different layers
- Collaborations among objects at different abstraction levels
- Collaborations among objects of your design and objects designed by someone else
- Collaborations among your objects and objects that come from a vendor-provided library

Whom an object receives a request from is a good indicator of how likely is it to accept a request at face value. Whom an object calls on determines how confident it can be that the collaborator will field the request to the best of its ability. It's a matter of trust.

## Trusted Versus Untrusted Collaborations

When should collaborators be trusted? Two definitions for collaboration are worth reexamining:

> Collaborate: 1. To work together, especially in a joint intellectual effort. 2. To cooperate treasonably, as with an enemy occupation force.
> —*The American Heritage Dictionary*

The first definition is collegial: objects working together toward a common goal. As shown in Figure 8-1, when objects are within the same trust region, their collaborations can be conscientiously designed to be more collegial. Both client and service provider can be designed to assume that if any conditions or values are to be validated, they need be done only once, by the designated responsible party.

Not every object needs to take responsibility for ensuring reliable collaborations. If every object took a paranoid stance, most of the time would be redundantly spent checking for preconditions to be established and busily guaranteeing that postconditions are satisfied. Once you've made sure that appropriate parties perform their assigned responsibilities, you can cut out a lot of design redundancy.

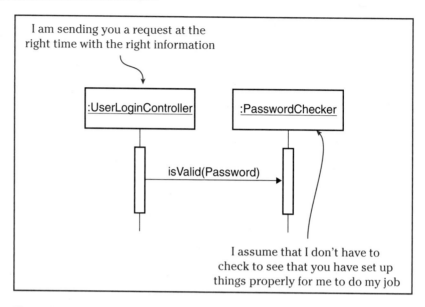

Figure 8-1
*Objects often trust their collaborators.*

In general, when objects are in the same layer or neighborhood, they can be more trusting of their collaborators. And they can assume that objects that use their services call on them appropriately.

The second definition requires you to think critically. When collaborators are designed by someone else or when they are in different layers, or a library, your basic assumptions about the appropriate design for that collaboration need to be carefully examined. If a collaborator can't be trusted, it doesn't mean that it is inherently more unreliable. But a more defensive collaborative stance may be appropriate. A client may need to add extra safeguards, potentially both before and after calling an untrusted service provider.

If a request is from an untrusted or unknown source, extra checks may be made before a request is honored. There are several situations to consider:

- When an object sends a request to a trustworthy colleague
- When an object receives a request from a trusted colleague
- When an object uses an untrusted collaborator

- When an object receives a request from an unknown source
- When an object receives a request from a known untrustworthy source

***Collaborations among trusted colleagues.*** A client that provides a well-formed request expects its service provider to carry out that request to the best of its ability. When an object receives a request from a trusted colleague, it typically assumes that the request is correctly formed, that it is sent at an appropriate time, and that data passed along with the request is well formed (unless there is an explicit design decision that the receiver takes responsibility for validating this information).

During a sequence of collaborations among objects within the same trust region, there is little need to check on the state of things before and after each request. If an object cannot fulfill its responsibilities and is not designed to recover from exceptional conditions, it could raise an exception or return an error condition, enabling its client (or someone else in the collaboration chain) to responsibly handle the problem. But the object may be legitimately designed to not check. In this case it won't even notice when things fail. In a trusted collaboration there is no need to check for invalid collaborations. So if trust is ever violated, things can go terribly wrong.

***When using an untrusted collaborator.*** When collaborators are untrusted, extra precautions *may* need to be taken, especially if the client is designed to be responsible for making collaborations more reliable. You may pass along a copy of data instead of sharing it with an untrusted collaborator. Or you may check on conditions after the request completes.

***When receiving requests from an unknown source.*** Designers of objects that are used under many different situations—such as those included in a class library or framework—must balance their objects' expected use (or misuse) with overall reliability goals. There aren't any universal design rules to follow. Library designers must make a lot of hard choices. You can design your object to check and raise exceptions if data and requests are invalid (that's certainly a responsible thing to do, but it's not always necessary) or to ignore such exceptions (that's the simplest thing, but not always adequate). Your goal should be to design your framework or library to be consistent and predictable and to provide enough information so that clients can attempt to react and recover when you raise exceptions.

There are exception-handling mechanisms to put in place to assist with untrustworthy collaborations, and there are additional exception-handling mechanisms that have nothing to do with trustworthiness, such as "out of stock." In spite of trust, things can still go wrong.

### When receiving requests from an untrusted client.

Requests from untrusted sources often are checked for timeliness and relevance, especially if your goal is to design an object that works reliably in spite of untrustworthy clients. Of course, there are degrees of trust and degrees of paranoia. Designing defensive collaborations can be expensive and difficult. In fact, designing every object to collaborate defensively leads to poor performance and potentially introduces errors.

## Implications of Trust

Objects generally don't check on who calls upon their services at run time. Decisions about whether requests are trusted or untrusted are typically design decisions, not run time ones. So responsibilities are typically implemented assuming a specific degree of trust.

Determining trust regions for a system is straightforward. After you determine them, it is easier to decide where to place extra responsibilities for making collaborations more reliable.

In the Speak for Me application, all objects within the core of the application are designed to work together and are considered to be within the same trust region. Objects in the application control and domain layers all assume trusted communications. Objects at the "edges" of the system—within the user interface and in the technical services layer—are designed to take precautions to make sure that outgoing requests are honored and incoming requests are valid. For example, the Selector debounces user eye blinks and presents only single "click" requests. And the MessageBuilder quite reasonably assumes that it receives trusted requests from the objects at the edges: the Selector and the Timer. Objects controlled by the MessageBuilder assume that they are getting reasonable requests, too. So requests to add themselves to a message or to offer the next guess are done without questioning the validity of input data or the request. Trusted collaborations within the core of the system greatly simplify the implementation of the MessageBuilder, the Dictionaries, the Guesser, the Message, and Letter, Word, and Sentence objects' responsibilities.

Objects at the edges of the system have additional responsibilities for detecting exceptions and trying to recover if they can or, if not, to report them to a higher authority (someone at the nurse's station). When a message cannot be reliably delivered, extra effort is made to send an alarm to the nurse's station and raise an audio signal.

In a large system, it is useful to distinguish whether collaborations among components can be trusted and furthermore to identify the guarantees, obligations, and responsibilities of each component.

After these constraints are agreed on, each component can be designed to do its part to ensure that the system as a whole works more reliably.

---

The telco integration application receives service order requests and schedules the work to provision the services and set up billing systems. The architecture of the system consists of a number of adapter components that interface to external applications. Collaborations between an adapter and its "adapted" application are generally assumed to be untrusted, whereas collaborations between any adapter and core of the system are trusted.

The order taking adapter component receives requests to create, modify, or cancel an order from an external Order Taking application. These requests are converted into an internal format, which is sent to the scheduler component. The order taking adapter does not trust the Order Taking application to give it well-formed requests; it assumes that any number of things can be wrong (and they often are). It takes extraordinary efforts to guarantee that requests are correctly converted to internal format before it passes them to the scheduler.

Even so, it is still possible to receive requests that are inconsistent with the actual state of an order: For example, a request to cancel an order can be received after the work has already been completed. It is business policy not to "cancel" work that has already been completed. So although collaborations between the Order Taking adapter and the scheduler are trusted, well-formed requests still can fail.

---

## IDENTIFYING COLLABORATIONS TO BE MADE RELIABLE

At first, you may not know just exactly what measures to take to increase your system's reliability. The first step is to identify several areas where you want to ensure reliable collaborations. Revisit your initial design and take a stab at improving it. You might consider the following:

- How collaborations support a specific use case or task
- How an object neighborhood responds to a specific request
- How an interfacer handles errors and exceptions encountered in an external system
- How a control center responds to exceptional conditions and errors raised by objects under its control

After you've identified a particular collaboration to work on, consider what needs to be done. Maybe no additional measures need to be taken; objects are doing exactly what they should be doing. More likely, you will want to add specific responsibilities to some objects for detecting exceptional conditions, and to others for reacting and recovering from them. The first step in making a collaboration more reliable is to understand what might go wrong.

## What Use Cases Tell Us

Ideally, some requirements document or use case should spell out the right thing to do when things go wrong. But even if use case writers have written quite detailed descriptions, rarely have they considered everything. Alistair Cockburn, in *Writing Effective Use Cases,* assigns four precision levels to use cases. Only those in the most precise level identify failure conditions and describe how the system should respond to them. Cockburn cautions use case writers not to write in too much detail too early:

> "[Describing exceptions] is often tricky, tiring, and surprising work. It is surprising because quite often a question about an obscure business rule will surface during this writing, or the failure handling will suddenly reveal a new actor or new goal that needs to be supported. Most projects are short on time and energy. Managing the precision level to which you work should therefore be a project priority."
> —*Alistair Cockburn*

Just because someone describes a possible exception doesn't mean it will actually happen. Your design may have successfully side-stepped the potential problem.

No wonder exception-handling strategies often remain unspecified until design! Use cases generally describe software in terms of actors' actions and system responsibilities and not in terms of objects and exceptions. At best, use case writers will identify a few problems and briefly describe how some of them should be handled.

But that doesn't relieve you of the responsibility for identifying real problems and resolving them as you encounter them. As you dig into design, you are likely to identify many exception conditions and devise ways of handling them. When your solutions are costly or represent compromises, review them with all who have a stake in your software's overall reliability. They should weigh in on your proposed solutions.

## Distinguish Between Exceptions and Errors

It is easy to waste a lot of time considering things that might go wrong or pondering the merit of partial solutions when there is no easy fix. To avoid getting bogged down, distinguish between errors and exceptions. *Errors* are things that are wrong. Errors can result from malformed data, bad programs or logic errors, or broken hardware. In the face of errors, there is little that can be done to fix things and proceed. Unless your software is required to take extraordinary measures, you shouldn't spend a lot of time designing your software to recover from them.

For the most part, errors can be ignored. On the other hand, *exceptions* aren't normal, but they happen and you should design your software to handle them. This is where the bulk of your energy should go—solving exceptional conditions. If a use case identifies exceptional conditions, it may also have identified how they should be accommodated:

> Invalid password entered—After three incorrect attempts, inform the users that access is denied to the online banking system until they contact a bank agent and are assigned a new password.

To translate this policy into appropriate objects' responsibilities, you'll need to assign some object the responsibility for validating the password; several more are likely to be involved in recovering from this problem. This is pretty easy. There is nothing difficult or challenging in designing an object to validate a password or report an error condition to the user.

But wait. Is the event an error or an exception? Mistyped passwords are a regular, if infrequent, occurrence. We want our software to react to this condition by giving the user a way to recover, so we view it as an exception and not an error. In fact, most use cases describe exceptions that cause the software to veer off its normal path. Some will be handled deftly, and users will be able to continue with their original task. These are *recoverable exceptions*. With others, users won't be able to complete their original task. The use case will end abnormally, but the application will keep running. From the user's perspective, these are *unrecoverable exceptions*. Rarely will use cases mention errors unless their authors are experienced at describing fault-tolerant software.

"I have long (but quietly) advocated dealing with exception handling issues early in the design of a system. Unfortunately, there is a natural tendency to focus on the main functional flow of a system, ignoring the impact of exceptional situations until later."

—John Goodenough

List exception conditions you expect at whatever level you are working at. If you have use case descriptions that you are designing for, start with those. But don't expect them to be a complete or particularly detailed guide as you design reliable collaborations.

## Object Exceptions Versus Use Case Exceptions

Let's get one thing clear: Exceptions described in use cases are fundamentally different from exceptions uncovered in a design. Use case exceptions reflect the inability of an actor or the system to continue on the same course. Object exceptions reflect the inability of an object to perform a requested operation. During execution of a single step in a use case scenario, potentially several use case-level exceptions could happen. However, the execution of a single use case step could result in thousands of requests between collaborators, any number of which could cause object exceptions. There isn't a one-to-one correspondence between exception conditions described in use cases and object exceptions. Nevertheless, we need to make our application behave as its use case writers desire. We also need to make it reasonably handle the many more exceptional conditions that arise during execution.

## Object Exception Basics

Invariably, an exception condition detected during application execution leads some object or component to veer off its normal path and fail to complete an operation. Depending on your design, some object may *raise* an exception, whereas another object may *handle* it. By handling an exception, the system recovers and puts itself into a predictable state. It keeps running reliably even as it veers off the normal path—to an expected but exceptional one. Left unhandled, however, exceptions can lead to system failure, just as unhandled errors do.

"A program must be able to deal with exceptions. A good design rule is to list explicitly the situations that may cause a program to break down."

—Jorgen Knudsen

It is up to you to decide what to do when an exception condition is encountered. Many object-oriented programming languages define mechanisms for programmers to *declare* exceptions and error conditions, *signal* their occurrence, and to write and associate *exception-handling code* that executes when signaled (see Figure 8-2).

Alternatively, you could design an object to detect an exception condition, and, instead of raising an exception, it could return a result indicating that an exception occurred (see Figure 8-3).

In part, it's a matter of style, but largely it's the implementation language that determines whether you design your objects to raise exceptions or report exception conditions. Either design described would "handle the exception condition" of an invalid password.

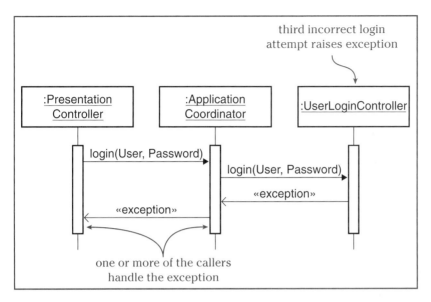

Figure 8-2
*Execution transfers directly to callers' exception-handling code.*

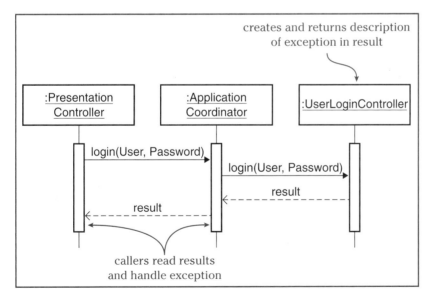

Figure 8-3
*A caller can check for an exception condition returned in a result.*

The first design (Figure 8-2) uses exception facilities in the programming language; the second (Figure 8-3) returns values that signify an exceptional condition. Both techniques convey the exceptional condition to the client. Yet another design alternative is to make a service provider smart. It might remember that an exception condition has occurred and provide an interface for querying this fact.

Let's look further at what it means to define and use exception facilities in an object-oriented programming language. When an object detects an exception and signals this condition to its client, it is said to *raise an exception*. In the Java programming language, the term is *throw an exception*. To throw a specific exception, a programmer would declare that a particular type of *Throwable* object (which contains contextual information) will be sent along with the exception signal. An object throws an exception by executing a statement:

```
if (loginAttempts > MAX_ATTEMPTS) {
    throw new TooManyLoginAttemptsException();

}
```

The handler of an exception signal has several options. It could fix things and then transfer control to statements immediately following the call that raised the exception (resumption). Or it might re-signal the same or a new exception, leaving the responsibility for handling it to a possibly more knowledgeable object (propagation). In most cases, instead of grinding to a halt, it is desirable to make progress. This involves a cooperative effort on the part of the object raising the exception, the client sending the exception-causing request, and one or more objects in the collaboration chain if the requester chooses not to handle the exception then and there.

In Java, there are subclasses of Error—for exception conditions that need not be handled—or subclasses of Exception—for conditions that are required to be handled or implicitly rethrown.

There must be enough information available that the object that takes responsibility for handling the exception can take a meaningful action. The design of appropriate exception objects that are returned to the client when an exception is raised is a topic we won't explore in great detail. Be aware that when you design an exception object, you can declare information that it will hold. When the object that detects the exception condition creates an exception object, it populates it with this information. Typically, exception objects are information holders.

We offer the following general guidelines for declaring and handling exceptions.

***Avoid declaring lots of exception classes.*** The more classes of exceptions you define, the more cases an exception handler must consider (unless it groups categories of exceptions). To keep exception-handling code simple, define fewer classes of exceptions and design clients to take different actions based on answers supplied by the exception object.

> Deep exception class hierarchies and wide exception class hierarchies are seldom a good idea. They significantly increase the complexity of a system, but the individual classes are seldom actually used. Compare the complexity of an IOError class hierarchy with 20 subclasses (probably arranged in some sub-hierarchy structure) with one I/O error class that knows an error code with 20 possible values. Most programmers can remember and distinguish 5–7 clearly different exception classes, but if you give them 20–30 exception classes with similar names and subtle distinctions, they will never be able to remember them all and will have to continually refer to the system documentation.

Identify exception classes in the same way you identify any other classes—via responsibilities and collaborations. Unless two exceptions will have distinct responsibilities or participate in different types of collaborations, they shouldn't need different classes. Outside the world of exceptions you wouldn't normally create two distinct classes simply to represent two different state values, so why create multiple exception classes simply to represent different values of an error code?

> It makes sense to have different exception classes for FileIOError and EndOfFile exceptions. Some people might try to treat EndOfFile as a FileIOError, but this wouldn't be a good design choice. FileIOError represents a truly exceptional and unexpected occurrence. Its collaborators are likely to have to take drastic actions. EndOfFile is usually an expected occurrence, and its collaborators are likely to respond to it by continuing the normal operations of the program. Seldom, if ever, do you want to respond in the same way to both of these exceptions. But you are quite likely to want to respond in an identical manner to all FileIOErrors.

***Name an exception after what went wrong and not who raised it.*** This makes it easy to associate the situation with the the appropriate action to take (see Figure 8-4). The alternative makes it less clear why the handler is performing specific actions. An exception handler may also need to know who originally raised it (especially if it was delegated upward from a lower-level collaborator), but this can easily be defined to be included as part of the exception object.

```
try {
    loginController.login(userName, password);
}
catch (TooManyLoginAttemptsException e) {
    // handle too many login attempts
}
```

Figure 8-4

*TooManyLoginAttemptsException explains what happened and not who threw it.*

***Recast lower-level exceptions to higher-level ones whenever you raise your abstraction level.*** When very low-level exceptions percolate up to a high-level handler, there is little context to assist the handler in making informed decisions. Recast an exception whenever you cross from one level of abstraction to another. This enables exception handlers that are way up a collaboration chain to make more informed decisions and reports. Not taking this advice can lead your users to believe that your software is broken, instead of just dealing with unrecoverable errors:

A compiler can run out of disk space during compilation. There isn't much the compiler can do in this case except report this condition to the user. But it is far better for the compiler to report "insufficient disk space to continue compilation" than to report "I/O error #xxx." With the latter message, the user may be led to believe there is a bug in the compiler rather than insufficient resources, something that can be corrected by the user. If this low-level exception were to percolate up to objects that don't know how to interpret this I/O error exception, it will be hard to present a meaningful error message. To prevent this, the compiler designers recast low-level exceptions to higher-level ones whenever subsystem boundaries are crossed.

***Provide context along with an exception.*** What's most important to the exception handler is to identify the exception and to gain information that will aid it in making a more informed response. This leads to the design of exception objects that are rich information holders. Specific information can be passed along, including values of parameters that caused the exception to be raised, detailed descriptions, error text, and information that can be used to take corrective action. When recasting exceptions, as shown in Figure 8-5, some designers also embed lower-level exceptions, providing a complete trace of what went wrong.

***Assign exception-handling responsibilities to objects that can make decisions.*** There are many different ways to handle an exception: One way is to log and rethrow it (possibly more than once) until someone takes corrective action. Who naturally might handle exceptions? As a first line of defense, consider the initial requester. If it knows enough to perform corrective action, then the exception can be taken care of right away and not be propagated. As

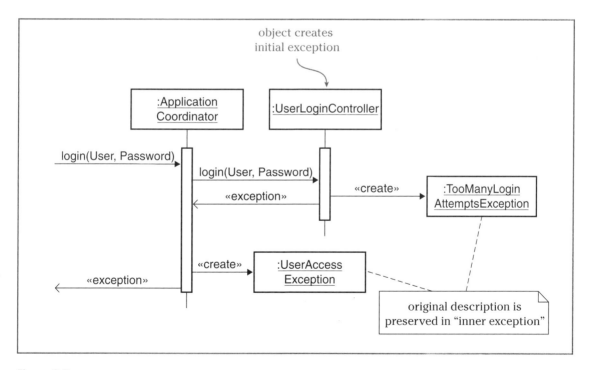

Figure 8-5
*Exception information is preserved in inner exceptions.*

a fallback position, it is always appropriate to pass the buck to some object that takes responsibility for making decisions and controlling the action. Controllers and objects located within a control center are naturals for handling exceptions.

***Handle exceptions as close to the problem as you can.*** One object raises an exception, and somewhere up the collaboration chain another object handles it. Sure, this works, but it makes your design harder to understand. It can make it difficult to follow the action if you carry this to extremes.

External interfacers often take responsibility for handling faulty conditions in other systems they interface to, relieving their clients of having to know about lower-level details and recovery strategies. Service providers often take on the added responsibility to handle an exception and retry an alternative means of accomplishing the request.

***Consider returning results instead of raising exceptions.*** Instead of raising exceptions, you always can design your exception taking object to return a result or status that is directly checked by the requester. This makes it more obvious who must take at least some responsibility: the requester.

## Exception- and Error-Handling Strategies

"The major difference between a thing that might go wrong and a thing that cannot possibly go wrong is that when a thing that cannot possibly go wrong goes wrong it usually turns out to be impossible to get at or repair."

—Douglas Adams

In the case of errors as well as exceptions, handling them is a matter of how much effort and energy you want to expend. Highly fault-tolerant systems are designed to respond by taking extraordinary measures. A highly fault-tolerant system might recover from programming errors by running an alternative algorithm, or from a suddenly inaccessible disk by printing data on an alternative logging device. Most ordinary software would break (gracefully or not, depending, again, on the design and the specific condition).

There are numerous ways to deal with a request that an object can't handle. Doug Lea, in *Concurrent Programming in Java™* (Addison-Wesley, 1999), poses the question, "What would you do if you were asked to write down a phone number and you didn't have a pencil?" to explore several options. One possibility is what Lea calls *unconditional action*. In this simple scheme, you'd go through the motions of writing *as if you had a pencil*, whether you had one or not. Besides looking silly, this is acceptable only if nobody cares that you fail to complete your task.

Employing this strategy often leads to unpredictable results. In real life, you likely wouldn't be so irresponsible, and your software objects shouldn't behave this way either. If an object or component or system that receives a request isn't in the proper state to handle it, nothing can be guaranteed. An unconditional act could cause the software to trip up immediately or, worse yet, to fail later in unpredictable ways. Ouch! There are more acceptable alternatives:

- Inaction. Ignore the request after determining it cannot be correctly performed.

- Balk. Admit failure and return an indication to the requester (by either raising an exception or reporting an error condition).

- Guarded suspension. Suspend execution until conditions for correct execution are established; then try to perform the request.

- Provisional action. Pretend to perform the request, but do not commit to it until success is guaranteed.

- Recovery. Perform an acceptable alternative.

- Appeal to a higher authority. Ask a human to apply judgment and steer the software to an acceptable resolution.

- Rollback. Try to proceed but, on failure, undo the effects of a failed action.

- Retry. Repeatedly attempt a failed action after recovering from failed attempts.

These strategies impact the designs of clients as well as objects fulfilling requests and, possibly, other participants in recovery activities. No one strategy is appropriate in every situation.

Inaction is simple but leaves the client uninformed. When an object balks, at least the requester knows about the failure and can try an alternative strategy. With guarded suspension, the object would patiently wait until some other object gave it a pencil (the means by which someone knows what is needed and supplies it is unspecified).

Provisional action isn't meaningful in this example, but it makes sense when a request takes time and can be partially fulfilled in anticipation of later completion. Recovery could be as simple as using an alternative resource—a pen instead of a pencil. Appealing to a higher authority might mean asking some human who always keeps pencils handy and sharp to write down the number instead. Rollback doesn't make much sense in this example because nothing has been partially done—unless the pencil breaks while the

> Inaction, balking, and guarded suspension can be categorized as pessimistic, or check-and-act, policies. Provisional action, appealing to a higher authority, rollback, recovery, and retry are try-and-see, or optimistic, policies.

> "Decisions about these matters usually need to be made relatively early in the design of an application. . . . Choices among policies impact method signatures, internal state representation, class relations, and client-visible protocols."
>
> —Doug Lea

requester is writing down the number. In this case the object would throw away the partially written number. Rollback is a common strategy in which either all or nothing is desired and partial results are unacceptable. Retrying makes sense only when there is a chance of success in the future.

There will *always* be consequences to consider when you're choosing any recovery strategy:

> "The designer or his client has to choose to what degree and where there shall be failure. Thus the shape of all designed things is the product of arbitrary choice. If you vary the terms of your compromise...then you vary the shape of the thing designed. It is quite impossible for any design to be 'the logical outcome of the requirements' simply because the requirements being in conflict, their logical outcome is an impossibility."
> —David Pye

Mixing or combining strategies often leads to more satisfactory results. For example, one object could attempt to write down the phone number but broadcast a request for a pencil if it fails to locate one. It might then wait for a certain amount of time. But if no one provided the waiting object with one, ultimately it might ignore the request. Meanwhile, the requester might wait a while for confirmation and then locate another object to write the phone number after waiting a predetermined period of time.

It isn't always possible to devise simple solutions to difficult problems. Systems that make concerted efforts to handle exceptions often employ complex strategies.

The best strategy isn't always obvious or satisfying. Compromises don't always feel like reasonable solutions even if they are the best you can do under the circumstances.

## Determining Who Should Take Action

But objects do fail to fulfill their responsibilities. Because objects do not work in isolation—they collaborate to fulfill larger responsibilities—a key question to consider is which objects should take on additional responsibilities for guaranteeing success in spite of individuals' failures. In the case of writing a phone number, other than doing the job yourself, the most assured way of guaranteeing success is to hand in a new pencil along with each request! However, providing the resources an object needs to ensure success isn't always practical, nor is it guaranteed to avoid all further failures. Objects and systems fail for many reasons: They can lack the resources they need; they can call on other objects that fail; the underlying operating systems and networks can fail. Although it is extremely difficult to build completely fail-safe objects, you certainly can make them more reliable.

You can do so by placing the burden for success on the requester, shifting some of it onto the object providing the service, splitting some extra responsibilities between them, or even designating others to get involved when things go wrong. Each choice has consequences.

## Asking the Client to Check Before Making a Request

Here are some considerations when you're deciding to burden the requester with checking beforehand that an object can do what it is asked:

***Can clients easily check for success?*** Is it easy to check whether the service provider is in a state that guarantees success? If not, you may need to expand the service provider's interface and assign it public responsibilities for reporting on what initially seemed like private implementation details. For example, we could give our object the added responsibility of reporting whether it has a pencil. Even if you do this, someone (most likely the initial requester) still must take some responsibility for reacting appropriately when the answer is no.

What guarantees are there that after an object has been checked for readiness, it stays ready? In concurrent systems, objects and resources are shared, and their state changes from moment to moment. If your service provider is shared or if it turns around and uses shared resources to fulfill its responsibilities, then between the time you ask whether it can honor a request and the time you ask it to perform the request, conditions could change. The pencil may have broken or may have been passed along to another. To avoid this, allow clients to check and reserve with a single request.

***Is the cost of checking prohibitive?*** Are conditions for success readily checked beforehand without incurring too much overhead? What if the consequences of asking whether an object has a pencil causes it to ask every one of its backup resources whether it has a pencil, and this takes a long time? Sometimes, determining whether a request will be successful involves more computation than simply performing the request and responding to exceptions.

***Does checking produce undesirable side effects?*** Checking may cause undesirable side effects. What if asking whether an object has a pencil causes it to drop everything and order one from a supplier? Would that be appropriate?

### Giving the Client Some Responsibility for Recovery

If you give a client some responsibility for guaranteeing success, there are many things to consider. How much responsibility should it take? Is it reasonable for each client to employ individual recovery strategies as it sees fit, or should you design some common recovery facilities that requesters can use? Or should some object better equipped to handle the situation be told of the failure?

### Giving the Service Provider Some Responsibility for Recovery

Even if you decide to shift some responsibility to the service provider for error recovery, don't be surprised by the demands this strategy can place on clients. Clients may have to understand the consequences of alternate courses of action taken by the service provider.

***Is it acceptable to introduce pauses or delays?*** Is it OK for the client to wait, perhaps indefinitely, for the service provider to acquire what it needs? What if the service provider queries its backup resources when it doesn't have a pencil? Sometimes these queries are quickly answered, and at other times, when they are busy, the responses can take a long time. If the client must turn around and give the phone number to another object within a prescribed time limit, intermittent and indeterminate pauses introduced by a more responsible service provider won't be acceptable.

***What is the probability that unavailable resources can be acquired?*** If the service provider doesn't have what it needs, can it reliably acquire it? If other users of this resource are ill behaved, then their performance impacts the service provider's ability to fulfill its responsibilities. A service provider is only as reliable as the resources it depends on.

***Are there alternative ways to fulfill failed requests?*** Does it make sense for the service provider to have a different means of accomplishing a request at its disposal, or is this overengineering? For example, what if our service provider had pens, pencils, and a variety of paper stock always on hand?

***Is it easy to detect failure?*** Of course, it is easy for people to know whether they've written down a phone number. They can scan a piece of paper and see a legible sequence of numbers. But sometimes, it isn't so easy for an object to know whether its actions have had the desired effects, especially if it collaborates with or changes the state of external devices or systems. The more collaborations involved in fulfilling a request, the harder it is to guarantee that each subrequest has the intended effect.

## DESIGNING A SOLUTION

So far, we've considered strategies for handling failures for a single request. Making larger responsibilities more reliable can get much more complex. After you've identified a particular collaboration sequence that you want to make more reliable, think through all the cases that might cause objects to veer off course.

Start simply and then work up to more challenging problems. Given the nature of design, not all acceptable solutions may seem reasonable at first. You may need time for a solution to soak in before it seems right.

### Brainstorm Exception Conditions

Complex collaborations can fail in numerous ways. Even simple collaborations can have many places where things can go wrong. Thinking through all the ways a collaboration might fail is difficult work. Make a list. Enumerate all the exceptional conditions you can think of for a specific chunk of collaborative behavior. Whether you are working with the collaborations in support of a use case or designing a collaboration deep inside your system, list everything that you reasonably expect could go wrong. Consider the following:

- Users behaving incorrectly—entering misinformation or failing to respond within a particular time
- Invalid information
- Unauthorized requests
- Invalid requests
- Untimely requests
- Time out waiting for a response
- Dropped communications

- Failures due to broken or jammed equipment, such as a printer being unavailable
- Errors in data your software uses, including corrupt log files, bad or inconsistent data, missing files
- Critical performance failures or failure to accomplish some action within a prescribed time limit

This list is intended to jog your thinking. But be reasonable. If some condition seems highly improbable, leave it off your list. Put it on another list (the list of exceptions you didn't design for). If you know that certain exceptions are common, say so. If you don't know whether an exception might occur, put a question mark by it. You may not know what are reasonable and expected conditions if you are building something for the first time. People *and* software *and* physical resources can cause exceptions. And the deeper you get into design and implementation, the more exceptions you'll find.

## Limit Your Scope

Take exception design in bite-sized increments. If you've already designed your objects to collaborate under normal conditions, start modestly to make the collaboration more reliable. Pick a single exception that everyone agrees is common and that you think you know how to handle. If you are designing collaborations for a specific use case, tackle one unhappy path situation. What actions should occur when there are insufficient funds when a user tries to make an online payment? What if the user blinks her eyes too rapidly and makes a false selection? What if the file is locked by another application?

After you've decided on what seems a reasonable way to handle that situation, design a solution using the object-oriented design techniques we've described. Minimize or purposely ignore certain parts of your design in order to concentrate on those objects that will take the exception and those that will resolve it. You needn't reach all the way from the user interface to the lowest technical service objects. Here is what we consider to be both in and out of scope for the exceptional case of insufficient funds:

Make a Payment Collaboration: Insufficient Funds

- Assume a well-formed request (no data entry errors).
- Ignore backend system bottlenecks.
- Ignore momentary loss of connections or communication failures (they will be handled by connection objects in the technical service layer).
- Offer the user an opportunity to enter an alternative amount.

***Determine who should detect an exception and how it should be resolved.*** Assume that everything goes according to plan up to the point where the particular exception you are considering is detected.

We know that the existing backend banking system returns an error code indicating insufficient funds to our external interface component. Now what?

The backend banking component reports the exception via a Result object to the FundsTransferTransaction that is responsible for coordinating the transaction. The FundsTransferTransaction interprets this as an "unrecoverable exception," which causes it to halt and return a Result (indicating failure) to the UserSession.

Collaboration ideas will change as you get closer to a working implementation. You can spend a lot of time spinning your wheels revising collaborations every time you make a slight change. Concentrate on who should be responsible for handling an error or exception. Designate places where the buck stops and where recovery actions will happen.

***Describe additional responsibilities of collaborators.*** Service providers, controllers, and coordinators are often charged with exception-handling responsibilities. In our example, the FundsTransferTransaction—a service provider/coordinator—coordinates the work of performing a financial transaction. It makes relatively few decisions, altering its course only when the result is in error. It is responsible for validating funds transfer information, forwarding the request to the backend banking interface component, logging successful transactions, and reporting results.

Objects within the application server component are within the same trust region. They receive untrusted requests from the UI component and collaborate with the backend banking component (each of those collaborations spans another trust boundary). The backend banking component interfaces to the backend banking system, a trusted external system that either handles the request or reports an error. Occasionally, communications between the backend bank system fail, and then our software must take extraordinary measures.

Objects at the edges of a trust region can either take responsibility for guaranteeing that incoming requests are well formed, or they can delegate all or part of that responsibility.

If you have the luxury of designing a group of objects to work together, you can assign certain objects responsibility for guaranteeing that information is correct or that requests are timely and relevant, and then turn around and relax some of the responsibilities of objects within a trusted boundary.

> In the online banking application, any incoming request from the user component is validated. The UserSession object receives and validates requests from the UI component and then creates and delegates the request to specific service providers. In the earlier example, a FundsTransferTransaction is created. It has responsibility for validating the funds transfer information and reacting to errors reported from the backend system.

Make sure you have considered the following:

- Who validates information received from untrusted collaborators
- Who detects exceptions
- How exceptions are communicated between collaborators (via raised exceptions or error results)
- Who recovers from them
- How recovery is accomplished
- Who recovers from failed attempts at recovery
- Who recasts exceptions or translates them to higher levels of abstraction

## Record Exception-Handling Policies

After you've decided how to solve one exceptional condition, tackle another. Often, you can leverage earlier work. If you decide that "these types of exceptions" are very similar to "those," you'll likely want to handle them consistently.

> There are two conditions that can cause a funds transfer request to fail: The account has a "hold" status that prohibits any monetary transactions, or the backend system might be too busy to handle the request within a reasonable time. In each case, the specific condition is reported to the user and the funds transfer fails.
>
> In the online banking application, both the FundsTransferTransaction and the UserSession react to exception conditions returned from requests. The FundsTransferTransaction is responsible for transaction-specific exceptions; the UserSession, a controller, takes on broader exception-handling responsibilities including unauthorized account access, invalid requests, and communication failures.

Write down general strategies you will attempt to follow. Deciding on exception-handling policies can save a lot of work:

> ### System Exception Policies
>
> **Recoverable software exceptions.** These are caught exceptions that do not necessarily mean an unstable state in the software (corrupt message, time-outs, etc.). The strategy to be followed in these cases is to first log the exception and then try to handle it (if retrying is likely to succeed). If not, raise the exception so that it can be handled (if the caller is within the same process); or return an error (if the caller is not within the same process).
>
> **Unrecoverable software exceptions.** These are caught exceptions that presumably can lead to an unstable state, such as running out of memory or a task being unresponsive. The response in these cases is to log the cause of the exception and to restart the application unless the severity of that specific condition is "hold&do not restart."

## DOCUMENTING YOUR EXCEPTION-HANDLING DESIGNS

You will likely want to beef up existing collaboration stories with exception-handling details. But don't pile on details. You can easily make a collaboration story incomprehensible or a diagram illegible, obscuring the main storyline. Instead, draw new diagrams to show how specific exceptions are handled. Leave existing diagrams alone.

Any new diagram will look nearly identical to the normal case but will include additional details about how exceptions are detected, communicated, and dealt with.

***Describe your solution.*** Your readers will get a much better sense of your exception design if you explain it. Describe which exceptions you considered, how each is resolved, and what you consider to be out of scope:

---

The online banking application is designed to cover communications failures encountered during a financial transaction. A full set of single-point failures was considered. Some double-point failures were explicitly not considered because they are unlikely and covering them adds undue complexity to the processing of transactions.

In each case, the general strategy is to ensure that transaction status is accurately reflected to the user. Failures in validating information will cause the transaction to fail, whereas intermittent communications to the external database or to the backend banking system during the transaction will not cause a transaction to fail. Here are the exceptions common to every transaction:

1. Network fails during attempt to send request to backend: Detect that response times out. Retry request after communications are restored. If too much time elapses, inform user of system unavailability and fail the transaction.

2. Failure to log transaction results to local database: Continue, but report condition to alternate log file and active console.

3. Failure to receive acknowledgment from backend system: Report system unavailability to user and report backend request status when connection is reestablished.

---

***Add a running commentary to existing collaborations.*** Accompany a happy path collaboration diagram with commentary that describes exceptions that you considered at each step. This is an extremely effective way to present your design. Reviewers are unlikely to get the big picture by looking at many diagrams, trying to piece together whether you've covered all the bases. So tell them what might go wrong at each step.

***Understand the limits of what can be explained with a diagram.*** If you show an exception being raised, you won't necessarily know which object handles it unless you explicitly add that detail. When an object detects an exceptional condition, it can either *raise an exception* or *return a result* whose value indicates an exception condition.

In UML, an exception is modeled as a signal. To show that an object raises an exception, draw an asynchronous message between it and the client whose request caused the exception. This is drawn as a line with a stick arrowhead (see Figure 8-6). Designate the line as an <<exception>>. Label it with the name of the exception to distinguish it from other asynchronous signals.

If you are returning a result to indicate an exception condition, add a return to your diagram. It is drawn as a dashed line with an open arrow. The value that is returned can be recorded above the line.

You can describe both normal and exceptional paths on the same diagram (see Figure 8-7). Show multiple paths emerging from the same point in the diagram. Label each with a guard condition that describes the conditions that cause one path to be selected over another. One branch continues with the normal path; others take exceptional ones.

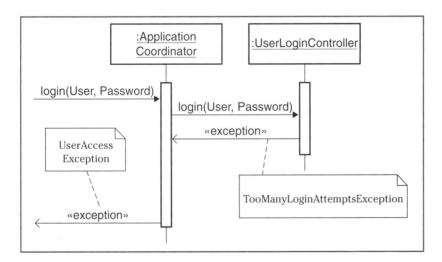

Figure 8-6
*Labeling exceptions with notes clarifies what's going on.*

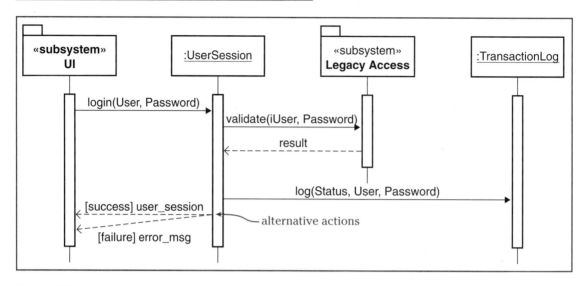

Figure 8-7
*FundsTransferTransaction takes one of two branches, depending on whether or not the transaction is successful.*

***Limit the number of diagrams.*** Create new diagrams only to illustrate key exception-handling cases or obscure solutions. If certain exceptions are handled similarly, say so, don't draw so.

***Limit the number of exceptions shown on any single diagram.*** Don't show more than one or two exceptions on a single diagram. Piling on details makes diagrams incomprehensible.

***Add notes to diagrams to clarify exception-handling responsibilities.*** You can't tell whether or not an object receiving an exception handles it. To make it absolutely clear that an object handles an exception, add an explanatory note (see Figure 8-8).

To show that an object recasts an exception, add a note (see Figure 8-9).

***Add exceptions to class definitions.*** The specification of a class in UML includes a declaration of operations, attributes, and relationships. An operation can be declared in syntax specific to the programming language. This enables you to precisely specify the exceptions raised by each operation. We typically do not go to this level of detail, leaving it for code comments and documentation.

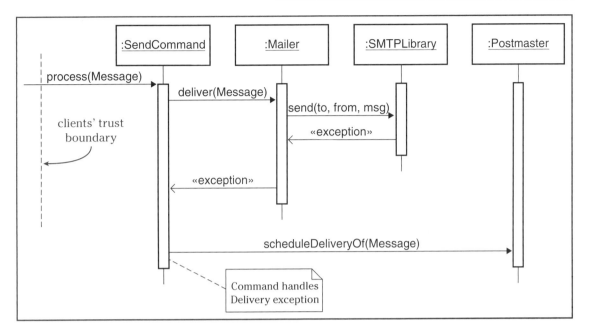

Figure 8-8
*Clients can trust the commands to handle any exceptions.*

**Add details sparingly.** Just because you can embellish a sequence diagram with exception details or show exception declarations in method signatures, don't go overboard. The more you pile on, the harder it is for viewers to discriminate what's important. Show those things that your readers cannot find elsewhere. If your exceptions can be found by browsing class documentation, do you really need to include them on class diagrams? Think carefully whether these embellishments add value or clarity or only another opportunity for code to get out of sync with your design.

"...the low-level design handling of particular exceptions is felt by many developers to be most appropriately decided during programming or via less detailed design descriptions, rather than via detailed UML diagrams."

—Craig Larman

## Specifying Formal Contracts

The interplay between collaborators can get complex. In a given collaboration, objects are designed according to a set of expectations, demands, and obligations on both the client and the provider of the service. When you need to get precise, use contracts to specify how collaborators should responsibly interact.

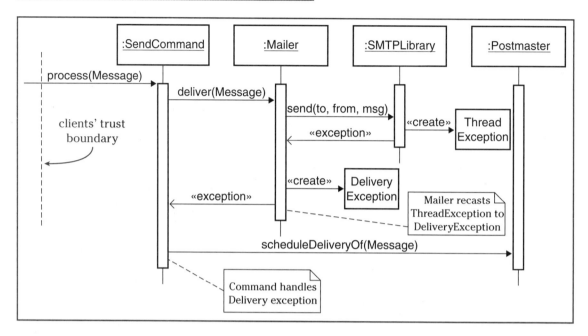

**Figure 8-9**
*Additional notes explain your exception-handling strategy.*

Eiffel was the first language to let programmers define preconditions that must be true before a body of code executes and postconditions that must be true after a body of code executes. Writing assertions that can be checked during program execution adds teeth to object contracts.

Bertrand Meyer views *contractual relations* between collaborators as an important specification tool. Contracts can be written to define the expectations and obligations of both client and service provider for any request. According to Meyer, any contract entails obligations as well as benefits for both parties; an obligation for one usually can be restated as a benefit for the other.

> "In relations between people or companies, a contract is a written document that serves to clarify the terms of a relationship. It is really surprising that in software, where precision is so important and ambiguity so risky, this idea has taken so long to impose itself. A pre-condition-postcondition pair . . . will describe the contract that the routine (the supplier of a certain service) defines for its callers (the clients of that service)."
> —*Bertrand Meyer*

Obligations can be stated in terms of *preconditions* that must be true before a request is honored, and *postconditions* that will be guaranteed by the service provider:

- A precondition obligates a client. It defines the conditions under which a request is valid. It is an obligation for the client—to make sure that preconditions are met—and a benefit for the service provider. Meyer goes so far as to say that if the requester does not satisfy the preconditions, then the service provider is not bound to satisfy the request.

- A postcondition obligates the service provider. It defines the conditions that must be ensured after the request is complete. It is a benefit for the client and an obligation for the service provider.

So if a service provider wanted to be very lazy indeed, its contracts would place high demands on what must be true before it starts (strong preconditions) and guarantee nothing in return (weak postconditions). Only if the preconditions are met will it start to work.

For a trusted collaboration, the service provider expects well-formed requests and the client expects reasonable attempts at performing the request. In untrusted collaborations, a client might take special preparations before making a request and possibly make extra checks afterwards to verify that the service was performed correctly.

Table 8-1 shows how we might state a contract outlining the obligations and benefits of a request that spans a trust boundary from the online banking system to the backend bank system to request a funds transfer.

> A contract specification is a job description for the service provider: Its work will start from the initial state of the system as characterized by the preconditions, and it will deliver results defined by the postconditions.

Table 8-1 *A contract explains both obligations and benefits.*

| Request: Funds Transfer | Obligations | Benefits |
|---|---|---|
| Client: online banking application | (precondition) User has two accounts. | Funds are transferred and balances adjusted. |
| Service provider: backend banking system | (preconditions) Sufficient funds were in the first account. Honor request only if both accounts are active (postcondition) Both accounts' balances are adjusted to reflect transfer. | Only needs to check for sufficient funds and active accounts, need not check that user is authorized to access accounts. |

Meyer's notions of obligations and benefits is contrary to *defensive* collaborations, in which nothing is trusted and everything is checked. In fact, if you spelled out the contractual obligations between collaborators in great detail, you could theoretically implement only a minimum number of checks. The hardest part in implementing objects that fulfill their obligations is ensuring that postconditions are met. This is especially difficult when a service provider collaborates with many others to get its job done.

You and your coworkers may go back and forth dickering over what constitutes "reasonable" benefits and obligations for a specific contract. This is a good exercise. After you decide who should take responsibility, you can implement collaborators to work within these constraints.

If you are designing a component that must work reliably in spite of untrusted requests, you can purposely design it with a defensive posture—checking everything before it does anything. If checks are expensive, you should probably assign more obligations to the service provider. Decisions about who should take responsibility for guaranteeing preconditions is partly a matter of style and partly a matter of the trust between objects.

Defining contracts is good way to reason about the obligations and benefits of a particular collaboration. But it's also a lot of work. Not all collaborations warrant this extra attention. Contracts are especially useful for defining the obligations and benefits between your software and external systems:

> In the online banking application, it is reasonable to put the obligation on the backend bank to keep track of funds in accounts. Other transactions can be made by other banking applications that affect account balances, independently of the online banking application. Even if the online banking application can check beforehand via an expensive communication, it can't guarantee that the funds will still be available by the time it actually makes the request.

Contracts make absolutely clear what is expected. They are especially important for describing collaborations that need to be reliable and that cross trust boundaries.

## REVIEWING YOUR DESIGN

Even with the best intentions, you can't spot all the flaws in your work. Have you ever had an "Aha! moment" when you explained something to someone else? Simply talking about your design with someone else helps you to see things clearly. A fresh perspective will help spot gaps in your design.

The most common bugs in exception-handling design, according to Charles Howell and Gary Veccellio in *Advances in Exception Handling Techniques* (Alexander Romanovsky, ed., Springer 2001), who analyzed several highly reliable systems, crop up when the following things happen:

- When writing exception-handling logic, you fail to consider additional exceptions that might arise. Don't let your guard down! Any action performed when an exception is handled could cause other exceptions. Often, the appropriate solution to this situation is to raise new exceptions from within the exception-handling code.

- You map error codes to exceptions. At different locations in your design, various objects may have the responsibility to translate between specific return code values and specific exceptions. The most common source of error is to incompletely consider the range of error codes—mapping some, but not all, cases. Mapping is often required when different parts of a system are implemented in different programming languages.

- You propagate exceptions to unprepared clients. Unhandled exceptions will continue to propagate up the collaboration chain until either they are handled by some catchall object or they are left to the run-time environment. Designers usually want some graceful exception reporting or recovery. What they'll get instead, if clients aren't designed to handle an unexpected exception, will be program termination.

- You think an exception has been handled when it has merely been logged. Exception code should do something meaningful to get the software back on track. As a first cut, you may implement a common mechanism to log or report an exception. But this doesn't mean it has been handled. You've done nothing but report the problem—something that is only slightly more useful than taking no action at all.

In addition to these potential sources of error, look for places where complexity may have sneaked in:

> "Redundant checking . . . is a standard technique in hardware. The difference is that in a hardware system some object that was found to be in a correct state at some point may later have its integrity destroyed because of reasons beyond the control of the system itself. . . [but] software doesn't wear out when used for too long; it is not subject to line loss, to interference or noise."
>
> —Bertrand Meyer

- Redundant validation responsibilities. When you aren't certain who should take responsibility, sometimes you put it in several places. Different levels of validation may be performed by different objects in a collaboration—first checking that the information is in the right format, next checking that it is consistent with other information. It is OK to spread these responsibilities among collaborators. But avoid two different objects performing identical semantic checks.

- Unnecessary checks. If you aren't sure whether some condition should be checked, why not check anyway? The reason is that it can decrease system performance and give you a false sense of security. This is an easy trap to fall into. By doing this, you've done absolutely nothing to increase your software's reliability and are likely to confuse those who will maintain your design.

- Embellished recovery actions. At first, extra measures seem to be a good idea . . . but wait. Is it really necessary to retry a failed operation, log it, *and* send e-mail to the system administrator? Look for places where extra measures detract from system performance, make your system more complex, and, on a really bad day, clog someone's inbox.

At the end of a review, you should be convinced that your exception-handling actions are reasonable, cost-effective, and likely make a difference in your system's reliability.

## Summary

As a first step in increasing your software's reliability, you need to understand the consequences of system failure. The more critical the consequences, the more you can justify the effort and energy of designing for reliability. To clarify your thinking, distinguish between exceptions—unlikely conditions that your software must handle—and errors. Errors are things that go wrong—bad data, programming errors, logic errors, faulty hardware, broken devices. Most software doesn't need to be designed to recover from errors, but it can be made more reliable by gracefully handling common exceptional conditions.

Approaches for improving reliability are rarely cut and dried. The best alternative isn't always clear. To decide what appropriate actions should be taken involves sound engineering as well as consideration of costs and impacts on the system's users.

Objects do not work in isolation. To improve system reliability you must improve how objects work in collaboration. Collaborations can be analyzed for the degree of trust between collaborators. Within the same trust boundary, objects can assume that exceptions will be detected and reported and that responsibilities for checking on conditions and information will be carried out by the appropriately designated responsible party. In some programming languages, exceptions can be declared. When an exception is raised, some other object in the collaboration chain will take responsibility for handling it. An alternative implementation technique is to return values from calls that can encode exceptional conditions.

When collaborations span trust boundaries, more precautions may need to be taken. Defensive collaborations—designing objects to take precautions before and after calling on a collaborator—are expensive and error-prone. Not every object should be tasked with these responsibilities. When you need to be very precise, define contracts between collaborators. Bertrand Meyer uses contracts to specify the obligations and benefits of the client and the provider of a service. Spelling out these terms makes it absolutely clear what each object's responsibilities are in a given collaboration.

## FURTHER READING

Doug Lea has written a very handy book called *Concurrent Programming in Java™: Design Principles and Patterns, Second Edition* (Addison-Wesley, 2000). This book is invaluable, even to non-Java programmers. It is packed with in-depth discussions and examples and good design principles. Even if you aren't building highly concurrent applications, this book is worth careful study.

*Advances in Exception Handling Techniques* (Alexander Romanovsky et al., eds., Springer Verlag, 2001) grew out of a workshop on exception handling for the 21st century. It is a collection of chapters written by programming language researchers, database designers, distributed system designers, and developers of complex applications and mission critical systems, who share their vision of the current state of the art of exception handling and design. You will find very readable papers that discuss exceptions from multiple perspectives.

Bertrand Meyer's book *Object-Oriented Software Construction (Second Edition)* (Prentice Hall, 2000) is the definitive work on software engineering using the principle of Design by Contract. It is a weighty book. But two chapters—Design by Contract: Building Reliable Software, and When the Contract is Broken: Exception Handling—are a good exposure to thinking in terms of preconditions, postconditions, invariants, and collaboration contracts.

Henry Petroski talks about the role of failure analysis in successful design in *To Engineer Is Human: The Role of Failure in Successful Design* (Vintage Books, 1992). Software designers clearly don't understand the laws that govern software failures as well as structural engineers understand physics and materials. But you can learn many lessons from this book.

# Chapter 9

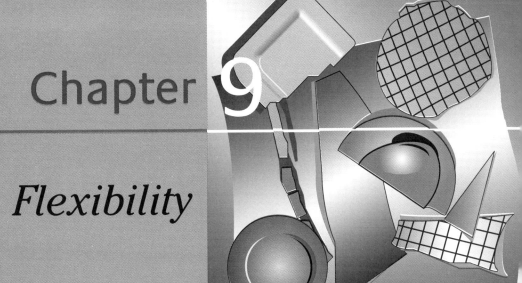

## *Flexibility*

Seemingly effortless improvisation—whether in music or software—requires you to quickly identify and fit something new alongside what's already there. You slip in and go with the flow. Coming up with variations with little apparent effort is what improvisation is all about. Composing on the spot. Making it look easy.

Only after you've acquired the basic skills can you begin to improvise. To get really good at it takes talent, sure, but also lots of practice and experience. How can you get to this level? If your software has been carefully designed, it's much easier. Software that has been designed to flex is set up for ready extension. It has the structures in place that allow for change, so you can look good without having to work so hard.

## WHAT DOES IT MEAN TO BE FLEXIBLE?

Most people think object software inherently is flexible. It isn't. Flexibility, even in object software, takes extra effort. It must be explicitly built into your design. Flexibility is a measure of how easily software can adapt to a range of design parameters. The larger the scope of these parameters' effects, the more flexible the software is.

> Flexible: Capable of responding or conforming to new or changing situations.
> —*Webster's Seventh New Collegiate Dictionary*

Designing software as a collection of roles, responsibilities, and collaborations is the first step toward creating flexible software. Flexible software has fewer hard-wired assumptions, fixed values, or static connections between collaborators. It's looser. Things can be slipped in. It is designed to include "knobs" that can be turned to adjust things. There are explicit places in the design that have been prepared for adaptation.

Flexible software may dynamically alter its own behavior as it executes, reacting to changes in its environment. Or the end user may be able to customize how the software works. That's flexibility, too. Or flexible software may be extended by a developer who adds new behaviors in prescribed ways—creating new subclasses, defining new methods, or plugging in new collaborators. In all these cases, software can be adapted to fit changing requirements.

There is a difference between an adaptable system and a flexibly designed one. Software can react to various situations even if its design is inflexible. What distinguishes a flexible design from other solutions is that it incorporates mechanisms—hooks, if you will—that enable it to be changed. Designers have anticipated future adaptations and have structured their design to accommodate them. They've placed extra mechanisms into the software in anticipation of its flexing. They have made educated guesses about how the software will need to be tweaked and have incorporated design elements that specifically enable additions and modifications and extensions. If they've make sound choices about where to incorporate these flexion points, their work will have a big impact on maintenance.

What does it take to make software flexible? In part, it depends on who makes the adjustments. If the person making changes is a programmer or designer, there will be obvious clues and special hooks installed in the design. Some of these hooks will exist regardless of

---

"Music is your own experience, your thoughts, your wisdom. If you don't live it, it won't come out of your horn."

—Charlie Parker

From the user's point of view, flexible software accommodates varying conditions or requirements. From a developer's point of view, flexible software can be modified or extended with ease.

A design that meets its stated objectives may or may not be able to flex and adapt to a new condition.

who makes the changes. But when a system is designed to be extended, there is even more work involved. Special attention may have been paid to designing and documenting class hierarchies with specific extension points. Ideally, when developers need to alter some behavior or extend the software's feature set, they should follow a well-understood procedure: Add a class here or override a method there. This works only if preparations have been made.

In a good design, flexibility isn't an accident; it's a byproduct of careful preparation. It takes extra machinery and inventions and design discipline as well as extra attention to design and coding details. You might need to identify common roles and document how class hierarchies can be extended. You might need to include additional embellishments that enable programmers to dynamically configure collaborators or varying information. It takes energy to describe and make points of extension evident. It's more work to develop coding examples that illustrate how to make an adaptation or write recipes that describe how to tinker with the flexible machinery.

Anticipating future changes is a bit of a gamble, sure, but the payoffs can be immense. Flexibility enables design improvisation.

> "People never understand how arranged Bill Evans's music really was. Sure, it was free and improvised. But the reason we could be so free is that we already know the beginning, the middle, and the ending."
>
> —Chuck Israels

## DEGREES OF FLEXIBILITY

The ways software *could* flex are limitless. There is never enough time and energy to realize every idea. Not every good design is a flexible one. And not every object needs to be flexible to make a system flexible. You should emphasize flexibility when

- It is clearly justified in support of tangible requirements
- It doesn't compromise other project goals
- Your software will live in an environment with a history of change
- Your software needs to adapt to different environments
- It is of high value to you, your teammates, and other project stakeholders

When's the right time to think about flexibility? As soon as you start partitioning responsibilities into related chunks, you can start thinking about flexible solutions. Monolithic software can be hard to change. It is easier to add flexibility to software that is organized into well-defined components and subsystems.

If you need to adapt to varying environmental conditions, it's better to structure your system so that points of potential change and

> "Patterns are a cornerstone of object-oriented design, while test-first programming and merciless refactoring are cornerstones of evolutionary design. To stop over- or under-engineering, balance these practices and evolve only what you need."
>
> —Joshua Kerievsky

variation are insulated from the rest of the system. You can intentionally *wrap* potential points of variation to prevent dependencies
on specific features from permeating other parts of the system. The
sooner you make these decisions, the easier it will be to keep your
options open. Very early decisions can dramatically increase or
inhibit your software's ability to flex.

But during exploratory design there are also many decisions that
impact flexibility. Choices you make as you assign responsibilities to
objects and design collaborations affect flexibility. Many of the practices we have mentioned in this book improve your design and, as a
side effect, make it easier to change. Responsibilities are design
placeholders where various object types and behaviors can be
plugged in to replace others. The ways you choose to divide responsibilities among objects enable you to neatly encapsulate any behaviors that might change. But only when you add explicit hooks—which
allow responsibilities to be modified or collaborators to be replaced
without affecting working code—do you really support flexibility.

> Whether it be extension,
> modification, or run-time
> configuration, flexibility isn't
> something that just happens.
> It must to be identified and
> designed into software.

Design patterns typically allow small groups of objects to flex in specific ways. How you use patterns impacts the ways your software
flexes. Consider the Command pattern. It encapsulates an action in
an object. You can add new operations by inventing new types of
Command objects (see Figure 9-1). You can do so relatively easily as

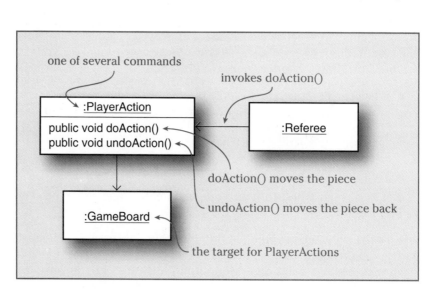

Figure 9-1
*The Command pattern supports varying actions on a target.*

long as a new Command object operates under the same assumptions as existing Command objects. The mechanism for supporting a new command is preestablished, leaving the design of the new command's behavior for you to concentrate on.

Your choice of patterns and the way your design is organized impact how amenable your software is to adaptation. But flexibility concerns don't stop there. At the most detailed level, seemingly small choices affect your software's ability to flex. How you construct methods, specify signatures, declare interfaces, and use inheritance impact flexibility. Identifying shared roles and then defining common interfaces make your software more flexible. Encapsulating private details inside objects makes clients less dependent on others' inner workings, thus making it possible to change how they work without rippling changes throughout the design. Code refactorings, described in Martin Fowler's *Refactoring: Improving the Design of Existing Code* (Addison-Wesley, 1999), improve the structure and quality of the implementation. Refactorings are intentional restructurings that preserve a design's intent while preparing it to better absorb an anticipated change. Whether you refactor during design or coding, refactorings tend to shift responsibilities among collaborators or move them around in an inheritance hierarchy.

## THE CONSEQUENCES OF A FLEXIBLE SOLUTION

Flexibly designed software offers many advantages. The ways to support specific variation have been preestablished. Hooks are in place, waiting for you to plug in a new variation. Instead of spending time devising new mechanisms, you follow set design rules. You just have to dig in and implement a variation that follows them. Are you improvising? Yes. But you don't have to be terribly clever. You have patterns and proven mechanisms to extend and augment.

> If a new banking service is similar to the design of an existing one, adding it is fairly easy. Objects that coordinate the new financial service need to be designed and coded. But the pattern for doing so is preestablished. It is a matter of fitting this new service provider into preexisting patterns of collaboration and calling on existing backend banking services. Sometimes, additional backend banking system functions may need to be wrapped and utilized. That takes more work.

A design chock full of ready-to-extend abstractions and brilliantly factored responsibilities can be daunting. Patterns can be applied too heavily, making the design complex, flexible, and hard to decipher. This is because it is harder to think abstractly than to think concretely.

The learning curve for highly flexible software can be steep. Understanding complex software takes time. Understanding complex, flexible software takes even longer. And if you dwell in a complex system for a while, you tend to create complex solutions, whether or not they are warranted. It's a matter of fitting in and following the established style. Yes, software can be too flexible for its own good! Raphael Malveau and Thomas Mowbray in *Software Architect Bootcamp* (Prentice Hall, 2000) caution against "flexibility disease," whose symptoms include the following:

- Overly complex procedures. If the recipe for making an extension has many complex steps to follow, it can be difficult and error-prone.

- Many documented conventions. Sometimes a design is so flexible that the only way to extend it properly is to follow complex coding conventions. The only thing that prevents you from breaking things is to pay excruciating attention to detail.

- Extra code. To use a configurable service, clients must parameterize their requests. And the service provider may be more complex in order to handle all the options. Extra complexity can pile up on both sides of a flexible interface.

The major drawback of a flexible design is added complexity. But creating an inflexible solution isn't the antidote. Inflexible designs are difficult to revise and improve on. No one wants to build software that is creaky, difficult to maintain, and subject to ugly hacks. So the easier it is to make software adapt, the longer it will stay true to its original design. The key is to build in flexibility in just the right places.

## NAILING DOWN FLEXIBILITY REQUIREMENTS

Not every object needs to be flexible, and not all parts of a design need to flex. You create a flexible design when you see the similarities and variations on common behavior and subsequently identify roles that can be shared by different kinds of objects.

> Letters, words, sentences, and commands are core concepts of the Speak for Me domain. Realizing that they are all variations of another concept, a "guess," simplifies the design and makes it easy to extend. There is no explicit statement in the requirements that "the system will offer several different kinds of guesses to the user." The concept had to be invented. But once they were there, we pushed on it . . . and extrapolated that message Destinations could also be a kind of guess.

The more variations you see surrounding a common theme, the more fodder you have to create good abstractions that support a range of variations. So even without expending lots of extra effort, you may discover that certain parts of your design may have the potential to be more flexible, even though flexibility hasn't been your focus. But how can you determine where you should concentrate your efforts?

***Identify the real problem.*** Flexibility requirements are rarely spelled out in explicit detail. No one says, "Build me the coolest framework and make it hum!" Often, only when you look closely at how to satisfy other requirements do you see that a flexible solution might be the right solution to propose:

> A stated objective for the online banking framework was that it should be configured and installed at a new location within a month. The project sponsors also wanted installations to require little or no programming or design rework because it was difficult to negotiate time-and-materials contracts and customers were used to fixed installation costs.
>
> These requirements led us to conclude that facilities needed to be designed into the software to make it easily tunable during installation.

Flexibility is rarely the problem that needs solving. Proposing a flexible solution may allow you to support frequent revisions or adapt to different environments or users or to add new functionality in a predictable way. The real need is to support new changes. Flexibility isn't a requirement; it's only one design option.

***Establish the vision.*** When you spot an opportunity to propose a flexible solution, it is important that you paint pictures of the future with and without a flexible solution. Make it clear that a flexible solution will make a difference.

> The telco integration framework will need to support cases in which different software components share information and in which data will need to be collected from more than one source. Rather than integrate various applications via point-to-point solutions, the framework will serve as the central means to coordinate work among various applications that it integrates. Limiting visibility between applications allows for changing external systems without changing each interdependent application.

Making an application flexible takes extra work. So it is important that the requirements warrant the effort. When requirements specify configurable behavior, or extensibility, or robust reactions to unanticipated conditions, that is where we start.

***Honestly assess whether a flexible solution is affordable.***
Although a flexible solution may be important to a project's success,
you have spotted a *potential* opportunity and not necessarily the
only workable solution. And because flexibility incurs extra development costs, you'll need to convince yourself and others that a flexible solution is the appropriate solution.

It is tempting to overdesign
and invent abstractions to
accommodate any number
of imagined design changes.
That's just another form of
feature creep.

> The system architect of the online banking system was fresh off
> another very successful project. A brilliant programmer, he loved the
> special challenge of building generalized frameworks, something that
> was explicitly demanded in his previous project. He brought his
> excitement (and assumptions about requirements) to the online bank-
> ing project. But this project was on a tight schedule, with little room
> for invention or error. When he became consumed by his desire to
> implement a customizable framework, his colleagues had to spend
> many long hours to fill in the gaps and meet tight project deadlines.

Flexibility in a design can be of great value. But the variations that you
support should be of value. When you are on a tight schedule, it is
dangerous to spend precious time designing for the unforeseen future.
You can't sacrifice other project goals just for the sake of flexibility.

***Identify places where your architecture should flex.*** There
may be areas in your design where a flexible solution offers clear
advantages. If you believe that to be true, push on that part of the
design for a bit and don't let go until you understand more. Before
you can design in flexibility, characterize what variations your software needs to support. Then pinpoint appropriate places where a
flexible design solution is warranted.

> A small number of design constraints were proposed for the telco
> integration project. These included statements such as these: It
> should provide transparent integration between different business
> applications. It will not provide only hardwired point-to-point com-
> munications. Instead, components in the integration framework will
> encapsulate the differences among instances of a particular type of
> application.
>
> This led us to partition the architecture into adapters that interfaced
> with core business processing functions. Adapters were responsible
> for transferring requests and information between external applica-
> tions and a business process coordination core. Each adapter inter-
> faced to a specific application. Resource managers were responsible
> for locating information maintained by external applications. Com-
> munications between adapters and the core were through a common
> set of framework-specific commands.

***Demonstrate real benefits.*** It can be difficult to quantify benefits and estimate the cost of designing a flexible solution, especially when you are building something from scratch. We can't stress this enough: Flexibility doesn't come for free! But the need for developing a flexible solution should be defensible. Identify the benefits that a more flexible solution provides over a less flexible one.

---

With the telco integration framework, a new application can be supported by defining its services, fitting them into current or new business processes, and developing an adapter component. Currently we must ask each vendor to bid on software modifications and customized interfaces to other applications. The vendors are in control, and we have little opportunity to manage development costs.

If the billing system fails, requests will be queued in the integration framework. Currently, the entire order must be reentered, which is error-prone. If the billing application's database becomes corrupted and needs to be restored, the framework could "replay" previous billing adjustments. This is possible because all orders are stored in a database. Currently, the billing system is restored with manual entries via a complex user interface. Only one or two highly skilled billing analysts can perform this task with any reliability.

The telco integration framework was sold to management on the basis of reduced customization costs, increased control over a constantly evolving environment, and increased reliability.

---

But be careful. Don't oversell or propose a difficult solution when a simpler one is adequate.

***Find out what you don't know.*** What you don't know can compromise your design efforts. Ask crucial questions before investing a lot of energy in wasted effort. You can mitigate risks by following an incremental, iterative development process that places tight controls on how much you will invest in making things flexible. In a nutshell, define an increment; identify a set of features that will prove the merits of some flexibility you want to support in your software; then design and implement a flexible solution that supports those features. Evaluate your results and replan for the next increment. Don't let unplanned embellishments slip in. Don't let too much time slide by without taking a critical look at your design solution. Each increment buys information about the choices you've made and lays a foundation for future increments. If you are planning to build a very flexible system, defining the right-sized increments and watching your investments in flexibility will be key to your success.

"An architecture is a plan, and it is said that no plan survives first contact with the enemy. The enemies in this case are change and ignorance. . . . What we don't know can change our architectural assumptions to the breaking point."

—Raphael Malveau and
Thomas Mowbray

> The first deliverable for the telco integration application was a proto-type, implemented in Java. This was delivered in six months. It handled simple service orders for two types of products. The project deliverables also included a design model for the core framework and adapters, a documented subsystem architecture, and a list of issues and recommendations.
>
> An important objective of the initial telco framework prototype project was to identify issues that must be addressed in a production-quality system. After the prototype was completed, the architecture, design, and issues were reviewed by a select group of internal and external reviewers. Their feedback was used in planning the next iteration.

Incremental development lets you validate what you think you know instead of pressing on in ignorance.

## RECORDING VARIATIONS

Hot spots, recorded on index cards, are informal tools for capturing rough ideas about the points of variation you want to support in your software. Index cards are indeed a flexible tool—you can use them to record variations as well as describe candidate objects.

If you are developing flexible software, it is important to characterize the types of variability your software needs to support. You can start by asking the following:

- What functions will change over time or work differently because of certain conditions? A list of points of variation, or hot spots, can focus your efforts.

- What is the desired degree of flexibility for each hot spot? Must the flexible functionality be changeable at run time or by end users? How flexible does the software need to be? An honest assessment of how flexible your software needs to be can help you plan the effort.

Whether you are building a framework or simply trying to design software that supports some variations, hot spot cards are a great way to briefly characterize some flexible behavior. Wolfgang Pree introduced the notion of a hot spot or variation card at an OOPSLA tutorial in 1995. Like CRC cards, they are a low-tech tool you can use to describe the essence of a variation.

A hot spot card is divided into three sections (see Figure 9-2). The top section includes the name of the hot spot. The middle section summarizes the functionality that varies. This high-level general description leaves out details. The bottom section is used to sketch

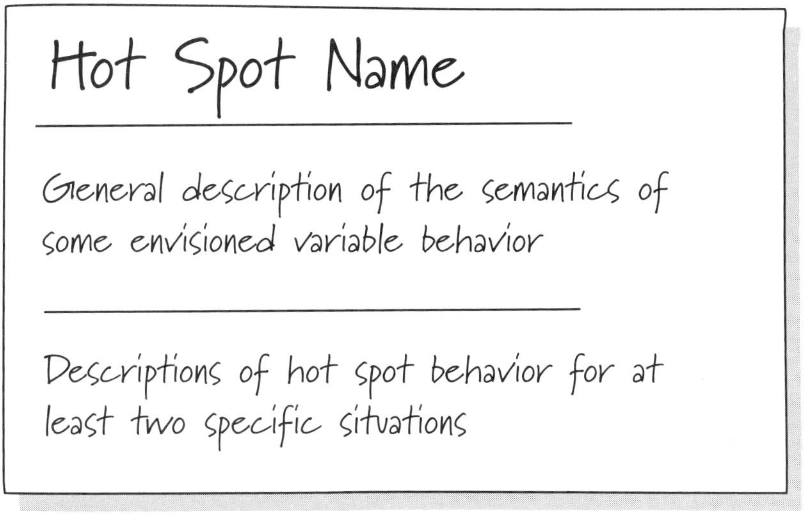

Hot Spot Name

General description of the semantics of
some envisioned variable behavior

Descriptions of hot spot behavior for at
least two specific situations

Figure 9-2
*The hot spot card describes and demonstrates variations.*

two specific examples of the variation. Ideally, you should capture just enough detail that you can discriminate similarities and differences as you consider potential design strategies.

Who fills out hot spots cards? During requirements gathering, people who articulate business needs—business analysts or end users—can work with designers to jointly fill out the cards. These cards can be a tool to briefly characterize run-time flexibility or the possibility of end-user-directed adaptations (see Figure 9-3). Anyone describing a hot spot should realize that added flexibility incurs some cost. A reasonable design solution will include additional mechanisms that will allow the software to flex in support of the hot spot.

You can also use hot spot cards during design. Document variations that you spot at the beginning of a design iteration. Use hot spot cards to reverse-engineer your design—characterize existing variations—before planning how to absorb new requirements. Ask what's already there and how it varies. Understand what you have before altering your design to slip in a new adaptation.

Imagine if the Sun Java development team had used hot spot cards to describe desired variable behaviors before inventing design mechanisms and new interfaces and classes! In Java, all collections contain a number of elements in a certain data structure. Different

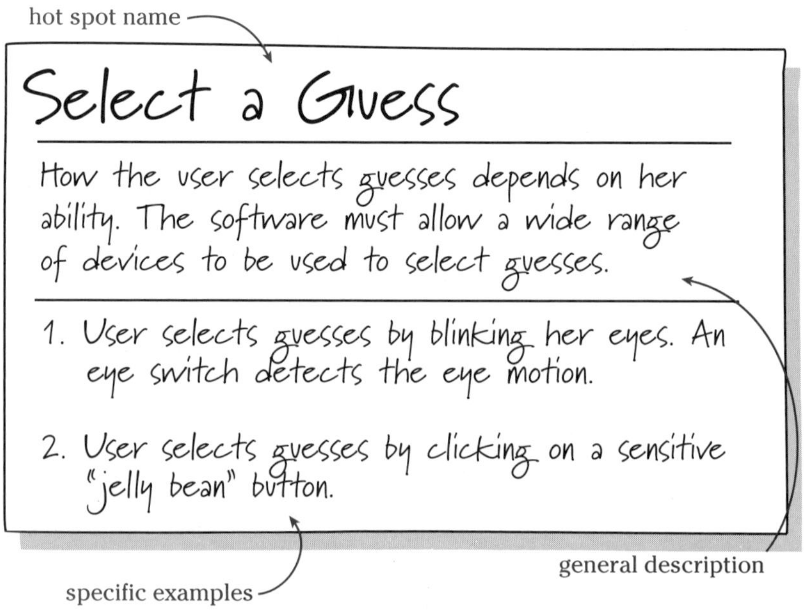

hot spot name

Select a Guess

How the user selects guesses depends on her
ability. The software must allow a wide range
of devices to be used to select guesses.

1. User selects guesses by blinking her eyes. An
   eye switch detects the eye motion.

2. User selects guesses by clicking on a sensitive
   "jelly bean" button.

general description

specific examples

**Figure 9-3**
*A guess can be selected in several different ways in Speak for Me. It's a hot spot.*

classes of collections define different structures, optimized for specific access and usage patterns. Linked lists and hashtables are two specific examples. An iterator is a mechanism for accessing elements of a collection without having to know anything about its underlying structure. In Java, an interface has been defined that describes three basic operations of an iterator: hasNext(), next(), and remove(). Figure 9-4 shows a description of collection traversal that might have hatched the Java iterator concept.

A hot spot card should describe the variation and not pose a design solution.

There are obvious limits to what can be written on a hot spot card. Complex algorithms don't easily fit. If you need to characterize a variation in more detail, do so. Use cards to sketch out the basic ideas, and keep them simple. Don't solve the flexibility requirement on the card—just sketch what varies. Nothing says you can't write more or that you must limit your thoughts to what fits on a card. Use the card to sketch what varies and not to solve the flexibility requirement. A slightly expanded hot spot description might sketch out several possible solutions.

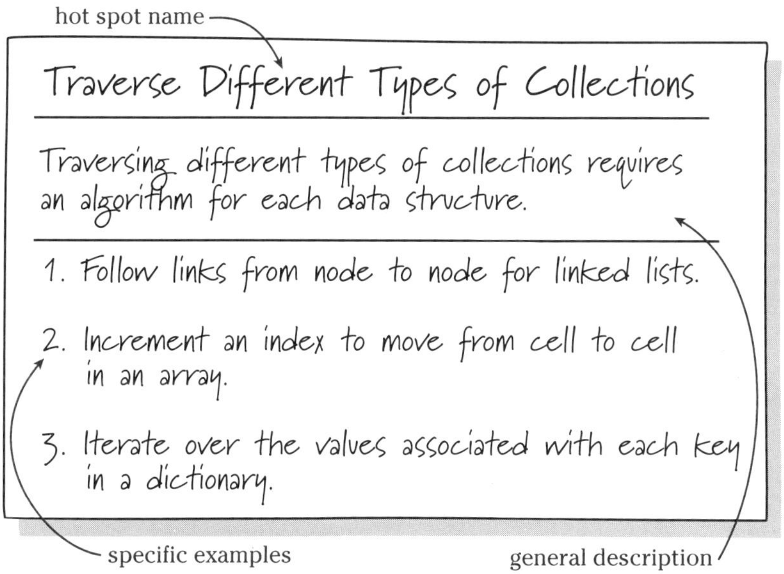

hot spot name ——

## Traverse Different Types of Collections

Traversing different types of collections requires an algorithm for each data structure.

1. Follow links from node to node for linked lists.

2. Increment an index to move from cell to cell in an array.

3. Iterate over the values associated with each key in a dictionary.

—— specific examples                                general description

Figure 9-4
*Iteration is a hot spot in collection class libraries.*

Early in the telco integration project, a 10-page document was written that described seven hot spots. It also described initial thoughts on how best to support them. The project sponsors and business analysts didn't want to give the team detailed guidance on design choices, but they wanted the team to focus on the right things. This document was one tool used to gain buy-in and support for an extensible framework and pinpoint exactly how the integration framework should flex. It was also used by the team to guide design discussions.

Hot spot descriptions are tools to guide your flexibility design efforts. Discussing hot spots helps a team to come to a deeper understanding of design variations that need to be supported. Use them to characterize how flexible a design needs to be.

## VARIATIONS AND REALIZATIONS

To "solve" a hot spot, you will likely introduce new design mechanisms that enable your design to flex. This boils down to making specific responsibilities tunable, replaceable, or extensible. After you've characterized a hot spot, you can get very specific. You can then do the following:

- Identify the focus and scope of the variation. How big an impact will it have on your design? Does it require a minor tweak, a modest investment, or a major design effort? Is it an extension or modification of what's already there, or does it require something new?

- Explore strategies for realizing the flexibility. Solutions can be as simple as tweaking a single responsibility or something much more elaborate.

- Evaluate your solution for gaps, unnecessary complexity, and usability.

- Describe to other designers and, potentially, to your software's users how to make the software flex.

## Identifying the Impact of a Variation

The *focus* of a variation is a set of system responsibilities that directly support the variation. A narrowly focused variation—one that affects one or two responsibilities—is likely to have a limited impact on a design.

> Enabling the design of Speak for Me to accommodate different preferences in the ordering of the spoken alphabet affects two objects: the UserPreferences object, which is responsible for knowing the preferred ordering, and the Alphabet, which is responsible for offering the next bid to the Guesser.

The *scope* is a measure of how pervasive that variation is—how much of the design, it affects. A variation could have a narrow focus and still have a large scope. This isn't necessarily the sign of a poorly factored design, but rather one that needs to be reshaped to accommodate a variation. Affected responsibilities may need to be factored into different objects or subdivided into smaller ones that can be tuned or replaced. Interfaces to services may need to be reconsidered. Responsibilities may need to be reassigned, and new objects may need to be inserted into the design.

## Exploring Strategies for Realizing Flexibility

Identifying the scope and focus of an adaptation sets the stage for devising mechanisms to support a variation. If a variation is simple, with a narrow focus and limited scope, you might get away with implementing a solution that isn't flexible. Your solution would support some variation but would not include mechanisms that would permit easy adaptations to support other, similar variations. On the other hand, if you expect similar variations to continue to crop up and stretch your design, develop a flexible solution.

Here are two examples that push at two ends of the spectrum. The first example is a variation with a narrow focus. It can be solved with a simple but inflexible design tweak. The scope could be fairly broad (it is hard to tell from the description), but even so, it seems that a reasonable design strategy would be to define a state variable (encapsulated in an information holder object) that could be checked:

> A trial version of software checks for a registration when it is launched. After that first check, it doesn't check again until the next launch. If the user isn't registered, the software disables several features (such as printing or creating work products larger than a specified size). **A check-once variation**.

In contrast, supporting a new product in the telco integration application has a broad scope and benefits from a flexible solution:

> When a new product is defined, the software needs to adjust in several places: New billing rules and provisioning tasks must be defined. A description of how to translate between an external order and the framework's representation of the order must be described. Initially, this analysis of the hot spot's scope surprised the project sponsors. They didn't expect that adding a new product would affect so many parts of the system. **A variation that requires definition of new information and translation rules**.

This variation is more challenging because the executable behavior of several parts of the design must change. The scope is broad, and the affected responsibilities are complex: New billing rules must be

When is a flexible solution warranted? It is hard to characterize how responsibilities vary until you have several variations to compare and contrast. Don't invent a flexible solution until you can test it with at least three tangible examples.

described, a provisioning task structure must be specified, and the external order must be translated into an internal one. This involves more than a few design tweaks. Each affected area of the design needs careful consideration and a flexible solution.

## Using Templates and Hooks to Support Variations

There are other techniques for making software flexible, but the Template Method pattern is a basic mechanism that enables responsibilities implemented in a class hierarchy to flex.

In addition to conditional logic and branching, there is one basic technique for making individual object behaviors flex that exploits inheritance: template methods. As described in *Design Patterns* (Erich Gamma, et al., Addison-Wesley, 1995), a *template method* is a skeleton of an algorithm. It specifies steps in an operation and identifies specific steps that can be tuned or replaced. A template method is a skeleton of an algorithm because it is incomplete; some steps are deferred.

As a designer you are likely to apply the Template Method pattern when you recognize that there will be differences in how subclasses should implement certain steps. The template method implements the fixed parts of an algorithm once, defines the ordering of steps, and leaves it up to subclass designers to implement the steps that vary. Code in template methods tends to call one of several kinds of methods:

- Concrete methods—methods defined in either abstract or concrete classes that do not require hooks to be replaced in order to work. A concrete method may implement default behavior that can be overridden in a subclass, or it may implement fixed behavior that is not replaceable.

- Primitive operations—basic operations defined by the specific programming language environment.

- Factory methods—methods that return new objects.

- Hook methods—placeholder methods that define spots where specific steps in the algorithm need to be plugged in to flesh out the skeleton. Often, designers provide default hook method implementations in abstract classes.

A *hook method* is a placeholder that gives other developers who are creating subclasses a chance to insert new behavior at a specific step in an algorithm. By calling upon a hook, developers can alter behavior for a particular step without having to alter any template method code. The template code stays fixed, whereas the contents of a hook varies and objects returned from factory methods vary (while supporting the same interface). The algorithm defined in a template method is flexible and is extensible by a developer who creates a subclass that implements hook methods.

> The general algorithm for performing any online banking request is as follows:
>
> 1. Obtain connection to backend banking system (a concrete action).
> 2. Prepare request (a hook).
> 3. Submit request to backend banking service (a hook).
> 4. Release connection (a concrete action).
> 5. Log results to transaction history database (a concrete action).
> 6. Report results to user (a concrete action).
>
> In the online banking application, a template method is defined in the abstract class `OnlineTransaction`. Subclasses are designed to coordinate specific transactions. Subclass designers must implement two hook methods: `prepareRequest()` and `submitRequest()`. All other steps of the algorithm are implemented by concrete methods defined in the `OnlineTransaction` (see Figure 9-5).

The Template Method pattern describes one specific technique to adapt a configurable algorithm whose steps need to vary. But there are other ways to make specific responsibilities tunable. More generally, a hook, according to Gary Froehlich and his colleagues who wrote about them in *Building Application Frameworks* (Mohamed Fayad, ed., John Wiley, 1999), is any point in the design that is meant to be adapted. It is a specific spot where variation is supported. There are several ways that behavior can be adjusted. Each hook uses at least one of these techniques:

- Enabling or disabling a feature
- Replacing a feature
- Augmenting a feature
- Adding a feature
- Configuring a feature

In support of an individual hot spot you might define several hooks or points in your design that are adaptable. To instrument these hooks you will need to introduce specific design mechanisms that allow other designers to adjust your design's behavior. For example, to enable or disable a feature, you might introduce a new variable

Normally, hook mechanisms wouldn't be part of your design. You introduce them whenever you want to support planned variations.

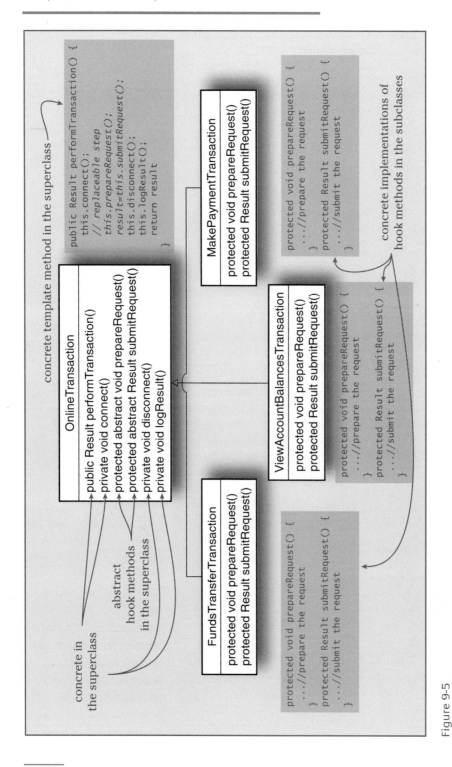

Figure 9-5
*Template and hook methods designate which parts are frozen and which spots are hot.*

whose value is checked in one or more places to alter the path taken through a method. To replace a feature, you might need to define new interfaces that allow designers to introduce new classes. Augmenting a feature may involve refactoring your design and making an extensible class hierarchy that incorporates template and hook methods. Or you may need to redesign a controller to activate a new feature.

***Determine when something needs to vary.*** The degree of difficulty of implementing support for a variation increases whenever software needs to adapt while it is executing. You may have to add support for synchronizing a number of related adjustments or structure your software so that the subsequent requests follow new rules, while a currently executing operation performs under conditions that were established when it started. Because dynamically adjustable software can be more complicated, don't assume it's a necessity. One question to ask when you're designing to support a variation is when it needs to be accommodated. Are conditions established when the application is launched, or are they dynamically checked to alter behavior during execution? There is a range of options.

---

User access rights to accounts are checked when a user logs in. The software doesn't check again until the next time the user logs in. **A check-once variation.**

The user of an e-mail application sets parameters that affect how mail is displayed, when to check for mail, whether to check for spelling errors, what signature to append to a message, how to encode a mail message, and so on. These variations affect many parts of the software. Whenever the user changes any setting, the software responds. **Numerous variations enabled by user-initiated events.**

To install a new upgrade to software controlling a card in a complex control system, the operator issues a command. The system reboots the card and reinitializes the card only after it has successfully downloaded the software and stored a backup copy in nonvolatile RAM. If the card isn't carrying any active traffic, an upgrade can be loaded at any time. **A dynamic reconfiguration with rollback/recovery constraints.**

---

Consider when your software needs to flex, and design it accordingly. Sometimes, simpler solutions meet flexibility requirements even though they don't support dynamic variation of system behavior.

There isn't a sharp line you can draw between what is considered "normal" conditional checking and control flow in an application and a flexible, configurable solution. Most object designs can be made to flex. A good design includes an appropriate degree of flexibility.

Supporting a different input device for the Speak for Me application involves installing a new device driver, defining and implementing a new interfacer to that device, and adding the device to the user's configurable preferences. Although Speak for Me could support dynamic loading of new devices whenever they are detected, this isn't strictly necessary. End users do not plug in new devices; hospital staff do. It is rare that a user is switched from one input device to another. In this case it is perfectly acceptable to configure the user's preferences and then restart the application.

"When faced with alternative approaches, choose the simplest first and change to a more complex one as needed."

—Martin Fowler

***Choose the simplest solution.*** When there is little reason to choose one design alternative over another, follow the simplest course of action. There are very simple ways to support variations that involve enabling or disabling a feature or setting a configurable parameter to a range of values.

To support optional functionality, you can design your objects to ask and respond to feature availability. Behavior is tuned by setting parameters whose values are queried. Depending on the value of a particular parameter, different branches can be chosen. In a non-object-oriented solution, these tunable parameters could be implemented as *flags*. A more object-oriented solution is to create an information-holder object with responsibility for maintaining configurable information. It is queried by objects whose responsibilities adjust accordingly.

Certain variations require no coding changes. Parameters stored externally in a file or database are read to initialize system behavior. Whether a developer or an end user, whoever edits that information may need to know what values are valid and understand dependencies that exist between parameters.

In the online banking application, certain bank installations support automatic online activation, whereas others require that users submit information that is later manually verified by a bank agent against bank records before online access is activated. A BankConfiguration object is queried to determine whether or not Auto Activation is enabled. The application alters its behavior to display the appropriate registration screen and to either invoke automated authorization services or queue a registration request for manual activation, depending on the answer to a simple question.

***Concentrate variable information into information holders.*** Often, many parameters control an application's variable behavior. You could locate each of these settable parameters in different objects whose behavior is directly affected. Alternatively, each affected object could turn around and ask a common source a question and then vary its behavior depending on the answer.

> In the online banking application there are dozens of parameters that can be used to tune the application's behavior: number of user retries before failing login, time elapsed before session time-out, and default language, to name a few. The BankConfiguration object is initialized by reading values from an external source.

We recommend the second approach. Bundled together, configurable information can be dealt with as a unit. Sprinkling configurable values among many objects makes this information hard to locate and manage. But don't let your information holder become too bulky. Instead of letting it get bloated with disconnected information, you can always divide and conquer. Create a number of smaller information holders that encapsulate related information. Give the original information holder responsibility for managing these smaller information holders. Redesign it to hold on to larger-grained information.

> Grouping related information into smaller focused information holders allows parts of the application to ask about specific feature sets. In an e-mail application, a number of user-specific information holders might be created and maintained by a UserPreferences object: IncomingMailOptions, OutgoingMailOptions, UserIdentity, ReplyOptions, and DisplayOptions, to name a few.

***Insert design placeholders.*** You aren't likely to discover all variations at once. But if you are following an incremental, iterative design process, you can plan to grow your design in specific ways. Placeholders can be introduced into your design to encapsulate behavior and information that you expect will grow and vary. You can invent several placeholders and grow their responsibilities with successive iterations. This isn't a technique so much for enabling variation as it is for keeping it contained to well-known spots.

Steven Jones, in *Building Application Frameworks,* introduces the notion of a Placeholder pattern. If you want to reserve a spot for anticipated improvements in later iterations, define and implement one or more placeholders and insert them into the design, to be fleshed out later. As an example, Jones describes a class hierarchy that includes a specific placeholder for application-centric features. Using this framework, application developers are expected to define a new class and add it to this hierarchy for each application they implement.

Planned for but unused flexibility increases a design's complexity. So do poorly factored hacks in support of unplanned variations. But appropriately located placeholders can preserve a design's integrity.

The abstract class `Application` defines common default behaviors for starting, initializing and shutting down any application. The class `CommonApplication` is a subclass of `Application`, and a placeholder that provides a home for additional behaviors that will have a global effect on all applications. Instead of subclassing `Application`, to fit into this application framework, developers create their own specific application's startup and control behaviors by subclassing `Common-Application`. The following future behaviors might be added to `CommonApplication`:

- Checking on whether a particular version of the application can be started on a specific machine.
- Verifying licensing keys or user registration.
- Maintaining banners or welcome messages.
- Registering a distributed application with a naming service.
- Specifying the operational mode of the application—is it in debug mode or normal operation? Is access limited, or is it under normal operation?

Some programmers are likely to argue against placeholders; they consider overdesigning to be bad practice. Designers who've been burned on prior projects might argue fervently for their favorite placeholder. The value of a placeholder is that it limits the impact of subsequent design changes. New responsibilities can be given to a placeholder, with minimal impact on the rest of the design (see Figure 9-6). Creating an explicit spot—a placeholder—allows for variations to be localized, encapsulated, and managed.

Debate about whether a placeholder is necessary or sufficient is healthy for a design, as long as camps don't form and positions become entrenched. The real test will be in the future—when new adaptations are rolled into the design.

In the online banking application there are several placeholders—too many for some designers' tastes. Several placeholders were introduced by the architect as a result of his past development experiences. Not all team members bought into the need for introducing so many of them. One noncontroversial placeholder is the BankConfiguration object—a spot where bank-specific configuration information is maintained. A more controversial placeholder is the user class hierarchy. Although there are only three known kinds of users—the bank agent, a system administrator, and end users—an ApplicationUser inheritance hierarchy was designed. It is intended to support anticipated user-specific capabilities and defines specific places for extension. The placeholder classes weren't easily accepted by the design team because early releases of the application supported only end users.

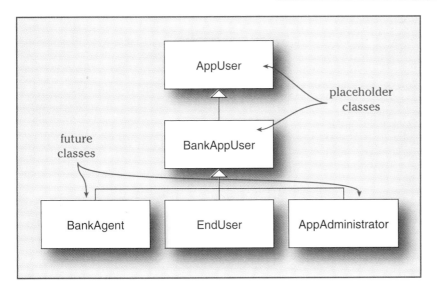

Figure 9-6
*Two placeholder classes—BankAppUser and AppUser—reserve spots for future behaviors.*

***Create appropriate knobs for developers to turn.*** As a flexibility designer, you can make other developers' jobs easier by providing extra support—adding "knobs" to your implementation that assist developers in making changes. The alternative is to give them free rein to the code and let them have at it. Sure, it's possible to implement variations without extra support. But it is especially important when several hooks must be implemented in a particular order to realize a single variation. Without such support, making extensions can get tricky.

If several parts of your system need to be configured as a unit and the ordering of changes is important, consider providing a single method—a master knob, if you will—that contains the code that configures a variation in one atomic operation. Rather than call on several methods to configure a feature, the developer invokes only one method to make a set of related changes. This is much more reliable than letting developers write their own scripts.

Sometimes, configuring a variation may involve reading and interpreting externally stored settings. Rather than let developers or users change settings by using a low-level text editor, you might want to create a tool that assists them in making consistent changes. A tool can also check and report inconsistent settings.

Sometimes, to implement a variation, extensive programming is required. It is difficult to provide knobs in this case. But at the very least, you can provide examples to emulate and can outline the steps developers should follow. Rather than provide a knob, provide them with a starting point.

There is one more knob that is a hallmark of disciplined development practices: a "test" knob. After making a change, a developer can turn a test knob to check whether an adaptation hasn't broken anything. A test knob typically invokes preexisting test code that asserts whether values are correctly initialized, whether newly installed objects respond appropriately to standard questions, and whether new variations of behaviors perform according to established scripts.

## THE ROLE OF PATTERNS IN FLEXIBLE DESIGNS

Design patterns use composition, inheritance, and abstraction as tools to enable adaptations. Design patterns make software "soft" and amenable to extension and modification in prescribed ways. We've already seen that the Template Method pattern defines basic building blocks for constructing skeleton algorithms. A design pattern typically affects a small segment of the design—a few collaborating objects or a class in an inheritance hierarchy. Let's look more closely at three patterns described in *Design Patterns* to see where they flex.

## Varying an Object's Behavior with the Strategy Pattern

The Strategy pattern lets you define a family of algorithms. The Strategy pattern encapsulates a single algorithm in an object. Usually called on by clients fulfilling larger responsibilities, this pattern lets developers use any object playing the role of the strategy interchangeably.

> The Strategy Pattern factors a responsibility (often a private one) out of an object, replacing it with a collaboration with another object that performs that responsibility. It is particularly useful when the responsibility is complicated or might vary. After a responsibility has been factored into its own object, it can be replaced with other strategies, enabling the original object's behavior to vary.

Speak for Me presents the letters of the alphabet in different sequences according to the wishes of the user. The Guesser delegates the work of guessing letters to the Alphabet. If the Alphabet plugged in different AlphabetOrder strategy objects according to the user's preferences, that would change the way letters are guessed.

The Strategy pattern presents a design alternative to having the client select the appropriate algorithm based on conditional logic and directly executing it. Sure, the client might need to be aware of different strategies in order to pick the right one. But the appropriate strategy might be provided by some other third party that knows which strategy to choose. The responsibility for performing different variants on the same algorithm has been factored into several different kinds of strategy objects. Introduce a new strategy, and you've extended your design.

## Hiding Interacting Objects with Mediator

One bugaboo of flexibility is tight coupling. To collaborate with an object, the client must acquire a reference to that object. If references are fixed, communication paths and collaborations aren't flexible. The Mediator pattern's sole purpose is to promote looser coupling by keeping objects from directly calling on one another's services.

By representing the responsibilities of the objects that it delegates to, a Mediator assumes all of their combined responsibilities.

In the Mediator pattern, an object that plays the role of a mediator is responsible for coordinating the interactions of a group of objects. Rather than collaborate with each other directly, the objects know only about the mediator. The mediator is the hub of communication. It instigates and manages inter-object communications.

> Speak for Me's MessageBuilder is a mediator. Coordinators often play the role of a mediator. It responds to the application events and hides the domain objects and their responsibilities from the objects in the user interface. The user interface objects know about mediator, but that's all. The mediator, in turn, knows about the event-handling responsibilities of all of the domain objects that it delegates to, but these domain objects and their responsibilities are hidden from the user interface objects. A mediator acts as a channel for interactions.

The Mediator pattern trades off complexity of interactions between individual objects for knowledge and visibility of those objects by an object playing the role of mediator. With this looser coupling, your design is more flexible. Any object that plays one of several preestablished roles known to the mediator can be plugged in and used interchangeably.

The distinction between a mediator and a coordinator is a subtle one. Your intention when inventing a coordinator is to solve a control problem by creating an object that coordinates activities of other objects. A designer may choose to adapt the Mediator pattern as a solution—designing that coordinator to play a mediator role, or not. A coordinator can manage the activities of other objects without having to be a mediator.

## Making a Predefined Object or System Fit Using Adapter

You apply the Adapter pattern when something you want to use isn't malleable enough to suit your purposes as is and you can't change it. Rather than warp the rest of your design to use an object or component that has an undesirable interface—it could be clunky, or too low-level, or not fit in with the rest of the design—you wrap it with a more desirable one and plug that into your design.

> The telco integration software coordinates the work of a number of business applications developed by independent software vendors. In order to insulate the integration core from application specifics, the system is partitioned into a number of adapters, which transform requests from the external application into integration software common commands and/or translates requests from the integration software into application-specific API calls (see Figure 9-7). Each adapter runs in its own process, allowing for asynchronous processing. Parts of the system can be brought up at different times, and adapters can be allocated to separate processors.

The Adapter pattern allows you to fit new elements into your design without compromising it. By creating adapters, you preserve your design's integrity and don't let low-level details or a clunky interface "leak out" and affect other objects.

## How Do Patterns Increase Flexibility?

Many of the design patterns described in *Design Patterns* encourage the distinction between an interface to a set of operations and its implementation. To be plugged in and used, an object need only support a common interface and not a common implementation. This allows objects that share common roles to be used interchangeably. Clients are unaware of the classes of objects they use; they only depend on their interface. This greatly reduces implementation dependencies among objects and gives designers the flexibility to replace one interface-compatible object with another.

Variations in behavior that are obtained by composing objects that support predefined interfaces promotes "black box" use. No internal details of those objects are visible to their clients. Regardless of whether you apply a particular pattern, you can always increase flexibility by defining interfaces and having clients rely on them instead of referring to concrete classes. Declaring an interface as the type of

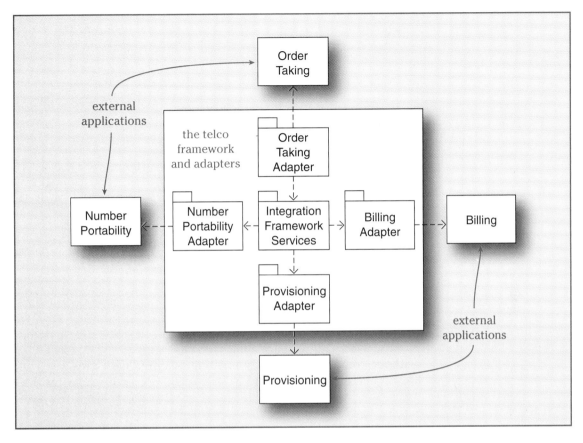

Figure 9-7
*The Adapter pattern can be used to make different objects or components present a similar interface.*

an argument as the value returned by a method, or as the type of a variable effectively establishes a contract for service without specifying what class of object will perform it. It's all the same to the client, but only an object's creator needs to be aware of its class. If a client's only view of a collaborator is its interface, different objects that support the same interface can be interchanged.

Another technique used in many design patterns is delegation: An object that receives a request forwards it to an appropriate delegate (see Figure 9-8). For example, both the State pattern and the Strategy pattern change the behavior of an object by changing whom requests are delegated to. Delegation makes it easy to support run-time variation. By swapping delegates on-the-fly, you can adjust an object's behavior.

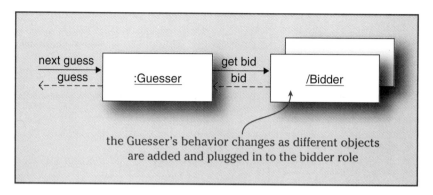

Figure 9-8
*Delegation to replaceable collaborators makes a design flexible.*

## HOW TO DOCUMENT A FLEXIBLE DESIGN

"Delegation is a good design choice only when it simplifies more than it complicates. It isn't easy to give rules that tell you exactly when to use delegation, because how effective it will be depends on the context and on how much experience you have with it. Delegation works best when it's used in highly stylized ways—that is, in standard patterns."

—Erich Gamma et al.

How can you denote a potential point of variation in a collaboration, or show where an object playing a specific role can be plugged in to a design? You might think that the first thing to do is to create appropriate class and sequence diagrams that identify "flexible elements"—but exactly how do you show that? UML provides basic mechanisms for showing classes, roles, interfaces, collaborations, and patterns. But it doesn't provide facilities for explicitly denoting hooks or identifying related template and hook methods.

Although frameworks and extensible software have been developed for a wide range of applications, UML as it stands today still lacks adequate ways to describe points where a design can be extended. Recently, the Unified Modeling Language community has started to define *profiles*, which are subsets or extensions of UML targeted for specific uses. That's one reason the authors of *The UML Profile for Framework Architectures* (Marcus Fontoura et al., Addison-Wesley, 2001) developed a specific profile aimed at aiding framework designers and architects in describing extensible software.

In defining UML-F, Marcus Fontoura, Wolfgang Pree, and Bernhard Rumpe have made a first attempt at describing points of design flexibility. It remains to be seen whether their proposed notations become widely adopted or make it into future versions of the UML standard.

Several notations in UML-F are worth a close look. Designs that have a large number of classes and interfaces can be difficult to grasp. For many systems, a complete class diagram that shows every class and interface as well as associations would be incomprehensible. It is common to show a partial set of classes on a diagram and to repeat classes on many different diagrams. It is a necessity to break down a large design into comprehensible chunks.

But this can be confusing, too—especially when classes are depicted in greater or lesser detail on different diagrams. On one diagram a class may include attributes and operations; on another, only a sub-set of operations may be enumerated. Yet a third diagram might show the class with no attributes or operations. This is perfectly legal in UML, and it is good to remove extraneous details so that you can emphasize what's important. However, developers studying a design model in order to make a variation could benefit from a clearer understanding of exactly what they are seeing.

To address this issue, the UML-F authors extended UML with two tags that make it explicit whether or not a class, or any other design element, is fully specified (see Figure 9-9). Tagged with a "©" means that it is complete. Tagging a design element with a "..." means that it is incomplete (there's more detail but it is not shown). By default, any element not tagged with "©" or "..." is deemed incomplete.

UML-F also lets you annotate individual methods with an explanation of their intent and implementation. This allows a designer to specify whether a method's implementation is

- Abstract and needs to be overridden by subclasses (shown with a diagonal slash through the rectangle)
- Inherited and not redefined (shown with an unfilled rectangle)
- Newly defined or completely redefined by a class (shown with a gray-filled rectangle)
- Redefined but uses behavior defined in a superclass via a call to the superclass's method (shown with a rectangle that is half gray, half unfilled)

This is particularly useful for visualizing how inheritance is used when you specify configurable algorithms using template and hook methods (see Figure 9-10). You can see at a glance whether a method has been replaced or superseded in subclasses without having to read code.

Finally, we introduce one more UML-F construct: template and hook tags. Methods, classes, and interfaces can be tagged as being

UML profiles are being proposed to address specific modeling issues of targeted application areas. For example, people are working on a UML profile for fault-tolerant designs. Other UML profiles being proposed at the time this book is being written range from enterprise application integration to workflow and business process modeling.

When you are looking at a UML diagram, you can never be certain whether you are looking at a complete or a partial specification of a class or inheritance hierarchy. Sometimes it is easy to forget this and read more (or less) into a design than was intended. That's why the UML-F authors included the "..." notation to tag design elements as incomplete. This forces your attention to the fact that you are seeing only part of a design.

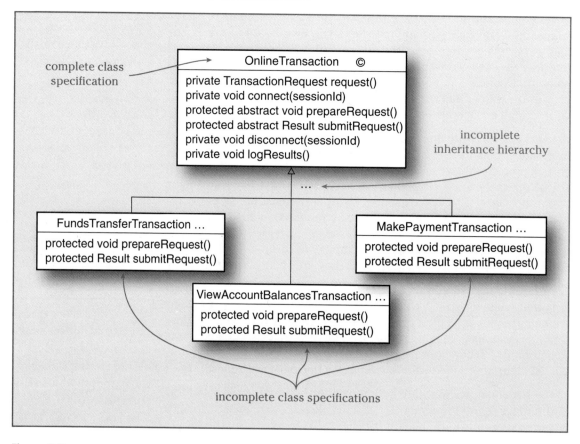

Figure 9-9
*Adding UML-F tags makes it clear whether you are looking at a partial or a complete specification.*

templates or hooks. A group of related template and hook tags can be named. Thus it is possible to see the complete suite of template and hook methods that support a specific variation (see Figure 9-11).

There is more to UML-F than we describe here. And there is more to describing how a design supports a variation than can be shown on any diagram. The main value of UML-F is the ways it can be used to express design variations and their implementation details.

When you look at any UML diagram it's hard to know how much is left out. There are many valid reasons to leave out design elements; to emphasize certain aspects and remove clutter are two.

## Consider Your Audience

Although you can document details in UML, consider your audience. What levels of detail do your readers need (or want) to see? Consider the detailed diagram in Figure 9-12, which shows the implementation of many hooks in Speak for Me.

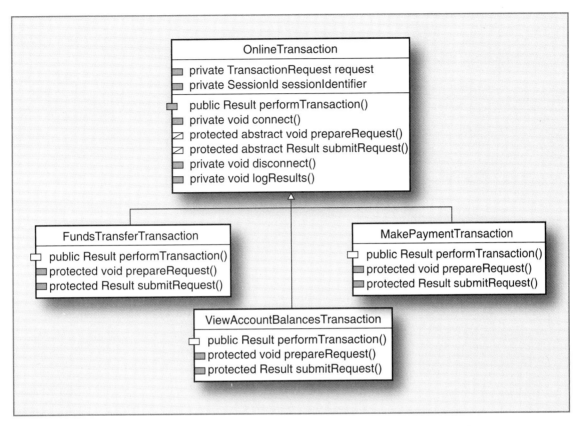

Figure 9-10
*UML-F has notations for showing implementation inheritance characteristics.*

Contrast Figure 9-12 with a second, conceptual picture (Figure 9-13) that generally explains hooks and where they are located in the design.

Different stakeholders are likely to prefer one view over the other. Some will prefer a big picture overview. Your fellow designers may want to examine your design in all its glory—and may not be satisfied with any level of detail you can show using UML. No single picture or diagram can communicate these different perspectives.

## Describing How to Make a Variation

If the person making a variation is a developer, he or she will need to understand at some level how the design works before making it vary. Diagrams can help, but they aren't the whole story. Explanations,

Without knowing whether you are looking at the whole story and where aspects of the design have been explicitly elided, drawings can only be viewed as representations, with the real answers to be found by reading code.

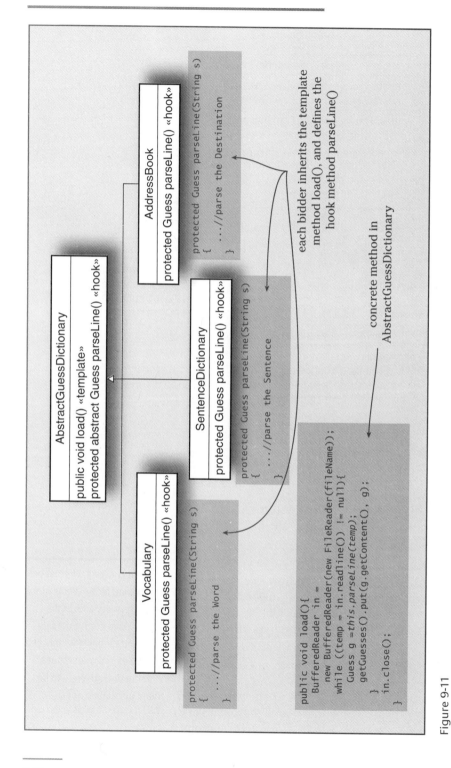

Figure 9-11
*GuessDictionaries share a common algorithm for loading data, but each parses its data differently.*

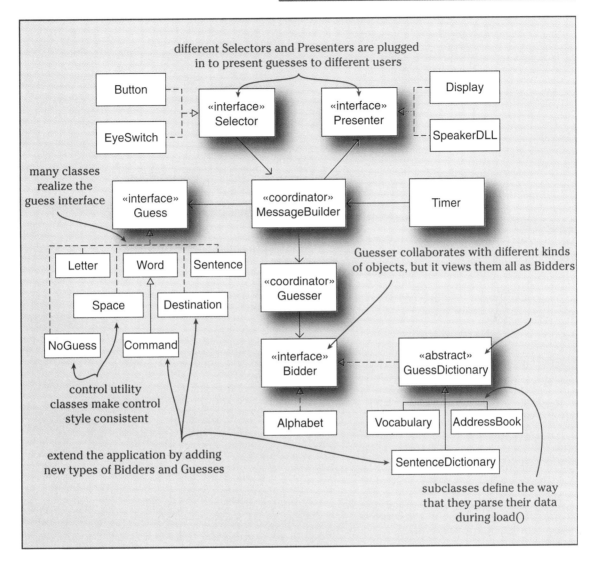

Figure 9-12
*UML class diagrams show flexibility in interfaces, abstract classes, and inheritance hierarchies.*

words, written procedures to follow, and code examples all help. But before you launch into an extensive documentation effort, consider what the person needs to know in order to make a variation.

If the level of support you have provided for making an adaptation is high, then developers may not require deep knowledge. Perhaps you

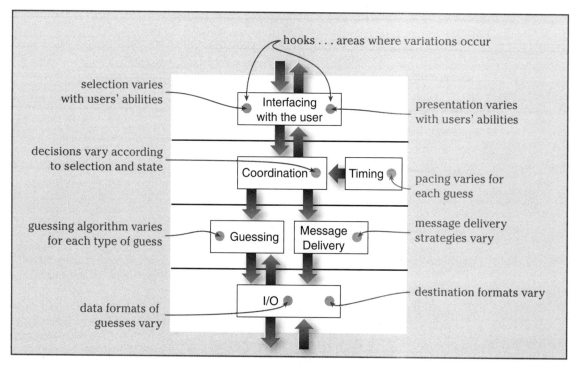

**Figure 9-13**
*A conceptual diagram can also be used to show how the Speak for Me application can flex without showing classes and interfaces.*

Sometimes multiple views of your design are appropriate. Don't expect everyone to understand your design's flexibility at the same level of detail. Vary your descriptions according to your audience.

have created a number of prebuilt components or classes. To implement a variation, a developer simply chooses an existing component and plugs it in to a particular collaboration by invoking a single "setter" method. If this is so, designers won't require deep knowledge of your design or a complex set of instructions. They are likely to need only a simple set of instructions—a basic recipe to follow.

*A Basic Recipe for Selecting a New Device Driver:*

Choose from one of . . .

Configure into system by doing . . .

Restart and test by calling . . .

More likely, the developer must change or add at least one class and modify code in other classes to implement a variation. Examples or pointers to places where similar variations have been implemented could be helpful.

---

### How to add a new banking option

1. Add a method to the BankConfiguration object that can query whether this feature is enabled.

2. Add a variable declaration in the bank configuration file named xxxFeature.

3. Initialize the system.

4. General procedure to follow: Code in the affected classes can be altered to query the Bank object for SupportsXXX and if so, alter behavior. Typically, Bank features affect specific transactions, specific display, or logging and recovery functions. For an example, see how supportsAutoActivation is used to vary the behavior of the RegisterTransaction.

---

More complex variations require more extensive knowledge. A good recipe needs to provide only enough information to guide someone making an adaptation. It doesn't have to tell everything. Here is a basic recipe template adapted from *The UML Profile for Framework Architectures*:

---

**Recipe Name:** Usually starts with "How to"

**Intent:** The reason to use this recipe

**Design Description:** Which classes and interfaces are involved and need to be understood, what roles do they play and what collaborations are involved. What responsibilities are adapted via the variation . . . backed up by supporting UML or UML-F diagrams and other descriptions.

**Related Recipes:** Alternative ways to accomplish a similar variation; or related sub-recipes. If the recipe is complex it may need to be broken down into several sub-recipes.

**Steps** 1. First create a class that implements the xyz interface. . .

2. In it define a method named. . .

3. And another method named. . .

4. . . .

---

*Sometimes people who create a design don't know how to limit their descriptions. The key to writing a good recipe is to get into the mindset of the users. Ask, "What do they need to know?" instead of thinking, "What should I tell them?"*

> **Discussion:** This could mention problems that might crop up, how to test that a variation is correctly installed, or what should not be attempted using this approach.

If the end user is making the variation, the recipes aren't likely to mention objects or how the software adapts behind the scenes. If it is more than a single action, users are likely to want step-by-step procedures, just as developers do—but procedures written at a level that describes how the user interacts with a tool to make changes.

End users and developers need to understand how to make variations, but typically at different levels of abstraction. Often, both need to understand the limits of the software. Certain changes are easy. Others take time and extra preparation. Good recipes should tell people what to expect, present options, and tell them what they need to know to keep on track.

## CHANGING A WORKING SYSTEM'S DESIGN

Software, unlike the pyramids, is seldom built as a memorial, never again to be touched. To withstand time, shifting user needs, or the latest OS release, software must be flexible.

So far we've talked about increasing flexibility as if you were approaching a design with a clean slate. When there are existing obstacles, bumps, wrinkles, and constraints that you have to put up with and cannot change, introducing flexibility is more challenging. If you could have divined the future and accurately predicted future requirements, you would have designed your software to absorb changes with minimal impact. Barring that, you need strategies for wedging variations into your existing software. How can you extend your software without compromising it?

Earl Ecklund, Lois Delcambre, and Michael Freiling introduced the idea of change case analysis in a paper presented at OOPSLA 1996. They suggest you characterize the focus, scope, and degree of definition of any proposed change before designing a solution. The scope of a change refers to how much it pervades the software; but to these authors, scope is more than the impact on the design. After software is in use, a proposed change can have far-reaching effects on users, existing requirements, use cases, design documentation, and testing procedures. *Degree of definition* refers to how well known the details of a proposed change are. After a proposed change is well defined and its impact has been assessed, then Ecklund and his colleagues propose that you shift your emphasis to design.

Not every change to your software is an opportunity to make your software more flexible. But it is an opportunity to rethink your design and ask, "Is now the right time to refactor my design, or should I simply make the change as quickly as possible?"

Of course, not all changes warrant creation of a flexible solution. You may need to bolt on a new feature that doesn't fit with or naturally extend the existing parts of your design. However, if a change represents a variation on existing behaviors, then you can consider a flexible solution. If changes occur frequently, and follow common patterns, you are likely to have designed your system to be flexible to begin with.

> Tax laws change every year, so tax preparation software changes every year. But it changes in predictable ways: Specific calculations and tax rules change and new tax forms are invented (with their own rules and calculations). Various items on forms are linked to other items. Tax preparation software is designed to support rules, calculations and relationships. Because forms and rules and calculations vary from year to year, the software designers have developed a framework for defining rules and relationships between line items, for defining new forms, and for performing calculations. If new rules don't fit into their existing toolkit of predefined calculator objects, they invent new calculators and fit them into the existing framework. If new forms are needed, they invent those. But the basic structures— forms with line items—and ways of performing calculations remain the same. It's only when new functionality is required, such as electronic filing of taxes, that major design work is required.

However, even though you know it is coming, if a change is ill defined, it is hard to plan ahead.

> Knowing that new software will continue to be integrated into the telco integration framework doesn't mean that the designers can make many preparations. Integrating any new software system will require developing a usage model and then writing an adapter to interface between it and the existing framework core. But beyond that, they can't "prepare" their design to absorb the new software. Not until a clear model is made of how the new software is to be used and how it interacts with the existing system can any detailed plans for design rework or new design features be made.

When does making a change compel you to a flexible solution instead of merely applying a fix? Rarely is this a simple decision. When the scope of a change is broad and will radically alter existing system behavior, it's a good time to step back and explore your options. Redesigning your software to increase flexibility may be the most expedient way to absorb this type of change. Or it may not be.

Martin Fowler's *Refactoring* describes many ways to readjust your code in preparation for a design change. Instead of patching in a change, you might need to refactor code before changing your design.

When the scope of a change is small—perhaps localized to a single object—the tendency is to patch in the change. That might be OK. But the next time you patch that patch, things could get ugly. It is a matter of deciding whether to pay for redesign now or defer the decision until later when you know more. You may not know enough about potential variations until you make that third or fourth change. When you start to see a pattern, consider refactoring your design and developing a more flexible solution. Patches may be the quickest solution, but they impact your software's ability to flex in the future. The more patches you make, the harder it is to see your design and to introduce support for adaptations.

## SUMMARY

Flexibility is a measure of how readily software adapts to a range of design parameters. Only those parts of a system whose behaviors need to be adjusted—by either a programmer or an end user—need to be flexibly designed. Flexibility does not necessitate large frameworks. To support any variation, you can introduce a modest amount of flexibility into your software. Hot spot cards are a low-tech tool for analyzing your software's flexibility requirements. The essential characteristics of variations, or hot spots, can be quickly described on index cards. After you've described a hot spot, you can pinpoint the areas of your design that are affected and strategize how best to alter your design to support the hot spot.

Many design techniques that you are already familiar with can be used to introduce flexibility into your design. Your intention is to make your design adaptable along specific dimensions. This requires extra work. To support any hot spot, you will likely introduce extra mechanisms—or hooks—into your design that allow others to tune or extend your design. You are likely to identify shared roles and define common interfaces. You may create new abstractions, define abstract classes, and use inheritance to your advantage. You may introduce placeholders—objects that have minimal behavior and are intended to accrue more responsibilities in later iterations. Many design patterns allow for specific extensions and variations. In addition to these design mechanisms, you may develop sample code for others to emulate or write recipes that explain how to perform an adaptation.

## FURTHER READING

*The UML Profile for Framework Architectures* (Addison-Wesley, 2001) by Marcus Fontoura, Wolfgang Pree, and Bernhard Rumpe describes a set of extensions to UML specifically targeted for developers describing extensible designs. This slim volume is divided into two parts. The first section describes the UML-F profile; the second is devoted to case studies and examples showing actual designs and recipes of extensible frameworks.

You can learn much about building flexible solutions by studying extensible designs. Two books, *Building Application Frameworks* (1999) and *Implementing Application Frameworks* (1999), edited by Mohamed Fayad, Douglas Schmidt, and Ralph Johnson, are full of experiences recounted by framework designers and architects. There is much practical advice to be mined from these books!

There are many techniques for introducing flexibility into a design. Most are based on inheritance, composition, and configuration. We want to point you to one more interesting idea—called Adaptive Object Models—introduced at the intriguing technology session at OOPSLA 2001. The idea behind an Adaptive Object Model is very simple: Let end users define objects, their relationships, and behaviors. Provide tools that let users describe objects and their semantics. Then construct your software to interpret and execute these self-describing models. Talk about the ultimate in end-user adaptation! Joseph W. Yoder, Federico Balaguer, and Ralph Johnson presented the paper "Architecture and Design of Adaptive Object Models" at the OOPSLA 2001 conference. Another paper, "The Adaptive Object Model Architectural Style," coauthored by Yoder and Johnson, describes in more detail techniques for constructing adaptive object modeling systems.

Wolfgang Pree, in *Building Application Frameworks*, introduces the notion of a *framelet*—an architectural unit that is small (fewer than 10 classes), does not take over main control of an application, and has a clearly defined and simple interface. A framelet can be extended and specialized, but by intent is small and narrowly focused.

# Chapter 10

## On Design

Lewis Thomas, noted physician and science writer, observed, "I'm not as fond of the notion of serendipity as I used to be. It seems to me now that as you get research going. . . things are bound to begin happening if you've got your wits about you. You create the lucky accidents." From time to time, object designers make startling discoveries, too—insights that make you want to stand up and shout. New ideas that you just know you should push on. Revelations that lead to deep understanding about how your software should work and what its limitations are. But amid these discoveries, you must keep working on the problem and not get distracted. That's the hard part: keeping design challenges in perspective while making progress and delivering on your promises.

## THE NATURE OF SOFTWARE DESIGN

As a designer, you are expected to be a good problem solver. You skillfully handle new challenges as they come up, balance conflicting priorities, and do what's needed to get the job done. In spite of uncertainty, you are counted on to devise good solutions.

You can be well prepared with a toolkit full of design techniques and practices, but design is never predictable. There are always surprises, additional complexity, and new twists. To keep on track, it helps to fit your design problems into one or more of these categories:

- *Core* design problems. The core is the core because without it, there is no reason to build the rest. Your application won't meet its users' needs or stand up to the rigors of use without a well-designed core. Core design problems must absolutely, positively be dealt with.

- *Revealing* design problems. Revealing problems, when pursued, lead to a fundamentally new, deeper understanding about the nature of your software. Just because some part of a design is difficult or tricky, however, doesn't make it revealing.

- The *rest*. Although not trivial, the rest requires hard work but far less creativity or inspiration.

Each type of problem warrants a different approach and has a different rhythm to its solution. Core problems must be solved. This is engineering at its best. You've got to give it proper attention. If you don't, your project will fail.

Revealing problems are squishy and hard to characterize or even know when they are completely solved. Each time you look further into a revealing problem it teaches you something new. Revealing problems deserve special recognition and attention. They can't always be solved in tidy ways. They must be tamed.

But the rest can't be ignored either. It may include mundane, tedious, or mildly interesting design work. It is always present and pressing. If you don't budget your time, it can soak up all your spare cycles. The rest needs your attention but not your total devotion.

This chapter presents strategies for designing responsibly in the face of uncertainty, complex problems that have no obvious answers, and lots of tedious details. We present ways to approach different kinds of design problems. To work effectively, you need to flex and adapt, react and respond, and work steadily on all aspects of your design.

## TACKLING CORE DESIGN PROBLEMS

Designing the core parts of your system requires energy and focused attention. It can be all too easy to get distracted by minutiae or wander off on a quest to solve a difficult problem. The core of your design must be well known and solid. It requires steady, persistent consideration. The key to balancing core design work with other design activities is to put everything else in perspective. The rest will always be with you and must be done after the core is well in hand. Revealing problems can crop up at any time. You can't plan for them. They just happen. Work on revealing problems progresses in fits and spurts. Rarely can revealing problems be solved by relentless attention. Core design problems are most often at the front of your work queue until you nail them and move on.

But what exactly is in the core? It depends. Designing an optimizing compiler is very different from designing online banking software. Core to an optimizing compiler is an internal representation of a computer program and code optimization algorithms. Design of an appropriate program representation goes hand in hand with the design of efficient optimization algorithms. The appropriate choice of structures to represent a program is critical to the algorithm design.

The core of the online banking system includes the design of online transactions and a common interface to backend banking services. Sure, the user interface is important to the project and its sponsors, but the quality of its design isn't central to the application's success. It just must be there. However, design features that enable performance to scale and the system to keep running under certain failure conditions are critical. Without a solid design for these core parts, the system won't be deployable.

Core problems include those fundamental aspects of your design (no, not every part can be fundamental) that are essential to your design's success. Depending on your design requirements, you might nominate for the core these elements of your design:

- Mechanisms that increase reliability. These could include the design of exception-handling mechanisms, recovery mechanisms, and connection and synchronization with other systems.
- Key objects in the domain model that your software manipulates.
- Important control centers.
- Support for user interactions.
- Key algorithms.

Whether you classify something as part of the "core" or part of the "rest," you'll still have to deal with it—it's a matter of emphasis. The main point is to give things the attention they deserve and be clear on your priorities.

How do you decide what's in and what's out? When there's debate on whether something is in the core, ask what the consequences would be of fudging that part of the design. What would happen if you didn't work so hard or come up with such an all-encompassing design? Would the project fail? Would other parts of your design be severely impacted? Then it's definitely core.

If you encounter disagreement about whether something is core, dig deeper. Are there fundamentally different expectations for that part of your design, or does someone know something important that no one else has thought about? You may be glossing over something important.

## FRAME THE PROBLEM

"When you turn on a light, you probably think of your movement of the control button and the illumination of the light as a single event. In fact, of course, something more complex is going on."

—Michael Jackson

Most software designs are too big to jump in and solve all at once. You break design into bite-sized chunks and work on them piece by piece. Depending on the nature of your software, you naturally focus on different things. Michael Jackson, in *Software Requirements & Specifications* (Addison-Wesley, 1995), identifies five general categories of problems—or *problem frames*—that software addresses. Many software systems can be thought of a set of related and interconnected subproblems and as a consequence may comprise several different problem frames. Each class of problem has its own concerns and design issues:

- *Control problems* occur when software controls state changes of external devices or machinery according to prescribed rules. The most obvious questions surround whether your design needs to determine whether its commands that supposedly have changed some external thing have had the desired effect. If so, you will likely design ways to probe whether things are as you expect. And if they aren't, well, you'll need to consider whether the problem is with your software or an external device.

- *Connection problems* occur when software receives or transmits information indirectly through a connection. Sometimes connections break down, and information gets lost or gets garbled. How reliable does your software have to be? Depending on the answer, you may need to go to great lengths to establish an alternative path or get the connection working again.

- *Information display problems* involve presenting information in response to queries about things and events known by your software. Typically, the quality and timeliness of information and the precision and nature of queries are a concern. Does your design have to accommodate imprecise questions or partial answers? Are users interested in the current information? Is history important, or timeliness of responses? If so, what do you need to do to meet these requirements?

- *Workpiece problems* occur when your software serves as a tool that allows users to create and manipulate computer-processable objects, or *workpieces*. Just as a lathe is a tool for woodworking, software helps users create documents, compile and write programs, compose music, perform calculations, manipulate visual images, and generate reports, to mention a few tasks. Design considerations for workpiece problems involve the nature of the workpiece and the usability of the tool.

- *Transformation problems* involve converting some input to one or more output formats according to well-defined transformation rules. Transformation problems can be tricky. There may be constraints on speed or memory utilization. Sometimes what constitutes an acceptable loss of information is at issue. Sometimes the reversibility of a transformation is important.

Jackson advocates that you fully understand the nature of the problems your software is trying to solve before you start design. That would be ideal. But if you live in a world of imperfect knowledge and incomplete specifications, you can still prepare yourself by characterizing the problems your design will solve. Even if you don't have all the answers, you'll know what questions to ask and which aspects of your design are likely to deserve your extra attention.

"Problem frames amount to coherent sets of useful questions to ask about the problem domain in order to invent a problem to solve."

— Ben Kovitz

Consider Jackson's characterization of connection problems:

> "In many problems you'll find that you can't connect the [software] machine to the relevant parts of the real world in quite the way you would like. You would prefer a direct connection. . . instead you have to put up with an indirect connection that introduces various kinds of delays and distortion into the connection."

If you find that connections between your software and some other system cannot be ignored—they are not transparent, nor do they always work flawlessly—then your design will have to address their quirky behavior. There are two basic strategies for dealing with connection issues. You could readjust your view and consider that your software is really interacting with "something in the middle" that is connected to "something out there" that doesn't always work. Jackson presents a classic example of a patient monitoring device as a connection problem:

> A monitoring system collects real-time readings of a patient's temperature, blood pressure, etc. through the use of analog devices. Analog devices are sometimes unreliable. This must be considered in the design of your monitoring software. If a patient's temperature reading is 132 degrees, considering the normal range of temperature variation, this reading is invalid. Your design should detect that a temperature sensing device isn't functioning properly and raise an alarm.

To accommodate a faulty connection means treating the analog device as an untrusted collaborator. Instead of blindly accepting its input, you validate information transmitted through a faulty connection.

Alternatively, if you determine that there will be interactions among your software, the connection, and the thing it connects to, all of which need to be considered, your design problem takes on an added degree of complexity. You must consider how your software should react in the face of potential time delays and conflicting states between connected systems as well as faulty connections.

> In the telco integration framework, there is a bidirectional connection between the order taking application and the framework: The framework receives orders from the order taking application and transmits notifications about the state of the order back to the application. Occasionally, communications between the order taking application will break down. To accommodate this, queues have been implemented to hold incoming requests and outgoing responses. Additionally, the interfacer component to the order taking application is designed to retry transmissions several times before queuing them and to notify system administrators when communications channels aren't working. Sometimes, as a result of delayed communications, cancel orders are received after orders have already been completed. Because the framework can't undo work that has been completed, it considers the cancel order a problem it can't solve and notifies a person charged with troubleshooting problem orders.

Characterizing the nature your design—or as Jackson phrases it, identifying relevant problem frames—helps you to sort through what's important and identify potential core design problems. Framing problems isn't only for analysts or business folks writing specifications. As a designer, you should be asking those questions that help you frame your design problems. Although you can look to use cases or requirements or user stories for guidance and clarification, they describe only what your system should do and not the nature of the problems you are solving.

Even if you have framed the problem and think you know what you're in for, there are often surprises. Sometimes, you stumble onto a meaty problem that can't be solved through skillful design alone.

## DEALING WITH REVEALING DESIGN PROBLEMS

Revealing design problems are always hard. They may be hard because coming up with a solution is difficult—even though that solution may eventually be straightforward. A revealing problem may not have a simple, elegant solution. It may not be solvable in a general fashion; each maddening detail may have to be tamed, one at a time. It may require you to stretch your thinking and invent things that you have never before imagined.

Sometimes when you work on a core problem, you discover it to be a revealing one, too. Not all core problems are revealing ones. But those that are deserve special recognition. What distinguishes revealing problems from core problems is their degree of difficulty and the element of surprise, discovery, and invention. To solve them you may need to experiment. They may not be easily solved. People may disagree on whether any solution is good enough. It may take a while to know what the real problem is. Working on revealing problems involves periods of intense concentration, design, reflection, and implementation, interspersed with open, honest communication about your progress.

Solutions to revealing problems can touch on any aspect of a design. They could impact an application's control architecture, the key responsibilities of core objects, the design of central services, and complex algorithms or interfaces to external systems. They can cause you to completely shift your worldview and discard what you had assumed to be a fundamental truth about your design, replacing it with something more complex. If you find yourself saying, "Nah—that could never be!" to a design challenge, you may have uncovered a revealing problem.

Let's look at some revealing design problems and see what we can learn.

### A Story About Managing Shared Information

The telco integration software glued together several disparate applications. The system was designed to streamline and, where possible, automate the process of taking an order, provisioning products that were ordered, and setting up customer billing. The applications that were integrated by the framework included

- Applications that managed customer service requests and orders
- Applications that managed the tasks involved in, and the provisioning of, telecommunications equipment and services
- Applications that billed customers for service

Each application had its own worldview and and proprietary databases and complex ways of interacting with users. None was designed to be plugged in to other applications to provide a comprehensive automated system. Right up front, the team faced a big decision that proved to be an ongoing, revealing design challenge: How should the framework handle information maintained by each application? Who should be the keeper of information about customers, their products, and orders? Should there be a master source? Not only did each application have its own worldview, but their views overlapped and sometimes contradicted one another. Addressing this fundamental question revealed several deep insights.

One design option that was considered and rejected was that the integration framework could maintain a master copy of orders, customers, and products and be charged with keeping everything in sync. Alternatively, the framework could take a more arm's length view of other systems and their information. It could be designed to know to ask other systems about the resources they maintained and coordinate their work.

Past experiences and war stories led the architects to conclude that the integration framework software should not actively manage all common information. This was too hard and fraught with data synchronization problems. Instead, the framework was designed to discover information in these other systems as it processed an order.

Working through an appropriate way to manage and change resources that are in other systems proved difficult. But deep insights were gained only after migrating data in one billing system to another. In a new release, the framework was chartered with supporting converted products. Sometimes, what was converted didn't match any official product. Still, the integration software was expected to gracefully handle converted products. This led to the design of strategies for limited support of nonstandard products and new rules for processing disconnect orders for products with ambiguous definitions.

The difficulty in solving how to handle converted products hammered home the lesson that it isn't always possible for the framework to interpret information that is validly being used by external applications. Still, the framework had to provide solutions to tame the difficult problem of product information that didn't fit standard definitions. It wasn't acceptable for the framework not to handle these products. The compromise, which didn't satisfy all the stakeholders, was for the framework to support these products in a limited way. The framework simply didn't have enough information to do anything else.

## A Story About Connection Problem Complexity

This next revealing problem was uncovered after the telco integration software had been in production for several months. Handling changes to in-progress orders proved to be a revealing problem.

To support the modification of an in-progress order, the designers developed a complex algorithm to compare a resubmitted order against the current one and to create new tasks to undo or modify work in progress. On further investigation, it was concluded that a change to an existing order could have several effects: Provisioning tasks might need to be modified; work that had already been completed might need to be undone; or additional work might need to be scheduled. And nothing prevented users from repeatedly submitting change requests. This was difficult, tricky work, but still not revealing. The revealing problem surfaced when the designers tried to handle several exceptional conditions that could happen when a user attempted to change an order.

It wasn't always possible to undo work that had been completed. And sometimes, even though the framework knew about errors, it couldn't report them to the order entry application because that application wasn't in a state to accept an error report. The framework couldn't "kick" this other system and make it receive a report. The other system couldn't be modified to accept error reports. It wasn't an option. This led to the creation of a problem order queue, where the software logged orders with problems that could be resolved only by extremely knowledgeable systems engineers.

Modifying orders that are being worked on by disparate systems proved to be a very hard problem. The analogy of trying to put toothpaste back into the toothpaste tube comes to mind. When tackled, it led to deep insights and the revelation that some problems with orders can be solved only by human intervention and judgment. That's what made it revealing, as well as plain difficult.

No matter how clever you are, software has its limits. Even with extraordinary effort you can't always design software to put things back the way they should be. Ask Humpty Dumpty if you don't believe us! Synchronizing systems can be very difficult. It isn't possible to transparently handle every anomaly with a software solution. Asking intelligent human beings to intervene sometimes may be not only the best solution, but also the only solution.

## A Story About a Design Problem That Never Got Easier

This is a story about the design of an optimizing compiler for Java. In order to aggressively optimize the code for a method, a compiler needs to model the possible control flow paths within the method. In other words, the compiler needs to understand all possible paths that execution may take through the method. This enables the compiler to do things such as eliminate code that will never be executed and eliminate duplicate computations whose results have already been computed earlier along a control path. Compilers typically model control flow by grouping statements into *basic blocks*. A basic block is simply a sequence of statements that is always executed from beginning to end. You can model complex control flow, such as loops and if statements, by building a graph whose nodes are basic blocks and whose edges are the possible control transfers between blocks. Because control transfers within a procedure are normally explicitly expressed as statements (if, case, for, while, etc.) in the programming language, normally it is fairly easy for a compiler to build and maintain the control flow graph.

Programming language features that support exception handling significantly complicate the modeling of control flows because exceptions can cause implicit transfers of control that are not explicitly shown in the code of a method. Because of this complication, many compilers simply do not attempt to optimize methods that throw or handle exceptions. Because it is quite common for Java methods to handle or throw exceptions, the designers concluded that their optimization objectives would not be met if they did not optimize such methods. So they adapted the control flow model to account for implicit control flow transfers caused by exceptions and enhanced optimization algorithms to deal with this model.

They succeeded, but not without a lot of work. During testing, the team kept uncovering optimization bugs that were the result of this design decision. As they continued to compile more programs, they continued to find even more sticky problems related to the optimization of exceptions. Even after the compiler had been shipping for several years, it remained the case that the majority of newly discovered optimization bugs were related to exceptions.

The designers didn't change or relax their design goals. They stuck to their initial decision and kept tweaking their design. When they started, they had no idea that optimizing exception handling would be a continuing source of bugs and new insights. In general, optimizing compilers are hard to design and debug because there are so many subtle language features that interact with one another. You can demonstrate only that a compiler correctly compiles the programs you have thrown at it. After it successfully compiles a suite of programs, there are no guarantees that it will compile the next tortured piece of code.

Any design handles only those problems its designers can conceive of. As with many other kinds of software, the number of different inputs a compiler must accept and process is infinite. Only over time and with enough test data can complex designs be adequately stressed and tamed. Most compilers or any other complex program will probably never be free of bugs. For systems such as these, designers simply cannot predict all problems beforehand nor develop the ultimate test suite. Christopher Alexander, in *Notes on the Synthesis of Form*, sums this up nicely: "The process of design, even when it becomes self-conscious, remains a process of error-reduction."

> When you cannot anticipate all situations your design must stand up to, you should expect to repeatedly confront a revealing problem until you've thrown enough rigorous cases at your design to harden it.

## Can Revealing Problems Be Wicked, Too?

In 1973, Horst Rittel and Melvin Webber coined the term *wicked problems* to describe questions that can't be solved using traditional approaches. Although Rittel and Webber were talking about problems in planning and setting public policy, their characterizations of wicked problems strike an eerie chord with our software design experience. Wicked problems generally have these characteristics:

- They have no definitive formulation. It's hard to state concisely what the problem is, and each time you do so, you gain a new insight.
- It's difficult to know when one is solved.

- Solutions aren't true or false, but rather good or bad. For better or worse, it may be difficult to get various stakeholders to agree on the quality of your solution. Some may consider it good enough, and others may not.

- There is no obvious way to verify that a solution fixes the problem.

- Every solution has unforeseen consequences. As you fix one problem, sometime later more problems may pop up.

- They don't have a well-described set of potential solutions.

- Each is essentially unique. You can reuse your brain and problem-solving skills, but you will likely craft a unique solution to each wicked problem.

- Each can be considered a symptom of another problem. The nest of interconnected concerns can be hard to untangle. There is no simple cause and effect.

- The causes can be explained in numerous ways. Different people will have different theories on what's really causing the problem.

- The planner can't be wrong. This means that you, the designer, still must invent some acceptable solution. You can't ignore the problem.

We never said it was easy! Solving wicked problems can involve intensely creative design activity or skillful negotiations. These problems call on many different problem-solving skills. Revealing problems may share one or more characteristics of wicked problems. They're closely related. Most revealing problems don't have obvious solutions. Sometimes they require you to redefine the problem. If you are lucky, you may invent a nifty solution. But there may not be a tidy solution to your revealing problem. Sometimes the solution represents a compromise. The hallmark of any revealing problem is that it forces you to think deeply about your software design.

Mary Poppendieck says that "wicked projects arise when a project is organized as if it were tame—thus creating a monster." To tame wicked projects, Poppendieck advises that they "are best served by an adaptive process instead of traditional methodologies."

## STRATEGIES FOR SOLVING REVEALING PROBLEMS

You don't sit down and try to solve a revealing problem through brute force or sheer willpower. You must look at the problem, roll it around, and consider perspectives. Viewing the problem from different angles gives you fresh insights. Revealing problems aren't often solved in predictable ways. George Polya, mathematician and author of *How to Solve It*, contrasts how insects and animals and humans approach problem solving:

> "An insect tries to escape through the windowpane, tries the same hopeless thing again and again, and does not try the next window which is open and through which it came into the room. A mouse may act more intelligently; caught in the trap, he tries to squeeze through between two bars, then between the next two bars, then between other bars; he varies his trials, he explores various possibilities. A man is able, or should be able, to vary his trials still more intelligently, to explore the various possibilities with more understanding, to learn by his errors and shortcomings. 'Try, try again' is popular advice. It is good advice. The insect, the mouse, and the man follow it; but if one follows it with more success than the others it is because he varies his problem more intelligently."

We are great problem solvers because we don't give up and don't often repeat dumb mistakes. Because rarely are we lucky enough to hit on a solution right away, we keep trying to find a good angle. We don't give up, and we are clever. We're very good at finding solutions because we weave our past experiences into a solution by what Polya calls "action of contact": Our current line of thinking makes contact with some past experience that may be relevant. Whenever you shift your perspective, you contact a different set of potentially relevant experiences. This means that the more experience you have with a particular class of problems, the more adept you are at shifting quickly to revealing angles and forming fruitful connections.

Problem solving requires these fundamental skills:

- The ability to shift your perspective and vary the problem

- The ability to gauge whether an approach, if pursued, is likely to bear fruit

- Knowing when you've hit a dead end

Most revealing problems require intense concentration. People get tired when they concentrate on the same point for very long. So to stick with it, you must redirect and look at different aspects of the problem. If there are new points to consider, you stay interested. If not, your interest lags. To keep working productively on a problem, you need to take breaks from time to time or shift your point of view.

The principal means we use to vary a problem, according to Polya, are generalization, specialization, analogy, decomposition, and recombination. These are an amazing fit with object-oriented design techniques! By using these techniques as a designer, you keep your basic reasoning skills sharp. But to solve a revealing problem you'll need to think through a problem at many different levels. You may

Before crafting an object-oriented solution, think about the nature of the problem and the solution in general terms. After you've identified a plausible design strategy, you can then apply these techniques to craft a solution. Don't mistake the mechanisms used in the solution for the general solution.

form complex chains of reasoning, or bounce around and recombine a number of half-baked solutions to finally come up with a three-quarters-baked solution. It's a lot of hard work!

## Redefining the Problem

Sometimes you can solve a problem by completely shifting your point of view. Instead of trying to solve the problem, turn the problem on its head. Imagine that everything worked as you wanted and the problem you are trying to solve doesn't exist. Live in that world awhile. Describe it. Envision how the machinery of your application might work in this ideal scene. Now, step back and figure out what you need to do create that ideal scene.

> Instead of trying to optimally schedule routes for transporting packages, FedEx redefined the problem. Instead of working on algorithms to optimize "a traveling salesman problem", it defined a whole new way of doing business. All packages are flown to a central location, sorted, and then loaded on the appropriate plane. Even packages shipped within the same city are routed through this central hub.

This makes scheduling easier but makes sorting harder. Let's consider a software example:

> A programming language that uses garbage collection, such as Java, C#, or Smalltalk, will automatically recover memory from objects that are no longer being used. Early implementations of object-oriented environments used reference counting to manage memory. Every time a new reference to an object was made, its reference count was incremented. Each time a memory reference to an object was overridden, its reference count was decremented. If the count went to zero, the memory for the object was freed. Reference counting is simple, but very expensive in terms of computational overhead. To speed up garbage collection algorithms, implementers of the languages redefined the problem—and now use a sophisticated scavenging algorithms.

Did replacing referencing counting techniques with sophisticated management of multiple object spaces and efficient marking strategies simplify the design of garbage collectors? No. But it did allow dramatic improvements in the performance of most applications. Solving a problem by redefining it doesn't necessarily simplify your design. It only opens up new possibilities.

## Synthesizing a Solution

Another approach to solving a revealing problem is to combine several parts of some almost-OK solutions. Even though you know that these potential solutions are flawed in one way or another, you can examine each for its strengths and weaknesses. Then propose a solution that combines the strengths of several flawed solutions and doesn't have their weaknesses. When designing reliable collaborations for writing a phone number, we devised a strategy that combined several recovery techniques because no single strategy proved satisfactory:

> An object would attempt to write down the phone number but broadcast a request for a pencil if it failed to locate one. It might then wait for a certain amount of time. But if no one provided it with one, ultimately it might ignore the request. Meanwhile, the requester might wait awhile for confirmation and then locate another to write the phone number after waiting a predetermined period of time.

Although rather complicated, this solution does handle several exceptional conditions. It's better than any individual simple solution, but is it a good solution? A simpler solution is always preferable. But if simple solutions aren't adequate, it's appropriate to consider a more complex solution. Sometimes there aren't any simple solutions or easy answers.

To solve revealing problems requires concentrated periods of thought and reflection, interspersed with time away from the problem. You need time to let things soak in. You need to let your background mental activity kick in and make connections between the problem and your experiences.

But on any project there's a ton of work to do. There's the core. And because it's been identified as being central, it usually gets the attention it deserves. And then there are revealing problems, which have their own rhythms—intense periods of concentration interspersed with background mental processing. Revealing problems are always either squarely demanding your undivided attention or lurking in the background. When they require soak time, take a break and work on something else. There's plenty of other stuff that needs your attention, too.

## Working on the Rest

The rest is what you work on day in and day out, week after week, when nothing else demands your attention. What items might be included in the rest?

- Common error logging or reporting mechanisms
- Data conversion
- Exception handlers
- Basic features that are similar to ones you've already implemented
- Unhappy path scenarios
- Optional features
- Alternative strategies for accomplishing some behavior
- Support for different ways that users accomplish basic tasks

Several items are on this list just to provoke your thinking. It's easy to get caught up in a debate of what's core and what's in the rest. Don't waste time debating whether common error logging and reporting mechanisms are considered core design work or part of the rest. If you know that something is just basic design work that has to be there—nothing special, nothing fancy—it's probably part of the rest. What about exception handling? Why *isn't* the 90% of your design work that supports the unhappy scenario a core design task? Well, depending on your project, it might be. Or it might not. When your team agrees that some design task is critical to the success of your design, add it to your list of core items. But not every design task is equally critical. Not everything can have the highest priority. Core problems should be given more attention. That doesn't mean the rest gets slighted. It just isn't at the top of your list.

The way you organize your design work, and how much time you spend working in uninterrupted stretches, can be critical to your success. Design and programming involve thinking, problem solving, and concentrated efforts. If you don't give core design activities your undivided attention, you can expend a lot of energy starting, stopping, and restarting. Alistair Cockburn, in *Agile Software Development,* describes why distractions can be so maddening:

> "Software consists of tying together complex threads of thought. The programmer spends a great deal of time lifting and holding together a set of ideas. . . . If she gets called to a meeting . . . her thought structure falls to the ground and she must rebuild it after the meeting. It can take 20 minutes to build this structure and an hour to make progress. Therefore, any phone call, discussion, or meeting that distracts her for longer than a few minutes causes her to lose up to an hour of work and an immense amount of energy."

It isn't always the meeting or the phone call or the overheard conversation that causes you to lose focus. Quitting a design session without coming to a good stopping point can also do you in.

> At the end of the day, it is tempting to leave CRC cards scattered around a table and white boards full of scribbles and sketches. Drop everything, the day is over! Time and time again we've found that spending just a minute or two to summarize where you are and where you might pick up your work can have a big payoff. Scribbling a couple of notes about the "state of your design" on a whiteboard before dashing off helps your team to reconnect with the design the next morning. Even taking a few seconds to group or rearrange CRC cards, instead of collecting them into a big pile, can help.

The worst thing you can do to break your flow is to put a rubber band around a stack of CRC cards, throw them in a drawer, and pick them up after a week.

Whether you are working on some core problem or on something slightly less important, take time to mentally wrap things up whenever you break away from design. Because the rest of your design work fits into days full of meetings, programming, conversations, and distractions, this isn't always easy. But it helps if you conclude (rather than halt) a design episode before switching to another task.

Above all, don't lose sight of the big picture. The core must be solid, the rest needs attention, and usually there are places where you'll need to cut corners. If you adopt development practices that help you honestly set and revisit your priorities, you will be much more comfortable making these design trade-offs.

It's hard to keep things on track and give design your proper attention when you are constantly distracted. Block off a chunk of time—at least an hour at a stretch—to work on any significant design task. Unless you are really caught up in your work, you need short breaks to keep your energy level high.

## DESIGNING RESPONSIBLY

"Fudging" on a software project is the equivalent of drawing pictures that distort the size and relative importance of things. Ever see a drawing of the United States with New York looming large in the forefront and the rest so small as to be indistinguishable? The tiny bits on the drawing are analogous to the parts of your design you are fudging on. You make 'em really small and insignificant in order to leave room for the "important" stuff. Different developers—and different development methods—fudge on different things.

Michael Jackson, in *Software Requirements and Specifications,* talks about the consequences of fudging. If you fudge on the wrong things, your software development effort is doomed. In Jackson's opinion, most object-oriented design methods pay attention to developing abstractions and inventing class hierarchies and understanding object interactions, but they fudge on correctness. He further argues that dividing a system into objects and classes makes it easier to fudge on understanding larger patterns of behavior. In contrast, formal methods are very careful about correctness and mathematical precision. But they fudge on how software should relate to its users and environment.

If you view software development (and object design) as only a narrow set of activities—focused on producing an object-oriented application—Jackson's assessment may be accurate. We think Jackson's view of object design and development practices is too limited. As designers, we naturally think in terms of software objects and their roles and interactions. You can zoom in and study individual collaborators, or you can shift your perspective to look at paths of collaboration among object neighborhoods and components. But although objects take center stage in our work, designing responsibly means fitting our work into a larger context of people, processes, and organizations. Design is a collaborative activity that at its heart involves melding the strengths of a group of individuals in order to produce something of value: a software design that meets customer needs. To keep on track, your team must do more than design responsibly. It must adopt development practices that support your project's values. People, development practices, and attention to design are equally important to a project's success.

Any development method or team emphasizes certain practices and, as a consequence, will slight others. Is fudging a bad thing? It is, but only if you ignore something that shouldn't be swept aside. The practices you adopt should support those things you value. If you need to be more formal, that is something you shouldn't fudge on. Don't use object technology and informal techniques as an excuse for fudging. You can add more precision and rigor to your design. But each project must adapt a set of development practices that supports its specific goals. There is much more to a successful project than a set of good design practices and techniques. There are

---

One of the parts of UML that we've fudged on mentioning in this book is the Object Constraint Language, or OCL. It is a modeling language that is part of UML. Using OCL, you can formally specify constraints in your model. If you need to precisely specify preconditions, postconditions, guards, relations, and operations in your design model, OCL is one formal language you can use.

---

"Basketball is a team sport filled with individual talent. Software development is similar. Collaboration—joint production of work products, collaborative decision making, and knowledge sharing—builds high-performance teams out of groups of individuals."

—Jim Highsmith

certainly more good design techniques than those we've mentioned in this book.

Designers of highly interactive systems will need additional practices that help them to identify and design effective user-system interactions. Embedded software designers often spend a lot of time on reliability and make trade-offs between memory utilization and execution speed. They may need to develop complex models that represent the state of their system, its hardware, and its software. Yet these designers can still reason about their software in terms of objects having roles and responsibilities. Although every project's concerns are slightly different from those of other projects, its primary tool—the power of abstraction used to create a model of software objects—remains constant.

An intriguing trend in software development is toward "agile" development practices. The agile movement embraces the notion that teams and organizations should flex and adapt to changing conditions. According to Jim Highsmith, those who pursue agile development practices "seek to restore credibility to the concept of methodology. We want to restore a balance. We accept modeling, but not in order to file some diagram in a dusty corporate repository. We accept documentation, but not hundreds of pages of never-maintained and rarely used tomes. We plan, but recognize the limits of planning in a turbulent environment."

Agility advocates want to be nimble. Development practices that worked well last week may need tuning or changing tomorrow. Fundamental to agile practices are the following beliefs:

- Organizations exhibit both *chaos* and *order* and cannot be managed by predictive planning and execution practices.

- Collaborative values and principles are vital to a project's success.

- Barely sufficient methodology lets a development team concentrate on those activities that create value.

Responsibility-Driven Design offers techniques that fit with and complement agile practices. Our emphasis is on *software responsibilities*. Following this approach, you start with rough ideas and refine them. You add as much precision as you need in your design work. Initially, you identify candidate objects, characterize them, assign them responsibilities, and develop an understanding of your application's control style. You might identify and apply design patterns or work through issues of trust among collaborators. Or you might develop exception-handling mechanisms. If you need a flexible design, you

Agile methods do not equate to good, and non-agile (or rigid) methods to bad. There are many places where agile, adaptable practices are vital. But there are situations when software should be developed in a rigorous fashion. Software that controls life-critical systems demands more formal methods and practices.

would pinpoint hot spots and then strategize how best to support planned variations in your software's behavior. Along the way you might develop and document collaboration stories to highlight key points in your design. Depending on your development practices, you could either keep these as part of your permanent design record or discard them after you've effectively communicated to others.

Responsibility-Driven Design offers tools and techniques, along with a galvanizing way of viewing your design. Thinking and reasoning about software in terms of objects, their roles, and their collective responsibilities provide a powerful perspective—one that doesn't fudge on a model of software as an organization of responsible, collaborating objects.

## FURTHER READING

*How to Solve It* by George Polya (Princeton University Press, 1971) presents many strategies for developing solutions to problems. Polya, a mathematician, freely uses mathematical examples. If you are not mathematically inclined, you can get past those parts quite nicely by not puzzling over them. Instead, concentrate on Polya's logical discussions and advice. The book contains summaries of various problem-solving strategies and questions to ask that are fundamental to any kind of problem solving.

Agile development practices are garnering a lot of attention. If you want to read a thoughtful discussion of the common principles behind agile development and survey six different agile methods, pick up Jim Highsmith's *Agile Software Development Ecosystems* (Addison-Wesley, 2002).

# Bibliography

Adams, Douglas. *Mostly Harmless (Hitchhiker's Guide Series #5)*. Random House, 1993.

Albers, Josef. "One Plus One Equals Three or More: Factual Facts and Actual Facts." In Albers, ed., *Search Versus Re-Search*. Hartford, 1969.

Alexander, Christopher. *Notes on the Synthesis of Form*. Harvard University Press, 1970.

Amyot, Daniel, "Frequently Asked Questions, with Answers," http://www.usecasemaps.org/, March 23, 1999.

Auer, Ken, and Roy Miller. *Extreme Programming Applied: Playing to Win*. Addison-Wesley, 2002.

Bass, Len, Paul Clements, and Rick Kazman. *Software Architecture in Practice*. Addison-Wesley, 1998.

Beck, Kent, and Ward Cunningham. "A Laboratory for Teaching Object-Oriented Thinking," *OOPSLA '89 Conference Proceedings*, pp. 1–6.

Bellin, David, and Susan Suchman Simone. *The CRC Card Book*. Addison-Wesley, 1997.

Bennett, Doug. *Designing Hard Software*. Prentice Hall, 1997.

Booch, Grady, James Rumbaugh, and Ivar Jacobson. *The Unified Modeling Language User Guide*. Addison-Wesley, 1999.

Budd, Timothy. *An Introduction to Object-Oriented Programming*. 3rd ed. Addison-Wesley, 2002.

Buschmann, Frank, Regine Meunier, Hans Rohnert, Peter Sommerlad, and Micahel Stal. *Pattern-Oriented Software Architecture: A System of Patterns*. John Wiley & Sons Ltd., 1996.

Clay, Jean, "Albers: Josef's Coats of Many Colours," *Realities,* August 1968, p. 68.

Cockburn, Alistair. *Agile Software Development.* Addison-Wesley, 2002.

Cockburn, Alistair. *Writing Effective Use Cases.* Addison-Wesley, 2001.

Constantine, Larry, and Lucy Lockwood. *Software for Use: A Practical Guide to the Models and Methods of Usage Centered Design*. ACM Press, 1999.

Coplien, James O., and Douglas C. Schmidt, eds. *Pattern Languages of Program Design*. Addison-Wesley, 1995

Davis, Alan. *201 Principles of Software Development.* McGraw-Hill, 1995.

Douglass, Bruce Powel. *Real-Time UML: Developing Efficient Objects for Embedded Systems*. Addison-Wesley, 1998.

Ecklund, Earl, Lois Delcambre, and Michael Freiling, "Change Cases: Use Cases That Identify Future Requirements," *OOPSLA '96 Conference Proceedings*.

Edwards, Betty. *Drawing on the Artist Within: An Inspirational and Practical Guide to Increasing Your Creative Powers*. Fireside, 1987.

Fayad, Mohamed E., Douglas Schmidt, and Ralph Johnson, eds. *Building Application Frameworks*. John Wiley & Sons, 1999.

Fayad, Mohamed E., Douglas Schmidt, and Ralph Johnson, eds. *Implementing Application Frameworks*. John Wiley & Sons, 1999.

Fontoura, Marcus, Wolfgang Pree, and Bernhard Rumpe. *The UML Profile for Framework Architectures*. Addison-Wesley, 2002.

Fowler, Martin. *Analysis Patterns: Reusable Object Models*. Addison-Wesley, 1997.

Fowler, Martin. *Refactoring: Improving the Design of Existing Code*. Addison-Wesley, 1999.

Froehlich, Gary, H. James Noover, Ling Liu, and Paul Sorenson. "Reusing Hooks." In Mohamed E. Fayad et al., eds., *Building Application Frameworks*. John Wiley & Sons, 1999.

Galton, Francis. *Inquiries into Human Faculty and Its Development.* London: Dent, 1907.

Gamma, Erich, Richard Helm, Ralph Johnson, and John M. Vlissides. *Design Patterns: Elements of Reusable Object-Oriented Software.* Addison-Wesley, 1995.

Goodenough, John. In Alexander Romanovsky et al., eds. *Advances in Exception Handling Techniques.* Springer-Verlag, 2001.

Harel, David, "From Play-In Scenarios to Code: An Achievable Dream," Technical Report MCS00-06, The Weizmann Institute of Science, February 2000.

Harrison, Neil et al., eds. *Pattern Languages of Program Design 4.* Addison-Wesley, 2000.

Highsmith, Jim. *Agile Software Development Ecosystems.* Addison-Wesley, 2002.

Hofstadter, Douglas. *Le Ton Beau De Marot: In Praise of the Music of Language.* Basic Books, 1998.

Howell, Charles, and Gary Veccellio. "Experiences with Error Handling in Critical Systems." In Alexander Romanovsky et al., eds., *Advances in Exception Handling Techniques.* Springer-Verlag, 2001.

Ingalls, Daniel. "A Simple Technique for Handling Multiple Polymorphism," *OOPSLA '86 Conference Proceedings*, pp. 347–349.

Israels, Chuck, quoted in Paul F. Berliner, *Thinking in Jazz: The Infinite Art of Improvisation.* University of Chicago Press, 1994.

Jackson, Michael. *Software Requirements & Specifications: A Lexicon of Practice, Principles and Prejudices.* Addison-Wesley, 1995.

Jackson, Michael. *Problem Frames: Analyzing and Structuring Software Development Problems.* Addison-Wesley, 2001.

Jacobson, Ivar et al. *Object-Oriented Software Engineering: A Use Case Driven Approach.* Addison-Wesley, 1992.

Jones, Steven R. "A Framework Recipe." In Mohamed E. Fayad et al., eds., *Building Application Frameworks*. John Wiley & Sons, 1999.

Kay, Alan, quoted in Cade Metz, "The Perfect Architecture." *PC Magazine*, September 4, 2001, http://www.pcmag.com/print_article/0,3048,a=10175,00.asp.

Kerievsky, Joshua, "Stop Over-Engineering!" *Software Development,* Vol. 10, No. 4 (April 2002).

Klee, Paul. *Altes Fraulein, 1931.* Paris: Spadem, 1976.

Kovitz, Benjamin L. *Practical Software Requirements: A Manual of Content and Style.* Manning Publications, 1998.

Kruchten, Philippe. *The Rational Unified Process: An Introduction, Second Edition.* Addison-Wesley, 2000.

Larman, Craig. *Applying UML and Patterns: An Introduction to Object-Oriented Analysis and Design and the Unified Process.* 2d ed. Prentice-Hall, 2001.

Lea, Douglas. *Concurrent Programming in Java™, Second Edition: Design Principles and Patterns.* Addison-Wesley, 2000.

Malveau, Rapahel, and Thomas Mowbray. *Software Architect Bootcamp.* Prentice Hall, 2001.

Martin, Robert C. et al., eds. *Pattern Languages of Program Design 3.* Addison-Wesley, 1998.

Metsker, Steven. *Design Patterns Java™ Workbook.* Addison-Wesley, 2002.

Meyer, Bertrand. *Object-Oriented Software Construction.* 2d ed. Prentice-Hall, 2000.

Minsky, Marvin. *The Society of Mind.* Simon and Schuster, 1988.

Norman, Donald. *The Design of Everyday Things.* Basic Books, 2002.

Page-Jones, Meilir. *Fundamentals of Object-Oriented Design in UML.* Addison-Wesley, 2000.

Peter, Laurence J., and Raymond Hull. *The Peter Principle.* William Morrow, 1969.

Petroski, Henry. *To Engineer Is Human.* Vintage Books, 1992.

Pirsig, Robert. *Zen and the Art of Motorcycle Maintenance: An Inquiry into Values.* William Morrow, 1975.

Polya, George. *How to Solve It.* Princeton University Press, 1971.

Poppendieck, Mary, "Wicked Problems," *Software Development,* Vol. 10, No. 5 (May 2002).

Pree, Wolfgang. *Design Patterns for Object-Oriented Software Development*. Addison-Wesley, 1995.

Pree, Wolfgrang. "Framelets—Small Is Beautiful." In Mohamed E. Fayad et al., eds., *Building Application Frameworks*. John Wiley & Sons, 1999.

Pye, David. *The Nature and Aesthetics of Design*. Van Nostrand Reinhold Company, 1978.

Reenskaug, Trygve, Per Wold, and Odd Arild Lehne. *Working With Objects: The OOram Software Engineering Method*. Manning Publications, 1996.

Rittel, Horst, and Melvin Webber. "Dilemmas in a General Theory of Planning." In *Policy Sciences,* Vol. 4. Elsevier Scientific Publishing, 1973.

Romanovsky, Alexander et al., eds. *Advances in Exception Handling Techniques*. Springer, 2001.

Rumbaugh, James. *OMT Insights*. SIGS Books, 1996.

Strunk, T., and E.B. White. *The Elements of Style*. Macmillan Publishing Co., 1972.

Tufte, Edward R. *The Visual Display of Quantitative Information*. Graphics Press, 1983.

Vlissides, John M. et al., eds. *Pattern Languages of Program Design 2*. Addison-Wesley, 1996.

Vygotsky, Lev S. *Thought and Language*. Rev. ed. MIT Press, 1986.

Wilkinson, Nancy. *Using CRC Cards: An Informal Approach to Object-Oriented Development*. Cambridge University Press, 1995.

Wirfs-Brock, Rebecca, and Brian Wilkerson, "Object-Oriented Design: A Responsibility-Driven Approach," *OOPSLA '89 Conference Proceedings,* pp. 71–75.

Wirfs-Brock, Rebecca, "Adding to Your Conceptual Toolkit: What's Important About Responsibility-Driven Design," in *The Report on Object Analysis and Design*, Vol. 1, No. 2 (1994).

Wirfs-Brock, Rebecca, "Designing Scenarios: Making the Case for a Use Case Framework," *The Smalltalk Report*, Vol. 4, No. 3 (1994).

Wirfs-Brock, Rebecca, "The Art of Meaningful Conversations," *The Smalltalk Report*, Vol. 4, No. 5 (1995).

Wirfs-Brock, Rebecca, Brian Wilkerson, and Lauren Wiener. *Designing Object-Oriented Software*. Prentice Hall PTR, 1990.

Wirfs-Brock, Rebecca. "Characterizing Your Objects," The Smalltalk Report, Vol. 2, No. 5 (1993).

Wirfs-Brock, Rebecca. "Designing Objects and Their Interactions: A Brief Look at Responsibility-Driven Design." In John Carroll, ed., *Scenario-Based Design: Envisioning the Work and Technology in System Development*. John Wiley & Sons, 1995.

# *Index*

## A

Abstract classes, 17, 80
Actors (UML), 51
Adapter design pattern, 340, 341
Adaptive Object Model, 353
Aftereffect guarantees, object contracts, 7–8
Applications
    application-specific objects, 10–12
    Application objects, Page-Jones domain divisions, 135
    architecture (*See* Architecture of applications)
    definition, 3
    policies, design description, 57
Architectural objects, Page-Jones domain divisions, 135
Architecture of applications
    basics, 27–28
    object collaborations, building models, 192
    object collaborations, influences on, 172–173
Architecture of applications, control styles. *See also* Architecture of applications, styles; Controllers, object role stereotype
    centralized, 30, 197, 198–200
    centralized, advantages/disadvantages, 198, 201–203

control centers, 196, 205
control centers, designing for similar systems, 230–236
delegated, 31–32, 33, 197, 200–201
delegated, advantages/disadvantages, 198, 201–203
dispersed, 30–31, 197
dispersed, advantages/disadvantages, 198, 203, 204–205
Guesser object/dictionaries neighborhood, 225–229
MessageBuilder object event, 205
MessageBuilder object event, basics, 206–208
MessageBuilder object event, centralizing control, 208–220
MessageBuilder object event, decision making, moving responsibilities, 224–225
MessageBuilder object event, decision making, refactoring into state methods, 220–221
MessageBuilder object event, final design, 229–230
object collaborations, 155
overview, 196
Architecture of applications, styles. *See also* Architecture of applications, control styles
    blackboard, 28

Architecture of applications, *(continued)*
  layered, 28, 29, 32–34
  layered, locating objects, 34–36
  pipes-and-filter, 28, 30

## B

Blackboard architectural style, 28
Builder design pattern, object collaborations, 171
Business objects, Page-Jones domain divisions, 135
Business rules, design description, 57

## C

Candidate objects
  characterizing in larger context, 98–99
  clustering/connecting, 99–101
  collaborators, 80
  conceptual objects, 58–60
  defending, 104–105
  descriptions, 93–98
  discarding, 103–104
  exploratory design stage, 60–61
  naming, 88–93
  responsibilities, 80
  reviewing, 105–106
  role stereotypes, 93–98
  roles, 79–80, 101–103
  search strategies, basics, 84–85
  search strategies, themes, 85–87
  steps in finding/assessing, 78–79
  transitioning to classes and interfaces, 80
  writing stories, 80–83
  writing stories, collaborations, 152–153, 154
Candidates, Responsibilities, Collaborators. *See* CRC cards
Case statements, 20
Classes
  abstract, 17, 80
  components, 18
  concrete, 80
  finding candidate objects, 80
  inheritance, 16–17
  instances, 13–16
  libraries of classes in frameworks, 25

superclasses and subclasses, 16–17
Collaboration of objects. *See* Object collaborations
Collaborators, finding candidate objects, 80. *See also* Object collaborations
Command pattern, 64–66
Components, 18
Composite design pattern, object collaborations, 171
Composition, object models, 16
Conceptual objects, 58–60
  judging merit, 60–61
  running collaboration simulations, 182
Concrete classes, 80
Concrete method, 330
Conditions-of-use guarantees, object contracts, 7–8
  collaborations, 156
Consequences, pattern elements
  definition, 20
  Double Dispatch pattern, 24
Consistency in design, 73–74
Context, pattern elements
  definition, 20
  Double Dispatch pattern, 24
Contracts, object collaborations, 156, 307
  basics, 7–8
  contractual relations, 308
  definition, 3
  obligations and benefits, 309–310
  preconditions and postconditions, 308–309
Control styles, application architecture. *See also* Architecture of applications, styles; Controllers, object role stereotype
  centralized, 30, 197, 198–200
  centralized, advantages/disadvantages, 198, 201–203
  control centers, 196, 205
  control centers, designing for similar systems, 230–236
  delegated, 31–32, 33, 197, 200–201
  delegated, advantages/disadvantages, 198, 201–203
  dispersed, 30–31, 197
  dispersed, advantages/disadvantages, 198, 203, 204–205
  Guesser object/dictionaries neighborhood, 225–229

MessageBuilder object event, 205
MessageBuilder object event, basics, 206–208
MessageBuilder object event, centralizing control, 208–220
MessageBuilder object event, decision making, moving responsibilities, 224–225
MessageBuilder object event, decision making, refactoring into state methods, 220–221
MessageBuilder object event, final design, 229–230
object collaborations, 155
overview, 196
Controllers, object role stereotype, 4. *See also* Control styles, application architecture
candidate descriptions, 93–94
collaborations, simulating, 179
in layered style applications, 34–35
object collaborations, 163
object collaborations, *versus* coordinators, 164
Conversations, design description, 54–55, 56
Coordinators, object role stereotype, 4
candidate descriptions, 93–94
in layered style applications, 34–35
*versus* mediators, 229
object collaborations, 163, 164
CRC cards
candidate objects, collaborations, recording, 151–152
candidate objects, connecting/clustering cards, 99
candidate objects, defining, 93–94
candidate objects, filling out, 100
candidate objects, finding patterns, 100–101
candidate objects, information required, 61–62, 63, 67
object collaborations, running simulations, 182
origin, 36
recording object responsibilities, 122–123

## D

Descriptions (design)
analysis, 49–50
application policies, 57
basics, 36
business rules, 57
design notes, 57
exceptions, 56–57
object responsibilities, 131–132
Responsibility-Driven Design, 44–47
UML (Unified Modeling Language), 241
usage, 50–51
usage, conversations, 54–55, 56
usage, scenarios, 53–54, 56
usage, use cases, 51–53, 56
Design patterns
Adapter, 340, 341
basics, 18–19
benefits to developers, 20, 25
Command pattern, 64–66
delegation technique, 341–342
Double Dispatch pattern, 20–25, 175, 176, 177
increasing flexibility, 340–342
Mediator, 339
object collaborations, 170–171
object collaborations, building models, 192
State, 341
Strategy, 337–338
Template Method, 330–331
Design process. *See also* Descriptions (design)
agile development practices, 373
analysis, 45–47
basics, 40–42
collaboration objects, responsibilities and control styles, 70–71
conceptual objects, 58–60
conceptual objects, judging merit, 60–61
connection problems, 358, 363–364
consistency, 73–74
control problems, 358, 362–363, 364–365
core problems, 356, 357–358
CRC cards, 61–62, 63, 67
design decisions, guidelines, 67–68
design decisions, testing designs with details, 68, 70
"fudging", 371–374
general problems, 370–371
problem frames, 358–361
problems, 356
responsible design, 371–374
revealing problems, 356, 361
revealing problems, and wicked problems, 365–366
revealing problems, redefining before solving, 368

Design process, *(continued)*
  revealing problems, solving, 366–368
  revealing problems, synthesizing before solving,
    369
  transformation problems, 359
  workpiece problems, 359
Design reviews for reliable collaborations, 311–312
Dialogs. *See* Conversations
Domain objects
  basics, 8–10
  object collaborations, building models, 192
  object responsibility restrictions, 135–136
  Page-Jones domain divisions, 135
Double Dispatch design pattern, 20–25
  object collaborations, 175, 176, 177

## E

Errors/exceptions
  basics, 288–294
  definition, 287
  design, limiting scope, 300–302
  design, listing possibilities, 299–300
  design description, 56–57
  handling, 294–296
  handling, documenting designs, 303–307
  handling, recording policies, 302–303
  of objects *versus* use cases, 288
  responsibilities, 296–299
Events (objects)
  collaborations, 169–170
  collaborations, building models, 192
  collaborations, running simulations, 180–182
  sources of object responsibilities, 123–124
Exceptions. *See* Errors/exceptions
External interfacers, object role stereotype
  candidate descriptions, 93
  collaboration identification, 165–166

## F

Facade design pattern, object collaborations, 171,
  173, 174, 175
Factory method, 330
Flexibility, 71–72
Flexibility in design, 71–72

documentation, audience considerations,
  344–345, 347, 348
documentation, descriptions of variations, 345,
  347–350
documentation, UML-F (Unified Modeling Language, frameworks), 342–344, 345, 346
documentation, UML (Unified Modeling Language), 345, 347
documentation, 342–344, 345
variations, describing for documentation, 345,
  347–350
variations, working into existing software,
  350–352
Flexible design
  advantages/disadvantages, 319–320
  decisions, objects needing flexibility, 320–324
  degrees of flexibility, 317–319
  overview, 316–317
  patterns, Adapter, 340, 341
  patterns, delegation technique, 341–342
  patterns, Mediator, 339
  patterns, State, 341
  patterns, Strategy, 337–338
  patterns, Template Method, 330–331
  patterns, ways to increase flexibility, 340–342
  Responsibility-Driven Design, 71–72
  variations, creating knobs for developers to
    turn, 337–338
  variations, hot spots, recording on cards,
    324–327
  variations, hot spots, solving, 327–328
  variations, inserting design placeholders,
    335–337
  variations, placing variable information into
    information holders, 334–335
  variations, strategies for realizing variations,
    329–330
  variations, supporting with template and hook
    methods, 330–333
  variations, times needed, 333–334
Flyweight design pattern, object collaborations,
  171
Forces, pattern elements
  definition, 19
  Double Dispatch pattern, 24
Foundation objects, Page-Jones domain divisions,
  135
Framelets, 353

Frameworks
    advantages/disadvantages to developers, 26–27
    basics, 25–26
    control styles, 201
    UML-F (Unified Modeling Language, frameworks), 342–344, 345, 346
Fundamental objects, Page-Jones domain divisions, 135

## G–H

Glossaries, 58

Hook method, 330
Hot spots, variations in design
    cards, 71, 72
    cards, recording variations, 324–327
    solving, 327–328

## I–K

Information holders, object role stereotype, 4
    candidate descriptions, 93
    in layered style applications, 34–35
    object collaborations, 159–160
    variable information in flexible designs, 334–335
Inheritance, classes, superclasses, and subclasses, 16–17
Instances of classes, 13–16
    inheritance, 16–17
Integrative and incremental processes, 42–43
Interfacers, object role stereotype, 4
    candidate descriptions, 93
    in layered style applications, 34–35
    object collaborations, 164–166
Interfaces
    basics, 12
    finding candidate objects, 80
Internal interfacers, object role stereotype
    candidate descriptions, 93
    collaboration identification, 165

## L–M

Layered architectural style, locating objects, 34–36

Libraries of classes in frameworks, 25

Mediator design pattern, 339
    object collaborations, 171
Model-View-Controller roles, assigning responsibilities of objects, 129–130, 131
Multiple stakeholder perspectives, 49, 50, 71

## N

Names, pattern elements
    definition, 19
    Double Dispatch pattern, 23
Naming objects, 88–93
Narratives. *See* Stories
Neighborhood of objects, 17
Neighborhoods of objects
    collaborations, 151

## O

Object collaborations
    architecture's influences, 172–173
    basics, 150
    control styles, 70–71, 155
    definition, 3
    degree of trust, 155–157
    design, based on use cases or events, 169–170
    design, patterns, 170–171
    design stories, 152–153, 154
    feasibility of collaborations, 187–188
    guidelines for design, 183–184
    guidelines for design, exceptional conditions, 190–191
    guidelines for design, Law of Demeter case study, 184–187
    guidelines for making connections, 188–190
    identification strategies, 158–159
    neighborhoods, 17
    preparations, 150–151
    raw materials for model building, 192
    recording candidates on CRD cards, 151–152
    roles-responsibilities-collaborations model, 5–7
    subsystems, 17
    troubleshooting problems, 173–176

# Index

Object collaborations, reliability
  contracts, 307
  contracts, contractual relations, 308
  contracts, obligations and benefits, 309–310
  contracts, preconditions and postconditions, 308–309
  design reviews, 311–312
  errors/exceptions, basics, 288–294
  errors/exceptions, definition, 287
  errors/exceptions, design, limiting scope, 300–302
  errors/exceptions, design, listing possibilities, 299–300
  errors/exceptions, handling, 294–296
  errors/exceptions, handling, documenting designs, 303–307
  errors/exceptions, handling, recording policies, 302–303
  errors/exceptions, of objects *versus* use cases, 288
  errors/exceptions, responsibilities, 296–299
  failures, consequences, 278–279
  information from use cases, 286
  overview, 285–286
  system reliability, 280
  trust regions, 280
  trust regions, decisions on placement of responsibilities, 284–285
  trusted collaborations, 280–281
  trusted collaborations, *versus* untrusted, 281–284
Object collaborations, responsibilities
  connecting objects, 166–167
  connecting responsibilities, 151–152
  control styles, 70–71
  factor in frequency of objects, 153–155
  subresponsibilities, 168–169
Object collaborations, role stereotypes
  controllers, 163
  controllers *versus* coordinators, 164
  coordinators, 163, 164
  information holders, 159–160
  interfacers, 164–166
  service providers, 162
  structurers, 160–162
Object collaborations, simulations
  basics, 176–177
  goal setting, 178

  planning, 177–180
  running, 180–182
Object collaborations, stories
  basics, 240
  description guidelines, 264–270
  development strategies, 241
  final stories, 273–274
  limitations of UML diagrams, 258–262
  listing items to cover, 243
  organization basics, 270–273
  preserving stories, 274
  scope, depth, and tone, 242–243
  selecting forms best-suited for stories, 263–264
  views, bird's eye, 244–245
  views, collaborators only, 245–250
  views, focused interactions among collaborators, 253–254
  views, implementations, 254
  views, in-depth, 250–253
  views, sequences of interactions among collaborators, 250
Object models
  composition relationship, 16
  inheritance relationship, 16–17
Object role stereotypes
  candidate descriptions, 93–94
  controllers, 4, 34–35
  coordinators, 4, 34–35
  information holders, 4, 34–35
  interfacers, 4, 34–35
  service providers, 4, 34–35
  sources of object responsibilities, 121
  structurers, 4, 34–35
Object roles, 3–4
  candidate objects, 79–80, 101–103
  collaborations, simulating, 178
  implementing responsibilities, 141–143
  roles-responsibilities-collaborations model, 5–7
Objects
  application-specific, 10–12
  candidates (*See* Candidate objects)
  class components, 18
  classes, instances, 13–16
  contracts (*See* Contracts, object collaborations)
  controllers (*See* Architecture of applications, control styles)
  definition, 3
  designer perspective, 11–12

domains, 8–10
events (*See* Events (objects))
interfaces, 12
naming, 88–93
patterns (*See* Design patterns)
responsibilities (*See* Responsibilities of objects)
software *versus* physical machinery, 2–3
user perspective, 11–12
Observer design pattern, object collaborations, 171

## P–Q

Packages (UML), 244–245
Page-Jones domain divisions, 135
Patterns (design)
    Adapter, 340, 341
    basics, 18–19
    benefits to developers, 20, 25
    Command pattern, 64–66
    delegation technique, 341–342
    Double Dispatch pattern, 20–25, 175, 176, 177
    increasing flexibility, 340–342
    Mediator, 339
    object collaborations, 170–171
    object collaborations, building models, 192
    State, 341
    Strategy, 337–338
    Template Method, 330–331
Pipes-and-filters architectural style, 28, 30
Predictability in design, 73–74
Problems
    design process, 356
    design process, connections, 358, 363–364
    design process, controls, 358, 362–363, 364–365
    design process, core problems, 356, 357–358
    design process, general problems, 370–371
    design process, problem frames, 358–361
    design process, revealing problems, 356, 361
    design process, revealing problems, and wicked problems, 365–366
    design process, revealing problems, redefining before solving, 368
    design process, revealing problems, solving, 366–368
    design process, revealing problems, synthesizing before solving, 369

design process, transformations, 359
design process, workpieces, 359
pattern elements, definition, 19
pattern elements, Double Dispatch pattern, 23
Profiles, Unified Modeling Language, 342
Project definition, 44
Project planning, 44

## R

Reliability in design, 73
Responsibilities of objects
    collaborations, connecting, 151–152, 166–167
    collaborations, factor in frequency, 153–155
    collaborations, subresponsibilities, 168–169
    definition, 3
    finding candidate objects, 80
    overview, 110–111
    recording on CRC cards, 122–123
    roles-responsibilities-collaborations model, 5–7
    testing for well-formed objects, 145–146
Responsibilities of objects, assignment strategies
    basics, 125–126
    coherent statements, 135
    distributing system intelligence, 133–134
    eliminating nonessential or overlapping responsibilities, 136–138
    general statements, 128–129
    initial assignments, 128
    judging ability of object to divide or share work, 132
    keeping behaviors with related information, 133
    limiting scope, 133
    limiting sharing of information, 134–135
    Model-View-Controller roles, 129–130, 131
    POSA, 129–131
    recording on CRC cards, 126–128
    restricting to single domain, 135–136
    troubleshooting problems, 138–140
    varying description length, 129–131
    word choices, 131–132
Responsibilities of objects, implementations, 140–141
    designing methods supporting responsibilities, 144
    implementation-specific responsibilities, 124–125

Responsibilities of objects, sources
  basics, 111–112
  design stories, 117–119
  implementation-specific responsibilities,
    124–125
  important object events, 123–124
  object role stereotypes, 121
  private responsibilities supporting public ones,
    121–123
  relationships between candidates, 123
  system behaviors, 112–115
  system behaviors, filling needs between system
    behaviors and use cases, 116–117
  themes, 117–119
  theoretical chains of reasoning, 119–120
  use cases, 112–115
Responsibility-Driven Design
  analysis, 45–47
  basics, 40–42
  collaboration objects, responsibilities and con-
    trol styles, 70–71
  conceptual objects, 58–60
  conceptual objects, judging merit, 60–61
  consistency, 73–74
  CRC cards, 61–62, 63, 67
  descriptions, 44–47
  descriptions, analysis, 49–50
  descriptions, application policies, 57
  descriptions, business rules, 57
  descriptions, design notes, 57
  descriptions, exceptions, 56–57
  descriptions, usage, 50–51
  descriptions, usage, conversations, 54–55, 56
  descriptions, usage, scenarios, 53–54, 56
  descriptions, usage, stories, 52–53
  descriptions, usage, stories for collaborations,
    152–153, 154
  descriptions, usage, use cases, 51–53, 56
  design decisions, guidelines, 67–68
  design decisions, testing designs with details,
    68, 70
  design patterns, 62, 64–67
  flexibility, 71–72
  glossaries, 58
  interactive and incremental processes, 42–43
  multiple stakeholder perspectives, 49, 50, 71
  predictability, 73–74

project definition, 44
project planning, 44
reliability, 73
stages, exploratory, 47, 60–61
stages, refinement, 48, 70–71
Roles of objects, 3–4
  candidate objects, 79–80, 101–103
  collaborations, simulating, 178
  definition, 3
  finding candidate objects, 79–80
  implementing responsibilities, 141–143
  roles-responsibilities-collaborations model, 5–7
Roles of objects, stereotypes, 4–5
  candidate descriptions, 93–94
  in layered style applications, 34–35
  sources of object responsibilities, 121
Roles-responsibilities-collaborations model, 5–7

## S

Scenarios
  design description, 53–54, 56
  sources of object responsibilities, 112–115
Search strategies for candidate objects
  basics, 84–85
  steps in finding/assessing, 78–79
  themes, 85–87
Semantic objects, Page-Jones domain divisions,
  135
Service providers, object role stereotype, 4
  candidate descriptions, 93–94
  in layered style applications, 34–35
  naming, 89
  object collaborations, 162
Solutions, pattern elements
  definition, 20
  Double Dispatch pattern, 24
Sources of object responsibilities
  basics, 111–112
  design stories, 117–119
  implementation-specific responsibilities,
    124–125
  object role stereotypes, 121
  private responsibilities supporting public ones,
    121–123
  relationships between candidates, 123

system behaviors, 112–115
system behaviors, filling needs between filling
    needs between and use cases, 116–117
themes, 117–119
theoretical chains of reasoning, 119–120
use cases, 112–115
Stages of design
    exploratory, 47, 60–61
    refinement, 48, 70–71
Stakeholder perspectives in design, 49, 50, 71
State design pattern, 341
    object collaborations, 171
Stereotypes of object roles
    candidate descriptions, 93–94
    controllers, 4, 34–35, 163
    controllers, *versus* coordinators, 164
    coordinators, 4, 34–35, 164
    information holders, 4, 34–35, 159–160
    interfacers, 4, 34–35, 164–166
    service providers, 4, 34–35, 162
    sources of object responsibilities, 121
    structurers, 4, 34–35, 160–162
Stories
    design description, 52–53
    design description, guidelines, 264–270
    final stories, 273–274
    finding candidate objects, 80–83
    limitations of UML diagrams, 258–262
    listing items to cover, 243
    object collaborations, 152–153, 154
    organization basics, 270–273
    preserving stories, 274
    selecting forms best-suited for stories, 263–264
    sources of object responsibilities, 117–119
    views, bird's eye, 244–245
    views, collaborators only, 245–250
    views, focused interactions among collabora-
        tors, 253–254
    views, implementations, 254
    views, in-depth, 250–253
    views, sequences of interactions among collabo-
        rators, 250
Strategy design pattern, 337–338
    object collaborations, 171
Structural objects, Page-Jones domain divisions,
    135
Structurers, object role stereotype, 4
    candidate descriptions, 93

in layered style applications, 34–35
    object collaborations, 160–162
Subclasses, 16–17
Subsystems of objects, 17
Superclasses, 16–17
Switch statements, 20
System behaviors, sources of object responsibili-
    ties, 112–117

T

Template method, 330–331, 332
Template Method design pattern, 330–331
Themes
    object collaborations, building models, 192
    sources of object responsibilities, 117–119
Troubleshooting problems
    object collaborations, 173–176
    object responsibilities, assignment strategies,
        138–140
Trust regions, 280
    decisions on placement of responsibilities,
        284–285
Trusted collaborations, 280–281
    *versus* untrusted, 281–284

U

UML-F (Unified Modeling Language, frameworks),
    342–344, 345, 346
UML (Unified Modeling Language)
    actors, 51
    design descriptions, 36
    documentation, flexible design, 345, 347
    exception handling, 305–307
    for frameworks (*See* UML-F (Unified Modeling
        Language, frameworks))
    packages, 244–245
    profiles, 342
    relationships between candidate objects, 123
    stories, 241
    stories, limitations of UML diagrams, 258–262
    stories, views, bird's eye, 244–245
    stories, views, collaborators only, 245–250
    stories, views, focused interactions among col-
        laborators, 253–254

UML (Unified Modeling Language), *(continued)*
    stories, views, implementations, 254
    stories, views, in-depth, 250–253
    stories, views, sequences of interactions among
        collaborators, 250
    systems and subsystems, 244–245
Unified Modeling Language. *See* UML (Unified Mod-
    eling Language)
Use cases
    collaborations, building models, 192
    collaborations, simulating, 179
    conversation form, 54–55
    design description, 51–53, 56
    essential, 75
    narrative form, 52–53
    object collaborations, 169–170
    scenario form, 53–54
    sources of object responsibilities, 112–115,
        116–117
    Use case map, 276

User interfacers, object role stereotype
    candidate descriptions, 93
    collaboration identification, 164–165

## V–Z

Variations, flexible design
    creating knobs for developers to turn, 337–338
    hot spots, recording on cards, 324–327
    hot spots, solving, 327–328
    inserting design placeholders, 335–337
    placing variable information into information
        holders, 334–335
    strategies for realizing variations, 329–330
    supporting with template and hook methods,
        330–333
    times needed, 333–334
Visitor design pattern, object collaborations, 171